D1450388

THIS BOOK DOES
 CIRCULATE

DISCARDED
SDSU LIBRARY

# MAGILL'S
# LITERARY ANNUAL
# 2015

*Essay-Reviews of 150 Outstanding Books*
*Published in the United States During 2014*

———————————————

*With an Annotated List of Titles*

Volume One
A-K

*Edited by*
EMILY GOODHUE
MATTHEW AKRE

SALEM PRESS
A Division of EBSCO Information Services, Inc.
Ipswich, Massachusetts

**GREY HOUSE PUBLISHING**

HILTON M. BRIGGS LIBRARY
South Dakota State University
Brookings, SD 57007-1098

DISCARDED
SDSU LIBRARY

Z1035
.A1
M32
2015
v.1

#3644785

*Cover photo:* Photograph of best-selling author Lily King at her Yarmouth, Maine home. © Carl D. Walsh/Porland Press Herald/Getty Images

Copyright © 2015, by SALEM PRESS, a Division of EBSCO Information Services, Inc. All rights in this book are reserved. No part of this work may be used or reproduced in any manner whatsoever or transmitted in any form or by any means, electronic or mechanical, including photocopy, recording, or any information storage and retrieval system, without written permission from the copyright owner. For permissions requests, contact permissions@ebscohost.com.

*Magill's Literary Annual,* 2015, published by Grey House Publishing, Inc., Amenia, NY, under exclusive license from EBSCO Information Services, Inc.

∞ The paper used in these volumes conforms to the American National Standard for Permanence of Paper for Printed Library Materials, Z39.48-1992 (R1997).

**Publisher's Cataloging-In-Publication Data**
(Prepared by The Donohue Group, Inc.)

Magill's literary annual.

    volumes ; cm

    Annual
    Began with: 1977.
    Editor: 1977- , F.N. Magill; <2010-2014>, John D. Wilson and Steven G. Kellman; <2015->, Emily Goodhue and Matthew Akre.
    Includes bibliographical references and index.
    ISBN: 978-1-61925-685-9 (2015 edition : set)
    ISBN: 978-1-61925-869-3 (2015 edition : vol. 1)
    ISBN: 978-1-61925-870-9 (2015 edition : vol. 2)
    ISSN: 0163-3058

    1. Books--Reviews--Periodicals. 2. United States--Imprints--Book reviews--Periodicals. 3. Literature, Modern--21st century--History and criticism--Periodicals. 4. Literature, Modern--20th century--History and criticism--Periodicals. I. Magill, Frank N. (Frank Northen), 1907-1997. II. Wilson, John D. III. Kellman, Steven G., 1947- IV. Goodhue, Emily. V. Akre, Matthew.

PN44 .M333
028.1

FIRST PRINTING
PRINTED IN THE UNITED STATES OF AMERICA

# CONTENTS

# CONTENTS

# PUBLISHER'S NOTE

*Magill's Literary Annual, 2015* follows a long tradition, beginning in 1954, of offering readers incisive reviews of the major literature published during the previous calendar year. The *Magill's Literary Annual* series seeks to critically evaluate 150 major examples of serious literature, both fiction and nonfiction, published in English, from writers in the United States and around the world. The philosophy behind our selection process is to cover works that are likely to be of interest to general readers that reflect publishing trends, that add to the careers of authors being taught and researched in literature programs, and that will stand the test of time. By filtering the thousands of books published every year down to notable titles, the editors have provided librarians with an excellent reader's advisory tool and patrons with fodder for book discussion groups and a guide for choosing worthwhile reading material. The essay-reviews in the *Annual* provide a more academic "reference" review of a work than is typically found in newspapers and other periodical sources.

The reviews in the two-volume *Magill's Literary Annual, 2015* are arranged alphabetically by title. At the beginning of each volume is a complete alphabetical list of all covered books that provides readers with the title and author. In addition, readers will benefit from a brief description of each work in the volume. Every essay is approximately four pages in length. Each one begins with a block of reference information in a standard order:

- Full Book Title, including any subtitle
- *Author:* Name, with birth year, and death year when applicable
- *First published:* Original foreign-language title, with year and country, when pertinent
- Original language and translator name, when pertinent
- Introduction, Foreword, etc., with writer's name, when pertinent
- *Publisher:* Company name and city, and the number of pages
- *Type of work* (chosen from standard categories):

| | |
|---|---|
| Anthropology | Film |
| Archaeology | Fine arts |
| Autobiography | History |
| Biography | History of science |
| Current affairs | Language |
| Diary | Law |
| Drama | Letters |
| Economics | Literary biography |
| Education | Literary criticism |
| Environment | Literary history |
| Essays | Literary theory |
| Ethics | Media |

| Medicine | Poetry |
| Memoir | Psychology |
| Miscellaneous | Religion |
| Music | Science |
| Natural history | Short fiction |
| Nature | Sociology |
| Novel | Technology |
| Novella | Travel |
| Philosophy | Women's issues |

- *Time:* Period represented, when pertinent
- *Locale:* Location represented, when pertinent
- Capsule description of the work
- *Principal characters* (for novels, short fiction) or *Principal personages* (for bibliographies, history): List of people, with brief descriptions, when pertinent

The text of each essay-review analyzes and presents the focus, intent, and relative success of the author, as well as the makeup and point of view of the work under discussion. To assist readers further, essays are supplemented by a list of additional "Review Sources" for further study in a bibliographic format. Every essay includes a sidebar offering a brief biography of the author or authors. Thumbnail photographs of book covers and authors are included as available.

Three indexes can be found at the end of volume 2:

- Category Index: Groups all titles into subject areas such as current affairs and social issues, ethics and law, history, literary biography, philosophy and religion, psychology, and women's issues.
- Title Index: Lists all works reviewed in alphabetical order, with any relevant cross references.
- Author Index: Lists books covered in the Annual by each author's name.

A searchable cumulative index, listing all books reviewed in *Magill's Literary Annual* between 1977 and 2015, as well as in *Magill's History Annual* (1983) and *Magill's Literary Annual, History and Biography* (1984 and 1985), can be found at our Web site, **www.salempress.com**, on the page for *Magill's Literary Annual, 2015*.

Our special thanks go to the outstanding writers who lend their time and knowledge to this project every year. The names of all contributing reviewers are listed in the beginning of Volume 1, as well as at the end of their individual reviews.

# COMPLETE ANNOTATED LIST OF TITLES

## VOLUME 1

Adultery *is a magical realist novel about a young woman who engages in an extramarital affair in an effort to find passion in her life.*

*A novel-within-a-novel,* Afterworlds *relates Darcy Patel's foray into young-adult publishing as she redrafts her debut paranormal romance novel about Lizzie, a girl who can cross into the afterlife and interact with the dead.*

*In* Age of Ambition, *winner of the 2014 National Book Award for nonfiction, Evan Osnos describes how in the early twenty-first century, Chinese people strive for economic success and some modicum of personal freedom even as the Communist Party maintains a tight grip on political power.*

*Dinaw Mengestu's third novel,* All Our Names, *chronicles the intense love affair between Helen, a Caucasian social worker in the American Midwest, and Isaac, an African foreign student, in the early 1970s. Helen tells how they fall in love in the United States, and Isaac remembers his time in Uganda during a time of political repression.*

*All the Birds, Singing is a lyrical, suspenseful novel told from the point of view of a young woman, alienated from fellow humans and from nature itself, who is attempting to come to terms with and move beyond a horrific past.*

*This novel interweaves the stories of Marie-Laure LeBlanc, a blind French girl, and Werner Pfennig, a German boy, during World War II. As they come of age, they become increasingly involved in the war—and with a mysterious jewel—while their fates converge.*

*In* American Fun: Four Centuries of Joyous Revolt, *John Beckman contrasts numerous examples of real fun (happy, spontaneous, participatory, and democratic) with bogus enjoyment (passive, consumer-oriented, and controlled by big business).*

COMPLETE LIST OF ANNOTATED TITLES

The Bees *(2014) follows a lowly worker bee, Flora 717, as she learns the rules of her hive and transcends her ignoble origins to live a richer and more varied life than any single bee—save perhaps a queen—should be able to experience.*

*An unorthodox mystery novel,* Bellweather Rhapsody *relates the profound life changes that several characters experience when a young girl is found dead in a manner that exactly mirrors a tragedy that happened in the same hotel room fifteen years earlier.*

The Betrayers *is a novel about two men with a strained history, one an Israeli politician raised in the former Soviet Union and the other a disgraced KGB informant, who meet coincidentally in Yalta and discuss the events that have led to their current life situations.*

*Lawrence Goldstone's masterful account of the patent war between aviation pioneers Wilbur and Orville Wright and their rival Glenn Curtiss offers a fascinating look at a pivotal decade in the early history of American aviation.*

Black Moon *is an intriguing first novel about what happens when the world is overtaken by an epidemic of sleeplessness. As the sleepless slip into a kind of delirium, the importance of dreams emerges.*

*Presented as a series of journal entries, written accounts, interviews, and reviews,* The Blazing World *paints a compelling portrait of a complex artist and her experiments with perception and personal identity.*

The Bone Clocks *is a fantasy fiction novel consisting of six interconnected stories that reflect on the machinations of immortal beings living in secret societies spread across the world.*

The Book of Strange New Things *is, above all, a love story. It relates the ways in which the relationship of Peter and Beatrice Leigh is tested by Peter's mission to the planet Oasis while conditions on Earth deteriorate, illuminating the strength of faith and the limits of love.*

*Many lives join together in* The Book of Unknown Americans, *collectively narrating the pain and progress of Latin American immigrants to the United States. The central protagonists, the three members of the Rivera family, do not stay long in the country, though their presence has a profound impact on their neighbors in their ramshackle apartment complex. This book tells their collective stories.*

Boy, Snow, Bird *is a fantasy novel about several generations of women living in a family with hidden sociological secrets.*

*Set in the Jamaica and United States of the 1970s through the 1990s,* A Brief History of Seven Killings *chronicles an assassination attempt on a reggae singer and the ultimate fates of his would-be assassins.*

*In this literary memoir, author Jacqueline Woodson uses free verse to chronicle her experiences growing up as an African American in the 1960s and 1970s and the joy she began to take in the act of writing.*

California *is a dystopian novel about a couple living amid the ruins of California after a vague environmental collapse leads to the seeming end of the national government.*

Can't and Won't *is Lydia Davis's first collection of short stories since her anthology* The Collected Stories of Lydia Davis *was published in 2009.*

Can't We Talk about Something More Pleasant? *is a graphic memoir about a grown child caring for aging, eccentric parents.*

*Ian McEwan's latest novel explores science, faith, and good judgment through the eyes of a High Court judge in London.*

Citizen *is an innovative collection of prose poems, essays, and scripts for situational videos. It includes artwork alongside anecdotes and reflections, often dealing with racial discrimination in the United States.*

*Haruki Murakami's* Colorless Tsukuru Tazaki and His Years of Pilgrimage *is a moving fictional portrait of a young man's isolation, which he cannot move beyond unless he is willing to revisit the relationships of his past.*

Console Wars *follows the six-year tenure of Tom Kalinske as president and CEO of Sega of America, during which time he helped Sega break Nintendo's stranglehold on the video-game market and shaped the future of the industry for a decade to come.*

*In filmmaker David Cronenberg's debut novel,* Consumed, *a couple of freelance cyberjournalists investigate a murder case that involves disease, cannibalism, and conspiracy.*

Cubed *examines the inextricable link between the growth of offices as places of business and the current condition of the white-collar worker. It traces the history of the office from its inception through the offices of the twenty-first century, ultimately questioning the meaning and role of work in contemporary society.*

Deep Down Dark *tells the exclusive story of the thirty-three men trapped 2,300 feet below ground for sixty-nine days after the collapse of the San José Mine in the Atacama Desert near Copiapó, Chile, on August 5, 2010.*

*Jenny Offill's second novel—her first in fifteen years—employs a breezy, yet arresting fragmented structure to illustrate love, marriage, parenthood, and infidelity.*

*In Joseph O'Neill's strange yet affecting new novel, an unnamed New York lawyer struggles with persistent guilt as he navigates the ambiguities of Dubai.*

Duty *presents an insider's look at the Department of Defense under two different presidents, from different parties, during a time of constant international conflict. American troops were at war in either Iraq or Afghanistan (and at times both) during Robert Gates's entire tenure as secretary of defense.*

COMPLETE LIST OF ANNOTATED TITLES

*This novel in two parts tells the separate but entangled stories of a young, contemporary British girl and a fifteenth-century Renaissance painter. The novel pushes the boundaries between history and fiction, past and present, and life and death as it unfolds these stories of a tortured adolescent and an ambitious painter, both navigating the pitfalls of love and loss and exploring ambiguous gender and sexual identities.*

*Caitlin Moran's first novel,* How to Build a Girl, *tells the story of a smart but unhappy, pudgy girl from a British working-class background who reinvents herself as a ferocious teenage music critic. As the heroine joins the world of Britain's rock-and-roll scene in the early 1990s, she experiences a sexual awakening.*

*Poet Matthea Harvey's fifth collection of poetry and illustrations,* If the Tabloids Are True What Are You?, *strengthens Harvey's position as a successful experimental poet and illustrator.*

*In* The Impossible Knife of Memory, *Laurie Halse Anderson chronicles the devastating effects of post-traumatic stress disorder on seventeen-year-old Hayley and her veteran father.*

*A Polish American professor and poet with a mysterious family history attends a Zen Buddhist retreat at the former site of the Auschwitz-Birkenau death camp in Oswiecim, Poland.*

*Funded by the publisher of the New York Herald, the ship captain, George De Long, and thirty-two men set off to follow supposed warm water currents in a polar expedition to the North Pole. The story provides a tale of challenge and misfortune, reminding the reader that when humans are pitted against nature, nature wins.*

*Focusing on the Allied invasion of North Africa and Sicily in 1942,* In the Wolf's Mouth *explores the impact of war on both combatants and civilians by tracing the activities of an American infantryman, a British civil affairs officer, and several Sicilians whose lives have been affected by the Fascist takeover of their island before the war.*

## VOLUME 2

*Li Huasheng escapes after twenty years in a Chinese prison camp and heads to Beijing to strike a one-time deal, offering British intelligence services Chinese military secrets in exchange for a way out of China. His plan is perfect, except for the fact that everything has changed during the time he was imprisoned.*

Nobody Is Ever Missing *is the story of Elyria, a young woman who decides to leave her life behind and head for New Zealand, where she has only the vague promise of a place to stay from a passing acquaintance.*

*A young-adult novel with an unusual premise,* Noggin *tells the story of a teenager who must adjust when his cryogenically preserved head is attached to a healthy new body five years after his death, just when his family and friends have begun to move on.*

*In* No Good Men among the Living, *American journalist Anand Gopal argues that the United States brought back the defeated Taliban in Afghanistan by allying itself with a group of brutal, self-serving warlords. Gopal's book focuses on the Afghan experience of the post-2001 years through the eyes of three radically different Afghan people.*

Nora Webster *presents a moving story of a middle-aged Irish widow's struggle to find herself after the death of her husband.*

*In* 100 Essays I Don't Have Time to Write, *playwright Sarah Ruhl presents one hundred very short essays on a variety of diverse topics.*

*Andrew Smith's* 100 Sideways Miles *tells the story of a teenage boy's journey of self-discovery in which he learns about life and love and grows comfortable with the man he is becoming. The novel is a classic coming-of-age story geared toward young-adult readers.*

One More Thing: Stories and Other Stories *is an unusually innovative and generally hilarious collection of short stories and flash fiction. It features a wide range of recognizable, contemporary Americans and exhibits familiarity with current lifestyles and colloquial speech.*

*Award-winning writer Eula Biss draws on her skill as an essayist and poet to produce a very readable yet complex and subtle work about immunization and its importance in an age when many are ignoring the calls for influenza or childhood vaccinations.* On Immunity *deftly braids personal narrative and solid research.*

On Such a Full Sea *is a dystopian novel about a future earth highly stratified into three levels of existence in which a young woman leaves the confines of her territory searching for her lost lover.*

Orfeo *is a novel about a bio-artist whose work blends biological genome manipulation with music.*

The Painter *is a novel about an artist running from a troubled past who commits a crime and then must elude police while moving through the wilderness of the American West.*

*Yelena Akhtiorskaya's debut novel,* Panic in a Suitcase, *paints a detailed picture of its eccentric Russian American and Ukrainian characters tied closely to the places they inhabit, Brighton Beach in New York City and Odessa in the Ukraine.*

*In* Pay Any Price: Greed, Power, and Endless War, *James Risen offers a number of case studies detailing how the war on terror begun in the aftermath of September 11 has been the cause of various kinds of financial, moral, and political corruption that have threatened American values.*

*In Sarah Waters's sixth novel, Frances Wray, a spinster in postwar London, and her mother take on boarders to avoid financial ruin. Soon the fraught interactions between the Wrays and the lower-class Barbers simmer to a deadly boil.*

Penelope Fitzgerald: A Life *is the biography of a British writer who, despite a privileged upbringing, innate intelligence, and a first-class education, languished in poverty and obscurity before bursting forth in her sixties to become a widely respected and honored novelist and biographer.*

*In* The Port Chicago 50, *Steve Sheinkin documents the mutiny trial of fifty African American sailors and the social factors that led to their conviction.*

*Kaui Hart Hemmings's second novel depicts a mother trying to cope with the recent death of her twenty-two-year-old son while realizing that she may not have known him as well as she thought.*

*Atticus Lish's first novel,* Preparation for the Next Life, *is a modern love story about a pair of destitute and emotionally damaged people living in New York City.*

*Long-time Nation columnist Katha Pollitt's Pro offers a scathing indictment of the forces that seek to limit abortion rights in an effort to rally what she considers to be the pro-choice majority in the United States.*

Redeployment, *a collection of short stories about US Marines fighting in the Iraq War and their return from the battlefield, won debut author Phil Klay the 2014 National Book Award.*

Red or Dead *is a quasi-biographical retelling of the career and retirement of Bill Shankly, football player and manager of the Liverpool Football Club, who was responsible for transforming the club into one of England's most successful franchises.*

*In November 1961, Michael Rockefeller, heir to one of the wealthiest families in the world, disappeared off the coast of New Guinea in a territory populated by a tribe of people who practiced ritual cannibalism. Author Carl Hoffman travels to the region to find out whether Rockefeller drowned after his boat capsized or whether, as some suggest, he made it to shore only to be killed and eaten by the Asmat people.*

The Story of Land and Sea *follows the lives of a family living in North Carolina during the Revolutionary War.*

A Sudden Light *follows a fourteen-year-old boy who must uncover the secrets of his family's past in order to heal old wounds and save his parents' failing marriage.*

Take This Man *is the poignant, often humorous, and sometimes troubling memoir of Brando Skyhorse, who was born to Mexican American parents but raised as a Native American by his volatile mother, his cranky grandmother, and a succession of temporary surrogate fathers.*

*In* The Teacher Wars, *Dana Goldstein offers a historical overview of the teaching profession in the United States from 1815, when women first began to serve as professional instructors, through the twenty-first-century culture wars of teacher tenure, standardized testing, and charter schools. By taking a long view on the history of education in the United States, Goldstein pinpoints moments of promise as well as missteps and corrects many common misperceptions about the profession.*

*In* Tennessee Williams: Mad Pilgrimage of the Flesh, *theater critic John Lahr paints a lively and moving portrait of one of the United States' most esteemed playwrights.*

10:04 *is a novel about writing a novel about time. An intellectual extension of Ben Lerner's first novel,* Leaving the Atocha Station *(2011), this autobiographical work continues to question the boundary between life and art.*

*Lawrence Wright presents a gripping, day-by-day account of the 1978 conference at Camp David that led to peace between Israel and Egypt, the first official peace treaty between Israel and one of its Arab neighbors.*

This Blue *is a wide-ranging collection of usually brief lyric poems. It illustrates McLane's varieties of tones, voices, techniques, and talents.*

    World Order *summarizes the events that have forged various present-day interna-
tional situations. The book focuses on Europe, the Middle East, Japan, India, China,
and the United States. Kissinger offers both analysis and possible solutions by dis-
secting the historical, philosophical, and religious underpinnings of each specific
region's foreign policies.*

    *In his eleventh novel, Martin Amis offers a modern-day fable about love in the
most forbidding of places: the Nazi concentration camp at Auschwitz. His often-
humorous perspective on a deeply serious topic challenges readers to appreciate the
complexities of a frightful era in world history.*

# CONTRIBUTING REVIEWERS

Michelle Acciavatti

Richard Adler

Pegge Bochynski

Joy Crelin

Christina Dendy

Robert Evans

Jack Ewing

Keith M. Finley

Molly Hagan

Gina Hagler

Raymond Pierre Hylton

Micah Issit

Judy Johnson

Mark Joy

Kathryn Kulpa

Reinhart Lutz

Charles May

Laurence W. Mazzeno

Daniel P. Murphy

Julia Sienkewicz

Amy Sisson

Rich Stein

Kenrick Vezina

Tom Willard

# Adultery

**Author**: Paulo Coelho (b. 1947)
**Publisher**: Alfred A. Knopf (New York).
272 pp.
**First published**: *Adultério*, 2014, in Brazil
**Translated from**: the Portuguese by Margaret Jull Costa and Zoë Perry
**Type of work**: Novel
**Time**: 2013
**Locale**: Geneva, Switzerland

Adultery *is a magical realist novel about a young woman who engages in an extramarital affair in an effort to find passion in her life.*

Best-selling author of *The Alchemist*

PAULO COELHO

Adultery

(Courtesy of Knopf)

**Principal characters:**
LINDA, a Swiss journalist married to a rich investment banker who feels depressed at the monotony of her life
JACOB KÖNIG, her boyfriend as a teenager, now a politician
LINDA'S HUSBAND, an unnamed investment banker
MARIANNE KÖNIG, Jacob's wife

Paulo Coelho is the best-selling Brazilian author of all time and is considered one of the living masters of magical realism, a genre that uses surreal or "magical" elements in an otherwise realistic setting. The English translation of his 1993 breakout hit, *The Alchemist*, remained on the *New York Times* best-seller list for more than three hundred weeks and has been called one of the best novels of the last century. Coelho is also notable as one of a small number of authors whose fiction has been embraced as a form of pop-psychological or even spiritual literature. Many of his most successful novels straddle the line between fiction and philosophy, telling stories that contain insightful observations on human nature and spirituality.

Occasionally, Coelho produces a novel that puzzles his fans, straying from the pop-psychological or self-help-oriented themes that have made him popular. One such example is *The Winner Stands Alone* (2008), a brutal murder story that received mixed reviews from both critics and audiences, largely because the book lacked the hopeful elements found in the author's more popular works. Coelho's latest novel, *Adultery* (2014), tells the story of a privileged woman attempting to "find herself" through a series of adulterous sexual encounters. Though the novel contains identifiable psychological themes and involves aspects of magical realism, *Adultery* differs from most of Coelho's canon in its darker and far less uplifting theme.

The protagonist of *Adultery* is a Swiss reporter named Linda, who is never given a last name. The book is written entirely from Linda's point of view, in the first-person perspective, and much of each chapter deals with her internal dialogue rather than her interactions with others. Linda explains in the opening passages that she is quite wealthy, having married one of the wealthiest men in Geneva; that she has two children and an extremely successful job as a magazine journalist; and that she enjoys a life of privilege and luxury. However, Linda is also profoundly unhappy. The reasons for her unhappiness are vague but can be summed up as a sense of upper-class ennui, resulting in her feeling that her life has become mundane and predictable. Linda says that this underlying sense of depression was heightened by an interview she conducted for a magazine article in which her subject explained that he prefers to live "passionately" rather than "happily," exchanging the greater highs and lows of the passionate life for the mid-range satisfaction of a happy life. This seemingly innocuous statement causes Linda to reexamine every aspect of her life and to become increasingly detached from both her job and her family.

The reason for the title of the book becomes clear after Linda meets with Jacob König, a Swiss politician whom Linda knew as a teenager. When she was fifteen, the two shared a kiss, and Linda muses to herself that she may once have been in love with him. At the interview, Jacob makes a seemingly halfhearted pass at Linda, and Linda says that she hopes her comments about her children and wedding ring will make the point to Jacob that she is unavailable for a tryst. However, unexpectedly, Linda then initiates a sexual encounter, thus beginning her pattern of self-exploration through flirting with the destruction of her married life.

Much of the middle section of Coelho's novel follows Linda's narcissistic obsession with her own unhappiness and dissatisfaction. She becomes increasingly obsessed with Jacob, whom she meets several more times, though they do not at first engage in further sexual encounters; their meetings are spent exchanging pseudo-philosophical observations about life and depression, including a puzzling detour involving the revolutions of Saturn. As Linda believes she has fallen in love with Jacob again, she becomes increasingly obsessed with his wife, Marianne, or Madame König, and begins regarding Madame König as her nemesis. Linda goes so far as to purchase cocaine for the purpose of planting the drug on Madame König's person so as to destroy her rival and clear a path to be with Jacob romantically. The darkness of Linda's desires makes her unsympathetic, and Coelho provides no redemption for his heroine. Linda unapologetically voices the darkest urges of upper-class emotional angst with little to no justification and a complete disregard for the well-being of anyone who might be adversely affected by her actions.

Along her path of self-discovery, Linda follows a pattern familiar from Coelho's other novels, exploring psychology and spirituality in an effort to address her emptiness and depression. She begins by trying to speak openly with her husband and friends but finds these encounters unsatisfying. Linda then moves on to psychotherapy, but she is told that problems like those she is experiencing cannot be easily or quickly solved. A psychotherapist's musing that psychotherapists are not "shamans" leads Linda to seek the advice of a Cuban shaman who offers spiritual counseling. The shaman and Linda spend part of an afternoon together, talking and walking in a park, and the shaman advises her that she needs to see her quest to completion before what he calls the "lightness" in her can win out over the "darkness."

After a large portion of the book is spent following Linda's soul-searching monologues, attempts to find spiritual or medical solace, and apathetic commentary on her career and the daily events of her life, she finally meets with Jacob again. Coelho devotes considerable space to building up their next sexual encounter both in Linda's mind

*Paulo Coelho, an award-winning author of more than thirty novels and biographical books, has been cited as the best-selling Brazilian author in history. He is best known for O* Alquimista *(1988;* The Alchemist, *1993), which has been translated into eighty languages and has sold more than sixty-five million copies worldwide.*

and in teasing conversations and meetings between the two. When they finally meet to live out the titular thrust of the story, it is a rough and denigrating sexual encounter that seems to leave Linda with increasingly lurid and animalistic fantasies about Jacob, as well as the realization that what she wants from him is lust rather than love. As the affair continues, Linda continues to explore her psyche, meditating on the evolutionary psychology of sex and monogamy, ruminating on spirituality and magic, and ultimately delving into a full-blown affair with Jacob, which she describes as occurring over several weeks with both "conventional and unconventional intercourse."

The consequences of the affair, like the build-up and Linda's obsessive fascination with Jacob, occur largely in Linda's mind. She describes learning to methodically hide the evidence of her meetings with Jacob from her husband. As her double life becomes more and more profound to her, Linda compares herself to the literary characters of Dr. Jekyll and Frankenstein's monster. Much of the remaining book is filled with Linda's realizations about love and life that may seem trite, given the nature of Linda's behavior. Linda muses that "love is an art" and gradually seems to come to understand how her choices may affect her life.

The emotional climax comes when Linda, her husband, Jacob, and his wife all meet up at a reception given for a local television celebrity. Coelho, who has a home in Geneva, is uncomplimentary in his depictions of upper-class Genevan society, describing the people (through Linda) as shallow and insipid. Observations like this appear in several sections of the book, providing Coelho with a forum to express what read like personal criticisms of Swiss society. Intermixed with commentary on the shallow state of the upper crust, Linda's private and public lives come uncomfortably together, causing her to reexamine the course and consequences of her behavior and to decide what is really important to her. The climax leads Linda on a path to put her life in perspective and to repair the damage she has done, and yet Coelho provides few consequences for his protagonist. Despite her flirtation with self-destruction, she is not punished morally. In the end, Linda's experiences result in a set of familiar revelations about the nature of love, life, and happiness.

Coelho's *Adultery* received mixed to negative reviews from critics. Joseph Peschel, writing for the *Los Angeles Review of Books*, complained that Linda's character never seems to improve throughout the book and characterized the book's ultimate revelations as "questionable." In the *Independent*, reviewer Rebecca K. Morrison wrote that *Adultery* left a "strange aftertaste of falseness and a rushed job." Yet despite this criticism, *Adultery* became a best seller, likely propelled by the success of Coelho's previous novels.

Fans of Coelho's will recognize some of the author's familiar motifs, such as his tendency to intersperse his work with psychological platitudes and his use of surreal descriptions to heighten the emotional poignancy of the action. Though *Adultery* may be considered one of the author's less successful novels from a critical standpoint, his explorations of a darker and less sympathetic set of characters and environments reveal a different side to the author's personality and provide an unusual perspective on the state of love and sexuality in the modern world.

*Micah L. Issitt*

**Review Sources**

Klein, Julia M. Rev. of *Adultery*, by Paulo Coelho. *Chicago Tribune.* Tribune Interactive, 22 Aug. 2014. Web. 26 Nov. 2014.

McAlpin, Heller. "You Would Think *Adultery* Would Be a Little More Tantalizing." Rev. of *Adultery*, by Paulo Coelho. *NPR.* Natl. Public Radio, 19 Aug. 2014. Web. 26 Nov. 2014.

Morrison, Rebecca K. "New Novel Fails to Stimulate." Rev. of *Adultery*, by Paulo Coelho. *Independent.* Independent.co.uk, 14 Sept. 2014. Web. 26 Nov. 2014.

Peschel, Joseph. "All You Need Is Love: Paulo Coelho's New Novel, *Adultery*." Rev. of *Adultery*, by Paulo Coelho. *Los Angeles Review of Books.* Los Angeles Rev. of Books, 24 Aug. 2014. Web. 26 Nov. 2014.

# Afterworlds

**Author:** Scott Westerfeld (b. 1963)
**Publisher:** Simon Pulse (New York). 608 pp.
**Type of work:** Novel
**Time:** Indeterminate present
**Locale:** New York City

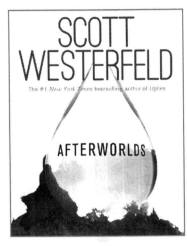

(Courtesy of Simon Pulse)

*A novel-within-a-novel,* Afterworlds *relates Darcy Patel's foray into young-adult publishing as she redrafts her debut paranormal romance novel about Lizzie, a girl who can cross into the afterlife and interact with the dead.*

**Principal characters:**
DARCY PATEL, an eighteen-year-old debut novelist
IMOGEN GRAY, her first girlfriend, a debut novelist
NISHA PATEL, her younger sister
KIRALEE TAYLOR, a young-adult novelist whom she has admired for years
LIZZIE SCOFIELD, the protagonist of her first novel
YAMARAJ, Lizzie's love interest within her novel
MINDY, the ghost of a young girl who was murdered
STANLEY DAVID ANDERSON, a highly successful author and social-media phenomenon

In *Afterworlds*, eighteen-year-old Darcy Patel has just landed a lucrative two-book contract on the strength of her first novel-length manuscript, which she wrote in a frenzy during National Novel Writing Month. Darcy breaks the news to her parents that she wants to take her six-figure advance and move to New York City, deferring college for a year so she can immerse herself in the New York publishing scene while she completes her novel's rewrites. In reality, though, Darcy is determined to make her publishing dream last as long as her money holds out, even if that means putting college off indefinitely.

As a new author with an impressive contract, Darcy finds herself welcomed into the young-adult publishing community, where she meets authors she has admired for years as well as several "sister debs," or authors whose first books will debut in the same year as Darcy's. She is quickly drawn to Imogen, who at age twenty-three seems worldly and sophisticated, and who shares Darcy's passion for writing. Imogen helps Darcy find an apartment, and the two quickly begin writing and exploring the city together.

As Darcy's first year in New York unfolds and she begins the long process of re-writing her first draft, the reader is shown the revised chapters of Darcy's novel, which is also titled *Afterworlds*. Darcy's protagonist, Lizzie, is returning from a visit to her father when terrorists attack the airport. When a 911 operator advises Lizzie to play dead to avoid the gunmen's attention, Lizzie sinks so deeply into a death-like trance that she actually crosses over to the afterworld, where a charismatic young man named Yamaraj protects her until it is safe to return to the real world. Initially presumed dead by the medical responders, Lizzie awakens as the only survivor of an attack that killed eighty-seven people, but she has been irrevocably changed in that she is now able to perceive the worlds of both the living and the dead. Yamaraj teaches Lizzie how to navigate the afterlife, telling her that she will be called at some point to help the recently deceased cross over, but there is some information he is reluctant to share. In an attempt to help the ghost of a little girl named Mindy, Lizzie takes matters into her own hands in order to prevent Mindy's killer from murdering again.

*Perhaps best known for his highly successful dystopian series* Uglies, *young-adult author Scott Westerfeld has also written the steampunk* Leviathan *series, the* Midnighters *trilogy, and a number of stand-alone novels.*

One of the most striking aspect of *Afterworlds* is the way the particulars of Darcy's life spill into her work. Both narrative threads, for instance, explore the themes of communication and trust. When Darcy accidentally sees a note in Imogen's diary that she believes is a criticism of her, she does not discuss it with Imogen immediately but rather lets her unhappiness fester for several weeks. The note did not actually refer to Darcy at all, but Imogen is so hurt at Darcy's lack of confidence in their relationship that she decides she needs a break from it. Similarly, Darcy's supportive aunt and younger sister both encourage Darcy to tell her parents about her new relationship, but Darcy balks. She has reason to believe that her parents will accept her homosexuality, but she still cannot bring herself to tell them, or even to let them read her novel before it is published. Within Darcy's novel, Lizzie too has trouble communicating with her mother and her friends. Fortunately, Darcy finally learns enough to begin trusting the people closest to her, and this transition is neatly reflected in her novel's new ending, in which Lizzie decides to tell her best friend everything about her recent extraordinary experiences.

Another theme within both stories is the importance of names. Because Darcy's paranormal romance novel involves malevolent spirits, it is not surprising that knowing another person's name can empower the ability to summon or bind that person. Attempting to navigate the unfamiliar afterworld, Lizzie makes the mistake of revealing Yamaraj's name to an evil spirit, with serious consequences. In Darcy's real life, names also carry weight and meaning, although in a more prosaic manner. Early in their relationship, Darcy learns that Imogen exclusively uses her pen name, Imogen

Gray, and she is surprised when Imogen initially refuses to reveal her legal name. Imogen tells Darcy that she is not proud of some things she had written on the Internet when she was less mature, and assuming a new name allowed her to become the person she wanted to be. Darcy eventually learns that Imogen chose her new name specifically as a tribute to a past girlfriend whom Imogen believes committed suicide. Later, when sales of Imogen's first novel are weak, Imogen believes that she may eventually have to change her name again in order to escape the publishing-industry stigma of a poor sales record. In this case, Imogen realizes that being forced to give up the name with which she has identified for years would be just as traumatic as having people discover her original name and believe her to still be that person. As Lizzie does in Darcy's fictional afterworld, Imogen discovers that names can confer both positive and negative consequences.

One aspect of *Afterworlds* that is perhaps somewhat less successful is the unrealistic ease with which Darcy enters both the publishing field and her relationship with Imogen, despite of her lack of experience in both areas. Although Darcy has never dated or even seriously kissed anyone, and in fact has never spent much time thinking about whether she was attracted to boys, girls, or both, she and Imogen feel an immediate attraction that they are both comfortable acting upon in spite of their differences in age and experience. They proceed from a first kiss to essentially living and presumably sleeping together quickly and without much note. Likewise, Darcy implies that her parents are overprotective and the reader therefore expects a great deal of resistance from them; in fact, her parents leave her almost entirely to her own devices, and are perhaps unrealistically supportive of her decisions. Darcy and Imogen's emotional relationship is treated more thoroughly than their physical one, in that Darcy works through the trust and insecurity issues that stem largely from her immaturity in a believable manner.

In terms of her career, not only has Darcy achieved a fairy-tale publishing contract a short time after sending her first query letter to an agent, she is immediately accepted into the young-adult publishing community as an equal. In addition to Imogen's support, Darcy is immediately taken under the wings of an acerbic yet kind author named Kiralee Taylor and a gregarious author and social-media phenomenon named Stanley Anderson, or "Standerson." Darcy gets prestigious blurbs for her novel and gets invited to tour with Standerson and Imogen even though her own novel debut is still several months away. Fortunately, Westerfeld's other observations about writing and publishing convey that world in a more realistic light. For instance, Darcy and Imogen discuss "imposter syndrome," or the irrational but common feeling that everyone will find out that they are not really talented enough to be published authors. Darcy's editor, Nan, reminds Darcy that while her first novel is an amazing achievement, it will never be perfect in Darcy's own eyes, and she may well look back on it someday as being incredibly naïve. Imogen also cautions Darcy about the "postpartum depression" most authors experience every time they complete a novel, no matter how many they have written. Finally, Westerfeld pokes good-natured yet accurate fun at authors who take themselves too seriously, particularly when they are concerned less about the craft of writing than about their public images. At the regular gathering of young-adult authors that Darcy attends, for instance, some of the writers constantly interrupt their conversations with one another to tweet the clever things they have just said to their followers. Refreshingly, Darcy and Imogen are more interested in writing than promoting their writing, although they understand that both are important.

On a more serious note, Westerfeld also examines the issue of cultural appropriation in literature and popular entertainment. After getting to know the more experienced writers, Darcy begins to worry that it was inappropriate to base her character Yamaraj on a Hindu god even though she herself is an East Indian American. While she does not practice Hinduism and so does not consider what she has done to be blasphemy, she wonders if she has been disrespectful by essentially turning a cherished religious deity into a romance-novel love interest. Darcy's fellow authors discuss the fact that while research and respectful treatment are necessary, in the end, almost everything fictional can be attributed to appropriation, whether of culture or specific experiences that may not belong to the actual author.

At nearly six hundred pages, *Afterworlds* moves at a surprisingly quick pace, in large part because both story lines are equally interesting. While Darcy's story is related in third person, Lizzie's tale employs first-person narration, effectively bringing the slightly removed secondary story line into more immediate focus. Ultimately, Darcy's astonishment at how quickly her first year in New York is passing mirrors the feeling that most young people have as they live through their first year of college or in a new job, thus creating an authentic emotional experience for the reader. While the lack of significant obstacles in Darcy's professional and personal lives is noticeable, Darcy's internal lack of confidence feels genuine, making it easy for the reader to root for her. Her sympathetic nature, coupled with the unique narrative structure and fast pacing, make this an eminently appealing young-adult novel, even more so because it feeds the reader's desire for a glimpse into the author's own world.

*Amy Sisson*

## Review Sources

Rev. of *Afterworlds*, by Scott Westerfeld. *Kirkus Reviews* 1 July 2014: 262. Web. 3 Feb. 2015.

Hilbun, Janet. Rev. of *Afterworlds*, by Scott Westerfeld. *School Library Journal* July 2014: 112. Web. 3 Feb. 2015.

Hunt, Jonathan. "Fierce Females." Rev. of *Afterworlds*, by Scott Westerfeld. *Horn Book Magazine*. Horn Book, Jan. 2014: 112. Web. 3 Feb. 2015.

Welch, Cindy. Rev. of *Afterworlds*, by Scott Westerfeld. *Booklist* 1 July 2014: 78. Web. 3 Feb. 2015.

Zacharek, Stephanie. "The Write Stuff." Rev. of *Afterworlds*, by Scott Westerfeld. *New York Times Book Review* 9 Nov. 2014: 33. *Book Review Digest Plus (H.W. Wilson)*. Web. 3 Feb. 2015.

# Age of Ambition
## Chasing Fortune, Truth, and Faith in the New China

**Author:** Evan Osnos (b. 1976)
**Publisher:** Farrar, Straus and Giroux (New York). 416 pp.
**Type of work:** Current affairs
**Time:** 2005–13; some flashbacks to earlier years from 1979 onward
**Locales:** Beijing, People's Republic of China; multiple other Chinese cities; Taiwan (Republic of China)

*In* Age of Ambition, *winner of the 2014 National Book Award for nonfiction, Evan Osnos describes how in the early twenty-first century, Chinese people strive for economic success and some modicum of personal freedom even as the Communist Party maintains a tight grip on political power.*

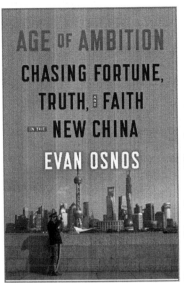

(Courtesy of Farrar, Straus, and Giroux)

**Principal personages:**

EVAN OSNOS, the author, a Chinese-speaking American reporter in Beijing

LIN ZHENGYI / YIFU, a Taiwanese officer who defects to the People's Republic of China

GONG HAINAN / HAIYAN, a young woman who launches an Internet dating website

ZHANG "MICHAEL" ZHIMING, a twenty-something devotee of English

HAN HAN, a popular Chinese blogger and car racer

CHEN GUANGCHEN, a blind, self-taught Chinese dissident lawyer who immigrates to the United States

AI WEIWEI, a celebrated Chinese dissident architect and artist

HU SHULI, a Chinese reporter and magazine founder

TANG JIE, a Chinese nationalist philosopher

LIU XIAOBO, a Chinese dissident imprisoned in 2008, who won the 2010 Nobel Peace Prize

Evan Osnos won the 2014 National Book Award for nonfiction for his incisive look at contemporary China, *Age of Ambition: Chasing Fortune, Truth, and Faith in the New China* (2014), which provides a perceptive look at how urban Chinese society changed from 2005 to 2013, the eight years he spent as a Chinese-speaking American reporter based in Beijing. Osnos calls this the time of "aspiration, a belief in the sheer possibility to remake a life" among the Chinese. About a quarter of a century since the death of Mao Zedong in 1976 and the end of the dark days of the Cultural Revolution, Osnos sees the once-uniform Chinese national history "splintering into a billion stories" of its people.

Since Osnos is a journalist and not a political scientist, his focus is on the stories of individuals. *Age of Ambition* successfully captures and describes the lives of those whom Osnos encountered and spoke with personally. He provides fitting economic data and statistics and the historical background against which the distinct stories unfold, which are always in the foreground as the fate of each person takes center stage. Osnos achieves his goal "to describe Chinese lives on their own terms"; when given the names of Chinese people, he follows the Asian custom of giving the family name first, an authorial decision a Western reader should keep in mind.

One remarkable life thus portrayed is that of Lin Zhengyi, whom Osnos admires for the audacity with which he "placed his bet on the new China." As Osnos retells the story, on the morning of May 16, 1979, Captain Lin Zhengyi defected from Taiwan, leaving behind his pregnant wife and small son. He did so by swimming the one mile of sea that divides the remote Taiwanese island of Quemoy, where he was posted, from the coast of mainland China. There, Lin changed his first name to Yifu, meaning "a persistent man on a long journey."

Lin embraced Communism "with the passion of the convert" and was allowed to study economics in Beijing. In 1982, he traveled to the United States to earn his PhD in economics from the University of Chicago and be reunited with his family. Upon returning to Beijing in 1987, he became a celebrated professor of economics. When Osnos met Lin for the last time in 2012, Lin reiterated his firm commitment that China needed a strong Communist government to ensure economic success. However, as Lin continued to defend the official position in the face of popular unease with Communist corruption, Osnos "sensed that he might always be an outsider." Osnos shares his admiration for Lin repeatedly with his readers. He calls Lin's insistence to make his own personal choices "by mainland Chinese standards, a radical act."

Another person admired by Osnos for her determination to make something big out of her life is Gong Hainan, whose parents were deemed "well-off peasants" and thus paired together during the Cultural Revolution. During her high school years, Gong had an accident, and because her school did not have the means to accommodate handicapped students, her mother carried her on her back from classroom to classroom until she recovered. Gong's medical bills ruined the family financially—an indictment of the Communists' failure to provide free health service to the poor. For a while, Gong joined other rural migrant women and worked in a city factory. Eventually, she attended Peking University. Like Lin Yifu, she followed the Chinese tradition of changing her first name at the start of a new period of her life; she became Gong Haiyan, in "reference to the small, hardy seabird in an old revolutionary poem by Maxim Gorky," the Russian poet. When she was cheated by one of the burgeoning online dating services, she founded her own quality online dating company, which was successful and made her a wealthy woman. She also met her future husband through the service.

Osnos skillfully uses Gong's story to reflect on the larger state of romance in contemporary urban China. As always in *Age of Ambition*, a concrete life observed leads the author to more general observations on a topic touched by that life. This approach works well in guiding readers into contemporary Chinese society from many different angles.

In the spring of 2008, Osnos met a young Chinese man whose ambition for fortune proved elusive. Zhang Zhiming came from a rural background and hoped that mastering and teaching English would become his personal path to success. Calling himself Michael, in part to reinvent himself like Lin and Gong, he served as a teaching assistant to the charismatic Li Yang. Li became successful through his brand of Crazy English, which instructs students to overcome their inhibitions about speaking English by shouting phrases instead. Eventually, Michael became disenchanted with Li and his methods and instead attempted to set up his own teaching method. At their last meeting in March 2013, Michael told Osnos how a Beijing publishing firm tried to steal his ideas and sell them as its own. At the time, Michael was about to leave the capital for his parents' home town, his fate a strong reminder that in contemporary China, many failed to realize their dreams.

After depicting various stories of success and failure in the "ravenous" quest for fortune in the first section of *Age of Ambition*, Osnos turns to the topics of truth and faith. At this point, the narrative becomes much darker in tone. Concerning the pursuit of fortune, Osnos likens what he saw in China to the United States' Gilded Age, which began after the Civil War and reached its heyday in the 1870s, in that some Chinese were able to amass gigantic fortunes comparable to those of the American railway barons. Yet the second part of *Age of Ambition*, regarding the pursuit of truth, clearly points at a key difference. Although Osnos never

*Evan Osnos became a reporter for the Chicago Tribune in 1999. In 2008, he and several other* Tribune *reporters won the Pulitzer Prize for investigative reporting.* The Age of Ambition, *based on articles he wrote for the* New Yorker *between 2008 and 2013, won the 2014 National Book Award for nonfiction.*

explicitly states it, this difference lies in the authoritarian and controlling influence that the Chinese Communist Party (CCP) has reserved for itself. While there was also corruption in the Gilded Age, there was nevertheless an atmosphere of vast personal freedom, including freedom of speech, which was lacking in Chinese life during the years that Osnos spent in Beijing. This situation is exemplified best when Osnos reports that in the summer of 2012, the CCP's Central Propaganda Department puts a warning on the Chinese search engine Weibo that "search results for 'the truth' have not been displayed."

In contemporary Chinese society, Osnos highlights the collision of two forces: the aspiration and ambition of the Chinese people and the unyielding authoritarianism of the Chinese government, the ruling Communist Party. With a certain irony, a tone that characterizes much of *Age of Ambition*, Osnos writes that to survive after the fall of Communism in the West in 1989, "the Chinese Communist Party shed its scripture but held fast to its saints; it abandoned Marx's theories but retained Mao's portrait on the Gate of Heavenly Peace." By 2014, Mao's head was still on all Chinese banknotes, underlining the veracity of Osnos's observation. Consequently, this account of contemporary China becomes much darker as it turns to the courageous Chinese who have suffered due to their opposition to the CCP's demand for compliance in return for some economic opportunities. There is the Internet blogger and car racer Han Han, who became a pop-culture celebrity for his irreverent account of official hypocrisy, yet retreated from his political criticism in the face of increasing censorship of the Internet and official repression.

*Age of Ambition* also features prominent Chinese dissidents, such as the blind, self-taught lawyer Chen Guangchen, who managed to immigrate to the United States; the famous dissident artist and architect Ai Weiwei; and Liu Xiaobo, who was awarded the Nobel Peace Prize in 2010 while in prison in China. Lesser-known fighters for a more open, transparent society, such as financial journalist Hu Shuli, who took on the issue of massive corruption by government cadres, are portrayed as well.

Osnos's portrait of the Chinese nationalist Tang Jie illustrates the CCP's attempt to monopolize public opinion. In 2008, Tang became famous for using the Internet to defend China against Western criticism of its human-rights record during the Beijing Olympics. Yet even Tang Jie's nationalist website was shut down for five months in 2011—an example, according to Osnos, of the CCP not allowing any opinion besides its own propaganda.

If there is one element lacking in Osnos's compelling *Age of Ambition*, it is the absence of any personal portrait of a member of a very important group in contemporary China: the Communist leaders and their children. Osnos apparently did not manage to approach personally any of the genuine elite of contemporary China who rule the country from within, a fact indicative of how the true possessors of political and economic power shield themselves from outside inquiry. Upstarts, outsiders, and common people were accessible to the American Osnos, but those in power kept to themselves.

*Age of Ambition* offers a fascinating, in-depth portrayal of Chinese people trying to chart their own lives in contemporary urban China. Osnos's account reaches deep behind the scenes to show how Chinese society is changing through its people and the struggle they are willing to endure in order to create a positive life. It is an award-winning book very worth reading for all who want to understand life in contemporary China.

*R. C. Lutz*

**Review Sources**

"China: Wild at Heart." Rev. of *Age of Ambition: Chasing Fortune, Truth, and Faith in the New China*, by Evan Osnos. *Economist*. Economist Newspaper, 31 May 2014. Web. 15 Dec. 2014.

Makinen, Julie. "Evan Osnos Observes China's Split Personality in *Age of Ambition*." Rev. of *Age of Ambition*, by Evan Osnos. *Los Angeles Times*. Los Angeles Times, 9 May 2014. Web. 15 Dec. 2014.

Pomfret, John. Rev. of *Age of Ambition*, by Evan Osnos. *Washington Post*. Washington Post, 16 May 2014. Web. 15 Dec. 2014.

Shapiro, Judith. "Striving for Wealth and Truth in China, in Face of Monolithic Government." Rev. of *Age of Ambition*, by Evan Osnos. *New York Times*. New York Times, 25 May 2014. Web. 15 Dec. 2014.

HILTON M. BRIGGS LIBRARY
South Dakota State University
Brookings, SD 57007-1098

# All Our Names

**Author:** Dinaw Mengestu (b. 1978)
**Publisher:** Alfred A. Knopf (New York). 272 pp.
**Type of work:** Novel
**Time:** 1970–74
**Locales:** Kampala, Uganda; Laurel, United States

*Dinaw Mengestu's third novel,* All Our Names, *chronicles the intense love affair between Helen, a Caucasian social worker in the American Midwest, and Isaac, an African foreign student, in the early 1970s. Helen tells how they fall in love in the United States, and Isaac remembers his time in Uganda during a time of political repression.*

(Courtesy of Knopf)

**Principal characters:**
ISAAC MABIRA, also known as BIRD and D——, a young Ethiopian man who immigrates to Uganda, then to the United States
HELEN, a Caucasian social worker in the American Midwest
AUBREY, her mother
DAVID, her supervisor
ISAAC, a poor young Ugandan man who becomes involved with a rebel group and takes the last name of its leader, his lover
JOSEPH MABIRA, a Ugandan politician from a powerful family turned rebel leader
HENRY, a retired Caucasian diplomat and friend of Joseph Mabira
THE PRESIDENT, an unnamed leader of Uganda modeled after the historical Idi Amin

The third novel of Ethiopian American author Dinaw Mengestu, *All Our Names* tenderly presents the interracial love story of Helen, a Caucasian social worker, and the man she knows as Isaac Mabira, a foreign student from Ethiopia. The novel is told in what has become Mengestu's trademark style of multiple points of view. The names of the novel's key African characters are fluid, which is alluded to in the title. Readers must watch carefully for clues as to who is who. Chapters entitled "Isaac" relate events in Uganda from August 1970 to spring 1973, prior to Isaac's arrival in the United States. Helen's chapters tell of the development of their romantic relationship from August 1973 to May 1974.

This bifurcation of the narrative corresponds to a similar approach in Mengestu's first two novels, including his award-winning debut, *The Beautiful Things That Heaven Bears* (2007), which also focuses on an interracial relationship. In *All Our Names*, Mengestu's structure works well to highlight the novel's key themes of lingering racial discrimination in the United States brought to the fore by an interracial relationship and inter-African violence. Neither the United States nor East Africa is a perfect place in Mengestu's novel. At the same time, the novel's structure stresses a second theme about each character's unique history, story, and viewpoint. The novel's only drawback is that Isaac's account of the events in Uganda is somewhat misaligned with historical reality.

*All Our Names* explores the themes of naming and identity. The novels first chapter, titled "Isaac," is set in Uganda's capital of Kampala in August 1970 at a university (modeled after the real Makerere University) with a strong reputation among African literary people. The narrator, originally from Ethiopia, meets Isaac, from northern Uganda. Both are outsiders, a fact that cements their friendship, but despite their outsider status, the narrator asserts that he and Isaac both "felt that was where [w]e belonged."

Helen's first chapter closely mirrors the opening of the first Isaac chapter. When Helen meets Isaac, she is thirty years old and somewhat adrift in her life. She is a disillusioned social worker for the fictional Lutheran Relief Services. Her most important goal in life is to be different from her mother Aubrey, who holds traditional, prefeminist values. Aubrey's devotion to her husband has not saved her from being abandoned by him, however. Aubrey and Helen live together in the fictional "quiet, semi-rural Midwestern town" of Laurel. The state is never given, though internal evidence suggests it is Missouri. Helen states that her town has finally been desegregated, even though oblique racism still lingers. Indeed, Missouri miscegenation laws prohibiting the marriage of white and black people were not repealed until 1967.

In August 1973, Helen's supervisor, David asks Helen to chaperone a new foreign student from Africa, whose name is Isaac Mabira. Helen muses that "One war had ended" by this time, a reference to the Paris Peace Accords of January 27, 1973, which ended American military involvement in Vietnam. From the point of view of Americans such as Helen, the Vietnam War had ended. In Vietnam, however, war continued until the forces of North Vietnam captured Saigon on April 30, 1975. Mengestu's novel accurately describes the feeling of the majority of Americans about their involvement in this war by the summer of 1973.

When Helen picks up Isaac, she notices "he wasn't bad-looking." Within one month of helping him settle into Laurel, she has become his lover. Mengestu convincingly shows how Helen is driven by her strong desire to be different from her mother. For Helen, loving Isaac is the most dramatic opposition to her mother's world, motivating her quick romantic action.

By choosing a state like Missouri, Mengestu can show the lingering effects of racism in middle America well into the early 1970s. This racism is exemplified when, in an act of defiance, Helen invites Isaac for lunch at a diner. Traditionally, this place served only white customers. People stare, and Isaac is served his food on a plastic plate while Helen's arrives on the customary porcelain.

Helen and Isaac engage in sexual activity in the evening only, when Helen goes to Isaac's apartment in the African American neighborhood. They make love without speaking much to each other, and she leaves for home before midnight. Readers may wonder why Isaac's African American neighbors are never shown to be curious about this Caucasian woman visitor.

While Helen tells of their relationship, the Isaac chapters highlight the troubles in an increasingly oppressive and violent Uganda. In the middle of *All Our Names*, Isaac is visited in Laurel by a former American diplomat, Henry, who tells him that his best friend in Uganda has died. When Helen inquires about the friend's name, she is finally told, "He had at least a dozen [nicknames] for me, but I only ever called him Isaac." Suddenly, readers realize that the narrator of the Isaac chapters has taken on the name and identity of the Ugandan Isaac. Thus, there are two Isaacs in *All Our Names*, serving to blur the lines of identity.

At a later dinner, Henry reveals he was friends with Joseph Mabira, who was not only an important rebel leader but also the boss and lover of the Ugandan Isaac. From a once powerful family forced out of political favor, Joseph took the young Ugandan Isaac under his wing, promising him a place in his rebel army. In veneration of his lover and mentor, the Ugandan Isaac took Joseph's last name, Mabira, which he passed on to the narrator when the latter sought to study in the United States. The Ethiopian Isaac, Helen's lover, was nicknamed Bird by his father in Ethiopia, but his real name is spoken only once by the Ugandan Isaac, rendered as D——.

Thus, Mengestu weaves a dense mystery around names and assumed identities in *All Our Names*. The revelation about her Isaac leaves Helen in despair. At the end of Isaac's spring semester, in May 1974, Helen decides they should take a trip to Chicago—where their eventual fate will resolve itself.

*Dinaw Mengestu is an Ethiopian American writer. He earned an MFA in writing from Columbia University in 2005. His first novel,* The Beautiful Things That Heaven Bears *(2007), won several literary prizes. He received a 2012 MacArthur Foundation grant.* All Our Names *(2014) is his third novel.*

The story of Helen and Isaac is told in a moving fashion. However, the narrator's presentation of Ugandan history is problematic. *All Our Names* carries the standard disclaimer that any resemblances to actual people and events is coincidental, which allows Mengestu artistic license to shape history according to his dramatic desires. However, in a novel that is clearly designed as a realistic story, and not as alternate history, Mengestu's authorial liberties with African history cannot be overlooked. *All Our Names* gives a version of the early years of Idi Amin's brutal rule that does not quite correspond to historical reality. The narrator arrives in Uganda and befriends the Ugandan Isaac "almost ten years" after independence. This must be around 1970, as Uganda became independent on October 9, 1962. Soon after, a new president "took power . . . after he staged the country's first coup." This is a clear reference to Idi Amin's coup, which took place on January 25, 1971.

The novel's Ugandan president, like the historical Amin, begins to crack down on civil society, including university students. In the novel, it is during this crackdown that Joseph Mabira takes the Ugandan Isaac as his lover. Mabira organizes an armed insurrection against the president. Things soon turn ugly and brutal. Isaac's chapters relate horrifying atrocities.

However, the depiction of anti-"Amin" forces inside Uganda fighting against the president is historically inaccurate. Ugandan rebels tried to invade from Tanzania in the south in 1972, but Joseph Mabira's rebellion occurs in the north and from within Uganda. Amin's troops massacred the Acholi and Lango people in the north, on the dictator's initiative, not in response to an uprising, as happens in the novel. As Mengestu has written nonfiction about the civil wars in Uganda, he must know the real history. His account in *All Our Names* more closely resembles what happened in Uganda's north much later, after 1986, and not from 1971 to 1972.

One possible reason for Mengestu's decision to retroject later events into an earlier decade of Ugandan history might have been a desire to juxtapose atrocities in East Africa next to racism in the United States. The kind of overt racial discrimination encountered by Helen and Isaac likely would not have occurred as readily in the late 1980s as it did in the 1970s. However, Mengestu's authorial decision detracts from the historical realism of his novel.

*R. C. Lutz*

## Review Sources

Hoffert, Barbara. Rev. of *All Our Names: A Novel*, by Dinaw Mengestu. *Library Journal* 15 Mar. 2014: 112. Print.

Jones, Malcolm. "Cultural Exchange." Rev. of *All Our Names: A Novel*, by Dinaw Mengestu. *New York Times*. New York Times, 19 Mar. 2014. Web. 5 Feb. 2015.

Kakutani, Michiko. "Out of Uganda, in the Midwest." Rev. of *All Our Names: A Novel*, by Dinaw Mengestu. *New York Times*. New York Times, 3 Mar. 2014. Web. 5 Feb. 2015.

# All the Birds, Singing

**Author:** Evie Wyld (b. 1980)
**First published:** 2013, in the United Kingdom
**Publisher:** Pantheon Books (New York). 240 pp.
**Type of work:** Novel
**Time:** Early in the second decade of the twenty-first century
**Locale:** An unnamed island off the coast of England, various locations in Western Australia

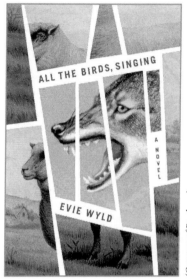

(Courtesy of Pantheon)

All the Birds, Singing *is a lyrical, suspenseful novel told from the point of view of a young woman, alienated from fellow humans and from nature itself, who is attempting to come to terms with and move beyond a horrific past.*

**Principal characters:**
JAKE WHYTE, the narrator, a self-sufficient young Australian woman who has moved to an island off the English coast to raise sheep
DOG, her dog
LLOYD, a mysterious drifter she takes in
OTTO, an Australian sheepherder who taught Jake and kept her as a sex slave

*All the Birds, Singing* (2013) opens with protagonist Jake Whyte standing over the mutilated body of one of her sheep as scavenging crows mock her from nearby trees. This somber scene effectively sets the tone for the rest of the novel, a dark and often gruesome examination of one woman's attempts to be self-reliant and come to terms with her past. Author Evie Wyld continues to display the talent apparent in her first book, *After the Fires, a Still Small Voice* (2009), for which she was named one of the best young British novelists of 2013 by *Granta* magazine. *All the Birds, Singing* has won several awards and earned her further critical acclaim.

Jake lives alone with her sheep and her dog, named Dog, on a farm on a remote island off the coast of England, which she purchased after moving from Australia three years earlier. She prefers her own flawed company, unwilling to interact with members of the local population except when absolutely necessary. The reasons for Jake's self-imposed exile and desire for solitude slowly become apparent as the novel proceeds, thanks to an imaginative structure that drives the story forward and backward simultaneously. The first-person narrative, divided in two, pulls in opposite directions, yet manages to provide a unified portrait of a woman with a unique personality: a survivor who withstands great hardships. Odd-numbered chapters, told in standard past tense, are set on the farm in the present day and move in chronological order; even-numbered chapters are relayed in present tense and are set in Australia, revealing Jake's past in reverse chronological order.

In the present-day chapters, readers are shown highlights of Jake's purposely standoffish lifestyle. She visits a farm shop to buy fresh fruits and vegetables, warily conversing with Marcie, the greengrocer's self-absorbed young daughter. She drives past a group of loutish teenagers and does not outwardly react when they make obscene gestures at her. She rebuffs genial farmer Don Murphy's neighborly attempts to draw her out, encouraging her to visit the local pub and mix with the natives. Jake keeps her shotgun loaded and a hammer close at hand as more sheep are mysteriously killed and she speculates about the possible perpetrator: human, animal, or something else? At night she tunes in to soccer radio broadcasts to drown out the ominous sound of the constant wind.

(© Roelof Bakker)

*Evie Wyld won the 2009 John Llewellyn Rhys Prize for her first novel,* After the Fire, a Still Small Voice *(2009). Her second novel,* All the Birds, Singing, *won the 2013 Encore Award, the 2014 Miles Franklin Award, and the 2014 European Union Prize for Literature, among other honors.*

Eventually, Jake visits the local police station to report the sheep killings. A condescending male sergeant barely listens to what she says and blames loose dogs, treating her like a helpless female and repeating Don's admonition that she should get out more and make friends. After returning home, Jake finds a drifter named Lloyd on her property. Although she is wary at first, Jake gives him shelter for the night, and eventually he remains on the farm, helping with odd jobs and slowly bonding with Jake and Dog as his own mysterious past is revealed.

Sheep continue to die, however, and both Jake and Lloyd glimpse a shadowy beast that they fear could be responsible—if it is anything more than imagination. Another suspect is Don's son Samson, fresh from juvenile incarceration, who comes to the farm, unaware that his father sold the property to Jake. Jake tries to rule out foxes or local children as the killer, but tension mounts as it becomes increasingly clear that she has chosen to live on the desolate island to escape something that may now be catching up to her.

Meanwhile, in the alternating chapters dealing with Jake's past in Australia, readers learn how and why she left for England. Jake is a successful shearer at an outback sheep ranch who, as the only woman on the crew, has earned grudging respect for her abilities. She has a regular lover, Greg, who is fascinated by the deep scars on her back; and an enemy, Clare, Greg's best friend, whom Jake replaced as a shearer. Clare tries to blackmail Jake for sex in exchange for his silence about something shameful he has learned about her earlier life. He says he has spoken with a man named Otto, who claims Jake stole his truck and money and killed his dog. Jake deals with Clare by knocking him out, but she cannot confront his allegations about her past and decides to leave for the distant British island.

In subsequent chapters, Jake's past is more deeply probed as the narrative moves backward in time. She is seen arriving at the sheep ranch, being introduced to other hands, participating in good-humored roughhousing and horseplay, and being taught the finer points of shearing. Later she is shown selling an old truck before being interviewed for the job on the sheep ranch, hinting that Clare's claims may have some foundation. And indeed, Jake is then shown stealing the truck from a crusty old sheep rancher named Otto and running over his vicious dog.

The reasons for Jake's actions become evident in later chapters as her relationship with Otto is unveiled. She is shown living with Otto in captivity, serving as his sex slave before eventually stealing his truck to escape. Otto is depicted as an eccentric who shifts between kindness and cruelty, regularly demanding she have sex with him yet at the same time exhibiting a prudish aversion to rough language. It transpires that Otto was a regular customer of Jake's when she worked as a prostitute, a job he "rescued" her from by inviting her to stay at his sheep ranch. There he teaches Jake his trade, but what seemed to her a way out soon proves to be a new torment. Prostitution, too, was originally Jake's attempt to make more money and improve her life, only to spiral into trouble. Only by the novel's conclusion do readers finally learn how deep the roots of Jake's trauma stretch, how she acquired her indelible physical and mental scars, and whether she may be able to finally escape them.

Though its overall tone is bleak, *All the Birds, Singing* is punctuated by bursts of dark humor that verge on slapstick, hinting that no matter how low one has sunk, the future holds the possibility of uplifting redemption. Wyld's technique of withholding information works well to make the novel a suspenseful, tension-filled read that offers several deep layers of meaning beneath the deceptively simple twin surface stories. Though the alternating narratives are a potential point of confusion, with few overt signs other than the shift in tense to alert readers to which story is unfolding, the strong writing and attention to detail ensure the structure's success.

*All the Birds, Singing* received widely positive reviews and earned Wyld the Miles Franklin Award, the Encore Award, and the Jerwood Fiction Uncovered Prize, as well as nominations for several other awards. The novel was praised as a worthy follow-up to *After the Fire, a Still Small Voice*, which had employed a similar narrative structure. The reviewer for *Publishers Weekly* commended the "searing" novel's "vivid storytelling," and others agreed that Wyld's skillful descriptions and excellent use of language carry the reader through the fairly brutal events depicted. Many critics especially praised the Australian sequences for their gripping and unflinching exploration of Jake's character and the forces that shaped it. In her review for the *New York Times*, Maile Meloy called the novel "swift and assured and emotionally wrenching."

Despite the general praise, critics did note some flaws in the book. Several reviewers felt the mystery elements of the novel are not given enough resolution, particularly the central question of what is killing the sheep and why. Though some readers may appreciate that Wyld leaves much of the conclusion open to interpretation, those looking for a more traditional mystery ending will not find it in Jake's present-day narrative. The reviewer for *Kirkus Reviews* felt that the lack of answers in the present-day island story detracts from Jake's development as a character, leaving her future too uncertain. Others agreed that it suffers in comparison to the Australian narrative, throwing the novel off balance. Finally, some critics warned that Wyld's menacing atmosphere may simply be too unrelenting for some readers to fully enjoy.

One of the major themes of the novel is that no matter how strong or self-reliant an individual might be, it is almost impossible to withdraw entirely from the human race: people need people as springboards for ideas, for companionship, for emotional support, and for mutual protection from dangers real and imagined. Another significant thread throughout *All the Birds, Singing* is suggested by the title: the sometimes uneasy relationship between humans and nature, as represented by animals. In both English and Australian environments, the novel emphasizes the constant presence of creatures. These range from the secretive and small but virulent, such as the venomous Australian redback spider, to the highly visible and audible, such as the different species of birds described throughout, and from the common and harmless sheep to the fearsome and unknown beast that is killing them. Jake is connected to nature through all of these, reflecting her inner psychology and her outer character. Wyld makes it clear that nature, like a person, can be mysterious, beautiful, nurturing, and dangerous, and she leaves it to the reader to interpret as they will.

*Jack Ewing*

## Review Sources

Rev. of *All the Birds, Singing*, by Evie Wyld. *Kirkus Reviews* 15 Feb. 2014: 286. Print.

Rev. of *All the Birds, Singing*, by Evie Wyld. *Publishers Weekly* 27 Jan. 2014:165–66. Print.

Meloy, Maile. "Isolation Unit." Rev. of *All the Birds, Singing*, by Evie Wyld. *New York Times Book Review* 15 June 2014: 10. Print.

# All the Light We Cannot See

**Author:** Anthony Doerr (b. 1973)
**Publisher:** Scribner (New York). 544 pp.
**Type of work:** Novel
**Time:** 1934, 1940–41, 1944, 1945, 1974, 2014
**Locales:** Paris, France; Saint-Malo, France; Schulpforta School, Germany; Zollverein, Germany

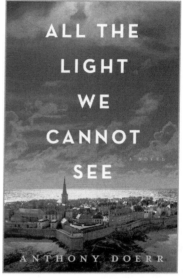

(Courtesy of Scribner)

*This novel interweaves the stories of Marie-Laure LeBlanc, a blind French girl, and Werner Pfennig, a German boy, during World War II. As they come of age, they become increasingly involved in the war—and with a mysterious jewel—while their fates converge.*

**Principal characters:**
MARIE-LAURE LEBLANC, a blind Parisian girl who flees the Nazi occupation
DANIEL LEBLANC, her father, master locksmith of the Muséum National d'Histoire Naturelle in Paris
ETIENNE LEBLANC, her reclusive great-uncle
WERNER PFENNIG, a German orphan and technological expert
JUTTA PFENNIG, his younger sister
SERGEANT MAJOR REINHOLD VON RUMPEL, a German officer and jeweler

Moving across space, time, and points of view, *All the Light We Cannot See* (2014) is a complex tale of war, families, and intertwined destinies. The novel revolves around two central characters, adolescents on opposite sides of World War II, who struggle to find their identities amid the realities of war. Doerr blends elements of historical fiction, mystery, fantasy, and coming-of-age story through rich prose that has gained the work widespread critical acclaim. A best seller that was named on many lists of the best novels of 2014, *All the Light We Cannot See* has been hailed as an achievement that stands out from the crowded field of World War II fiction.

Marie-Laure LeBlanc is the only daughter of master locksmith Daniel LeBlanc, who is employed at the Muséum National d'Histoire Naturelle in Paris, France. An attentive single father, LeBlanc rises to the challenge of lovingly raising his young daughter, who lost her eyesight due to congenital cataracts. Until the Nazi invasion, the two live a quiet, bonded existence in their neighborhood of Paris, which Marie-Laure has learned to navigate astutely by memorizing a scale wooden model that her father painstakingly carved for her. When the city falls under German occupation, the

LeBlancs flee to the seaside home of Marie-Laure's reclusive great-uncle Etienne in Saint-Malo, France.

In a darker corner of Europe, Werner Pfennig and his younger sister, Jutta, are raised in an orphanage in the coal-mining town of Zollverein, Germany. Both precocious and highly intelligent, Werner and Jutta stand out in the orphanage, and the former chaffs at his predestined life course working in the mines. When Werner finds and repairs a broken radio, the two children discover a larger world that can penetrate even into their sparse existence. However, the siblings' childhood bond is shattered when Werner's talent with radio machinery is noticed and the young boy is handpicked to attend the Schulpforta military academy of the Hitler Youth.

The novel unfolds by revealing different moments of Marie-Laure and Werner's stories in counterpoint, moving easily back and forth in time through their lives until their ultimate connection. Though the book does not follow a linear chronology, the characters' strong voices make it easy to follow the intertwining stories and time lines. The tensest drama takes place across six days in August 1944, during which the American bombing of Saint-Malo ends the German occupation of the city but causes devastating damage. Marie-Laure survives the bombing of the city in her great-uncle's home, only to face terror and uncertainty in its wake. Werner, serving as a radio specialist in a unit trained to detect and apprehend resistance radio transmissions, is also in Saint-Malo as he becomes increasingly aware of the moral consequences of his job. The dangers that both Marie-Laure and Werner face in the ensuing days are narrated in incremental steps throughout most of the balance of the novel, and these same steps gradually bring the two protagonists closer toward contact with one another in an intricately unfolding plot that is both suspenseful and skillfully recounted.

A third, and more mysterious, subplot complicates the novel, adding the sparkle of a treasure hunt to the darkness of the war narrative. As a small child, Marie-Laure heard tales of a priceless diamond, known as the Sea of Flames, locked in a deep inner recess of the natural history museum where her father works. The powerful stone, it is rumored, gives its owner eternal life but also the curse of an existence surrounded by tragedy. Unbeknownst to Marie-Laure, her father is entrusted with a significant role in concealing this artifact from the approaching Germans. Daniel LeBlanc does not know whether he carries the original diamond or a copy made to deceive the Nazis, but either way concealing the stone is an unwelcome burden. When Daniel disappears, arrested on false charges by the Germans, Marie-Laure and Etienne are unaware of the mysterious and dangerous rock he has left concealed in the home, though they remain tied to its influence.

Meanwhile, Sergeant Major Reinhold von Rumpel, a German officer and jeweler by trade, begins his search for the Sea of Flames. Initially begun out of curiosity, von Rumpel's quest becomes urgent after his diagnosis with terminal cancer. Slowly, he winds his way through forgeries and roadblocks, in search of the actual diamond that he hopes will act as his own fountain of eternal life. His tenacity brings him closer and closer to Saint-Malo, creating another plotline of tension and confluence that adds further drama to the novel.

In *All the Light We Cannot See*, Doerr focuses his narrative away from the broad impacts of World War II and onto the interlocking, nuanced, and imperfect lives of his protagonists. In their struggles, missteps, and frailties, Doerr's characters introduce the reader to the human tragedies of World War II through a perspective that is intimate and personal, rather than bloody, bombastic, and dichotomous. None of the central characters

*Anthony Doerr has published widely and to great acclaim. His publications include the novel* About Grace *(2004), the memoir* Four Seasons in Rome *(2007), and two volumes of short stories,* The Shell Collector *(2002) and* Memory Wall *(2010). He has been the recipient of numerous awards, including the Rome Prize and Guggenheim Fellowship.*

is in a position of great power, and none is capable of foreseeing the wider implications of his or her actions. During Werner's schooling, for example, he follows the prompting of a teacher and mentor in order to devise a system of triangulating radio waves that can enable him to locate a transmission point. Initially, he accepts the idea of his task being merely numbers and a problem to solve. Only after his invention is functional does Werner realize that its purpose is to hunt down and kill those using unauthorized radios.

Doerr presents strong development in his characters even as he makes clear their flaws and human limitations. During his military service, Werner is pushed to rethink his training as he faces the consequences of his mathematical calculations in the broken and lifeless bodies of his targets. Etienne, meanwhile, lives his life as a recluse, attempting to control the chaos and uncertainty of life by shutting down all possibility of missteps. He has not left his house in years when Daniel and Marie-Laure arrive on his doorstep. After Marie-Laure enters his life, however, Etienne begins to battle his own fears in order to nurture and protect the child.

Only Marie-Laure herself seems to move through the world with a guiding sense and prescience beyond her age. Despite her blindness, she astutely solves puzzles, immerses herself in literature with the benefit of volumes published in braille, boldly serves the French Resistance, and demonstrates great skill at self-preservation. Critics almost unanimously praised her character as one of the highlights of the book; in his review for the *New York Times* William T. Vollmann called her "an exquisitely realized creation." However, some found that other elements of the book did not work as well. Vollman found Doerr's treatment of Nazi characters, especially von Rumpel, stay too close to cliché and prevent the novel from reaching a higher level of literature. John Freeman, in a review for the *Boston Globe*, also noted that the basic plot elements can feel derivative, but asserted that Doerr's "startlingly fresh" language allows it to succeed. Indeed, even scenes that could easily appear overly sentimental are made poignant by Doerr's clear, simple, yet detailed writing.

Doerr's interest in capturing the human condition comes to particular life in the association between his central characters and powerful sensory experiences. Many critics noted the skillful way in which opposing sensations are drawn into a strong overarching metaphor. Marie-Laure cannot see, but she experiences the world through her incredibly astute senses of sound and touch. Fascinated with scientific study and natural history, her hands follow the characteristics forms of shells and rocks, and devour the prose of Jules Verne, but the brilliant internal refractions of light at the heart of the Sea of Flames are nothing to her. By contrast, Werner and Jutta are spellbound by voices that come to them over radio waves, especially the soothing and informative broadcasts of a French scientist, whose radio programs for children become the highlight of their evenings. Also belonging to the world of sound is Frederick, Werner's closest friend at the military academy. Frederick is fascinated with birds and can identify a birdcall from great distance without seeing the animal itself. As it turns out, he is also dangerously near-sighted—which leaves him vulnerable within the cruel training practices at Schulpforta. Doerr's compelling descriptions of sensation are part of what brings the novel to life. These sensitivities also draw connections across and among these characters. Ultimately, one of the implicit themes of the novel is a faith that art, which captures the imagination and the senses, can bring people together across the greatest chasms.

The book concludes with two larger chronological jumps, the first of which is set in 1974 and the second in 2014. These bursts into later decades allow Doerr to bring some closure to the complex strains of the narrative while at the same time acknowledging the impossibility of healing and recovery from certain types of wartime losses. A final connection between Marie-Laure and Werner is established through an accidental series of governmental and individual acts of repatriation and recompense. Ultimately, the items involved are small—decidedly insignificant in the greater scheme of world history when looking back across the years—yet their emotional significance in the lives of individuals is undeniable. Through these actions, the reader witnesses the slow healing of Europe as a generation who grew up in a war seeks to reconcile itself both to its history and to its survival.

*All the Light We Cannot See* is a powerful novel. In elegant prose, it weaves a complex cast of characters whose small lives develop urgency and enduring meaning across the pages of the book. Ultimately, this is a tale of human resilience coupled with frailty and obsolescence, and of continuities and connections that defy physical and national division. Rather than a love story, war story, or treasure hunt, this book offers a combination of all three, designed to probe large, small, and intangible qualities of the human condition.

*Julia A. Sienkewicz*

## Review Sources

Cha, Steph. "'All the Light We Cannot See' Pinpoints 2 Lives in War." Rev. of *All the Light We Cannot See*, by Anthony Doerr. *Los Angeles Times*. Los Angeles Times, 23 May 2014. Web. 10 Jan. 2015.

Maslin, Janet. "Light Found in the Darkness of Wartime." Rev. of *All the Light We Cannot See*, by Anthony Doerr. *New York Times*. New York Times, 28 Apr. 2014. Web. 14 Jan. 2015.

Freeman, John. Rev. of *All the Light We Cannot See*, by Anthony Doerr. *Boston Globe*. Boston Globe Media Partners, 3 May 2014. Web. 10 Jan. 2015.

Vaill, Amanda. Rev. of *All the Light We Cannot See*, by Anthony Doerr. *Washington Post*. Washington Post, 5 May 2014. Web. 10 Jan. 2015.

Vollmann, William T. "Darkness Visible." Rev. of *All the Light We Cannot See*, by Anthony Doerr. *New York Times*. New York Times, 8 May 2014. Web. 14 Jan. 2015.

# American Fun
## Four Centuries of Joyous Revolt

**Author:** John Beckman (b. 1967)
**Publisher:** Pantheon Books (New York). 432 pp.
**Type of work:** History, cultural history, social history
**Time:** 1600s–present
**Locale:** United States

*In* American Fun: Four Centuries of Joyous Revolt, *John Beckman contrasts numerous examples of real fun (happy, spontaneous, participatory, and democratic) with bogus enjoyment (passive, consumer-oriented, and controlled by big business).*

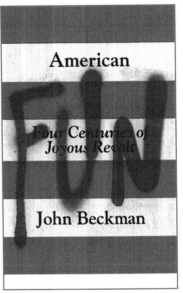

(Courtesy of Pantheon)

**Principal personages:**
JOHN ADAMS, patriot and second US president
SAMUEL ADAMS, patriot and Revolutionary War leader
P. T. BARNUM, business owner
FREDERICK DOUGLASS, former slave, a champion of rights for African Americans
ABBIE HOFFMAN, hippie and political activist
KEN KESEY, author, prankster, and advocate of drug use
THOMAS MORTON, fun-loving, disruptive colonist
MARK TWAIN, author and humorist

John Beckman's *American Fun* traces the history of the various ways in which Americans have amused themselves over the centuries, from the earliest days in Puritan New England to the present era. Beckman argues that some kinds of fun have been invigorating and rebellious and have often been associated with positive political and cultural changes, while other kinds—especially those involving "amusements" provided by big businesses or wannabe big businessmen (such as P. T. Barnum)—have tended to make Americans passive consumers of fun. This position ultimately does not seem much fun at all. Beckman admires fun associated with individual initiative and widespread participation by a broad cross section of "the people"; he is critical of fun in which people stand around (or, more often, sit around, as at the movies or in amusement parks) and expect to be entertained.

Beckman discerns a pattern repeated frequently in American history. In this pattern, a small group of nonconformists has so much fun flouting authority that more and more people join them. This process is democratizing, because people devoted to having active fun are people less likely to care about distinctions of race, class, gender, religion, and so on. A commitment to playful fun, therefore, can have serious social implications by undermining the power of rigid authority and authority figures. People out to enjoy themselves often break oppressive laws and even (as in the American Revolution) help overthrow tyranny. This kind of fun is "the fun of eluding laws *together*, in playful, active, comical ways that often"—paradoxically—"model good citizenship." Whether by dancing new dances together, playing new music together, gambling together, drinking together, taking drugs together, or participating in other often transgressive behaviors, Americans have always had fun that both springs from and contributes to a deep desire for freedom, Beckman asserts.

Beckman spends much time discussing the antics of the early New Englander Thomas Morton, who "schooled in English Renaissance hedonism, founded [the community of] Merry Mount thirty miles to the north [of Plymouth] and devoted himself and his band of rogues to all the excesses outlawed at Plymouth." While the Puritans amused themselves by tarring and feathering lawbreakers and eventually by persecuting witches, Morton was a "lover of the wilderness who consorted with Indians," behaving as "a radical democrat and reckless hedonist." His behavior offended sober-minded Puritans, who did what they could to suppress both him and his activities. His admiration of the local Indians was just one of many reasons the Puritans disdained him.

Similar contrasts between the humorous and humorless run through Beckman's book. For instance, the sober-minded John Adams is contrasted with his second cousin, Samuel, whose name is still associated with beer and good times. Beckman sets both figures within a larger context consisting of fun-loving seamen and the rebellious Sons of Liberty and lesser-known Sons of Neptune. The fun of these folks often resulted in riots and eventually paved the way, according to Beckman, for America's revolt against England. Contrasting the Adams cousins, Beckman, in awkward phrasing unfortunately common in the book, says that "while both men were pear-shaped Puritans with similarly piercing eyes, their temperaments could not have been more different. If John pinched his pennies, Samuel shot his wad." Sometimes Beckman tries a bit too hard to be colloquial, in ways that will make some readers wince. He says, for instance, that Morton "never copped" to the charge that he had taught American Indians how to shoot, while he says that the Puritans, having decided to suppress Morton, "got cracking."

Interestingly, Beckman argues that Frederick Douglass, the great champion of liberty for black slaves (who had been a slave himself), was one of the spoilsports of his day. He believed that many slaves were pacified by their commitment to enjoying good times, and he argued that African Americans, if they were serious about gaining their freedom, needed to be serious in other ways as well. But Beckman argues that the African Americans who wanted to enjoy themselves thereby created communal bonds and helped foster a distinctive black culture rooted in shared music, dancing, folktales, and aspirations. Slaves who frequently identified with mythic "tricksters" often undermined their masters' power while seeming merely interested in enjoying themselves. Ultimately their efforts led to the development of jazz, the quintessential American music.

Later chapters deal with the California gold rush and the freewheeling lifestyles of the miners' camps, where drinking, gambling, hoaxes, horseplay, and prostitution were common. Out of this milieu came Mark Twain, one of the greatest of all American funnymen. "The freedom with which Twain skewered politicians," says Beckman, "much like the freedom with which he needled public sympathies and roared away his nights with other drunken reporters, was enabled on some level by the permissiveness of the West, and by the viral mistrust of authority and control, but it also sprang from his fascination with community—especially reckless, chaotic community." In Beckman's book, the best fun is never merely private; it always involves forging deeper bonds with others.

On the other side of the ledger, there have always been folks who have consistently been serious about religion, sobriety, good morals, and other forms of proper behavior. By the mid-to-late nineteenth century, fun was often domesticated and tamed and could thus become a big business, appealing to the powerful as well as the masses partly because it caused no real trouble. Beckman thinks Barnum was the key figure in this transformation. He argues that Barnum managed "to concoct a 'fun' that seemed to resolve one of America's deep struggles: it pandered to Puritans while pleasing hedonists." Any kind of subsequent fun that has merely entertained Americans without demanding much active participation and rebelliousness is, Beckman believes, ultimately indebted to Barnum. Circuses, Wild West shows, minstrel shows, and other forms of passive (and sometimes demeaning) entertainment were products of "Barnumism." Even sports became increasingly organized rather than remaining spontaneous. Beckman asserts Barnum was no Thomas Morton: "He went to church, led carnies in prayer, and became a roaring voice for temperance. More to the point, he knew that alienating pious America was terrible for business." At best, the concoctions of Barnum and people like him served as relief valves for go-getting, urbanized Americans, who were expected to work long and hard if they hoped to prosper.

*A graduate of the University of Iowa and University of California, Davis, John Beckman is a professor of English at the US Naval Academy, specializing in American studies, creative writing, and critical theory. He has written a novel,* The Winter Zoo *(2002), and contributed to several national publications.*

Partly because African Americans were not expected to prosper, they were the folks (along with other ethnic minorities, such as the Irish) still most closely associated with genuine fun. In the 1920s, in particular, black influence on white culture became especially pronounced. This was largely because of jazz, which eventually led to rock and roll. Rock in turn eventually led to heavy metal, hip-hop, and other rebellious musical genres. For Beckman, the history of America is a history of "merry pranksters" challenging a staid status quo and eventually winning more freedom for everyone. It is hard to doubt the general truth of this narrative, and Beckman is clearly on the side of the rebels and nonconformists.

Only a few times does he gesture toward the dark underside of the story he tells. Alcoholism, drug and gambling addictions, broken homes, poverty, juvenile delinquency, sexual abuse, teenage pregnancies, sexually transmitted diseases, and the violence stoked by drugs and championed in some popular music (music that often demeans women directly and its fans indirectly, by encouraging irresponsible behavior)—all these possible topics figure only infrequently in this book. At one point, when discussing the 1960s, Beckman does mention in passing "a subculture of runaways and distracted idealists who exposed themselves to rampant hepatitis, VD, meth addiction, poverty, drug wars, rape, and frequent abuse by pimps (who seized on 'free love' teeny boppers), Hell's Angels (who treated weak hippies like servants), the Mafia (who bullied dealers into their drug trade), and, constantly, cops and Feds." AIDS, however, is never mentioned, nor is much said about all the other various pathologies, both literal and metaphorical, that have descended on an American society often addicted, unfortunately, to fun at any price.

*Robert C. Evans, PhD*

**Review Sources**

Rev. of *American Fun: Four Centuries of Joyous Revolt*, by John Beckman. *Kirkus Reviews*. Kirkus, 5 Jan. 2014. Web. 6 Feb. 2015.

Beck, Stefan. "A History of American Fun." Rev. of *American Fun: Four Centuries of Joyous Revolt*, by John Beckman. *Daily Beast*. Daily Beast, 9 Feb. 2014. Web. 6 Feb. 2015.

Chudacoff, Howard P. "The Pursuit of Happiness." Rev. of *American Fun: Four Centuries of Joyous Revolt*, by John Beckman. *New York Times*. New York Times, 4 Apr. 2014. Web. 6 Feb 2015.

Jackson, Buzzy. Rev. of *American Fun: Four Centuries of Joyous Revolt*, by John Beckman. *Boston Globe*. Boston Globe Media Partners, 1 Feb. 2014. Web. 6 Feb. 2015.

# American Innovations

**Author:** Rivka Galchen (b. 1976)
**Publisher:** Farrar, Straus and Giroux (New York). 192 pp.
**Type of work:** Short fiction
**Time:** Late 1970s; 1997–2013
**Locale:** New York City; Chapel Hill, North Carolina; Norman, Oklahoma; Key West, Florida; Singapore; Mexico City; unidentified American cities

(Courtesy of Farrar, Straus, and Giroux)

*The ten stories of Rivka Galchen's first anthology,* American Innovations, *focus on different female characters who are all to some degree alienated from the world around them, sometimes in supernatural ways. Many stories do not follow a conventional, linear narrative, and some leave the reader in suspense after their ending.*

**Principal characters:**

An ENVIRONMENTAL LAWYER, recently unemployed and beginning to detach from reality

ILAN, a philosopher who befriends a female engineering graduate

JACOB, his friend, also a philosopher

A MOTHER, a woman involved in a conflict over the proceeds from a real estate transaction

HER DAUGHTER, her opponent in the conflict

A STUDENT of library and information sciences who grows a third breast on her back

ROY, a young recovering heroin addict

TRISH, a pregnant woman writer whose husband, Jonathan, has just left her

EDDY, a tenant in a near-empty five-story town house up for sale

"ALICE," an American biologist who travels to Mexico City and strikes up an acquaintance with a band of local intellectuals

J, a married science-fiction writer who takes along her stepmother for a literary event on Key West

A NEW YORK CITY WOMAN in her mid-thirties who believes that her furniture has walked out of her apartment

In *American Innovations* (2014), Rivka Galchen offers ten fascinating short stories from the perspective of diverse women characters who all find themselves alienated from the world around them. In some stories, this alienation has realistic interior or exterior reasons. Other stories introduce supernatural elements that take the protagonists by surprise. Galchen's stories belong to the realm of literary fiction, with many cross-references to scientific ideas and American popular culture, as well as reflections on the nature of wealth and the absence thereof.

The title story veers suddenly from the quirkily realistic into the realm of the supernatural. After the breakup of a relationship, the youngish female narrator visits her rich sixty-something aunt in Singapore. Her aunt remembers that at night on September 11, 2001, she noticed a lump on her lower rib cage. Turning on the television, news of the terrorist attack in New York City, where it was still morning, reached her in Singapore, joining global and personal worries. It turned out one of the aunt's silicone breast implants had slipped down. She decided not to replace it and live with her naturally small breasts, defying surgical innovations.

More than a year later, the narrator wakes up one morning in her home in Chapel Hill, North Carolina. To her surprise, she discovers she has grown a third breast, on her back. She decides to be nonchalant about it. She wears loose clothes to her class as a student of library and information sciences. Nobody notices her transformation until she is with the troubled teenage girls she works with as project volunteer. The narrator decides to see a trusted Russian American woman physician for her condition at the climax of the story.

The title of "American Innovations" may allude to the American obsession with innovative cosmetic plastic surgery, which supernaturally backfires against the narrator. This pop-cultural preoccupation with innovative shapes for the female body is alluded to also by a reference to a three-breasted prostitute in the 2012 remake of the film *Total Recall* (1990).

The jacket text of the hardcover edition of *American Innovations* informs the reader that the stories in Galchen's collection "are secretly in conversation with canonical stories," meaning they are inspired by classic short stories. In the case of "American Innovations," the stated inspiration was Nikolai Gogol's story "Nos" (1836; "The Nose" 1842). Franz Kafka's *Die Verwandlung* (1915; *The Metamorphosis*, 1937) is another literary ancestor; whereas Kafka's Gregor Samsa is transformed into a hideous bug, Galchen's narrator receives one breast too many through a capricious turn of fate.

*Rivka Galchen received her medical degree from Mount Sinai Medical School in 2003 and later earned a master of fine arts from Columbia University. She started to teach creative writing at Columbia University in 2009. Her first novel,* Atmospheric Disturbances *(2008), won the William Saroyan International Prize for Fiction Writing in 2010.*

In "The Lost Order," deviation from the regular world is not external but rather in the mind of the female narrator. She is a married environmental lawyer who became unemployed four months prior. Staying at home and trying to cope with the sudden change in her once-busy life, she receives a call from a number with suppressed caller ID. To her amazement, a somewhat angry man orders delivery of garlic chicken, insisting that this time, she get the order right. Overwhelmed by the call, the narrator promises prompt delivery. Only when the caller hangs up does she realize what she has foolishly done. Her husband calls next, also from a suppressed line. He asks her to look outside for his wedding ring, which he lost while playing with their dog. Obstinately, the narrator refuses. When the other caller rings again and insults who he thinks is the Asian restaurateur at the other end of his line, the stunned narrator hangs up. She tries to make amends by looking for the ring outside. When her husband returns, it becomes clear that the narrator is disassociating from the world around her. As a darkly humorous character study, "The Lost Order" explores the alienation from her world that a stunned professional woman might experience under pressure.

"The Region of Unlikeness" develops into a soft science-fiction story about the possibility of time travel. In New York City, the narrator, a civil engineering graduate, becomes acquainted with an unlikely pair, handsome Ilan and overweight Jacob, two philosophizing friends. Once Ilan drops out of sight, Jacob tells the narrator that he died, which she does not believe. Eventually, Jacob asks the narrator to his apartment to propose a fantastic theory involving her, Ilan, and himself. While time travel and time paradoxes have long been standard science-fiction tropes, Galchen manages to infuse her version with a quirky atmosphere of its own.

"Sticker Shock" represents an experiment in narrative voice. The story of a mother-daughter conflict evolving from 1997 to 2011 over a piece of real estate in New York City is related in the jargon of a real-estate professional seemingly detached from the personal lives of the two antagonists. The clash of values, expectations, fears, and ultimate family bonds between a mother and daughter fighting over money and power is revealed through the clinically detached voice of the anonymous third-party narrator.

"Wild Berry Blue" takes readers convincingly into the world of a lonely nine-year-old Israeli girl living with her physician father and mother in Oklahoma in the late 1970s. The story is introduced by the adult woman remembering her first childhood crush and is believably told from the perspective of her younger self. The nine-year-old narrator enjoys her Saturday morning routine with her father, eating cookies dunked in milk while he reads his newspaper at the local McDonald's. The place has a policy of hiring recovering drug addicts and alcoholics, most of whom were former patients of her father's. Going up to the counter for another milk carton, the narrator notices a tattoo on one of the server's arms. She perceives it as "a fragment like ancient elaborate metalwork, that creeps down all the way, past the wrist, to the back of the hand" of the young man, whose name tag identifies him as Roy. She sees his blue eyes, and her crush blossoms.

Galchen creates a nice double layer for her narrative: the girl readies herself to play the role of the biblical Esther at the Jewish Purim festival in Tulsa. As the girl knows, "Esther married the gentile king" to save her people. Her crush on Roy, a recovering heroin addict, and her role as Esther account for some uncanny synchronicity. The next Saturday, the girl munches on colored candy that gives her "wild berry blue saliva" as she approaches blue-eyed Roy at the McDonald's counter. She tells Roy she is going to a medieval fair to buy a crown for her Esther costume, and Roy says he likes the plain wooden puppets sold there. The girl resolves to buy such a puppet for him. What will happen to her innocent crush constitutes the climax of this well-crafted story.

"The Entire Northern Side Was Covered by Fire" tells the story of pregnant writer Trish, who is left by her husband, Jonathan, on the day she sells the movie rights to her first novel. From her brother and her struggling writer friend David, Trish finds out her husband kept a blog called *I Can't Stand My Wife*. For her, the short story suggests, the sudden revelation of this blog is likened to the historic devastation caused by a meteor striking Siberia in 1904, setting the tundra aflame, as reported by contemporary eye witnesses.

"Real Estate" and the closing story, "Once an Empire," both deal with the supernatural. In the first story, the narrator's rich aunt asks her to house-sit her "pretty run-down five-story town house," which she has put up for sale. It is meant to be vacant, but one day in the lobby, the narrator encounters Eddy, who tells the narrator that her aunt let him stay on for a little while. When the narrator goes out to eat, she encounters a man who looks like her father, who has been dead for thirteen years. It turns out that the man may be the ghost of her father, just as Eddy may be a ghost. The story provides only an oblique explanation for this turn of events.

In "Once an Empire," the narrator, a woman in her mid-thirties, believes she sees her furniture walk out of her Brooklyn apartment next to the Jehovah's Witnesses Watchtower Building, which incidentally was sold to a developer on October 2, 2013, after Galchen's story was published. The strange furniture walk-out happens when the narrator returns from a movie "past midnight, which is when . . . the veil between the living and the dead is at its thinnest . . . its being the witching hour." The narrator reports the loss, but not its circumstances, to the police. A few weeks later, she finds her furniture deposited by a woman antiques seller near three dumpsters on a vacant lot. She likens her situation to that of "Britain, once an empire, now a small island off Europe." The reader may wonder whether the narrator has become delusional in the aftermath of a burglary or if a supernatural event has taken place.

The narrator of "Dean of Arts" is a married molecular biologist who, while on a trip to Mexico City, meets a group of Mexican intellectuals and decides to impersonate an American reporter who can make them famous. She clearly bears some resemblance to the protagonist of "The Lost Order." Her relationship with reality becomes also rather tenuous.

"The Late Novels of Gene Hackman" chronicles the paid-for trip of married science-fiction writer J and her elderly but sprightly Burmese American stepmother, Q, to a literary event on Key West. While they are there, they hear of the (real-life) event of Gene Hackman getting struck by a truck on January 13, 2012. While J worries about Hackman, Q is more confident, as she is throughout the trip, and believes he will survive, which the real Gene Hackman did, with only minor injuries.

The female narrators of *American Innovations* generally share a predilection for some disassociation from common reality. Often they are professional women in their thirties who encounter a crisis caused by either internal or external, sometimes seemingly supernatural, conflicts. A dead father figures in many stories. Husbands, if they exist, appear as a vaguely benign presence, sometimes bemused by the changes in their wives. Occasionally, there is an older aunt or stepmother supporting the protagonist mentally or monetarily.

The ten stories of *American Innovations* make for an unusual, exciting reading experience. A reader who does not demand a classic, linear plot but is willing to engage in occasionally meandering narratives, which may appear to just peter out at the end but reveal much throughout their narrative journeys, will be richly rewarded by Galchen's literarily ambitious short fiction.

*R. C. Lutz*

**Review Sources**

Bezmozgis, David. "The Unpossessed." Rev. of *American Innovations*, by Rivka Galchen. *New York Times*. New York Times, 16 May 2014. Web. 6 Feb. 2015.

Gartner, Zsuzsi. Rev. of *American Innovations*, by Rivka Galchen. *Globe and Mail*. Globe and Mail, 16 May 2014. Web. 6 Feb. 2015.

Langer, Adam. "Short Stories That Riff Playfully on Some Enduring Forebears." Rev. of *American Innovations*, by Rivka Galchen. *New York Times*. New York Times, 7 May 2014. Web. 6 Feb. 2015.

# Andrew's Brain

**Author:** E. L. Doctorow (b. 1931)
**Publisher:** Random House (New York). 224 pp.
**Type of work:** Novel
**Time:** 2001
**Locales:** New York, California

Andrew's Brain *follows the disjointed narrative of a cognitive scientist named Andrew, as delivered to an unknown interlocutor referred to as "Doc," in which he relates the series of disasters and tragedies that he presumes make up his life—and for which he assumes some agency.*

**Principal characters:**
ANDREW, a cognitive scientist and professor turned public school teacher, later a government official
DOC, the unnamed interlocutor to whom he tells his story
MARTHA, his ex-wife
BRIONNY, his deceased wife

(Courtesy of Random House)

E. L. Doctorow is perhaps best known for adapting large, historical moments to small, personal experiences of those moments, making the personal perhaps more significant than the historical. His sweepingly epic novels, such as *Ragtime* (1975) and *The March* (2005), immerse readers in immense historical landscapes as well as the depths of the characters who occupy them. These books take readers into the expansive South of the Civil War and into World War I–era New York, dropping them into the hearts and minds of characters both imagined and real. Typically, in Doctorow's novels, one pivotal event—war, depression, the execution of suspected Cold War spies—turns the spokes of the characters, all hooked to the same wheel. Doctorow's encompassing voice has earned great acclaim for the breadth of such storytelling.

*Andrew's Brain* (2014), his twelfth novel, feels smaller than these works in several ways. In it, Doctorow touches less firmly on a monumental event while trying to delve even deeper into the mind of one man, Andrew, whose life spiraled into desperation as a result of that event. However, the reader does not know this until the final third of the novel, and Andrew does not seem to understand it either.

In the opening lines of the novel, Andrew offers to tell the reader about "my friend Andrew, the cognitive scientist." He is speaking to an unknown listener, who occasionally interrupts the ensuing two hundred pages of narrative with guiding, even leading, questions and sometimes sympathetic, sometimes critical commentary. The reader does not know to whom Andrew is speaking (though Andrew dubs his interlocutor "Doc," suggesting a therapist), where he is talking, or why he has elected to share his stories with the listener. The reader does not even know for sure whether Andrew made that choice himself, of the free will that he continuously calls into question.

Doctorow has said that he began the novel as a conversation and that the model of that conversation took over. What follows is a circuitous recounting of the high points of Andrew's life that—inevitably, he implies—turned to tragedies: the death of a driver in an automobile accident, a hawk attack on his dachshund, the death of his first child, the death of his second wife. Andrew even finds affirmation of his self-assumed status as catastrophic agent from a particularly unsympathetic source, who calls him the Pretender and blames him for destroying anything he touches.

Andrew, for his part, seems pleased to accept this blame."My soul resides in a still, deep, beautiful, emotionless, calm cold pond of silence. But I am not fooled," he tells Doc. "A killer is what I am. And to top things off I am incapable of punishing myself, taking my own life in despair of the wreck I've made of people's lives, helpless infants or women I love." From beginning to end, Doctorow reveals only what Andrew tells Doc, and Andrew's nonlinear perspective and his self-absorption make his reliability dubious. What any other character says is uncertain. Time and again, Doc questions Andrew on the veracity of his story, but even his words are shared through Andrew's tinted lens.

Andrew begins by describing the night that he takes his infant daughter, Willa, to his semi-estranged ex-wife, Martha. He justifies his abandonment of Willa, whose mother, Brionny, has died, as an attempt to save the girl's life. Andrew blames himself for Brionny's death, just as he blames himself for numerous other catastrophic events in his life. Keenly narcissistic, Andrew at once professes culpability for the losses that he and others connected with him have suffered while simultaneously disclaiming any emotional sense of that agency.

More notably, throughout his telling, Andrew supplies philosophical observations on neuroscience that call into question the independent agency of the mind, undermining even his own conclusions. "We have to be wary of our brains. They make our decisions before we make them," he tells Doc. He is not merely unwilling to punish himself for his professed crimes; he is incapable. He is responsible for the unhappy events of his life, but not really, because he cannot help what he is or what he thinks or what he does. He cannot truly be held accountable, even though he repeatedly seems to blame himself. It is a dangerous cognitive game that

*The author of numerous short stories, plays, and essays, E. L. Doctorow has earned many honors for his work, including the National Book Award, three National Book Critics Awards, two PEN Faulkner Awards, and the PEN Saul Bellow Award. In 2014, he was awarded the US Library of Congress Prize for American Fiction. His other acclaimed novels include* The Book of Daniel *(1971),* Ragtime *(1975),* World's Fair *(1985),* The Waterworks *(1994),* City of God *(2000), and* The March *(2005).* Andrew's Brain *is his twelfth novel.*

Andrew plays, more with himself than with Doc, and a difficult one to believe of a character who feels more like a professor of literature and philosophy than of neuroscience.

*Andrew's Brain* maintains the lyrical, profound, and clever voice that Doctorow has used so well in his preceding novels. He repeatedly engages the reader with Andrew's darkly comical twists and turns and appeals to the reader's sympathy through the more touchingly soft moments in his story. Andrew is annoyingly evasive and full of bombast, but his quirky sense of self and his haphazard romanticism invest the reader in the mystery of his heartbreak. Throughout the novel, Doctorow leads the reader to feel Andrew's suffering and to want to find some redemption for him, just as most readers presumably seek their own.

However, the novel lacks the panoramic scope and empathetic follow-through that readers might expect. Though it centers on one man's thoughts and stories, Andrew's voice often waxes inauthentic. Well past the midway point, the novel turns to the pivotal, driving event of Andrew's story, but as *Washington Post* reviewer Ron Charles pointed out, it feels distracting and even contrived. The back end of the novel makes an abrupt turn that comes across as largely disassociated from the emotional investment of the first 150 or so pages. When Doctorow circles around in the final few pages, the terse resolution feels unresolved.

Perhaps because it deviates so strongly from Doctorow's other novels, *Andrew's Brain* did not receive the same critical acclaim as the award-winning *Ragtime*, *The March*, *World's Fair* (1985), and *Billy Bathgate* (1989). These and other of Doctorow's novels plunge the reader body and mind into the historical and geographic context of their settings, while the stories themselves feature a varied cast of characters whose lives entangle to produce complex and thrilling plotlines. In *Andrew's Brain,* the context for Andrew's reflections is often missing or treated in such trite fashion as to make it difficult to ground the reader. The focus is so narrow as to provide insight into only one character. Andrew's vantage is too precarious to convincingly deliver the other characters in his tale, and so he skews his wives, the husband, his in-laws, and even the unnamed but recognizable political personages of the period into two-dimensional creations of his own perspective. The reader is left with only Andrew with whom to feel any connection. Likewise, the plot centers on what Andrew reveals and is necessarily just as scattered and limited as his report. All of the elements of the story become too thin to hold on to—except Andrew.

All of this is likely intentional. Doctorow has demonstrated such a deftness of storytelling that the seeming deficiencies in *Andrew's Brain* seem more a trick than a failure. The conclusion of the novel comes across as disappointing and incomplete, but because of this, the reader is compelled to reread and investigate more deeply, to search out the punch line in the novel that *New York Times* reviewer Terrence Rafferty called "cunning." "It isn't hard to figure out that Andrew is an unreliable narrator," Rafferty concluded, "but by the end of this sly book Doctorow has you wondering if there's any other kind." He posited that Doctorow, as the author, has engaged in a sly pretense to amuse himself, perhaps at the reader's expense.

Andrew repeatedly brings the story back to the brain and its nefarious alter ego, the mind. Though unconvincing as a scientist, he delivers many theoretical insights that suggest the novel is less a reflection on its particular time and place and more a metaphor for human reality. At one point, Andrew says, "The great problem confronting neuroscience is how the brain becomes the mind. How that three-pound knitting ball makes you feel like a human being." *Andrew's Brain* is not about the character of Andrew or the events he experiences, but rather about Andrew's perception of events—and whether that perception can ever be trusted. Taken in this sense, the late entry of Doctorow's characteristic political and historical flavor makes more sense. The story of Andrew becomes less a story of one man and more an allegory for human civilization.

At its heart, *Andrew's Brain* is a story that its author wanted to tell. However, Doctorow does not make his reasons for writing as clear as in previous works, instead leaving it to the reader to figure out the meaning behind the tale. Though more limited in scope than earlier novels, *Andrew's Brain* challenges the reader to examine Andrew even as Andrew mockingly examines himself. During one session with Doc, Andrew suggests that the collective mentality of ant colonies will enable insects to outlive the more limited human species. Perhaps Doctorow's novel dares the reader to question the importance not only of Andrew's story but also of the broader, collective human story. Why does it matter? The punch line is in what meaning, if any, can be found. The taunt is in daring the reader to make one.

*Christina Dendy*

## Review Sources

Charles, Ron. Rev. of *Andrew's Brain,* by E. L. Doctorow. *Washington Post.* Washington Post, 13 Jan. 2014. Web. 28 Jan. 2015.

McAlpin, Heller. "E. L. Doctorow's New Novel 'Puzzling and Ultimately Disappointing.'" Rev. of *Andrew's Brain,* by E. L. Doctorow. *NPR.* NPR, 17 Jan. 2014. Web. 28 Jan. 2015.

Rafferty, Terrence. "The Mind's Jailer." Rev. of *Andrew's Brain,* by E. L. Doctorow. *New York Times Book Review* 12 Jan. 2014: 1. Print.

Ulin, David L. "E. L. Doctorow Gets Inside *Andrew's Brain.*" Rev. of *Andrew's Brain,* by E. L. Doctorow. *Los Angeles Times.* Los Angeles Times, 9 Jan. 2014. Web. 28 Jan. 2015.

# Annihilation
## Book One of the Southern Reach Trilogy

**Author:** Jeff VanderMeer (b. 1968)
**Publisher:** FSG Originals (New York). 208 pp.
**Type of work:** Novel
**Locale:** Area X

*A four-woman team is sent to explore Area X. The last eleven expeditions to Area X have failed. It is left to this team to successfully investigate the area, which is adjacent to a former military installation and said to be the site of a past environmental catastrophe of unknown consequences.*

(Courtesy of Farrar, Straus, and Giroux)

**Principal characters:**
THE BIOLOGIST, an expedition member and
    the narrator of the novel
THE SURVEYOR, a former military member who joins the expedition
THE PSYCHOLOGIST, the leader of the expedition
THE ANTHROPOLOGIST, a member of the expedition

*Annihilation* tells the story of four female scientists who are deployed on a mission to explore Area X. It is rumored that, years ago, a catastrophic ecological event took place in Area X. The borders are sealed, but there is some concern that the affected area may be expanding past its borders. Authorities are not certain what this will mean for the rest of the planet. As a result, they have sent several teams to investigate the area. None of the teams has been successful.

The scientists who make up the twelfth expedition are tasked with pursuing an investigation through their individual fields of study. No names are used on expeditions, so throughout the novel, the women are referred to by their primary occupation. Although each woman is tasked with keeping a journal, the story is told through the biologist's journal. This format results in a narrative that not only reports events but reports her emotional journey as well.

Details of the biologist's background are revealed in bits and pieces. She is divorced from a member of the eleventh expedition. She had an isolated childhood. She has volunteered for the expedition, not only for the unique opportunity it presents to observe the various habitats but also to discover what happened to the eleventh expedition.

The expedition quickly encounters things the team members cannot explain. The team members also soon realize they have not been given all of the information they need to survive. In fact, they have not even been given information that is entirely accurate. One of the first structures they discover is not on any of the maps they have been given. They know that the psychologist has hypnotized them for the purposes of the expedition, but there is soon reason to doubt her motives. Is she truly using hypnosis to further the purposes of the expedition or for purposes of her own? If her purposes are those of the expedition, then why is the information they received not fitting with her use of hypnosis? Each question builds the tension lurking just beneath the surface.

Area X is described as one that is lush in wildlife. The biologist enjoys her study of the area. The solitude and species diversity are more than she could have hoped for. The only obvious puzzle is in the form of a creature that moans in the night. The moaning is unsettling and leaves all of the women to wonder if they are truly alone. For her part, the biologist wonders just what type of creature it might be. The moaning creature adds to the pervasive feeling of being watched by the animals that almost seem human. They wonder if the animals are really observing them with the interest of a human, or if they are simply animals that are curious about the presence of humans. The knowledge that every earlier mission ended in failure adds to the unsettling atmosphere.

Answers to some of their questions do fall into place. As they do, they raise new questions. These new questions are ever more unsettling. The expedition members are left to wonder just what their mission truly is, whether they will be able to learn what happened to the prior missions, whether it was wise to volunteer, and what it will take for any of them to survive.

The mood in *Annihilation* is oppressive. The point of view and voice are exclusively that of the biologist. Her senses filter each interaction and discovery. She is not content to take anything at face value. Not only does she have a conversation with a peer, she dissects the conversation to parse the true meaning behind each word. She is similarly aware of potential bias in her interpretation of findings and events, and she works to circumvent this bias by methodically making her way through each event in excruciating detail.

Sara Sklaroff, in a review of the novel for the *Washington Post*, "About fifty pages into Jeff VanderMeer's new novel, *Annihilation*, I felt the onset of a panic attack. *Annihilation* is successfully creepy, an old-style gothic horror novel set in a not-too-distant future. The best bits turn your mind inside out."

The setting in *Annihilation* becomes a character in many ways. Whether or not that setting is menacing depends largely upon the perception of the character. In an interview with Matthew Rossi for *Electric Lit*, VanderMeer explained, "It is worth noting that the biologist in *Annihilation* doesn't see the natural environment as threatening at all. The clearest sight is the kind that understands that even when we think we are removed from the natural world that in fact we never have been and never will." This is significant because without her ease in the natural environment, there would be no way to separate what events are truly threatening. If the biologist were inclined to jump at every new discovery, there would be no way to tell which discoveries are truly alarming. Since hers is the only report, her ability to react appropriately to events and discoveries makes it possible to view the report as more than a paranoid, alarmist recitation.

*Jeff VanderMeer is an award-winning novelist and editor who has won the World Fantasy Award three times and been a finalist for the Nebula Award. He has edited or coedited more than ten fiction anthologies. He has also taught at the Yale Writers' Conference, lectured at the Massachusetts Institute of Technology, and served as codirector of Shared Worlds.*

*Annihilation*, the first of three novels in the Southern Reach Trilogy, was a New York Times Best Seller. Foreign rights have sold in seventeen countries. The movie rights have been acquired by Paramount Pictures. VanderMeer has been interviewed many times about the ways in which he uses his characters to tell a story and create an environment and mood.

In his interview with Rossi, VanderMeer spoke about the ways in which a character brings interpretation to an event: "Landscape in fiction always comes to us through character viewpoints. . . . Two people walk through a pristine wilderness. One notices the biting gnats and the mud and the ache in their knee. The other notices the night heron high on a branch and the way the pine forest transitions to swamp and a particular type of dragonfly." In *Annihilation*, there is a crucial difference in the ways each of the characters sees the environment.

As a result of the biologist's introspection, the sense of foreboding and of something menacing just around the corner is reminiscent of the mood in Daphne du Maurier's classic novel *Rebecca* (1938). The biologist's matter-of-fact approach to the discoveries in Area X harks back to H. G. Wells's science-fiction thriller *The Island of Dr. Moreau* (1896). VanderMeer transcends one genre by bringing this gothic horror feel into the present time in a believable fantasy world, without a single false step. In *Annihilation*, he has created a hybrid that is stronger than each individual genre. In so doing, he has pushed the boundaries of science fiction and fantasy.

In a review of the novel for the *Los Angeles Times*, Lydia Millet addressed the literary influences that have been ascribed to *Annihilation*: "*Annihilation* has been touted as part H. P. Lovecraft and part Margaret Atwood, but Vandermeer's calmly rational biologist narrator will read, to any [John] Wyndham fan, as a direct descendant of the botanist narrator in the postapocalyptic romance *The Day of the Triffids*." She added, "*Annihilation*, in which the educated and analytical similarly meets up with the inhuman, is a clear triumph for VanderMeer, who after numerous works of genre fiction has suddenly transcended genre with a compelling, elegant, and existential story of far broader appeal. That's not to say his genre readers should turn away—on the contrary. The cleverness of *Annihilation* is that, like Wyndham's stories, it's both genre and general."

Not every reader will enjoy *Annihilation* from the first word. Jason Sheehan expressed such criticism in a review for *NPR Books*. "I sat down with Jeff VanderMeer's new book, *Annihilation*, on a snowy afternoon, cracked it open, and hated it from word one. . . . You read something like that and you're on ice from the very start, fishtailing wildly through someone else's freaked-up daydream." However, Sheehan added that despite the novel's disorienting start, it nevertheless drew him in. "Didn't come up for air again for three hours, and finished the entire thing in less that a day, knowing it finally for the strange, clever, off-putting, maddening, claustrophobic, occasionally beautiful, occasionally disturbing, and altogether fantastic book that it is. *Annihilation* is a book meant for gulping—for going in head-first and not coming up for air until you hit the back cover."

Author Jeff VanderMeer has won multiple awards for his work in science fiction and fantasy. In his other work, as in *Annihilation*, VandeerMeer's characters are fully realized people who are faced with extraordinary challenges. The settings and characters feel real and familiar. There is just that little twist that takes it beyond the norm and into new territory. The other books in the trilogy, *Authority* and *Acceptance*, both released in 2014, take up where *Annihilation* leaves off, focusing on related aspects of the investigation, to bring the investigation of Area X to a satisfying conclusion.

*Gina Hagler*

**Review Sources**

LeClair, Tom. "Futuristic Thrillers." Rev. of *Annihilation*, by Jeff VanderMeer. *New York Times*. New York Times, 14 Feb. 2014. Web. 2 Mar. 2015.

Millet, Lydia. "In Jeff VanderMeer's 'Annihilation,' Fungal Fiction Grows on You." Rev. of *Annihilation*, by Jeff VanderMeer. *Los Angeles Times*. Los Angeles Times, 30 Jan. 2014. Web. 2 Mar. 2015.

VanderMeer, Jeff. Interview by Matthew Rossi. *Electric Literature*. Electric Lit, 8 Sept. 2014. Web. 2 Mar. 2015.

Sheehan, Jason. "You'll Get Lost In The Haunted World Of 'Annihilation.'" *NPR Books*. NPR, 7 Feb. 2014. Web. 6 Feb. 2015.

Sklaroff, Sarah H. Rev. of *Annihilation*, by Jeff VanderMeer. *Washington Post Books*. Washington Post, 25 Feb. 2014. Web. 6 Feb. 2015.

# Another Great Day at Sea
## Life Aboard the USS George H. W. Bush

**Author:** Geoff Dyer (b. 1958)
**Photographs:** Chris Steele-Perkins
**Publisher:** Pantheon Books (New York). Illustrated. 208 pp.
**Type of work:** Autobiography, memoir
**Time:** 2011
**Locale:** Arabian Sea

*Award-winning writer Geoff Dyer presents an engaging account of his stay aboard the aircraft carrier* USS George H. W. Bush. *Dyer's book is a fish-out-of-water tale, documenting his attempts to adjust to the life lived by the thousands of men and women serving on modern warships.*

(Courtesy of Pantheon)

**Principal personages:**
GEOFF DYER, the author
CHRIS STEELE-PERKINS, his "snapper," or photographer
ENSIGN PAUL NEWELL, the officer charged with chaperoning him
LIEUTENANT COMMANDER RON RANCOURT, the officer in charge of Flight Deck Control
CAPTAIN BRIAN LUTHER, commanding officer of the USS George H. W. Bush
REAR ADMIRAL NORA TYSON, commander of the Carrier Air Wing

British writer Geoff Dyer has distinguished himself as a novelist and essayist, winning many awards for his work. In 2011 Dyer was given the opportunity to spend two weeks aboard the *USS George H. W. Bush*, which resulted in a book recounting his experiences. Readers should not pick up Dyer's *Another Great Day at Sea* (2014) expecting a detailed description of the operations of a modern American supercarrier. Likewise, those hoping for loving and accurate evocations of modern military hardware will be sorely disappointed. Dyer's grasp of the technicalities of the planes and various weapons surrounding him is rather vague, despite the fact that he has fond memories of building Airfix models of warplanes in his youth. His invincible obliviousness extends to a disquieting persistence in labeling the *USS George H. W. Bush* a "boat," something anathema to naval veterans, for whom such a vessel will always and accurately be referred to as a "ship."

Dyer was not an embedded journalist in the conventional sense. Although part of his book appeared in the *New Yorker*, it is not really an exercise in reportage. Instead, Dyer was aboard the carrier as a result of a grant from the Writers in Residence association, which places writers and photographers in important organizations in an effort to stimulate the arts of the nonfiction essay and photojournalism. Other works in the series have looked at the International Monetary Fund and Bell Labs. In the United Kingdom, *Another Great Day at Sea* was originally published by Visual Editions, a publishing company that specializes in image-oriented works, in a format that highlighted photographer Chris Steele-Perkins's contributions; in the American edition by Pantheon Books, the pictures are relegated to a run-of-the-mill photo section, seemingly as an afterthought. Front and center, and comparatively naked, is Dyer's intentionally quirky rumination on naval life.

*Geoff Dyer is an award-winning novelist and nonfiction writer. His essay collection* Otherwise Known as the Human Condition *(2011) received the National Book Critics Circle Award for criticism.*

A casual reader of *Another Great Day at Sea* might think that the book is less about life on a supercarrier than it is about the author himself. By definition, an essay is a personal thing. Since the days of Michel de Montaigne, the art of the essay has married the autobiographical with the observational; a great essay is as much a window into its author's mind as it is a commentary on the world. In the hands of a brilliant essayist such as Montaigne, the vagaries of the author's personality can be plumbed to offer insight into the wider human condition.

In *Another Great Day at Sea*, however, Dyer emphasizes the idiosyncratic over the general. The authorial presence never fades into the background, which will often frustrate readers more interested in the carrier and its operations than Dyer. Those who are willing to accept the book for what it is—Geoff Dyer's impressions of two weeks at sea with the United States Navy—will find it intermittently delightful. At its heart, Dyer's essay is a comedy, a droll tale of a middle-aged writer literally at sea. Its comic effects come from one of the oldest tropes in literature, the clash of cultures, in which a stranger attempts to negotiate his way in a strange land. Dyer casts himself as a latter-day, rather effete Gulliver thrown in with several thousand youthful, patriotic, optimistic Middle Americans. For a Briton living in coastal California, this is terra incognita indeed.

In a work of this sort, the author's tone is everything, and Dyer's may be off-putting to some American readers. Dyer is resolutely British, in his social and cultural attitudes as well as his dry sense of humor. Unfortunately, humor is often difficult to translate across borders, even between cultures that share the same language. Dyer frequently attempts to be funny; some may find his efforts merely irritating. He chooses to exhibit the persona of a high-maintenance writer with finicky tastes and unrealistic expectations about comfort who finds himself lost amid the impersonal privations of a warship. This is the stuff of a sitcom or service comedy, painting him as a sort of middle-class Bertie Wooster ruefully missing the services provided by his Jeeves.

Dyer joins the *USS George H. W. Bush* as it is cruising in the Arabian Sea. After an uncomfortable flight from Bahrain aboard a US Navy transport, he is shocked to learn that there are no badminton or tennis courts available on the ship. Here, just a few pages into the book, he launches into an extended discussion of sleeping arrangements.

Space and privacy are at a premium aboard an aircraft carrier. Steele-Perkins shares a room with Dyer's guide, Ensign Paul Newell, and four other officers—comparative luxury on a ship where enlisted men sleep in two-hundred-person berthing areas. The thought of sleeping with others horrifies Dyer, who worries about his late-night typing and bathroom trips. Before arriving, he lobbied intensively for a single room, and his persistence pays off. When he arrives, he is conducted to the Vice-Presidential Room in a small cluster of VIP guest suites. He has some square footage for his solitary pursuits and a sink into which he can urinate at night.

Dyer also complains about the food. Though it is plentiful and hearty in the American manner, as far as he is concerned, there are not enough vegetarian options, and most of it he regards as canned glop. Dyer lives a spartan existence until he meets the captain's cook and is able to wangle some specially prepared meals. Another problem for Dyer is the narrow passageways and hatches that pose a constant risk to his tall and gangly frame. Movement becomes a process of endless ducking and weaving. While bewailing his troubles to the unflappably amiable Paul Newell, he is told that he will get used to life on the carrier. In the book, Dyer responds by noting that the essence of his character is not getting used to things. Wherever he may be, he refuses to get used to things. He continues to complain, here about the routinely malfunctioning toilets and the absence of alcoholic beverages. Dyer's resolute determination to not fully fit in may have made him a handful as a guest. It also enables him to assess what he saw on the carrier with a stubbornly original outsider's eye.

Dyer pays obligatory obeisance to the technical marvels around him. He notes that a modern supercarrier is essentially an extremely specialized industrial site, humming with activity as it goes about the dangerous business of launching and landing highly sophisticated and heavily armed warplanes. But first and foremost Dyer is interested in the people inhabiting the ship. He compares the *USS George H. W. Bush* to a small city, in particular a small American southern or midwestern city, something with which he is thoroughly unfamiliar. Herein lies the charm of the book: though he is very different from the people whom he finds himself in close quarters with, Dyer discovers that he likes and admires them. For Dyer, the *USS George H. W. Bush* becomes a microcosm of America—not the coastal, elite America that he is used to, but rather Middle America, the America of vast spaces and homely values so famously ignored by a *New Yorker* cartoonist many years ago.

Some of what Dyer encounters remains alien to him. A resolute atheist, he is struck by the religiosity of so many of the people aboard the carrier. He attends a Pentecostal service and is put off by the preaching, though he does like the music. He learns that Ron Rancourt, the officer who manages the carrier's flight deck, is retiring to homeschool his children so he can give them a Christian-based education that they would not receive in the public schools. Dyer deeply admires Rancourt as a man but cannot help regarding him as a Bible Belt zealot.

Yet even what repels Dyer is a manifestation of what he finds overwhelmingly attractive about the men and women whom he meets. They are dedicated, hardworking, and proud of what they do. They are believers, imbued with an ethic of service. Dyer becomes expert in American idiom, experiencing the varying nuances of "sucking it up." He finds a can-do spirit everywhere. He notes that the carrier is a place where "the rubber meets the road," an expression characteristic of a country where he believes the rubber dreams of meeting the road. For Dyer, the marriage of rubber and road is emblematic of the national drive and competency that put so extraordinary a ship as the *USS George H. W. Bush* in the waters of the Arabian Sea. He may wonder about the mission of these Americans in the heart of the Middle East, but Dyer remarks that in England, road and rubber no longer seem to meet. Though he does not explicitly say so, it is clear that for this scion of Great Britain, the torch of empire has irrevocably passed.

Another aspect of life aboard the carrier that impresses Dyer is the absence of the class consciousness that he associates with his homeland. Although there is obviously a hierarchy on a warship, Dyer sees it as a peculiarly American hierarchy, with the prerogatives of rank softened by the permeability of American society, allowing even the lowest ranked to hope rise above their current station. A high point of Dyer's essay comes near the end, when the carrier's crew holds the Steel Beach Party on the deck, a picnic featuring grilled steaks, country music blasting from speakers, and footballs flying through the air. Here he finds the ship's captain and the air wing's admiral in shorts and T-shirts, mixing easily with the other ranks. This relaxed and informal gathering seems to embody the decency and Middle American virtues that Dyer finds so attractive in the carrier's crew.

The title *Another Great Day at Sea* refers to Captain Brian Luther's daily broadcast to the ship's company. The captain declares every day, without exception, a great day to be at sea and working aboard the *USS George H. W. Bush*. For Dyer, reflexively British, self-deprecating, and quizzical, there is something distinctively American about this cheerful assertion of quotidian greatness. Such a confident assumption of excellence defies patronization.

Dyer was exhausted and glad to leave the carrier at the expiration of his two weeks, but he did not depart with a notebook filled with anecdotes and observations calculated to appease the prejudices of the intelligentsia about the American military. Dyer may have been a modern Gulliver, but his book is not a satire. Instead, he has written an offbeat but insightful homage to his hosts. Dyer delivers what was expected of him by the Writers in Residence series: an intensely personal meditation on life aboard a supercarrier.

*Daniel P. Murphy*

## Review Sources

Rev. of *Another Great Day at Sea*, by Geoff Dyer. *Kirkus Reviews* 1 May 2014: 51. Print.

Rev. of *Another Great Day at Sea*, by Geoff Dyer. *Publishers Weekly* 27 Jan. 2014: 176. Print.

Freeman, Jay. Rev. of *Another Great Day at Sea*, by Geoff Dyer. *Booklist* 15 Mar. 2014: 34. Print.

Hoffert, Barbara. Rev. of *Another Great Day at Sea*, by Geoff Dyer. *Library Journal* 1 Dec. 2013: 70. Print.

Martin, Clancy. "The Wordy Shipmate." Rev. of *Another Great Day at Sea*, by Geoff Dyer. *New York Times Book Review* 22 June 2014: 18–19. Print.

McGrath, Charles. "Wedged into Warship with Pen in Hand." Rev. of *Another Great Day at Sea*, by Geoff Dyer. *New York Times* 20 May 2014: C1+. Print.Wilson, Frances. Rev. of *Another Great Day at Sea*, by Geoff Dyer. *TLS* 15 Aug. 2014: 26. Print.

# An Untamed State

**Author:** Roxane Gay (b. 1974)
**Publisher:** Black Cat (New York). 368 pp.
**Type of work:** Novel
**Time:** Present
**Locales:** Port-au-Prince, Haiti; Miami, Florida; Nebraska

(Courtesy of Black Cat)

*Kidnapped in Haiti and held for ransom, a young Haitian American woman endures days of torture and sexual abuse, then faces a much longer struggle to heal her deep emotional trauma.*

**Principal characters:**
MIREILLE DUVAL JAMESON, a first-generation Haitian American immigration lawyer
MICHAEL JAMESON, her white, midwestern husband
THE COMMANDER, leader of the kidnappers who hold her captive
TIPIERRE, a kidnapper who tries to present himself to her as a protector
CHRISTOPHE, her infant son
SEBASTIEN DUVAL, her father, a wealthy Haitian businessman who was born poor and was educated in the United States
LORRAINE, her mother-in-law, who takes her in after the kidnapping
GLEN, her father-in-law, who, along with his wife, takes her in after the kidnapping

*An Untamed State* (2014) is the first novel from Roxane Gay, a writer who has already made her voice known as a blogger, essayist, op-ed contributor, and flash-fiction writer. Gay's nonfiction writing, both fearless and accessible, examines feminism, race, and body image through topics both cultural and personal; her published writings include a searingly honest memoir of sexual assault and a humorous essay about her adolescent obsession with the *Sweet Valley High* books. In *An Untamed State*, Gay takes on messy issues—class, privilege, sexual violence—and resists providing a tidy, simple resolution. Kidnapped as she leaves her parents' gated mansion in one of the world's poorest nations, the protagonist is turned into a focus for the rage of her captors, yet she resists their attempts to justify their actions as class warfare. Gang-raped, beaten, and imprisoned, Mireille Duval Jameson is stripped of her privileged identity, left with nothing except a fierce will to survive.

Each of *An Untamed State*'s forty-two chapters is headed by hash marks, as if marked on a wall by a prisoner counting the days of her captivity. Mireille's actual captivity lasts thirteen days, but her sense of bondage lasts much longer; when, toward the end of the novel, a therapist tells Mireille that she will get better but will never again be the person she was, Mireille thanks her for this honesty. Told almost entirely from Mireille's point of view, with only a few chapters focusing on events from her husband's perspective, *An Untamed State* is both compelling and uncomfortable to read. Gay's close first-person narration pulls readers into Mireille's consciousness, even as Mireille is forced to endure acts that unmoor her mind from her body. Again and again, Mireille describes herself as "no one": a person with no identity, someone who is already dead. To keep even a small island of sanity, she disassociates herself from the woman she was, the successful American lawyer, the wife of Michael and mother of Christophe, the daughter of a man who refuses to pay a million-dollar ransom to end her torture. At one point, Mireille begins

(© Jay Grabiec)

*Roxane Gay is a Haitian American professor and writer whose work has appeared in numerous journals and anthologies. She edits the online journal* the Rumpus *and founded the nonprofit literary arts collective* [PANK]. *Her first book,* Ayiti *(2011), a collection of stories about Haiti and the Haitian diaspora, was followed by her widely acclaimed essay collection* Bad Feminist *and her novel* An Untamed State, *both in 2014.*

talking about herself in the third person, as if her former identity has no connection to the person she has become. The first half of the novel is a taut, almost unbearably intense narrative of captivity and escape; the second half depicts, with almost equal intensity, the protagonist's struggle to reconcile the strong, unafraid woman she was before with the still-strong but scarred and wary survivor she has become.

A child of Haitian immigrants, Mireille Duval grows up American, with a life of privilege. She knows Haiti from childhood visits and is aware of the country's poverty, crime, and social unrest, but until her kidnapping, she never felt afraid there. Mireille's father, Sebastien, a builder, makes a fortune in the United States and returns to Haiti, where he lives in a gated mansion with armed guards. One day, when Mireille is visiting with her husband and her young son, their car is surrounded as they leave the gates. Criminals beat Mireille's husband and drag her away in front of a crowd of indifferent spectators.

At first hopeful that her captivity will be short, Mireille is defiant to her kidnappers, but the Commander, the leader of the men who took her, grows angry when Mireille's father refuses to pay the million-dollar ransom he demanded. In a horrifying sequence, the Commander allows his men to gang-rape Mireille, then burns her with cigarettes and rapes her. Later, one of the men, TiPierre, tells Mireille he has paid the other men to leave her alone, that he has "bought" her for himself. She is allowed to escape briefly and runs through the slums, then is brought back to her cell by the Commander, who tells her that she is complicit in the poverty she has seen. Refusing to absolve his crime, Mireille tells the Commander he is no less complicit.

As her captivity continues, with beatings, torture, sexual abuse, and increasingly desperate phone calls to her family and the kidnapping negotiator her father has hired, Mireille takes refuge in flashbacks to her first meeting with her husband, their courtship and marriage, and the birth of their son. Meanwhile, Michael, Mireille's American husband, is frantic with worry and angry that Mireille's father will not pay the ransom. (Sebastien believes that giving in to the kidnappers' demands would invite further kidnappings, ultimately leaving him destitute.) Together with a streetwise cousin of Mireille's, Michael goes looking for the kidnappers. They find TiPierre, who denies that his gang is responsible for the kidnapping. Later, when they realize the truth, Michael and the cousin return. Michael beats TiPierre and almost shoots him, but when he sees that the man, like him, has an infant son, Michael is unable to kill him.

Barefoot, bleeding, and disoriented, the ransomed Mireille is reunited with her family but is too traumatized to allow a medical exam. She and Michael leave Haiti for their home in Miami. But Mireille's terrifying flashbacks of being trapped persist, and she runs from Michael, driving across the country and finally ending up at his parents' farm in Nebraska. There, Lorraine, Michael's mother, provides Mireille with both the caring and the distance she needs to begin the process of healing, a process that eventually brings her back to Haiti some years later to face her aging father.

*An Untamed State* grew out of Gay's short story "Things I Know about Fairy Tales," which she originally published in 2009 in the online journal *Necessary Fiction*, and references to fairy-tale tropes recur throughout the novel. Mireille describes her kidnapping as the end of a fairy tale; she compares her captivity to that of the miller's daughter in "Rumpelstiltskin," forced to bargain away her firstborn son to fulfill her father's boastful lies, and later imagines herself as Persephone, trapped in the kingdom of Hades. A typical fairy tale might have ended with Mireille's miraculous rescue and return to her family, where she would live happily ever after. In Gay's version, Mireille's rescue is only the beginning of her long road back to herself—or, at least, to a version of herself that she can live with.

*An Untamed State* received positive reviews from most major review sources. Both *Library Journal* and *Booklist* gave starred reviews to the novel; *Booklist*'s Donna Seaman called it "ferocious, gripping, and unforgettable," and Ashanti White, in *Library Journal*, praised the novel's balance of external drama and internal turmoil. The *New Yorker* called *An Untamed State* a "commanding début" and found Gay's handling of Mireille's internal struggle to maintain her identity especially well handled. *Kirkus Reviews* noted the difficult subject matter of the novel and praised Gay's reserved, matter-of-fact handling of violence. "The more bluntly Gay describes Mireille's degradations," the reviewer wrote, "the stronger the impact." A few critics, such as Ron Charles for the *Washington Post*, found *An Untamed State* difficult to recommend simply because of the graphic depiction of the violence the protagonist endures and the unrelenting tension of her ordeal; Charles found the novel "riveting" and brilliantly written, yet so intense and brutal that it was "emotionally exhausting" to read.

In an April 2014 interview with Tomi Obaro for *Chicago* magazine, Gay said that the idea for the novel came from hearing her parents talk about kidnappings in Haiti. In creating a character that survives a series of violent sexual assaults, Gay also drew upon her own experience as a rape survivor. Some of Mireille's actions after the kidnapping—she refuses medical attention, leaves her husband and son, and puts herself in a dangerous situation in a bar, where she is nearly raped again—may seem irrational or self-destructive, but they are consistent with Gay's stated determination to create realistic characters who, like most people, sometimes make bad decisions. In *An Untamed State*, Gay creates a complex, fully developed protagonist who is smart, loving, and determined, yet can at times be stubborn, impulsive, and quick tempered. Mireille is, by any definition, a strong female character. She is strong enough to survive the unthinkable, yet she does not come through her ordeal without scars. This same multidimensionality can be found in all the characters in *An Untamed State*, even the kidnappers, whose lives of extreme poverty contribute to but do not excuse their actions; like everyone else, they bear their own scars.

*Kathryn Kulpa*

**Review Sources**

Rev. of *An Untamed State*, by Roxane Gay. *Kirkus Reviews* 1 Apr. 2014. Web. 1 Feb. 2015.

Rev. of *An Untamed State*, by Roxane Gay. *New Yorker* 4 Aug. 2014: 69. Print.

Charles, Ron. Rev. of *An Untamed State*, by Roxane Gay. *Washington Post*. Washington Post, 27 May 2014. Web. 1 Feb. 2015.

Locke, Attica. "An Unflinching Portrayal of Sexual and Spiritual Violence." Rev. of *An Untamed State*, by Roxane Gay. *Guardian*. Guardian News and Media, 7 Jan. 2015. Web. 1 Feb 2015.

Seaman, Donna. Rev. of *An Untamed State*, by Roxane Gay. *Booklist* 1 May 2014: 46. Print.

White, Ashanti. Rev. of *An Untamed State*, by Roxane Gay. *Library Journal* 1 Feb. 2014: 62. Print.

# The Assassination of Margaret Thatcher

**Author:** Hilary Mantel (b. 1952)
**Publisher:** Henry Holt (New York). 256 pp.
**Type of work:** Short fiction

(Courtesy of Henry Holt and Company)

*In a collection of ten odd and beguiling short stories, Hilary Mantel explores womanhood, marriage, misogyny, English politics, and the nature of fear. Her stories fall in the crevice between realism and fantasy, where everything is a little bit off-kilter, a little bit strange—or, at least, strange enough to make you look twice.*

Each of the short stories in *The Assassination of Margaret Thatcher* (2014) is like an arrow shot from a bow; Mantel's lean, clear-eyed prose moves with purpose and rarely misses its target. In the closing story, "The Assassination of Margaret Thatcher," for which the collection is named, Mantel imagines the sniper-style death of the conservative British prime minister at the hands of an Irish Republican Army (IRA) gunman in 1983. (The real Thatcher served as the prime minister of England from 1979 to 1990 and died in 2013 at the age of eighty-seven.) The story's controversial premise landed in Mantel in some hot water. One of Thatcher's former advisers called for a police investigation of the author, and the *Daily Telegraph*, a conservative-leaning national British newspaper, refused to publish the story even after it had paid a significant advance for it.

Mantel is no stranger to political controversy. Though she is one of Great Britain's most popular writers, among conservative circles she is also one of its most reviled. In the past, she has criticized the nation for fetishizing the British monarchy, particularly for its invasive obsession with Kate Middleton. (Mantel herself was made a dame in 2014.) And of course, on the topic of one of Britain's most divisive historical figures, Mantel is equally plainspoken. "I loathed her," she told Isaac Chotiner in an interview for the October 27, 2014, issue of *New Republic*, citing Thatcher's apparent contempt for her own history, women, the Irish, and the poor. Mantel continued, "She aroused such strong loathing in so many people. That's the fact that interests me. What is it we are hating? It goes beyond politics."

Mantel completed the story only a few months before the collection was published. Like the story's narrator, Mantel lived in the upper-middle-class London neighborhood of Trinity Place in 1983, when Thatcher visited a hospital there to undergo minor eye surgery. Mantel's window, like the narrator's, overlooked the hospital's entrance. "I saw her come out on the grounds of the hospital as described [in the story]," she told Chotiner. "And certain thoughts passed through my head."

Mantel's willingness to deconstruct complicated emotions—hatred, fear, and, in "Assassination," a devious violent impulse—is what gives her stories their heft, while her black-as-night sense of humor makes them sing. In the collection's opening story, "Sorry to Disturb," the wife of a British government worker navigates (and largely stagnates in) Saudi Arabia's male-centered culture in the 1980s. Whiling away the daylight hours in a stuffy apartment where furniture rearranges itself in the night, the woman opens a door to a Pakistani businessman named Ijaz who has come to borrow her phone. Ijaz keeps returning to the apartment, and the protagonist's attempts to avoid him are both frightening and farcical. Ijaz's demeanor grows more sinister as the story, physically pervaded by Jeddah's oppressive heat and dust, reaches its satisfyingly discordant conclusion. "Sorry to Disturb" is a subtle and precise exploration of misogyny and oppression, and like "The Assassination of Margaret Thatcher," it finds its mooring in Mantel's own life: the story was first published in the *London Review of Books* in January 2009 as a memoir.

In "Comma," two young girls spy on a wealthy invalid, but Mantel uses her story to highlight the subtle class differences between the girls themselves and the cruelty that manifests out of their relationship. In her review of Mantel's collection for the *New York Times Book Review*, Terry Castle described the tale as "spare and horrifying." She also wrote that it contained a noun that she had never encountered before; a bleb, she found, is a blister-like swelling on human skin or plants. The image of the girls hiding in the garden on a midsummer day, surrounded by roses "already scorched into heavy brown blebs on the stalk," mirrors the festering nature of the girls' relationship with one another, as well as the bulbous veil of skin attached to the invalid where a face should be. "You know you're in the hands of a master storyteller when, as here, some curious yet minor verbal oddity, some seeming rhetorical blip, turns out to be so cunningly related to a story's metaphoric unfolding," Castle wrote.

"Winter Break" is one of the darkest pieces in the collection. The story, about a husband and wife embarking on a winter holiday, brilliantly showcases Mantel's skill for the sinister. In her hands, a horror story is not merely scary; it is profoundly unsettling. The protagonist's rotten marriage and her unspoken desire to have children coalesce with the more immediate rough taxicab ride and the car's headlights cutting through the darkness in one horrifying moment, fully realized in the story's very last line. In a strong collection, "Winter Break" is an achievement all by itself.

But even the weakest stories in the book are admirable (and infinitely readable) for their insistence on their own strangeness. There is nothing tired about the collection; each story gleams with a freshness of intent. At first glance, "Harley Street" is an elongated punch line. One could say the same of "The Long QT," about a husband's infidelity (a recurring theme in the collection), which does not reach the depth achieved by some of Mantel's other pieces but is beguiling for a plot device that is so literal it is surreal. And in "Terminus," a commuter sees her dead father riding a passing train and spends the day wandering in search of him again. Mantel takes this thin premise further, meditating on the nature of living itself. "How many [people], I ask you, are connected at all points, how many are utterly and convincingly in the state they purport to be: which is, alive?" the commuter wonders. And then, a paragraph later: "For distinguish me, will you? Distinguish me 'the distinguished thing.' Render me the texture of flesh. Pick me what it is, in the timbre of the voice, that marks out the living from the dead. Show me a bone that you know to be a living bone. Flourish it, will you? Find one, and show me."

"Offenses against the Person" is also about male infidelity, but from the perspective of the cheating father's grown child, and in "How Shall I Know You?" an author travels to give a lecture for a reading club. The story, according to Maureen Corrigan for National Public Radio's *Fresh Air*, "starts out as a witty farce about a writer who accepts an invitation to lecture on her books at a book club in some dismal burg, but it curls round into something richer and stranger altogether: a chill meditation on the hierarchy of pity." "The Heart Fails without Warning," written from the perspective of an eleven-year-old girl named Lola, is another strong offering. In her diary, Lola chronicles her older sister's escalating struggle with anorexia. Lola's observations are glib—"the less of her the better"—but falsely so. As Mantel demonstrates in "Comma," which is also narrated by a young girl, familial stress breeds cruelty. Lola's bids for attention only deepen the rift between her and her parents, while her father, a cold and distant figure, becomes practically petulant in his inability to understand his daughter's disease. Most memorable in the story—which, at its core, is about the perils of being both a child and a girl—is the moment the sisters come across a dangerous image of submission, one that Mantel expertly transforms at the story's end.

*Hilary Mantel is the best-selling British author of the Thomas Cromwell series of novels. The first two installments,* Wolf Hall *(2009) and* Bring Up the Bodies *(2012), both won the prestigious Man Booker Prize, making Mantel one of only three authors to win the prize twice. She lives in Sunningdale, a large village outside of London.*

Finally, in "The Assassination of Margaret Thatcher," a middle-aged woman lets an IRA gunman into her apartment, assuming him to be the boiler man. For all the furor surrounding the story's premise—both the UK *Guardian* and the *New York Times* published the story before the book was released, giving it the opportunity to provoke outrage in daily commentary—Mantel's interest lies further from Thatcher herself than one might think. Through her comically bourgeois narrator, Mantel questions a certain dictum about violence in a postcolonial society—in this case, one run by a hawk known as the Iron Lady. "I had said to [the gunman] earlier, violence solves nothing," the narrator muses. "But it was only a piety, like a grace before meat. I wasn't attending to its meaning as I said it, and if I thought about it, I felt a hypocrite. It's only what the strong preach to the weak; you never hear it the other way round; the strong don't lay down their arms."

Thatcher provides a symbolic crux for Mantel's collection, which is about women and womanhood, and the related issue of control. How much control do Mantel's female characters assert over their own lives? Does the protagonist of "Assassination" submit to the will of the assassin; does she aim to please him, convince him that she understands the plight of the working class? Or is the assassin a physical fulfillment of an act she would like to commit herself but is too afraid to? As in all of her stories, Mantel asks the reader to think twice.

*Molly Hagan*

## Review Sources

Castle, Terry. "Within Her Sights." Rev. of *The Assassination of Margaret Thatcher*, by Hilary Mantel. *New York Times Book Review* 5 Oct. 2014: 1. Print.

Corrigan, Maureen. "'The Assassination of Margaret Thatcher' and Other Stories from Hilary Mantel." Rev. of *The Assassination of Margaret Thatcher*, by Hilary Mantel. *Fresh Air*. Natl. Public Radio, 15 Oct. 2014. Web. 1 Nov. 2014.

Lasdun, James. "Hilary Mantel's New Collection." Rev. of *The Assassination of Margaret Thatcher*, by Hilary Mantel. *Guardian*. Guardian News and Media, 24 Sept. 2014. Web. 1 Nov. 2014.

Sanai, Leyla. "Author Conjures Sinister Forces." Rev. of *The Assassination of Margaret Thatcher*, by Hilary Mantel. *Independent*. Independent.co.uk, 18 Oct. 2014. Web. 1 Nov. 2014.

Smith, Wendy. "Unnerving Short Stories by Hilary Mantel, Margaret Atwood and Joyce Carol Oates." Rev. of *The Assassination of Margaret Thatcher*, by Hilary Mantel. *Washington Post*. Washington Post, 29 Sept. 2014. Web. 1 Nov. 2014.

# The Ballad of a Small Player

**Author:** Lawrence Osborne (b. 1958)
**Publisher:** Hogarth (New York). 272 pp.
**Type of work:** Novel
**Time:** 2008
**Location:** Macau and Hong Kong, People's
Republic of China

(Courtesy of Hogarth)

*Lawrence Osborne's third novel features a
crooked English lawyer who has embezzled
the funds of a wealthy widow and absconded
to Macau, where he leads the life of a compulsive gambler.*

**Principal characters:**
FREDDY "LORD" DOYLE, a former English
    lawyer and embezzler who has become a
    fugitive and a compulsive, self-destruc-
    tive gambler
DAO-MING TANG, a Chinese woman of Tibetan ethnicity who came to Macau for a
    better life but became a prostitute
"GRANDMA" CHENG, a wealthy, fear-inspiring gambler from Hong Kong
MR. CHENG, her husband
CHANG SOUZA, a senior manager of the historical Lisboa hotel
SOLOMON MCCLASKEY, a British gambler and an acquaintance of Doyle's
ADRIAN LIPETT, a British gambler
YO YO, his Chinese girlfriend

In his second novel, *The Ballad of a Small Player* (2014), Lawrence Osborne combines a fascinating psychological in-depth portrait of a compulsive English gambler
with an atmospherically dense description of the casino world of Macau. After embez-
zling a fortune from an elderly British widow who entrusted him with managing her
wealth, former lawyer Freddy Doyle is spending his time in Macau gambling away
his stolen money. Because he dresses impeccably, wearing kid gloves at the gambling
tables, and cultivates an upper-class British accent, he is addressed as Lord Doyle by
Chinese players and casino and hotel staff. In reality, Doyle is from a lower-middle-
class background; in Macau, he has created the persona of a desultorily playing lord
for whom losing is as thrilling as winning.

A former Portuguese colony, Macau became a special administrative region of the
People's Republic of China in December 1999, when it reverted back to Chinese rule.
After the transition, Macau continued to allow casino gambling, which attracted a
considerable gambling clientele from mainland China. As Doyle states, in Macau, "the

game . . . is punto banco baccarat. It involves no skill, and that is why the Chinese like it."

For anyone familiar with the game, however, one major problem of *The Ballad of a Small Player* is that Osborne's description of how punto banco baccarat is played in casinos is wrong. Osborne correctly describes the formalized, unbending rules of how a

*Lawrence Osborne published his first novel,* Ania Malina *(1986), before turning to travel writing. Twenty-six years later, he published his second novel,* The Forgiven *(2012), to critical acclaim.* The Ballad of a Small Player *is his third novel.*

winning hand is calculated, but his depiction of the action of the game is wrong on two major points. While this may seem like a minor error, in a novel where the game plays a central role, such a mistake detracts severely from the story's veracity.

First, in punto banco baccarat, gamblers do not play against each other, as Osborne depicts. Near the beginning of the novel, Doyle considers an elderly Chinese woman known to all as Grandma and muses, "I enjoy the thought of skinning her alive with a few good hands." For all the drama implied, this is not how punto banco baccarat is played in a casino. Gamblers do not compete with each other directly; instead, they can wager on either the player's hand, punto, or the banker's hand, banco. This is akin to betting on a red or a black number in roulette, or on pass or do not pass in craps. The dealer then draws the cards for both banker and player hands, according to fixed rules that leave no room for skillful decision making. To say that two gamblers playing punto banco baccarat, one of whom bets on the bank's hand and the other on the player's hand, play against each other is like saying that in roulette, one gambler betting on red and the other on black play against each other. In reality, all these gamblers play against the casino. Additionally, the bets that gamblers place on either the punto (player) or the banco (bank) hand do not need to match up at all, as is asserted in the novel. In reality, many gamblers prefer to bet on the player hand, so there is rarely a matchup of banker and player bets. The only variant of baccarat in which gamblers do play against each other is the traditional version called chemin de fer, or in some privately organized baccarat games. These are different from the punto banco baccarat played in Macau casinos, and neither of these alternative version figures in *The Ballad of a Small Player*.

The second major error in Osborne's depiction is that in reality, the margin of one hand's win over the losing hand does not affect the ratio of the payoff. The punto, or player's hand, is always paid even money for a win. A winning bet of one thousand will always pay just one thousand, for instance, no matter how decisive the victory. The banker's hand, favored by the odds, is paid even money minus a 5 percent commission for the casino. Winnings are paid by the casino, not by other players.

In the novel, once Doyle is on a winning streak, his earnings are impossible in reality. Doyle begins with just a few thousand Hong Kong dollars that he has stolen from Dao-Ming Tang, a young Chinese woman who is about half his age. She is a prostitute who has fallen in love with him and rescued him when he was down and out. "I threw down five hundred," Doyle states. He wins with a nine, "a natural." He lets his money ride, and wins again with another natural. In reality, Doyle would have now won two thousand dollars. In Osborne's novel, however, Doyle states, "I raked in a hundred thousand." This could not have happened with his initial bet after just two wins at punto banco baccarat.

Setting this issue aside, however, *The Ballad of a Small Player* offers a fascinating psychological portrait of a compulsive gambler going through the highs and lows of his addiction. After losing the game with Grandma, Doyle manages to win at another one in the company of Dao-Ming Tang. Eventually, they leave together and check into a hotel for one night. Dao-Ming Tang says she is not a prostitute, but she accepts Doyle's money, indicating the opposite.

This brief encounter functions as catalyst for Doyle's ensuing downward spiral. At first, he seems to be having luck with the cards; however, when he plays against Grandma again, he loses all his money to her. Desperate, Doyle looks up fellow gambler Solomon McClaskey and begs him to return a prior loan of his, but the little money that he manages to extract is also quickly lost. Taking the ferry from Macau to Hong Kong, Doyle even considers suicide. He settles for a breakfast he cannot pay for at the Intercontinental Hotel. Just as he is confronted by the bill, Dao-Ming Tang appears and rescues him. She takes him to her home on Lamma Island, part of Hong Kong, and Doyle wonders about the welts around her neck as they make leisurely love. In the end, he cannot resist the allure of gambling; he steals her money and returns to Macau.

It is now that the novel turns to the supernatural. Hand after hand, Doyle wins big. In a display of narrative symmetry, he is approached by a losing British gambler, Adrian Lipett, and his Chinese girlfriend, Yo Yo, mirroring Doyle's own approach to McClaskey. Doyle's improbable lucky streak awakens the suspicions of senior hotel and casino manager Chang Souza, who permits Doyle one last game at his casino. The game is played against Mr. Chen, Grandma's husband. Doyle stakes all his money. From this moment on, *The Ballad of a Small Player* dips into the genre of the ghost story; Doyle appears to be surrounded by a strange aura.

Overall, for a reader willing to forgive Osborne his inaccurate depiction of punto banco baccarat, *The Ballad of a Small Player* offers a haunting depiction of the troubled psyche of a compulsive gambler. Drawing on his previous strengths as travel writer, Osborne portrays the atmosphere and flavor of Macau with far more veracity than he does the game on which his story is based. On balance, this novel is a flawed but still-enticing work.

*R. C. Lutz*

## Review Sources

Finnell, Joshua. Rev. of *The Ballad of a Small Player*, by Lawrence Osborne. *Library Journal* 1 Mar. 2014: 85. Print.

Shone, Tom. "Liar's Luck." Rev. of *The Ballad of a Small Player*, by Lawrence Osborne. *New York Times Book Review* 6 Apr. 2014: 12. Print.

Woodward, Gerard. Rev. of *The Ballad of a Small Player*, by Lawrence Osborne. *Guardian*. Guardian News and Media, 26 Apr. 2014. Web. 20 Jan. 2015.

# Bark: Stories

**Author:** Lorrie Moore (b. 1957)
**Publisher:** Alfred A. Knopf (New York). 208 pp.
**Type of work:** Short fiction
**Time:** 2003–12
**Locales:** Minneapolis, Minnesota; Washington, DC; Paris, France; Wisconsin; the Caribbean

(Courtesy of Knopf)

*Lorrie Moore's collection of eight stories focuses on the dark, unhappy side of human experience. Nevertheless, her characters indulge in humorous wordplay and self-deprecating comments about their sometimes absurd circumstances.*

**Principal characters:**

IRA, a recently divorced middle-aged Jewish man who is ready to date again

ZORA, a divorced pediatrician with a sullen teenage son

ROBIN ROSS, a theater professor who dies of cancer and appears as a ghost to three of her friends

KIT, a middle-aged woman who has one last family vacation with her husband and children before her divorce becomes final

RAFE, Kit's soon-to-be-ex-husband

BAKER "BAKE" MCKURTY, a minor historian whose left-wing political prejudices blind him to the suffering of others

LINDA SANTO, a lobbyist who survived the 9/11 attack on the Pentagon

KATHERINE "KC," a failed rock musician who charms an old man for his money

PETE, a middle-aged man breaking off his relationship with the mother of a mentally ill boy

TOM, a former drug runner recruited as secret agent by the US government

NICKIE'S MOTHER, a Wisconsin divorcée who attends the second wedding of her daughter's former nanny

With *Bark* (2014), Lorrie Moore offers her readers a new anthology of her popular short stories that balance the darkness in life and human relationships with a healthy level of self-deprecating humor and an eye for the absurd. The eight stories collected in *Bark* were written over the course of a decade and are arranged chronologically in order of their first publication, with only the last story having never been published. Together, these tales provide a view of mostly middle-aged American characters involved in toxic relationships defined by unhappiness and despair, from which they try to escape with a measure of dark humor.

The first story, "Debarking," contains two trademark elements of Moore's fiction: witty wordplay and tragedy. Ira, the historian protagonist, is a middle-aged Jewish man, recently divorced and living in Minneapolis. Ira tells his friend Mike, a fellow historian, that he is physically unable to remove his wedding band six months after his divorce. It is indicative of the penchant for self-pity and self-dramatization that links Ira to Moore's other characters that he remembers later that he did remove his wedding band once already, while taking a hot bath, but put it on again because he was terrified by the sight of his naked finger.

Moore's fondness for wordplay manifests itself throughout *Bark*. In "Debarking," she plays on the title of the collection when Mike sets up Ira with a divorced pediatrician named Zora. Remembering how his ex-wife accused him of barking at other people like a dog, Ira decides to be gentler with Zora—in effect, to debark his voice. Moore puts another twist on the word when Zora and Ira first make love, and Zora asks him, "Did you get off?" Startled, Ira remembers how he was asked this question once before, while in the process of "debarking from a plane." When Ira finds out that Zora has multiple issues of her own, including a drug habit and a para-oedipal relationship with her sullen teenage son Bruno, Ira settles on debarking from the new relationship. Here, and in her other stories, Moore spices up the narrative by juxtaposing, to humorous effect, the linguistic coincidences of the English tongue. Debarking can mean silencing a dog or, from French roots, leaving a ship or an airplane. Similarly, the lives of her characters contain many, often opposing, meanings and interpretations.

*Lorrie Moore's first collection of short stories,* Self-Help *(1985), founded her literary career. Her short story "People Like That Are the Only People Here" (1997) won the 1998 O. Henry Award. In 2004, she received the Rea Award for the Short Story. She worked as a humanities professor and creative-writing instructor at the University of Wisconsin–Madison from 1984 until 2013, when she left to accept an endowed chair at Vanderbilt University.*

"The Juniper Tree" represents Moore's foray into the ghost-story genre. Ostensibly, it is about Robin Ross, a drama professor at a Midwestern university who has died of cancer. The day after her death, Robin appears to a trio of her former colleagues, the story's narrator included, at her now-deserted house. First published in 2005, the short story gains further poignancy from its personal context: Moore dedicated the story to her real-life colleague at the University of Wisconsin–Madison, the late filmmaker Nietzchka Keene, who died of cancer in 2004; Keene's film *The Juniper Tree* (1990) is based on one of the more gruesome fairy tales collected by the Brothers Grimm. Thus, Moore's short story is also, in a way, an elegy for a departed friend.

"Paper Losses" offers a close look at the decay and death of a marriage, told in never-ending puns by the wife in this sorry tale. After twenty years of marriage, Kit and Rafe, two former peaceniks whom Moore fails to develop in any deep way, view each other with rage and resentment rather than love. As Rafe withdraws, Kit likens their marriage to "being snowbound with someone's demented uncle." To fulfill legal requirements, Rafe has Kit served with divorce papers while they still live under one roof with their children. For the kids' sake, the couple goes ahead with a planned family vacation to the Caribbean. It is a predictably unhappy trip that affords Kit plenty of opportunity to exercise her sarcasm.

In "Foes," Baker "Bake" McKurty is a minor historian deeply resentful of successful people. Sixty years old and married, Bake prefers to live with his antidepressant-induced sexual impotence rather than take medication to treat it. (As the story is set in 2008, Viagra has been on the market for a decade.) Bake and his wife, Suzy, attend a fundraiser in Washington, DC, for a struggling literary magazine. Bake, an ardent left-winger, is seated next to Linda Santo, an attractive lobbyist. As dinner progresses, Bake indulges in a political rant against Linda. Bake is so blinded by his self-righteousness that he fails to recognize his dinner companion's suffering until she points it out to him. It turns out that Linda is a survivor of the September 11, 2001, attack on the Pentagon; what Blake sneeringly mistook for botched cosmetic surgery is actually reconstructive surgery for her burn injuries. Humbled but still full of pettiness, Bake is on the verge of a pathetic breakdown in front of his wife after the dinner. His insecurity manifests as pretension when he uses a French phrase he cannot even pronounce correctly.

*Bark* includes two short stories that pay homage to two classic writers, whose original tales Moore gives a contemporary twist. "Wings" is modeled after Henry James's novel *The Wings of the Dove* (1902); in Moore's reimagining, James's plotting couple, Kate Croy and Merton Densher, become failed middle-aged rock musician KC and her freeloading boyfriend D. Encher, called Dench. Their target is the elderly widower Milton "Milt" Theale, named after James's young female protagonist Milly Theale. Completing Moore's reversal of genders, it is the male Dench who persuades the female KC to charm Milt into leaving her his money, while in the original, it is Kate Croy who puts Densher onto the idea of marrying the mortally ill Milly for her fortune.

KC encounters the aging, lonely Milt while walking her dog, Cat. Typical of Moore's wordplay, Cat is short for Katherine, KC's first name. Despite having been neutered, Cat still displays some rudimentary sexual behavior, though futile it may be, cruelly mirroring Milt's infatuation with KC. After bequeathing to KC his villa with two side wings, which give the short story its name, Milt wishes for a French kiss from her. In disgust, she turns away and has the old man committed to hospice care. From there, Moore's story diverges from James's tale, concluding on a wholly original note.

Moore's "Referential" is dedicated to "VN" in recognition of novelist Vladimir Nabokov. Inspired by Nabokov's short story "Signs and Symbols" (1948), "Referential" falls short of the source material's narrative quality. Nabokov's Russian American married couple has become a Midwestern widower and her boyfriend of eight years, the enigmatic Pete. As in Nabokov's story, the woman has a mentally ill sixteen-year-old son who is institutionalized; here, the teenage boy suffers from massive self-destructive urges to mutilate himself. After her son was committed, Moore's middle-aged narrator dedicated herself to an ascetic lifestyle, discarding all baubles and accessories and wearing her "graying hair undyed" in a severe bun. Pete has begun to drift away. After visiting her son for his sixteenth birthday, the woman tells Pete of a self-delusional scheme to bring him home. Pete extricates himself from this fantasy proposal and leaves the distraught narrator pondering what the future might hold for her and her son.

The last two stories in *Bark* are the weakest. "Subject to Search" tells the story of Tom, a former drug runner who becomes a secret agent for the US government. After meeting his American girlfriend in Paris, Tom suddenly has to leave as an incident resembling the Abu Ghraib prison scandal hits the world media. Meting out poetic justice, Moore's story has Tom end his days in a guarded government facility for the incurably deranged.

*Bark*'s concluding story, "Thank You for Having Me," toys with a distractingly ridiculous situation. Set in rural Wisconsin, it features a woman who decides to attend the second wedding of her daughter's former nanny, Maria. The mother incongruously dresses in a "synthetic leopard-print sheath" for the occasion. It turns out Maria had first married a local farmer's son, Ian, who signed his farm over to her. Maria then sold the farm and divorced Ian to marry another farmer's son. Ian serves as best man at this second wedding, which is interrupted by a local biker gang. The story has a delightfully funny premise, but it may alienate some readers with its obvious construction as a vehicle for forced aphorisms and wordplay.

The linear chronology of the stories appearing in *Bark* provides an unexpected survey of American politics and the forward march of entertainment technology in the early 2000s. Moore's largely left-wing characters give their perspective on political events ranging in time from the 2003 invasion of Iraq to Barack Obama's 2008 presidential campaign. Moore also inadvertently chronicles the technological progress in entertainment equipment, from the VCR in 2003 to the fourth generation of iPods in 2009. Perhaps sarcastically, the mother in "Thank You for Having Me"—the only new story in the collection—says, on the day after Michael Jackson's death in 2009, "Well, at least Whitney Houston didn't die." Houston died soon after, on February 11, 2012.

Critical reception of *Bark* has been mixed. At their best, Moore's stories shed light on human tragedy through a distant, self-deprecating irony. At their worst, they are bogged down by stereotypical characters that border on pathetic.

*R. C. Lutz*

## Review Sources

Kakutani, Michiko. "Passage to Midlife on Broken Pavement." Rev. of *Bark*, by Lorrie Moore. *New York Times*. New York Times, 19 Feb. 2014. Web. 22 Oct. 2014.

McAlpin, Heller. "Book Review: Lorrie Moore's *Bark* Looks at Bitter Disappointments of Relationships." Rev. of *Bark*, by Lorrie Moore. *Washington Post*. Washington Post, 24 Feb. 2014. Web. 22 Oct. 2014.

Rich, Nathaniel. "The Aliens Next Door." Rev. of *Bark*, by Lorrie Moore. *Atlantic*. Atlantic Monthly Group, 19 Feb. 2014. Web. 22 Oct. 2014.

Shilling, Jane. "Dead Frogs and Rat Kings." Rev. of *Bark*, by Lorrie Moore. *New Statesman* 14 Mar. 2014: 49. Print.

Sturgeon, Jonathon Kyle. "The Bite Is Always Worse: Lorrie Moore's *Bark* Is the Author's First Dud." Rev. of *Bark*, by Lorrie Moore. *New York Observer*. Observer Media, 27 Feb. 2014. Web. 22 Oct. 2014.

# The Bees

**Author:** Laline Paull
**Publisher:** HarperCollins (New York). 352
  pp.
**Type of work:** Novel, nature
**Time:** Unknown
**Locale:** A beehive

(Courtesy of Ecco)

*The Bees (2014) follows a lowly worker bee, Flora 717, as she learns the rules of her hive and transcends her ignoble origins to live a richer and more varied life than any single bee—save perhaps a queen—should be able to experience.*

**Principal characters**:

FLORA 717, a sanitation worker bee who displays unique characteristics and rises through her hive's caste system

SISTER SAGE, one of many Sage priestess bees who serve as the queen's deputies

LINDEN, a scrawny and sardonic drone who forms an unlikely friendship with Flora

THE QUEEN, a holy figure to the hive and the source of all life for the bee colony

Laline Paull's *The Bees* is unusual in that it is a serious literary work that almost exclusively features anthropomorphic animals, centered, of course, on the titular insects. However, this quality succeeds as much more than a gimmick, and the book has been favorably compared to two of the best-known other adult works starring only animal characters: *Watership Down* (1974) by Richard Adams and George Orwell's *Animal Farm* (1945). Yet Paull's debut novel also goes further than those two classics, introducing readers to the remarkably alien world of bees in ways beyond simple metaphors for human society. Mixing science and fantasy, familiar dramatic tension and strange sensations, *The Bees* is a unique and fascinating read.

The reader is introduced to the book's protagonist, Flora 717, on the day she claws her way out of the wax cell in which she is born. She is a honeybee of the lowest caste, a sanitation worker. Immediately, the hive's rigorous structure and group mentality is made apparent. She is inspected for any abnormalities by the police bees, as the hive cannot bear any deviations from the norm—they are the calling cards of disease and degradation. Because she is found to be too large and ugly, Flora is to be summarily executed. However, a bee from the Sage class of "priestesses" who report directly to the queen steps in and spares her out of apparent curiosity, sensing something different. Not only is Flora physically abnormal, but she can speak, unlike other members of her caste, and soon proves to have an independent psychological streak as well. Sister Sage takes Flora on her first trip through the hive, and readers encounter this strange world along with the young hero.

Paull blends the science of how bee communities actually work with imaginative layers of human emotion and society, making the characters and relationships relatable but foreign enough that they never feel like simple stand-ins for the human world. The very real strict hierarchy of bee society is tweaked to include echoes of highly structured religious traditions such as the Catholic Church and the Church of England, with the queen as the ultimate holy figure. There is a sense of a feudal realm mixed with science fiction throughout. Flora is part of the system, linked to her hive mates right down to the chemical signals they communicate with and are controlled by, yet she displays a unique individualism that becomes the main focus of the story.

As challenging circumstances begin to threaten the hive's existence, Flora's special abilities allow her to experience almost ev-

(© Adrian Peacock)

*Laline Paull is an author and playwright whose previous work includes a National Theatre play based on naturalist Charles Darwin's voyage on the* Beagle *titled* Boat Memory. The Bees *is her first novel.*

ery role available to members of the hive. It is discovered that she can produce royal jelly, and so receives the honor of helping to care for the queen's offspring. She is exposed to the world—and dangers—outside the hive as a forager. But Flora's differences from the other bees become heretical when she eventually begins to produce eggs of her own. What follows is a tale of adventure and survival, and while various connections to humanity may certainly be made, it must be taken above all as about bees and the natural world.

*The Bees* is first and foremost a triumph of imagination. The central conceit is at once literary and literal. Bee biology informs life in the hive, from the method of wax production to the hive's dramatic defense against an invading wasp. The relationship of the bees to their kin, the wasps, hornets, and ants, is particularly intriguing, with ants a sort of respectful and well-liked terrestrial equivalent to the bees and wasps and hornets acting as jealous cousins who cannot make honey and covet the treasures of the hive. When a wasp invades the hive, for instance, Paull borrows from the defensive technique of Japanese honey bees (her bees have no stated national origin). The workers swarm the invader and vibrate wings until, smothered in a ball of live bodies, the wasp eventually succumbs to the high temperature and lack of oxygen.

The arrival of drones—the rare, precious male offspring that carry a hive's seed into the wider world—is reframed as an event with as much pomp and circumstance as any prince might wish. Indeed, the drones are lazy, loutish, and obsessed with their masculine beauty. Their antics are often as amusing as they are lewd. Without spoiling their fate, suffice it to say that it follows bee biology in a horrifically cathartic fashion.

Paull also uses the relationship between bees and flowers, shaped by a deep history of coevolution, to paint a picture of pollination as a nearly erotic experience from the perspective of the creatures involved. Although anthropomorphization naturally takes over from science in such scenes, Paull's language does so in a way that stimulates greater interest in bee ecology. Many reviewers came away with a greater appreciation for bees and an interest in learning more, hinting at how such a work of fiction could be put to good use in science education.

*The Bees* has much in common with fantasy novels, particularly with touches like the spiders cast as predatory soothsayers and the mysterious panels in the hive's "library" that contain histories dating back further even than the life of the queen. Comparisons to landmark fiction such as *Watership Down* and the writing of Margaret Atwood are also well deserved. This is a novel firmly entrenched in the history of allegorical animals, even if Paull rather skillfully dodges the interpretation that her bees exist solely as mirrors for humankind. More than many other fantasy-animal novels, Paull keeps the focus squarely on the animals themselves. The book's only tangible connections to the human world are two brief framing chapters featuring the owner of the land where the hive sits, a scene of disruptive honey harvesting, and Flora's occasional encounters with human development outside of the hive.

The scenes hinting at humans' impact on the tightly interconnected natural world, including Flora's encounter with an apparently poisoned field of flowers and her near death at the hands of a radio tower, lend a definite sense of environmental damage to the proceedings, even if these concerns are never brought to the fore. As of the book's publication, honeybees are indeed in peril due to mysterious environmental concerns, and it is not hard to imagine the connection between dangerously diminishing bee populations and the hazards encountered in the book—fictionalized or not.

To be sure, the perils that face the hive from within and without are dramatic enough without the need for any outright moralizing over a global, human-caused catastrophe. The natural world can be dangerous on its own, as evidenced in two memorable scenes. When a mouse seeks shelter and food in the hive during a harsh winter, the resultant destruction and loss of life is brutally effective at emphasizing the alien dimensions of Flora's world. Similarly, the terror produced by the fertility police and their search for the traitorous, egg-laying bee is palpable throughout the hive, and these bees are no strangers to seeing their peers viciously put down in the name of the hive.

For all of Paull's engaging and richly textured prose, *The Bees* does suffer from a dragging midsection. As fascinating as Flora's day-to-day life is, it can sometimes feel like the narrative lacks a drive towards anything, content to simply react to the changing circumstances of each season and the biological compulsions that define life as a bee. Flora, for all her unusual strength and size, can read as a frustratingly unsure protagonist. She may have the capacity to do things no worker should, but she remains ambivalent at best about her motivations. She does not establish herself as a rebel, an iconoclast, or really even an individual with much of a personality. She may be gifted, but she is still a devoted worker, and even when she breaks the rules, it is for the good of the hive. Her decisions often seem driven by her unique biology and not by a strong personality. This is effective in keeping her realistically "bee-like," which gives the work its unique feel, but some readers may find such characterization hard to identify with at times.

Critical reception of *The Bees* was largely positive, with nearly universal praise for Paull's evocative language and creativity in leveraging biology to inform the world of the hive. Most reviewers agreed that the book's prose is exceptional and pulls the reader along for a captivating ride. Many also commented on the boldness of the narrative and its unique style, especially coming from a debut novelist. Reactions to Flora and the central plot threads, however, were somewhat varied. Emma Straub, writing for the *New York Times*, noted that the overarching direction of the story quickly becomes predictable but dismissed this as a quibble in the face of the novel's imagination and literary merit. "Some aspects didn't always work," Straub wrote, "but the tale zooms along with such propulsive and addictive prose that I didn't mind."

Others echoed the sentiment that *The Bees* has its share of flaws that are mostly outshined by its strengths. In her review for the *Guardian*, Gwyneth Jones voiced concerns with Paull's protagonist and the structure of her plot: "Our appealing insect heroine, authentically bee-like in her hive-mind limitations, can seem more like a narrative device than a person: a cipher leading us through the mazes of this strange and fascinating miniature world." Like some other critics, Jones pointed to the rich themes of race and gender that can be read into Flora's unusual development but questioned whether the narrative manages to deliver on these ideas. She also speculated about the debatable political overtones of Flora's origins and special abilities. Yet some reviewers, such as Amal El-Mohtar for *NPR*, preferred to interpret the novel's drama as encapsulated within the bees' experience without overlaying any specific political or social message. Indeed, perhaps the best way to experience Flora's world of hive, honey, and high adventure is to submit to her familiar-but-alien experience and fly alongside on her fascinating journey while leaving one's human preoccupations behind, allowing interpretations to come as they may.

*Kenrick Vezina, MS*

**Review Sources**

El-Mohtar, Amal. "From Flower to Factory, These Bees Are No Bumblers." Rev. of *The Bees*, by Laline Paull. *NPR Books.* NPR, 6 May 2014. Web. 22 Feb. 2015.

Jones, Gwyneth. "The Bees by Laline Paull Review—A Fantasy with a Sting in Its Tail." Rev. of *The Bees* by Laline Paull. *Guardian*. Guardian News and Media, 21 May 2014. Web. 22 Feb. 2015.

Straub, Emma. "Hive Mentality." Rev. of *The Bees*, by Laline Paull. *New York Times*. New York Times, 23 May 2014. Web. 22 Feb. 2015.

Ulin, David L. "Ideas Swarm in Laline Paull's 'The Bees'." Rev. of *The Bees* by Laline Paull. *LA Times*. Los Angeles Times, 2 May 2014. Web. 22 Feb. 2015.

# Bellweather Rhapsody

**Author:** Kate Racculia (b. 1980)
**Publisher:** Houghton Mifflin Harcourt (Boston). 352 pp.
**Type of work:** Novel
**Time:** 1997
**Locale:** The Hotel Bellweather, Clinton's Kill, New York

(Courtesy of Houghton Mifflin Harcourt)

*An unorthodox mystery novel,* Bellweather Rhapsody *relates the profound life changes that several characters experience when a young girl is found dead in a manner that exactly mirrors a tragedy that happened in the same hotel room fifteen years earlier.*

BERTRAM "RABBIT" HATMAKER, a high school musician participating in Statewide, a prestigious music festival
ALICE HATMAKER, his twin sister and fellow festival participant
NATALIE WILSON, his teacher and chaperone
FISHER BRODIE, the orchestral conductor at the festival and a former musical prodigy
JILL FACCELLI, a musical prodigy and festival participant
VIOLA FABIAN, Jill's mother and the festival director
MINNIE GRAVES, a young woman who years before witnessed a murder-suicide at the Hotel Bellweather
HAROLD HASTINGS, the longtime concierge at the Hotel Bellweather

In *Bellweather Rhapsody* (2014), twins Alice and Bertram "Rabbit" Hatmaker are excited to have been chosen as participants in the prestigious Statewide music festival, to which the most talented high school students in New York are invited each year. Together with their teacher and chaperone, Natalie Wilson, they drive to the Hotel Bellweather, a huge resort in the Catskill Mountains that is long past its prime.

While Rabbit is preoccupied with figuring out how to tell his twin sister that he is gay, Alice, whose boyfriend has recently broken up with her, must confront her own fears about her dreams and the future. Alice is initially thrilled that her assigned roommate for the festival is Jill Faccelli, a musical prodigy who has been playing the flute professionally since she was eight years old, but Alice inadvertently makes an enemy of Jill's famous mother, Viola Fabian, who is running the festival. Jill confesses to Alice that her life is miserable; shortly afterward, she appears to have hanged herself. Jill's body disappears, however, and Alice and the other festival participants learn that a murder and a suicide by hanging took place in the same hotel room exactly fifteen years before.

Although *Bellweather Rhapsody* is a mystery novel, it is somewhat nontraditional in its format and especially in its tone. The novel begins with a short prologue set in 1982, in which a twelve-year-old girl named Minnie Graves, who is at the Hotel Bellweather as a bridesmaid in her sister's wedding, runs off to explore the hotel, only to witness the murder-suicide of another bride and groom whose wedding also took place that day. The timeline then jumps ahead fifteen years to 1997, where it covers the four days, Thursday through Sunday, of the music festival. The book is divided into four sections, one for each day, and the sections are titled with tempo instructions, which construct the narrative as a musical performance. The theme of music as a powerful force is carried throughout the book, beginning when the festival's eccentric conductor, Fisher Brodie, demands that the students tell him what compels them to play. Jill, the only true musical prodigy among the students, storms out of the rehearsal in a rage. Although Fisher's unorthodox methods initially shock the students, several of them, especially Rabbit, eventually experience personal epiphanies as a direct result of his tutelage.

In addition to music, the author also explores the concepts of psychological trauma and healing. The most obvious example is Minnie, who is now twenty-seven but who has been haunted since childhood by the shocking deaths that she witnessed. The reader learns that in the intervening years, Minnie coped with her nightmares by watching such horror movies as *The Shining* (1980), based on the Stephen King novel of the same name, which takes place at an isolated resort hotel very similar to the Hotel Bellweather. She has also been shielding herself by gaining weight, which makes her feel physically safer. It is not until Minnie rescues a deaf dog that she begins to emerge from her shell, getting a part-time job in a library and writing movie reviews for a local newspaper. Armed with her newfound courage, Minnie decides to return to the Hotel Bellweather on the fifteenth anniversary of the deaths that she witnessed, in the hope that doing so will banish her remaining fears. When Jill apparently hangs herself in the same hotel room and her body subsequently disappears, Viola insists that Jill is unstable and is playing an elaborate prank on her, but both Minnie and Alice feel certain that Jill is really dead. Minnie decides that getting to the bottom of the mystery is the exact therapy she needs.

As it happens, Viola is also intimately connected to another character in need of healing: the twins' teacher and chaperone, Natalie Wilson, who during her high school years was one of Viola's music students. Natalie initially worshipped her teacher, but she quickly learned that Viola was not only psychologically but also physically abusive. Natalie was too ashamed to report the abuse, and eventually she lost her love of music. Many years later, after Natalie had married and built a life for herself as a music teacher, she suffered another trauma when she shot and killed an intruder who had broken into her home. She is still dealing with the aftermath of that tragedy, in part by drinking too heavily, when she is shocked to encounter Viola at the music festival. Natalie has her gun with her in the hotel and begins to entertain fantasies of at least scaring Viola, if not outright killing her.

Fisher Brodie, the conductor, requires yet another kind of healing. Like Jill, he was a musical prodigy as a child, performing professionally as a pianist until an accident resulted in the loss of three fingers on his right hand. As the novel progresses, the reader learns that Fisher had come to despise his life as a performer and to resent the parents who forced it upon him. The author adds another layer of mystery to this complex story when multiple characters refer to Fisher as having destroyed his own career, making the reader wonder exactly how he lost his fingers. His healing comes in the form of finding love for the first time, which allows him to reclaim his love of music.

In contrast to the characters trying to overcome their pasts, Alice and Rabbit are both worried about the future, as is appropriate for high school students on the verge of graduation. Rabbit's main concern is whether and how he should tell Alice that he is gay. He knows that he cannot go much longer without openly acknowledging his sexuality,

(© Sage Brousseau)

*Kate Racculia's novel* Bellweather Rhapsody *was named one of* Library Journal's *best books of the year. It is her second novel, following* This Must Be the Place *(2010).*

but he feels that Alice must be told first. He has difficulty finding the right moment until he realizes that the nature of the music festival, especially once the participants are snowed in by a severe blizzard, has given him the perfect opportunity to explore not only his own identity but also his generally submissive relationship with his twin. His first tentative steps toward autonomy alarm Alice, who always strives to be the center of attention. Alice, a gifted singer, feels that she is unattractive except when she performs, so she seeks every opportunity to do so. Not only does Rabbit's newfound independence make Alice fear that she will lose her greatest champion and admirer, she is also crushed by Viola's cruel insistence that Alice is nothing special. If that turns out to be true, Alice believes she will have no reason to live.

Another emotional thread carried throughout the entire novel is an exploration of compassion. When Minnie first arrives back at the Hotel Bellweather, she is terrified and concerned only with trying to assuage her own fears. However, just as she learned that rescuing her dog gave her a purpose in her own life, she discovers that it is more important to take care of some of the others affected by the previous tragedy and by Jill's current disappearance. When Minnie and Alice attempt to unravel clues about the mystery, Minnie is horrified that their questioning distresses Harold Hastings, the man who has been the concierge at the hotel for more than forty-five years, and she makes it her mission to do what she can to help him.

In sharp contrast, Viola appears to demonstrate no compassion whatsoever. Fisher, who like Natalie has a past relationship with Viola, refers to her as a sociopath, and the twins and Hastings instinctively recoil from Viola upon first meeting her, even though she is considered very beautiful. Alice, meanwhile, lies somewhere between Minnie's solicitude for others and Viola's contemptuous disregard for them. Alice is self-centered enough that she keeps a scrapbook and diary specifically intended for her eventual biographer, and her reaction upon meeting Jill for the first time is to plan how to use their new acquaintance to her own advantage at the festival. However, when Alice sees what Jill's life is really like and then joins forces with the overweight, socially awkward Minnie to investigate Jill's disappearance, she consciously recognizes that she is having the first truly compassionate experience of her life. In fact, while almost every character learns a great deal about him or herself over the course of the festival, Alice's transformation is perhaps the most moving, especially because it dovetails so neatly with her brother's metamorphosis.

In spite of the emotional depth of this novel, it also displays a quirky reverence for popular culture that simply makes it fun to read. Alice and Rabbit often refer to popular music from the 1990s with the typical intensity of teenagers, and Minnie uses her memories of brave characters, such as Sigourney Weaver as Ripley in the movie *Aliens* (1986), to bolster her own courage when necessary. In addition, Hastings enjoys reading about the adventures of fictional detectives such as Agatha Christie's Hercule Poirot and Miss Marple. These popular references are blended seamlessly with several of the characters' emotional reactions to more classical music, in particular the musicians' memories of the first time music truly moved them. This juxtaposition of popular and classical elements gives the novel a unique and refreshing tone.

Ultimately, *Bellweather Rhapsody* is a distinctive blend of entertaining mystery story and profound literary character portraiture. The author reveals critical information in carefully planned stages that feel natural rather than manipulative, creating suspense that infuses several plot threads. The ending is particularly satisfying because it feels complete while still leaving some of the characters' futures realistically unresolved. Even minor characters are richly drawn, and the major players each experience the type of significant change and growth that marks good storytelling, resulting in a remarkably accomplished novel.

*Amy Sisson*

**Review Sources**

Rev. of *Bellweather Rhapsody*, by Kate Racculia. *Kirkus Reviews* 1 Apr. 2014: 234. Print.

Rev. of *Bellweather Rhapsody*, by Kate Racculia     . *Publishers Weekly* 24 Feb. 2014: 151. Print.

Cart, Michael. Rev. of *Bellweather Rhapsody*, by Kate Racculia. *Booklist* 1 May 2014: 16. Print.

Fontaine, Nancy H. Rev. of *Bellweather Rhapsody*, by Kate Racculia. *Library Journal* 15 Apr. 2014: 79–80. Print.

Valby, Karen. Rev. of *Bellweather Rhapsody*, by Kate Racculia. *Entertainment Weekly*. Entertainment Weekly and Time, 14 May 2014. Web. 25 Nov. 2014.

# The Betrayers

**Author:** David Bezmozgis (b. 1973)
**Publisher:** Little, Brown (New York). 240 pp.
**Type of work:** Novel
**Time:** Summer 2013
**Locale:** Yalta, Crimea

*The Betrayers is a novel about two men with a strained history, one an Israeli politician raised in the former Soviet Union and the other a disgraced KGB informant, who meet coincidentally in Yalta and discuss the events that have led to their current life situations.*

(Courtesy of Little, Brown and Company)

**Principal characters:**
BARUCH KOTLER, an Israeli politician and former Soviet prisoner who has fled to Yalta after the public leak of a scandal
LEORA ROSENBERG, his former assistant who left Israel with him
SVETLANA TARASOV, an elderly woman living in Yalta on a pension
VLADIMIR TANKILEVICH, her husband, a former KGB informant and friend of Kotler's

Canadian author and filmmaker David Bezmozgis seems to find inspiration for his artistic expression in his family's history and the history of Jews in Europe and North America. Born in Riga, Latvia, Bezmozgis immigrated with his family to Canada in 1980, and the experience of eastern European Jews in Canada was the subject of Bezmozgis's award-winning collection of short stories, *Natasha and Other Stories* (2004), many of which were first published in the *New Yorker* and *Harper's*. His first novel, the critically acclaimed *The Free World* (2011), told the story of Latvian Jews temporarily forced to wait in Italy for visa clearance before continuing their planned immigration to North America. Bezmozgis used the viewpoints of different generations of the same family to create a sensitive and complex exploration of cultural transformation, assimilation, and the myriad motivations that underlie immigration.

Bezmozgis's second book, *The Betrayers* (2014), is a short novel, similar in structure and tone to many of the author's earlier short stories. In it, Bezmozgis again delves into the eastern European Jewish experience, this time telling the story of a celebrated Israeli politician and survivor of Soviet imprisonment who is given a fateful and coincidental opportunity to confront the former KGB informant responsible for his earlier prison sentence. Critics and interviewers have often mentioned how the 2014 Russian occupation of Ukraine's Crimean Peninsula complicated the plot of Bezmozgis's novel, which is set in the Crimean city of Yalta and was in the works when the Russian takeover began. Though the Yalta described in *The Betrayers* now exists in a past or alternate-reality Crimea in which Russia's military remains absent, Bezmozgis's novel is more about personality and interpersonal relationships than the broader political issues that have come to dominate the region.

The primary character in *The Betrayers* is Baruch Kotler, who provides the narrative voice for most of the novel. Kotler is a for-

*David Bezmozgis is an award-winning Canadian author and filmmaker known for his novels and short stories exploring Jewish history and the immigrant experience. He won the Reform Judaism Prize for Jewish fiction in 2004 and the Toronto Book Award and a Guggenheim Fellowship in 2005.*

mer Soviet Jew and "refusenik," a name given to the Soviet and other Eastern Bloc Jews who were denied permission to immigrate to Israel in the 1960s and 1970s. Following the Six-Day War between Israel and Egypt, Jordan, and Syria in 1967, a large number of Jews from the former Soviet Union and surrounding territories sought permission to immigrate to Israel. In many countries, Jews were refused permission to leave, partially out of fear of what a mass exodus might do to the economies and nations left behind. In the Soviet Union, the government used "security concerns" as justification to refuse visa applications. Protests resulted, and many Soviet Jews were imprisoned as "potential political threats" or even suspected spies. This tumultuous and tragic period in European Jewish history has become fertile ground for novels and histories of the Jewish experience. Reviewers have noted similarities between Bezmozgis's fictional Kotler and the real-life figure of Natan Sharansky, a Soviet prisoner who was later freed and came to Israel as a hero. Like Sharansky, the fictional Kotler was freed from the gulag, after a thirteen-year imprisonment, and was welcomed to Israel as a hero. Having been hardened by his time as a prisoner, Kotler has become a right-wing stickler who has a reputation for being stubborn and pugnacious.

At the beginning of the novel, Kotler is on the run. He is in Yalta, the famed Crimean resort city that sits on the coast of the Black Sea. In the midst of a sentimental journey, Kotler returns to the site where he and his parents spent a mythic summer during his youth to possibly recapture the sense of freedom and ease he had once felt looking out to the sea. As Kotler gradually explains through his narration, his hard-line stance on Jewish settlements in the West Bank brought him into conflict with other factions in the Israeli political environment. His enemies dug into his life and found evidence that Kotler, who is married with two children, had been having an affair with his much-younger assistant, Leora Rosenberg. Leaked photos revealing the affair have been running around the clock on the news, embroiling Kotler and his family in a tawdry political scandal. Unable to see a clear path out of the mess, Kotler flees with Leora, traveling to the one place where his memories remain pure and happy. Kotler has, in essence, become the first "betrayer." He has left his wife, Miriam, who spent thirteen years campaigning for his release while he sat in prison, and he has disappointed his two children.

Most of the story takes place over two days in Yalta. After arriving to find that their hotel has given their room away to another lodger, Kotler and Leora return to the bus station, where poor Crimean residents stand advertising rooms for rent. Two older women approach the couple. The first woman, Svetlana, advertises her room by saying that her husband is Jewish, from Kazakhstan. "Doesn't it say in the Torah that you should first help your own kind?" she asks, trying to lure the couple away from her competitor. Leora and Kotler accept Svetlana's offer, after some disagreement, and begin exploring Yalta. Bezmozgis's clever and often-humorous observations on culture are sprinkled throughout the novel, such as when Kotler and Leora find the statue of Lenin in Yalta's Lenin Square, looking "intently out to sea—and peripherally at a McDonald's." Through passages like this, and through the at-times-cynical musings of his characters, Bezmozgis periodically reflects on the bizarre terrain where political idealism meets the vagaries of real life.

The central drama in *The Betrayers* begins when Kotler realizes that Svetlana's husband, a man now calling himself Chaim Tarasov, is in fact Kotler's former university roommate in Moscow, the same man who informed on him to the Soviet KGB forty years earlier. The man, whose original name was Vladimir Tankilevich, told the KGB that Kotler had ties to the CIA, which led directly to Kotler's thirteen-year imprisonment in the gulag. Therefore, Tankilevich becomes the second betrayer in the story, a disgraced villain who provides a contrast to Kotler's political righteousness. Tankilevich has struggled to make a life for himself in the wake of his shame, being known as the man who betrayed the Jewish hero Baruch Kotler. The portrait of Tankilevich given in *The Betrayers* is sensitive and nuanced. As the story progresses, Tankilevich explains why he felt it necessary to give information to the KGB, a justification that does not excuse his actions but does complicate the morality of the issue, making it clear that both men were caught up in the violent persecution directed toward Soviet Jews.

Over the course of a tense day and night, Kotler and Tankilevich confront one another. Kotler wants to understand and force Tankilevich to live up to the reality of his actions, while Tankilevich wants public forgiveness from Kotler. Undeniably, the chance encounter between the two men is a product of strange coincidence, and this inevitably leads to discussions about fate, determinism, life, and spiritual belief. "Fate led; I followed. I chose to follow," Kotler says of the situation to Tankilevich's wife.

Some reviewers had difficulty with the fact that the conflict of *The Betrayers* hinged on such an unlikely act of providence or happenstance. *Los Angeles Times* critic David L. Ulin remarked that this central conceit strains credibility and makes Tankilevich and Kotler seem more like archetypes than real people. Ulin further noted that the "cosmic justice" of their fateful meeting seemed all the more out of place considering the seeming absence of justice in the real-life situation in Ukraine. In contrast, *Boston Globe* critic Brock Clarke wrote that while the premise of these two men having such an improbable encounter struck him as ridiculous, the fatalistic nature of their reunion gives the book a feeling of inevitability that highlights the deeper discussions of complex moral issues. While the setup for the meeting may seem contrived—a point Bezmozgis acknowledges by having Leora comment on it herself—the discussions that follow prove to be anything but black and white, successfully involving readers by prompting them to decide which of these "betrayers" actually deserves sympathy.

Most critics praised Bezmozgis's prose, specifically the way he employs dashes of humor and clever dialogue to emphasize meaningful observations and reflections about people and their environments. *New York Times* critic Boris Fishman called the novel a master class for fledgling writers and an inspiration for readers. Through two novels and his collected stories, Bezmozgis has explored the European Jewish experience and history from a variety of perspectives. Though some critics felt *The Betrayers* fell short of Bezmozgis's earlier efforts, his skillful prose and wit proved an interesting vehicle for a novel that had more of the pacing of a political thriller than Bezmozgis's earlier work. In the end, the novel comes across as a powerful commentary on morality that leaves readers an open ground to explore their own thoughts on fate, destiny, and forgiveness.

*Micah L. Issitt*

**Review Sources**

Clarke, Brock. Rev. of *The Betrayers*, by David Bezmozgis. *Boston Globe*. Boston Globe Media Partners, 27 Sept. 2014. Web. 21 Jan. 2015.

Cummins, Anthony. "Too Calculated." Rev. of *The Betrayers*, by David Bezmozgis. *Telegraph*. Telegraph Media Group, 7 Oct. 2014. Web. 21 Jan. 2015.

Fishman, Boris. "Yalta at This Time of Year." Rev. of *The Betrayers*, by David Bezmozgis. *New York Times Book Review* 19 Oct. 2014: 13. Print.

Theroux, Marcel. "Flight to Crimea." Rev. of *The Betrayers*, by David Bezmozgis. *Guardian*. Guardian News and Media, 29 Aug. 2014. Web. 21 Jan. 2015.

Ulin, David L. "Blame and Forgiveness in David Bezmozgis' *The Betrayers*." Rev. of *The Betrayers*, by David Bezmozgis. *Los Angeles Times*. Los Angeles Times, 18 Sept. 2014. Web. 21 Jan. 2015.

# Birdmen
## The Wright Brothers, Glenn Curtiss, and the Battle to Control the Skies

**Author:** Lawrence Goldstone (b. 1947)
**Publisher:** Ballantine Books (New York).
 428 pp.
**Type of work:** History
**Time:** 1905–15
**Locale:** United States

*(Courtesy of Ballantine Books)*

*Lawrence Goldstone's masterful account of the patent war between aviation pioneers Wilbur and Orville Wright and their rival Glenn Curtiss offers a fascinating look at a pivotal decade in the early history of American aviation.*

**Principal personages:**

WILBUR WRIGHT, the coinventor of the first airplane to achieve sustained mechanical flight and the chief instigator of a patent war

ORVILLE WRIGHT, his younger brother, coinventor, and business partner

GLENN CURTISS, a rival aeronautical pioneer whom they accused of patent infringement

MILTON WRIGHT, their father, a strict moralistic clergyman

THOMAS SELFRIDGE, a pilot, the first person to die in an airplane crash

JOHN MOISANT, an exhibition flyer

HARRIET QUIMBY, the first American woman to hold a pilot's license

LINCOLN BEACHEY, a famed daredevil stunt pilot

For generations, every schoolchild has been taught that Wilbur and Orville Wright's groundbreaking flight on December 17, 1903, at Kitty Hawk, North Carolina, was the beginning of modern aviation. However, according to the August 18, 1901, edition of the *Bridgeport Herald*, Gustave Whitehead, a German immigrant and resident of Bridgeport, Connecticut, had piloted a mechanical aircraft four days earlier—more than two years before the Wright brothers glided into the history books. Others also made first-in-flight claims, including French engineer Clément Ader and German inventor Karl Jatho, but these men remain a footnote in early aviation history. The Wrights continue to be universally acclaimed as the first to achieve controlled, powered, heavier-than-air human flight and are thus regarded as the inventors of the airplane.

 Yet the claims of Whitehead, Ader, Jatho, and others continue to spark vigorous debate among some scholars, demonstrating that the genesis of aviation was not as clear cut as the general public has been led to believe. And if the origins of mechanical heavier-than-air flight were messy, subsequent events during the early years of the budding industry were even more so, as the title of Lawrence Goldstone's meticulously researched *Birdmen: The Wright Brothers, Glenn Curtiss, and the Battle to Control the Skies* (2014) suggests. Goldstone convincingly portrays the Wrights' initial contributions as part of a broader story that includes larger-than-life personalities, brutal competition, and mean-spirited court battles that ultimately proved more destructive than beneficial to the development of aviation.

Goldstone begins his narrative with a brief survey of humankind's desire to take to the air. From Aristotle and Archimedes to Leonardo, Galileo, and Newton, giants of science contributed to the body of knowledge that would eventually lead to mechanical flight. Later, other researchers—including English polymath George Cayley, French-born American engineer Octave Chanute, and German engineer Otto Lilienthal—took up the task of investigating the principles of flight, and some attempted to build their own gliders and airplanes. Because of their foundational work, the pieces were in place that would enable the Wrights and their fellow inventors to construct viable flying machines.

Although Goldstone provides a detailed account of the technical challenges the Wrights faced and eventually overcame, his exploration of their upbringing and psychology is the greater attraction, providing fascinating insights into the reasons behind their commitment and drive. Sons of Milton Wright, a bishop of the Church of the United Brethren in Christ, Orville and Wilbur were raised in a strict but loving home. Wilbur was witty and intellectually brilliant but also socially awkward and antagonistic, and his difficult personality would prove to be both an asset and a liability. Goldstone tells the story of Milton, an archconservative, coming into conflict with more liberal members of his denomination. The situation became so heated that the liberal faction rebelled against Milton's authority and sought to break away from his congregation. Compelled by a sense of righteous indignation, Wilbur aggressively defended his father's views by writing derisive, bitingly sarcastic editorials and instituting lawsuits against the liberals who sought to gain control of church property. Wilbur's invective did nothing to sway the liberal majority, but his single-mindedness, superior attitude, and litigious temperament foreshadowed the behavior he would exhibit years later during the patent war with fellow aviator and inventor Glenn Curtiss. In contrast, Orville did not participate in Wilbur's campaign against Milton's enemies; while he shared his brother's moralistic perspective and sense of perceived injustice against their father, he was content to let Wilbur lead the charge against Milton's foes. His deference to his older brother would characterize their relationship for the rest of their lives.

In spite of his reserve, Orville possessed an entrepreneurial spirit, and he started a printing company in 1889. Wilbur's entrance into the enterprise laid the foundation for their lifelong collaboration as business partners and aeronautical pioneers. The Wright brothers presented a united front during their careers as printers, later as bicycle salesmen and manufacturers, and finally as aviators. While Orville made important contributions, Goldstone makes it clear that it was primarily Wilbur's technical expertise, creative vision, and driving ambition that fueled the brothers' quest to achieve mechanical heavier-than-air human flight.

Goldstone covers familiar ground as he describes the brothers' famous experiments at Kitty Hawk, North Carolina, from 1901 to 1903, which led to their discovery of three-axis control—the management of yaw, pitch, and roll—a crucial concept that is still used in modern aircraft. Orville contributed the idea of a rear rudder to control yaw, Wilbur proposed a wing-warping system to control roll, and a forward elevator managed pitch. The Wrights' patent on three-axis control acknowledged that other methods could be used to achieve lateral (roll) control but maintained that they owned the idea of it. Goldstone quotes from a letter from Wilbur to Chanute, written on January 20, 1910: "It is our view that morally the world owes its almost universal use of our system of lateral control entirely to us. It is also our opinion that legally it owes it to us." In asserting their alleged ownership of lateral control, the brothers attempted to establish a monopoly by preventing other inventors from incorporating this essential element into their aircraft designs—unless they paid licensing fees to the Wrights.

The litigious brothers, especially Wilbur, sought remuneration from several people whom they believed to have infringed on the Wright patent, but their main target was Glenn Curtiss. Like the Wrights, Curtiss was mechanically gifted and had been a bicycle shop owner and racer. Unlike the more cautious brothers, he had also been a daredevil motorcycle rider, setting groundbreaking speed records. Because of his motorcycle background and knowledge of powered vehicles, Alexander Graham Bell invited him to develop an engine that could propel an aircraft. Curtiss's work in aviation set him on a collision course with Orville and Wilbur. He, too, was interested in lateral control, but instead of using wing-warping technology, he employed ailerons to correct roll. The Wrights regarded his sale of airplanes using ailerons as a direct infringement on their patent and filed a lawsuit against Curtiss, who fought back by continuing to design innovative aircraft without bowing to the Wrights' demands.

*Lawrence Goldstone is the author or coauthor of fourteen books of fiction and nonfiction, including* Dark Bargain: Slavery, Profits, and the Struggle for the Constitution *(2005) and* Lefty: An American Odyssey *(2012). His first novel,* Rights *(1992), was the winner of the 1992 New American Writing Award, and his novel* The Anatomy of Deception *(2008) was a New York Times notable mystery.*

The Wrights' preparations for and accomplishments at Kitty Hawk are well known. Goldstone's narrative becomes more compelling when Curtiss is introduced a third of the way into the book. The rivalry between Curtiss and the Wrights gives the story a dramatic edge that quickens the pace and throws the personalities of the principal players into sharp relief. The Wrights' plan to establish an aeronautical monopoly makes them appear greedy, egotistical, and monomaniacal. While Curtiss was just as competitive and ego driven, Goldstone portrays him as more reasonable and less rigid than the inflexible Wright brothers.

Curtiss and the Wrights, and by extension the pilots they employed, were also adversaries during air shows, where flyers tried to outdo one another with increasingly death-defying stunts. Curtiss was enthusiastic about exhibition flying, while the

Wrights were less so. At first, the brothers refused to enter air competitions because they considered the contestants a "bunch of patent infringers." Yet they soon realized that the air shows, although expensive to run, were a selling tool and an opportunity to display the superiority of their airplanes. Profit motive won out over their reluctance, and in July 1910, the Wrights decided to participate in exhibition flying.

The air shows were huge hits among the American public and, depending on the location, could draw hundreds of thousands of people. It was not just the novelty of witnessing machines flying through the air that attracted such large audiences; the flamboyant daredevils who took to the skies were the real crowd-pleasers. Goldstone captures the competitive spirit between not only Curtiss and the Wrights but also the pilots who flew for them. The term "birdmen" aptly describes Thomas Selfridge, a US Army lieutenant and Wright flyer who would be the first to die in a powered airplane; John Moisant, who stunned onlookers as he circled the Statue of Liberty in his Blériot aircraft; Eugene Ely, a Curtiss pilot who was the first to perform a fixed-wing aircraft landing aboard a ship; and Lincoln Beachey, a fearless barnstormer whose breath-taking feats riveted spectators. There were "birdwomen," too: screenwriter Harriet Quimby was the first American woman to earn a pilot's license and the first woman to fly across the English Channel; Matilde Moisant, John's sister, became the second licensed American female pilot and broke the women's world altitude record.

As spectacular as the air competitions were, they often exacted a terrible cost—and the public's appetite for disaster seems to have been just as voracious as its craving for thrills. In his gripping account of Beachey's hair-raising stunts, Goldstone notes that "Beachey had no illusions about the source of his popularity. When asked to describe his appeal, he replied, 'People come to see me die.'" This comment underscores both the danger of exhibition flying and the dark side of human nature. Vividly portraying the aftermaths of various accidents, Goldstone highlights the ghoulish behavior of on-lookers as they rush to the scene to strip the pilot's dead body of goggles, gloves, and pieces of clothing and the plane of its parts to keep as souvenirs.

While the air shows drew huge crowds, Wilbur devoted more of his time serving supposed patent infringers with lawsuits than he did designing state-of-the-art aircraft. Meanwhile, Curtiss, who continued to improve his designs and introduce new con-cepts such as the hydroplane, gained the upper hand. In addition, European aeronauti-cal companies began to enter the market, and the Americans slipped to second place in the aviation race. Wilbur's all-consuming pursuit of litigation chipped away at and finally eradicated the brothers' lead in the industry. According to Orville, the stress of protecting the Wright patent damaged Wilbur's health. He died of typhoid fever on May 30, 1912.

In January 1911, Allan Ryan, president of the Aero Club, gave a speech in which he said, "It is my own belief that the future supremacy of this country in the aeronautic field is going to depend very largely upon the harmonious cooperation of the institu-tions and individuals interested in the great science." Goldstone's assessment echoes Ryan's remarks. He argues that the United States' fall to second place was primarily due to the litigation between the Wright brothers and Glenn Curtiss, which prevented the free flow of ideas and the necessary collaboration that could have bolstered the nation's worldwide leadership in the aviation industry. Yet the patent war itself was not the sole factor that kept the United States from forging ahead. Goldstone makes it clear that it was the self-seeking, arrogant, stubborn personalities of the principal players—he especially faults Wilbur—that stalled the development of mechanical flight. Had Wilbur Wright, Orville Wright, and Glenn Curtiss put their egos aside, perhaps the American aviation industry would have taken off sooner.

*Pegge Bochynski*

## Review Sources

Rev. of *Birdmen: The Wright Brothers, Glenn Curtiss, and the Battle to Control the Skies*, by Lawrence Goldstone. *Kirkus Reviews* 15 Mar. 2014: 2. Print.

Rev. of *Birdmen: The Wright Brothers, Glenn Curtiss, and the Battle to Control the Skies*, by Lawrence Goldstone. *Publishers Weekly* 20 Jan. 2014: 40–41. Print.

Boyne, Walter J. Rev. of *Birdmen: The Wright Brothers, Glenn Curtiss, and the Battle to Control the Skies*, by Lawrence Goldstone. *Aviation History* Nov. 2014: 62. Print.

Cataneo, Emily. Rev. of *Birdmen: The Wright Brothers, Glenn Curtiss, and the Battle to Control the Skies*, by Lawrence Goldstone. *Christian Science Monitor*. Christian Science Monitor, 7 May 2014. Web. 28 Oct. 2014.

Link, Forrest. Rev. of *Birdmen: The Wright Brothers, Glenn Curtiss, and the Battle to Control the Skies*, by Lawrence Goldstone. *Library Journal* 1 Sept. 2014: 64. Print.

Roche, Rick. Rev. of *Birdmen: The Wright Brothers, Glenn Curtiss, and the Battle to Control the Skies*, by Lawrence Goldstone. *Booklist* 15 Dec. 2013: 6. Print.

# Black Moon

**Author:** Kenneth Calhoun (b. 1966)
**Publisher:** Hogarth (New York). 288 pp.
**Type of work:** Novel
**Time:** Near future
**Locale:** Southern California; Utah; Idaho

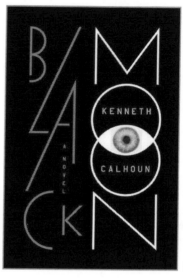

(Courtesy of Hogarth)

*Black Moon is an intriguing first novel about what happens when the world is overtaken by an epidemic of sleeplessness. As the sleepless slip into a kind of delirium, the importance of dreams emerges.*

**Principal characters:**
MATTHEW BIGGS, a former adman
CAROLYN, his wife, a victim of sleeplessness
CHASE, a besotted adolescent on the brink of
    adulthood
LILA FERRELL, a teenage girl whose parents have become sleepless
FELICIA, Chase's former girlfriend, who works at a university sleep clinic
JORDAN, Chase's high school friend and road-trip companion

*Black Moon* (2014) is Kenneth Calhoun's first novel, but the author is no stranger to storytelling. His short stories have been published in such exclusive literary magazines as *Tin House*, and his work was selected for the 2011 PEN/O. Henry Prize collection. He is also an accomplished graphic designer and filmmaker as well as a respected professor. *Black Moon* may be Calhoun's first foray into long fiction, but it is clearly the work of a master of creative force, and Calhoun's many professions add depth and poise unusual in a first novel.

In *Black Moon*, readers are introduced to a world where sleep has become impossible. In this dystopian near-future, only a few people are capable of sleeping naturally, and neither the reason for losing nor that for keeping the ability to sleep is known. What is known is that not sleeping destroys humanity. Sleeplessness breeds anxiety, desperation, rage, and eventually insanity. Civilization begins to collapse and crack, families are destroyed, and violence flourishes as the sleepless desperately try to find a way to cure themselves of their insomnia. With such a premise it would be easy to fall into a zombie-apocalypse drama, but Calhoun prefers instead to draw the reader into an intensely atmospheric work that evokes a dreamlike fog in which even the most incoherent sequences seem plausible and what is real becomes a less and less meaningful question.

Calhoun uses multiple characters and plot lines to tell his story. Matthew Biggs has recently walked away from a lucrative yet hollow career in advertising and is desperately trying to rescue his wife, Carolyn, from her sleepless state. College student

Chase reunites with his high school friend Jordan after his first year away at school, and they quickly become swept up in plotting to steal pharmaceutical sleep aids and get rich. Chase's former girlfriend, Felicia, finds herself thrust into a mothering role and working with the very people who may be able to find a cure. Lila is a young teenager trying to save her family. Each character has a compelling survival story, but that is not the point. These characters are central to the story not because of how they survive but because of who they are—or rather, who they could be, for they are all people who do not know who they are and are almost better defined by what they have lost than by what they have. Biggs has quit his job and is coasting through life until the sleeplessness epidemic gives him a purpose: finding his wife. Chase struggles not only with his sexual identity but also with his transition to adulthood, his lost childhood filled with fear and trepidation. Felicia accepts the maternal role thrust upon her but struggles with being an object of desire. Lila is caught as her parents' marriage disintegrates, but their love for her remains. Carolyn, a haunting and enigmatic character, is seen only through Biggs's eyes and thus remains almost entirely without an identity at all.

Calhoun weaves his story through his characters' negative spaces. As Biggs searches for Carolyn, who has vanished mysteriously, readers learn that she sees herself as an artist no longer able to create and a woman unable to conceive. Chase is incapable of introspection. Lila flees her increasingly unstable family, finding herself alone for the first time. Felicia is bound by promises that no longer matter. As the period of sleeplessness extends, the novel becomes more trancelike. New characters appear, only to fade away again into the fog. Things happen that may or may not be hallucinations. Time passes in short fits and long, cinematic sweeps. As the sleepless slip into hallucinatory states, dreams and reality become one. "It's dreams all the time now so nothing is nothing anymore," Chase says.

Dreams are what unite these characters. In interviews Calhoun has admitted to a fascination with dreams—their purpose, their value, their meaning. Lost and confused as they all are, each of Calhoun's characters has one or more dreams to which they cling. Some are simple, such as Chase's desire to prove he is heterosexual and win back Felicia, and provide the novel with much-needed elements of comic relief. Other dreams are more complex. Biggs and Carolyn are first brought together when he dreams about her, a dream Carolyn believes represents her metaphorical struggle against admitting her mother is dying. As the novel progresses, Biggs and Carolyn continue to connect in the dream world until Carolyn defines almost all of Biggs's reality. Lila dreams of finding safety and security, but as she tries to navigate the world of the sleepless, she finds herself ever more alone. In one of the bizarre sequences, she dons an owl mask to hide her face as she realizes survival almost certainly dependent on her ability to sustain her isolation. Felicia, the only character whose circumstances make a cure for sleeplessness a possibility, dreams of nothing more than a normal college life. Although she finds herself tending to the sleepless, she clings to the fantasy that maybe everything is not ruined. "Maybe is enough," she tells herself.

Apart from "why," "maybe" is perhaps the most repeated word in *Black Moon*. Calhoun breaks up the narrative with long lists of maybes. Multiple people think of maybe-lists of potential causes of the sleeplessness. Biggs rattles off numerous may-bes for Carolyn: maybe Carolyn is, maybe Carolyn thinks, maybe Carolyn did. And maybe Chase can win Felicia back. Nothing is certain.

Felicia realizes that "the world ha[s] been turned inside out." Felicia thinks, "All the outside things were now inside. Everything else that we kept in our heads, in hearts, has flooded out into the open air."Ever focused on Carolyn, Biggs hopes that salvation can be found in this new juxtaposition of the world. This almost poetic way of thinking is classic Calhoun, who can describe even the most dreadful events with soft, lyrical language. His prose is sometimes direct, sometimes delirious, depending on the scenario. He advances the plot in a mostly straightforward manner but manipulates time and reality in a way consistent with delirium.

While Calhoun never slips while juggling the multiple story lines, he can be a little heavy-handed with the plot. It is unclear whether he wants a comparison to be drawn between Biggs's desperate search for Carolyn and Chase's passion-fueled quest for Felicia. That Felicia just happens to be doing summer research at a sleep institute is a little too pat. And as Calhoun attempts to draw the multiple story lines together and to a close, they lose some of their integrity, perhaps because each layer was originally written as a short story. Basic attention to detail is sometimes ignored; for example, Calhoun has Lila explain how her community ran out of water but not how the characters are able to travel such long distances in seemingly impossible short periods of time.

Still, the novel does not suffer from any of these things as long as the reader stays swept up in the story. Calhoun largely avoids the pitfalls of a complicated storytelling mechanism by staying grounded in the humanity of his characters. He is tender toward those suffering from sleeplessness, making it clear that they are struggling to retain their humanity and cling to the familiar, even as their cognitive functions decline. His sleepless characters, despite shuffling and twitching, talking strangely, and tending toward homicidal violence, are not zombies but victims who have done nothing to deserve their wretched fates. The reader is never unaware of the desperation of the sleepless, nor of their humanity. They trash houses because they are looking for homes. They destroy pictures they do not recognize because they need to belong. They despair because they are not saved.

*Vandermeer, Jeff. "Insomnia Takes Over the World in Kenneth Calhoun's* Black Moon.*" Rev. of* Black Moon, *by Kenneth Calhoun. Los Angeles Times. Tribune Interactive, 7 Mar. 2014. Web. 6 Nov. 2014.Filmmaker and graphic designer Kenneth Calhoun is the author of numerous works of short fiction. He is also an assistant professor at Lasell College. In 2011 he was selected for the PEN/O. Henry Prize collection.* Black Moon *is his first novel.*

Calhoun is also a master of subtle humor. He clearly enjoys employing the scrambled speech he assigns to the sleepless, whose syntax is jarring and reminiscent of a yokel in the Old West. And Calhoun is unafraid to be lowbrow. When Chase thinks all has been lost, he is delighted to discover that the truck he has stolen, while bereft of anything he might use as clothing, has sheep. Having grown up in a suburb in southern California, Chase is somewhat in awe of nature, and the sheep take on spiritual significance for him. Chase is also the butt of most Calhoun's jokes, but as an adolescent on the cusp of adulthood, it makes sense that he is the most awkward and least competent character. As his situation spirals out of control, he serves as a metaphor for the type of self-absorbed society that could suffer an apocalypse. He mistakes his echo for his conscience yet is aware that he is lacking something. Eventually Chase realizes that "he was growing distant from that core he had always felt so compelled to protect, to hold tightly together . . . He was the opposite of all that he had been. He had been turned inside out." What Biggs and Felicia are capable of recognizing as happening to the world, Chase can only see as happening to himself.

Calhoun does fall a little short with the female characters. Neither Felicia nor Lila is given as much attention as she deserves. Yet through Lila, who is in the midst of the epidemic, and Felicia, who is largely sheltered from it, the novel draws a sort of soul. Their experiences are what allow the reader to truly feel the horror of what is happening. On the other hand, Carolyn remains a plot device throughout the novel, never developed as her own character. Yet she has the strongest presence of all the characters, and although Calhoun never allows her to speak for herself, she is in many ways the most human and only slightly less sympathetic than Lila.

It is clear that Calhoun identifies the most with Biggs, and the novel would have benefited from greater narrative distance. Still, because Biggs clings so tightly to Carolyn, Calhoun is able to demonstrate to the reader how dream, memory, and fantasy can overwhelm reality. At some point, it becomes clear that all the characters are not really seeking themselves but rather are looking for the way they thought of themselves in the past; this is the most obvious with Biggs, whose search for Carolyn becomes less and less about her and more and more about their relationship.

Toward the end of the novel, Calhoun veers closer to science fiction as the sleep clinic becomes more central to the story. The scientists at the clinic are caricatures of scientists, but their mission is not. They focus on finding a way to return sleep at all costs and must struggle with the consequences of their decisions. The scientists neither search for a cause of the sleeplessness nor leave the clinic boundaries to help the public, so their work is self-serving, though not without heart. They are dedicated to saving those that still reside within the clinic. They work to preserve the humanity of those they can reach, even at the cost of exploiting those who do not need a cure.

Throughout *Black Moon*, Calhoun manages to maintain the dreamlike atmosphere of the novel, at times infused with chaotic energy, other times with almost laconic despair. And he never tries to solve the mystery of dreams. Chase's friend Jordan explains that dreams are universal, whether one is sleepless or not. "It means," he says, "that it's where we really live, and when we're awake, we're just coming up for air." Much happens to humanity in *Black Moon*, but dreams remain.

*Michelle Acciavatti*

**Review Sources**

Rev. of *Black Moon*, by Kenneth Calhoun. *Kirkus Reviews* 15 Jan. 2014: 225. Print.
   Rev. of *Black Moon*, by Kenneth Calhoun. *Publishers Weekly* 13 Jan. 2014: 47.
   Print.
Heller, Jason. "*Black Moon* Imagines A Sleepless American Nightmare." Rev. of
   *Black Moon*, by Kenneth Calhoun. *NPR*. Natl. Public Radio, 6 Mar. 2014. Web.
   26 Nov. 2014.
Ophoff, Cortney. Rev. of *Black Moon*, by Kenneth Calhoun. *Booklist* 1 Feb. 2014:
   19. Print.

# The Blazing World

**Author:** Siri Hustvedt (b. 1955)
**Publisher:** Simon & Schuster (New York).
384 pp.
**Type of work:** Novel
**Time:** 1990s–2012
**Locales:** New York City; Nantucket

(Courtesy of Simon & Schuster)

*Presented as a series of journal entries, written accounts, interviews, and reviews,* The Blazing World *paints a compelling portrait of a complex artist and her experiments with perception and personal identity.*

**Principal characters:**
HARRIET "HARRY" BURDEN, a middle-aged artist largely ignored by the artistic community
MAISIE LORD, her daughter
ETHAN LORD, her son
BRUNO KLEINFELD, her boyfriend
RACHEL BRIEFMAN, her best friend since childhood
ANTON TISH, the first of Burden's artistic "masks"
PHINEAS Q. ELDRIDGE, the second artistic mask
RUNE, the third artistic mask
OSWALD CASE, a journalist
SWEET AUTUMN PINKNEY, Tish's assistant

Steeped in yet sharply critical of the art world, Siri Hustvedt's sixth novel, *The Blazing World*, raises important questions about what it is to be a woman and an artist in the late twentieth and early twenty-first century. The novel is ostensibly the nonfictional creation of a professor named I. V. Hess, who has compiled journal entries, personal accounts and interviews, and other written ephemera to produce a portrait of a deceased artist named Harriet Burden. Burden's work late in life, particularly her complex and controversial project *Maskings*, becomes the focal point of *The Blazing World*, which calls attention to issues of identity and perception as well as the biases of the artistic community.

Following the death of her husband, the respected art dealer Felix Lord, Harriet Burden struggles both with her intense grief and with her knowledge of her tenuous place in the artistic community. She is herself a talented artist whose art had been publicly displayed in her youth, but in the eyes of many who know or know of her, she is merely the widow of a more important member of the community and better known as the host of his parties and the mother of his children. Since her marriage to

Felix, her own art has received little notice, an injustice that she attributes not only to her overshadowing husband but also to the ingrained sexism of the art world, in which male artists are common and female artists much less so.

In the years after Lord's death, Burden decides to embark on a new project that she calls *Maskings*, one that she hopes will call attention to the biases of the art world and allow her to play with the idea of identity. She enlists a young artist, Anton Tish, to act as the public face of her work for an art exhibition titled *The History of Western Art*. The exhibition consists of a large sculpture of a sleeping woman covered with text and images, all references to art and artists, as well as a number of boxes containing scenes of humanoid figures. Although Burden is responsible for designing and creating the artwork, she allows Tish to take credit for it publicly and present himself as the art's creator, while she is relegated to the role of patron and occasional helper. The exhibition is widely successful and brings Tish significant praise—praise that Burden believes the exhibition would never had received had the public known its creator was middle-aged woman rather than an attractive man in his twenties. However, Tish struggles with the inauthentic nature of his fame, and his and Burden's working relationship soon breaks down.

Burden embarks on the second stage of her project with the help of Phineas Q. Eldridge, a performance artist whom she meets through her son, Ethan. Her second project, *The Suffocation Rooms*, consists of a series of rooms in which the figures and objects inside become progressively larger, the temperature increases, and the surroundings become more aged and worn as the viewer walks through them. This exhibition is likewise generally well received, although it does not attract the same amount of attention as *The History of Western Art*. This difference in reception could possibly be attributed to the fact that Eldridge is both mixed race and homosexual and thus has a more difficult time gaining acceptance in the art world than the white, heterosexual Tish. Burden and Eldridge become close friends, and they also collaborate on a number of smaller works.

It is the third of Burden's exhibitions that garners the most attention and has the most extreme effect on Burden herself. Her third artistic mask is an artist named Rune, who, unlike Tish and Eldridge, already has a significant following. The exhibition, titled *Beneath*, consists of a maze studded with "windows" that contain screens showing short films or boxes filled with a variety of meaningful objects. In her journal entries, Burden describes herself as the work's primary creator, as with the previous two exhibitions. However, her relationship with Rune abruptly falls apart in what Burden considers a betrayal. Believing that Rune is trying to steal the artwork from her, Burden decides to reveal the truth about the three exhibitions. She assumes the name of Professor Richard Brickman, an identity she created in a conversation with Rune, and sends a letter to the journal *The Open Eye*; in it, Burden-as-Brickman claims to have received a lengthy manifesto from Burden that reveals the three deceptions. Although *The Open Eye* does publish the letter, this tactic is only somewhat effective. Rune publicly denies that Burden was any more than a muse or patron, and although those closest to her believe her, others in the art community, particularly journalist and Rune biographer Oswald Case, remain convinced that Rune was the sole creator of *Beneath*.

The debate about Burden's role in *The History of Western Art*, *The Suffocation Rooms*, and *Beneath* continues after her death, and through this compiled book, the fictional I. V. Hess seeks to shed light on this mystery.

*The Blazing World* takes its title from a work by the seventeenth-century English duchess Margaret Cavendish, a writer and natural philosopher whom Burden cites as an inspiration in several of her journal entries. Cavendish's status as one of the few women publicly publishing and practicing natural philosophy during her time makes her an appropriate avatar of sorts for Burden, who feels strongly that her identity as an artist has been subsumed by her other feminine identities of daughter, wife, and mother. Even with her parents and husband dead and her children grown, she cannot escape the biases engrained in the art world, which she too has internalized to a degree. In many ways, *The Blazing World* is a feminist critique of not only the art world but also the ways in which society forces women to alter their identities and construct new ones.

(© Marion Ettling)

*Siri Hustvedt is the author of several novels, including* What I Loved *(2003) and* The Summer without Men *(2011), as well as numerous essays and other nonfiction works.*

As the supposed creation of Hess, the novel compiles written documents in a variety of styles. Hustvedt is apt at creating varied narrative voices, rendering all of the compiled sources distinct. Burden's journal entries are complex, incorporating numerous references to art and philosophy, which are explained by Hess in endnotes; in the guise of Brickman, Burden is just as erudite but nevertheless quite different in voice. Her daughter, Maisie, provides a relatively straightforward take on events, while Ethan's chapters are written as poetry. Even the reviews of the exhibitions are written in styles that render them distinct yet believable. These multiple viewpoints serve a variety of purposes in the novel. Had the story been told solely from Burden's perspective, it would have ended with her death. With its multinarrator structure, however, the novel is able to present Burden's death and some of the events afterward, providing further context for her work and a glimpse of how she was received posthumously. This is particularly important because the novel frequently raises examples of female artists who were largely ignored or dismissed during their lifetimes but who became somewhat celebrated after their deaths. Whether Burden is destined to join their ranks remains unclear, but the very existence of Hess's book suggests that she may.

Perhaps the most important function of the novel's structure, however, is the way in which it raises questions about truth, perception, and intent. It is clear from Burden's journal entries that she believes she has been dismissed and ignored as an artist, in large part because she is a woman and because she was Felix Lord's wife. It is this belief that fuels her work with Tish, Eldridge, and Rune. Likewise, her journal entries express her strong belief that she has been betrayed by Rune, whom she believes is trying to steal her work from her. The chapters narrated by journalist Oswald Case form a counterpoint to Burden's narrative, characterizing Rune as a genius martyr and Burden as a shrill, largely talentless hanger-on. Burden's and Case's perspectives essentially become the two opposite ends of a spectrum, and each calls the other into question. At the same time, the myriad other viewpoints in the novel—including those of Burden's children, boyfriend Bruno Kleinfeld, longtime friend Rachel Briefman, Eldridge, and Sweet Autumn Pinkney, Tish's assistant and Burden's friend—provide perspectives located between those of Burden and Case. They confirm some assertions and criticize others, provide details and insights only those closest to Burden could, and allow the reader to decide whether and to what extent Burden's perceptions are correct. For some readers, Burden may ultimately emerge not as the ignored, mistreated genius her journals present her as nor the shrill hysteric described by Case but as someone else entirely—someone complex, contradictory, and altogether human.

Critical response to *The Blazing World* was largely positive, and the novel was included on the long list for the prestigious Man Booker Prize in 2014. The novel is a complex work that invites interpretation, and much of the critical response reflects individual readers' perceptions of the book. Their differing interpretations even extend to details such as the meaning behind the name of the book's fictional author. In her review for the *Boston Globe*, Laura Collins-Hughes suggested that the name I. V. Hess may be related to the concept of a Hess image, a type of visual afterimage, which could tie in to the novel's focus on identity. Fernanda Eberstadt, writing for the *New York Times*, proposed that Hess's name may be an allusion to the sculptor Eva Hesse, while Amal El-Mohtar, in her review for *NPR*, suggested that the name may be related to the Hunt and Hess scale, used to evaluate brain hemorrhages. Critical responses to the narrative as a whole were likewise varied. In her review for the *Telegraph*, Lucy Beresford noted that she found the novel to be "dry and labored"; on the other hand, El-Mohtar wrote that the novel "gives off the warmth and light by which to read, understand, marvel at it." The difference between those two responses underscores the complex nature of the novel and, ultimately, of Harriett Burden herself.

*Joy Crelin*

**Review Sources**

Beresford, Lucy. Rev. of *The Blazing World*, by Siri Hustvedt. *Telegraph*. Telegraph Media Group, 25 Mar. 2014. Web. 21 Dec. 2014.

Rev. of *The Blazing World*, by Siri Hustvedt. *Kirkus*. Kirkus Media, 27 Nov. 2013. Web. 21 Dec. 2014.

Collins-Hughes, Laura. Rev. of *The Blazing World*, by Siri Hustvedt. *Boston Globe*. Boston Globe Media Partners, 12 Apr. 2014. Web. 21 Dec. 2014.

Cusk, Rachel. Rev. of *The Blazing World*, by Siri Hustvedt." *Guardian*. Guardian News and Media, 15 Mar. 2014. Web. 21 Dec. 2014.

Eberstadt, Fernanda. "Outsider Art." Rev. of *The Blazing World*, by Siri Hustvedt. *New York Times Sunday Book Review*. New York Times, 28 Mar. 2014. Web. 21 Dec. 2014.

El-Mohtar, Amal. "A Delicate Arson: 'The Blazing World' Consumes Its Readers." Rev. of *The Blazing World*, by Siri Hustvedt. *NPR Books*. NPR, 15 Mar. 2014. Web. 21 Dec. 2014.

# The Bone Clocks

**Author:** David Mitchell (b. 1969)
**Publisher:** Random House (New York). 640 pp.
**Type of work:** Novel
**Time Period:** 1800s–2043
**Locale:** England, Iraq, Ireland, Switzerland, Australia

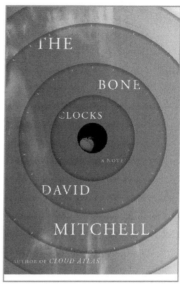

(Courtesy of Random House)

*The Bone Clocks is a fantasy fiction novel consisting of six interconnected stories that reflect on the machinations of immortal beings living in secret societies spread across the world.*

**Principal characters:**
HOLLY SYKES, an Englishwoman gifted with strange abilities who uncovers an ancient war between two dueling societies of immortals
HUGO LAMB, a college student in 1990s England with whom she has an affair
CRISPIN HERSHEY, a former novelist who becomes a friend of hers
DR. MARINUS, part of a group of immortals known as the Horologists, whose souls reincarnate into another human body after death

David Mitchell has been twice nominated for the Booker Prize in fiction, and reviewers have called him one of the most innovative writers of the last decade. Since his 2004 novel, *Cloud Atlas*, was turned into a blockbuster film, interest in his work has grown, and Mitchell has developed a dedicated fan base that follows his work. In most of his novels to date, Mitchell explores the way that lives are connected in unexpected ways across time and space. Many of his novels are written as collections of short novellas or stories that all link together through their contribution to an underlying plot or through the life of one or more central characters.

Perhaps the most unique thing about Mitchell's *The Bone Clocks* (2014) is the way the book connects to his other novels. Mitchell has said in interviews that he is developing what he calls an "über-book," in which all of his fiction can be said to take place within the same multiverse. Characters, elements of setting, the names of businesses, organizations, and other features of his fictional environments recur from book to book in different manifestations. Each book is not only its own story but also contributes to the larger fictional world that Mitchell has created. Before *The Bone Clocks* was published, Mitchell hinted that it would provide important new clues to unraveling the full reality of his über-book.

In interviews, Mitchell said that *The Bone Clocks* was inspired by pondering his own mortality. Like *Cloud Atlas*, *The Bone Clocks* is a six-part story that takes place in a variety of settings around the world and in a number of different time periods. In each part, Mitchell uses a new narrator with a unique voice and perspective. Each section is told from a first-person point of view, and each is connected to the lives of a small number of central characters who tie the sections together and often provide alternating voices for the story.

The first section of *The Bone Clocks* is seen through the eyes of Holly Sykes, the pivotal central character in Mitchell's broader narrative. She is introduced to readers as a fifteen-year-old living in the small town of Black Swan Green, England, in 1984. As a teenager, Holly has typical teenage concerns: she chafes against her mother and obsesses over her crush on a local boy, Vin. Readers also learn that Holly has unusual abilities; she hears voices, coming from what she calls "Radio People," and sees spectral figures that may or may not be real. Mitchell weaves in the supernatural elements of his story slowly over the first section of the book, using Holly's strange encounters to hint at the larger mystery. Through Holly, readers meet Miss Constantin, a ghostly figure that Holly encountered when she was seven; and Dr. Marinus, a Chinese child psychologist whom Holly has been visiting to cope with her unusual experiences. Holly also meets Esther Little, an elderly woman who asks Holly to grant her "asylum." Though Holly does not know what this means, she agrees, and readers later learn that Esther and Dr. Marinus are Horologists, an ancient race of immortals who benevolently inhabit new bodies after death in a sort of repeated transmigration. Toward the end of the section, Holly learns that her brother, Jacko, has gone missing. There is no immediate closure given to the Jacko story here, but the event and the character come back later with new significance as the book progresses.

The second section introduces readers to Hugo Lamb, a smooth-talking Cambridge undergraduate who is taking a break from college in 1991 to spend the New Year holiday in Switzerland. Here, Lamb meets Holly Sykes, who has been working as a waitress in a local bar, and the two have a brief affair. Miss Constantin, the woman from Holly's past, then reappears and introduces Hugo to the secret society of the Anchorites, a society that has achieved immortality by leeching the souls of the living, like psychic vampires. Hugo abandons Holly when he is invited into the Anchorites' secret society, and this fateful decision leads into the third section of the book, revealing a set of circumstances that lead Holly in a new direction.

The third section of the book, set in 2003 and 2004, is narrated by Ed Brubeck, a former war reporter who has becomes Holly Sykes's live-in lover. The couple have a daughter, Aoife, and are visiting England to attend the wedding of Holly's sister Sharon. This section is less chronologically fluid, as portions of it involve Ed's memories of his time in Iraq, alternating with contemporary scenes set in England. Ed accepts a new assignment in the Middle East, this time in Syria, where he dies. Again, the new narrator and new timeline provide a look at how Holly's life develops and leads readers further into the Anchorite and Horologist societies.

A number of reviewers have highlighted the fourth section of *The Bone Clocks* as one of the book's most gripping parts. The section is narrated by Crispin Hershey, a former star novelist whose latest book has received bad reviews. In retaliation, Crispin frames Richard Cheeseman—the reviewer responsible, in Crispin's mind, for tanking his novel—resulting in Cheeseman's arrest and incarceration. After Crispin details these tribulations in his career, Holly returns to the story, this time as the newly successful author of a book about her preternatural gifts, her childhood experiences, and the disappearance of her brother. Crispin and Holly become friends after meeting repeatedly at book festivals. Though the story gradually winds further into what the reader learns is an ancient war between the Anchorites and Horologists, reviewers appreciated the way Mitchell used the character of Crispin to drop in self-reflective commentary on the writing industry, literary criticism, and even his own ambitious "interlinking universes" approach to storytelling.

The fifth section takes place in 2024, and readers enter the mind of Dr. Marinus, a Horologist who is now in the body of a female psychiatrist. We learn that Esther, the other

© Paul Stuart

*David Mitchell is an English author whose books* number9dream *(2001) and* Cloud Atlas *(2004) were finalists for the Booker Prize for fiction. He has written six novels and has also published short fiction in* McSweeney's, Granta, *the* Guardian, *and the* New York Times. *A film adaptation of* Cloud Atlas *was released in 2012, starring Tom Hanks and Halle Berry.*

Horologist Holly met as a child, has taken refuge inside Holly's body. The fifth section is the longest and most fantastical of the book, delving directly into the pseudo-magical battle between the Horologists and the Anchorites. The Horologists enlist Holly to help them destroy the Anchorites' main headquarters, known as the Chapel. Esther, one of the oldest Horologists, is forced to sacrifice her soul, using its energy to destroy the Chapel. This section of the book is heavy with action and fantasy, with the two groups of immortals using strange powers to fight one another. Holly narrowly escapes, having helped the Horologists achieve their goal.

In the final section, readers return to Holly, who again becomes the narrator and is now seventy-four years old and living in Ireland. It becomes clear that in this dystopian future, environmental devastation has ravaged most of the world, and Holly is now caring for her two grandchildren after the death of her daughter and son-in-law in a "gigastorm." Digital communication has largely collapsed, the world has run out of petroleum fuel, and the area in which Holly lives has recently lost military protection and is presumably about to be overrun by a sort of postapocalyptic militia. The Horologists return to Holly, offering to save her grandchildren by giving them sanctuary in Iceland, where geothermal energy has allowed the country to avoid the devastation of the petroleum collapse. Holly agrees and sends her grandchildren away, but she remains in Ireland to face whatever fate is coming to her.

*The Bone Clocks* flip-flops through time periods, narrators, perspectives, geographical locations, and themes, building on the broader world-within-a-world that Mitchell has created through his linked novels. Several characters in *The Bone Clocks* have appeared in past novels as well. Marinus, for instance, appeared as a surgeon in Mitchell's 2010 novel, *The Thousand Autumns of Jacob de Zoet*. Learning that Marinus is a character who can appear as different people, in different time periods, because of his or her ability to transmigrate into new bodies gives an explanation for the character's reappearances. Reviewer Kathryn Schulz, writing in *New York* magazine, provided a chart mapping the appearances of characters throughout Mitchell's novels and found that twenty-three characters appear in two or three of Mitchell's six works to date. The Anchorites and Horologists introduced in *The Bone Clocks* thus redefine the appearance of immortals, "soul vampires," and enigmatic reappearing characters in all of Mitchell's earlier works.

Reviews of *The Bone Clocks* were primarily positive, though some reviewers felt that the novel was not as good as some of Mitchell's earlier works. Reviewer James Wood, writing in the *New Yorker*, criticized Mitchell's characterizations as seeming "too similar" and voiced doubts about the validity of his ambition in linking his fictions into a broader multiverse. Writing in the *Atlantic*, reviewer Derek Thompson called the book "almost perfect," with only minor missteps in what he saw as a superior novel based on excellent storytelling technique. Reviewers have compared Mitchell favorably to authors such as Michael Chabon, Thomas Pynchon, and Jonathan Franzen for his ability to create eloquent prose that serves the story. While reviewers focused on Mitchell's overarching "über-novel" strategy, *The Bone Clocks* is also an independent, stand-alone work of fiction that does not require readers to have followed his other books. Though it is an epic, *The Bone Clocks* is also a fantasy adventure that, while it has broader significance in terms of commentary and symbolism, reads like a secret society thriller.

*Micah L. Issitt*

**Review Sources**

Charles, Ron. Rev. of *The Bone Clocks*, by David Mitchell. *Washington Post*. Washington Post, 26 Aug. 2014. Web. 17 Oct. 2014.

Thompson, Derek. "*The Bone Clocks*: David Mitchell's Almost-Perfect Masterpiece." Rev. of *The Bone Clocks*, by David Mitchell. *Atlantic*. Atlantic Monthly Group, 2 Sept. 2014. Web. 17 Oct. 2014.

Wood, James. "Soul Cycle." Rev. of *The Bone Clocks*, by David Mitchell. *New Yorker*. Condé Nast, 8 Sept. 2014. Web. 17 Oct. 2014.

Worley, Sam. Rev. of *The Bone Clocks*, by David Mitchell. *Chicago Tribune*. Tribune Interactive, 12 Sept. 2014. Web. 17 Oct. 2014.

# The Book of Strange New Things

**Author:** Michel Faber
**Publisher:** Hogarth (New York). 512 pp.
**Type of work:** Novel
**Time:** Near future
**Locale:** London, England; the planet Oasis

(Courtesy of Hogarth)

*The Book of Strange New Things is, above all, a love story. It relates the ways in which the relationship of Peter and Beatrice Leigh is tested by Peter's mission to the planet Oasis while conditions on Earth deteriorate, illuminating the strength of faith and the limits of love.*

**Principal characters:**
PETER LEIGH, a Christian missionary to the inhabitants of the planet Oasis
BEATRICE LEIGH, his wife, who tells of catastrophic events on Earth
USIC, his employer, a mysterious corporation
ALEX GRAINGER, his advisor on Oasis
JESUS LOVER FIVE, an Oasan who befriends Peter

Writer Michel Faber has won much critical acclaim for his ability to transform stories from straight genre pieces to works of high literary merit, as demonstrated in his historical novel *The Crimson Petal and the White* (2002) and his science fiction novel *Under the Skin* (2000). In *The Book of Strange New Things* he returns to the general category of science fiction, though with a different scope and focus. In the near future, Peter Leigh journeys to the planet known as Oasis, light-years away from his wife on Earth. He is a Christian missionary to the planet's native population, employed on behalf of a corporation known only by the acronym USIC. From this deceptively simple setup Faber crafts a nuanced tale that takes on big questions about religion, love, and humanity. The result is another unique novel that has attracted wide praise from many reviewers.

From the start, it is clear that Peter would be happier if his wife, Beatrice, could accompany him on his interplanetary mission. He feels they function well as team, with each filling in where the other has shortcomings—in fact, it was she who introduced him to faith in the first place. He is a bit concerned that without Beatrice, he will fail to keep track of important details, or will misread a look or comment. Yet Peter is also deeply devoted to his sense of duty to his religion, and relishes working as a pastor. When it is clear that the offer to travel to Oasis is only available to Peter, the couple decides that the opportunity to be a missionary on a new planet, combined with the lucrative salary he will earn, is worth the time they will spend apart.

Faber creates a strong sense of the couple's relationship from the beginning, including the subtle differences that will soon be magnified by the huge distance between them. They are introduced as a perfectly happy pair, but a telephone call marred by static hints at the communication challenges that later increasingly manifest themselves in their interplanetary email exchanges. Peter felt their goodbye was said the day before his departure, while Beatrice wants to extend the farewell until the very moment he leaves. She does not quite make it to that last moment, however, telling Peter that she cannot stand there to be left alone and urging him to go ahead to his departure gate without her. Peter is reluctant to leave, yet at the same time he is anxious to begin is work on Oasis. His actual journey is a blur, reflecting Peter's own apathy toward some of the details of life. Once on Oasis, though, he is very quickly swept up in the whirl of new experiences.

Peter is enthusiastically welcomed by the inhabitants of Oasis, who are physically humanoid except for the face, which resembles "a massive whitish-pink walnut kernel," and their exotic language. He learns that instead of being the difficult converts he expected, they are already highly accepting of Christianity. Peter, it turns out, is a replacement for a previous missionary, who began teaching the Oasans before he disappeared; the mystery of just what it is that happened to that predecessor sets an uneasy tone despite the general air of friendliness on the planet.

Peter's unease is compounded when he observes that none of his fellow USIC employees are bothered by the fact that there is no outlet for news from Earth. None of them seem to have people they communicate with back home. Peter is in the unique position of having someone he cares for who can also tell him about what is going on. That brings him some comfort until an e-mail he sends to Bea is blocked, with a message advising him to seek assistance. He learns from his advisor, the prickly Alex Grainger, that all of his e-mails are read to ensure the content is appropriate before his messages are allowed to be sent. He is stunned when she does not find this objectionable.

*Michael Faber is a Dutch-born author whose novels include* The Crimson Petal and the White *(2002) and* Under the Skin *(2000). He has also written prize-winning short stories and worked in journalism.*

Peter decides to live with the Oasans rather than in the base with the other USIC employees. These are the people he is here to minister to. He wants to know them and share their daily life. He wants them to know that he is committed to their well-being and not simply running out to speak to them a couple of times a week. He adjusts easily to their routines and finds that sleeping outside works best for him. The Oasans accommodate this because he is of vital importance to them—the Bible is their "book of strange new things." Meanwhile, the more time Peter spends with the Oasans, the more uncomfortable he feels with the other humans on the USIC base. He is irreconcilably different from them, and they find him strange. He is the only one without a specific job title that meets some need of the base, and he is also the only one who is genuinely interested in speaking with each person.

His time away from base makes it impossible for him to communicate with Bea on a regular basis. The technology he requires to do this is not available where he stays and he does not insist upon it until it is too late. The tear in their relationship begins simply enough with the lag between e-mails, and is compounded by the fact that they have always previously experienced things together. Faber ups the emotional load by having Bea relate a series of catastrophic events on Earth. Some of them are world-wide, such as a tsunami that wipes out the Maldives, and some of them hit closer to home, as grocery stores run out of goods and garbage piles up on the sidewalks. Yet Peter cannot relate, and finds himself annoyed by both the tedious news and his own lack of interest. With all that is happening on Earth and all that is new to Peter on Oasis, the distance between them is far more significant than a mere million miles of space. The emotional bond between them is tested as the fabric of their relationship begins to unravel.

Peter lacks the emotional maturity to step up when Bea needs it. For her part, Bea is faced with the cataclysmic changes that signal the end of civilization as they have known it. She is furious with herself for needing Peter so viscerally, even as she is furious with Peter for allowing events and experiences outside the bond of their marriage to distract him from her needs. Peter is dumbstruck when Bea renounces God. Their mutual faith has been a linchpin of their relationship. Still, he has loved Bea for many years and through many struggles. His emotional growth is marked by his struggle to come to terms with the consequences of their choices and beliefs.

When his Oasan friend Jesus Lover Five is admitted to the infirmary, Peter realizes for the first time that he has insight into and deep attachment to two different worlds. As Grainger experiences dramatic shifts in her emotional well-being, and Jesus Lover Five is confronted by the limits of faith, Peter is left to wonder about his culpability in both their individual plights. It also forces him to confront his lack of true communion with Bea since he was introduced to the Oasans. Is his place on the failing Earth or among the utterly attentive congregation on Oasis?

Religion, faith, and relationships are integral themes of this novel. Peter is wholly invested in his role as a missionary, and the way Faber portrays his personal and public belief is highly realistic. The intricacies of communicating with an alien species are also well illustrated, with unfamiliar characters standing in as Oasan speech in the text to give the reader the same sense of disorientation. When Peter discovers that the Oasans are unable to pronounce many words from the Bible, he translates them into ones that fit their speech production. Faber brings up interesting issues of the relationship between pastor and congregation; Peter's great success with his new followers plays to his ego while forcing him to question his own faith and the reasons why things have gone so easily.

*The Book of Strange New Things* was met with mostly strong praise from critics, with many ranking it as a novel worthy of Faber's previous two efforts. Reviewers frequently cited his depth of characterization and strength of description as highlights. His storytelling abilities allow him to create an entirely new planet and make it seem real. He takes a refreshing perspective on science fiction, creating something that transcends the narrow classifications of genre by avoiding clichés and exploring deep ideas. Not all reviews were wholly positive, however. In her review for the *Boston Globe*, Rebecca Steinitz expresses her disappointment with the ultimate execution of the novel despite an intriguing premise: "If this strange, new setup seems promising, it doesn't deliver much. . . . Big issues are put into play—faith, love, redemption, prejudice—but they dwindle away into ambiguous banalities. . . . faith could be just a powerful placebo but maybe not; and passionate pain might be better than passive acceptance, except that those who feel it are miserable." Yet others feel the ambiguity of the questions Faber raises is a strength, revealing the complexity of the issues at play. In his *Washington Post* review Ron Charles writes, "If it feels more contemplative than propulsive, if Faber repeatedly thwarts his own dramatic premises, he also offers . . . a state of mingled familiarity and alienness that leaves us with questions we can't answer—or forget."

To fans of science fiction with literary aspirations or those looking for a nuanced portrayal of religion, *The Book of Strange New Things* is certainly worth reading. While it may not appeal to everyone, it brings something new to the table, and will likely spark many discussions on a wide variety of topics as it examines the challenges of love and faith.

*Gina Hagler*

**Review Sources**

Charles, Ron. Rev. of *The Book of Strange New Things*, by Michel Faber. *Washington Post*. Washington Post, 25 Nov. 2014. Web. 18 Feb. 2015.

Steinitz, Rebecca. Rev. of *The Book of Strange New Things*, by Michel Faber. *Boston Globe*. Globe Media Partners, 28 Oct. 2014. Web. 18 Feb. 2015.

Theroux, Marcel. Rev. of *The Book of Strange New Things*, by Michel Faber. *New York Times*. New York Times, 30 Oct. 2014. Web. 18 Feb. 2015.

# The Book of Unknown Americans

**Author:** Cristina Henríquez (b. 1977)
**Publisher:** Alfred A. Knopf (New York).
  286 pp.
**Type of work:** Novel
**Time:** ca. 2008
**Locale:** Delaware

*Many lives join together in* The Book of Unknown Americans, *collectively narrating the pain and progress of Latin American immigrants to the United States. The central protagonists, the three members of the Rivera family, do not stay long in the country, though their presence has a profound impact on their neighbors in their ramshackle apartment complex. This book tells their collective stories.*

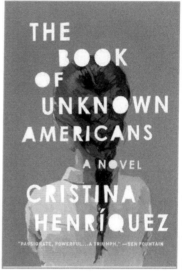

(Courtesy of Knopf)

**Principal characters:**
MARIBEL RIVERA, a teenage girl who has sustained a brain injury
ALMA RIVERA, her mother
ARTURO RIVERA, her father
MAYOR TORO, a teenage boy who becomes her love interest
CELIA TORO, Mayor's mother
RAFAEL TORO, Mayor's father

In *The Book of Unknown Americans* (2014), doting parents Arturo and Alma Rivera leave their comfortable, middle-class home in Mexico for the sake of their only child, Maribel, who was a precocious and active young teenager before an accident left her with physical, emotional, and mental damage. Now withdrawn and confused, she has retreated into herself, and her parents are desperately seeking treatment that will improve her condition. They are drawn to the United States in the hopes of offering their daughter the treatment and education she needs to recover.

As the novel begins, the Rivera family has completed a thirty-hour journey from their lifelong home in the small town of Pátzcuaro, Mexico, to the Wilmington area of Delaware. They have come legally and have expended most of their savings to do so. Arturo, a successful contractor in Mexico, has taken a position as a mushroom picker across the state line in Pennsylvania. It is grueling and abusive work. Alma will continue to be a homemaker. Maribel will, hopefully, be assigned to a nearby school for children with special needs. Their arrival at their grungy apartment in the middle of the night is inauspicious. They unload their few possessions from the flatbed of a pickup truck, including a mattress and television that their driver has found for them by the side of the road, and bring everything into the stinky, dirty apartment, where they fall asleep.

The Riveras' story unfolds from this arrival, sandwiched between the autobiographical narratives—perhaps better described as testimonies or eyewitness accounts—of the other residents of the apartment complex. As Fito Angelino, landlord and proprietor of the building, explains to the new residents, "Here is us! Venezuela, Puerto Rico, Guatemala, Nicaragua, Colombia, México, Panamá, and Paraguay. We have it all. . . . You'll fit right in." Although they do form a community of sorts, Fito's positive spin does not necessarily capture the spirit of the place. Theirs is not a community of privilege. The residents of the apartment complex navigate the city on public buses, since most lack access to cars. The power cuts in and out. While they are not close, however, these neighbors do find a support structure in one another. On Christmas Day, when the whole building loses power, they gather together in a single apartment, where they celebrate their common language of Spanish and bond through their shared immigrant experiences. Though the Rivera family's stay in the apartment complex does not last a year, the book captures a slice of life in this community life and offers a glimpse into the lives of new immigrants to the United States and their families.

Of all the Riveras' neighbors, the most significant relationships that they develop are with the members of the Toro family, originally from Panama. In contrast to the newly arrived Riveras, the Toros have been residents of the complex for almost two decades, and their two sons have grown up there. One is already off at college, but Mayor, the younger son, is in high school and still living with his parents. While the Toro parents long for home, their sons barely remember their native land. Celia Toro can think of nothing else but making a return visit, but her husband, Rafael, is reluctant to do so, fearing that he would find his home "unrecognizable." Instead, he conjures memories of its sights, smells, and sounds, reflecting to himself, "I would rather just remember it in my head, all those streets and places I loved. . . . That's the Panamá I want to hold on to."

Although they have been in the United States for a long time, the Toro family's situation is not stable. Rafael has worked as a line cook in the same restaurant the entire time, and as the nation falls into economic crisis, its impact takes a toll on the restaurant's business. Rafael worries for his job but will not allow his wife to seek work outside the home, determined to retain his status as the family breadwinner. The two argue ferociously about this issue throughout most of the novel. As if to emphasize the precariousness of Rafael's status as patriarch, the Toros receive a generous monetary gift from Celia's sister, who has received a hefty divorce settlement and decides to pay back the Toros for many years of favors.

In the midst of this family turmoil, Mayor attempts to safely navigate high school and puberty. Between encounters with bullies and athletic failure, he does not move through adolescence with confidence; indeed, he is punished for being a quiet and sensitive young man. However, as the narrative unfolds, he and Maribel strike up a close friendship that gradually develops into youthful romance. Through his affection for Maribel, his protectiveness of her, and his interest in bringing her further out of her shell, Mayor builds his skills of personal interaction. Also through this relationship, the reader learns much more about the mysterious, damaged Maribel.

The budding relationship between Mayor and Maribel is what provides *The Book of Unknown Americans* with its heart and momentum. A critic for *Kirkus Reviews* observed, "People think Maribel is dumber than she is and that Mayor is more predatory than he is. In this way . . . they represent the immigrant experience in miniature." Perhaps more interesting than this teenage romance, though, are the mature relationships of the parents. The Toros fight cruelly and constantly, yet over the pages of the novel, the reader learns the history and background of their relationship, particularly Rafael's difficult childhood and vagrant youth, from which his love for Celia rescued him. This tour through the ups and downs of their lives provides some perspective on their current difficulties and creates characters who are multidimensional rather than one-note.

Arturo and Alma Rivera, on the other hand, represent the ultimate love story. Both testify that they have been profoundly completed by their relationship with one another. Yet in the aftermath of Maribel's injury, the two have been pulled apart by grief, unhappiness, and especially silence. They still hold on to one another, but the communion that they have always felt in their relationship is gone. Over the pages of the novel, the reader feels them growing further apart, even as their daughter shows incremental signs of progress. It is a small but truly human drama, and it pushes the reader forward with the desire to find out if the couple will manage to make it through this dark period. The story leads up to a tragic event and then a sudden denouement, which unravels the interlocked lives of these two families.

*The Book of Unknown Americans* attempts to tell a broad, universal story of the Latin American diaspora, but the chapters that focus on the Toro and Rivera families are the most compelling portions of the novel. The chapters of the novel are narrated in first person by various inhabitants of the apartment complex. Those passages that advance the plot of the book are told primarily by Alma Rivera or Mayor Toro; the other testimonies tell of the residents' past experiences, life stories, and key emotional or intellectual experiences. The conceit of the book is that each of these characters is one of the titular "unknown Americans." As a class, their stories are unknown or even irrelevant. They are not wealthy, they are neither criminals nor public servants, and they occupy such a low social and economic rung that they pass beneath the radar.

*Cristina Henríquez's first novel,* The World in Half, *was published in 2009. She is also the author of the short-story collection* Come Together, Fall Apart *(2009). She is a graduate of Northwestern University and has studied writing at the Iowa Writers Workshop. The Book of Unknown Americans is her second novel.*

In these chapters, Henríquez attempts to show the diversity and individuality of these unknown voices, presenting the other apartment residents as real people with stories that have meaning. There is certainly a sense of universal humanity that arises from their stories. However, many critics felt that these asides distracted and detracted from the core plotline, and some felt that Henríquez's efforts in these chapters fell short of her goal. In her review for the *Guardian*, Sandra Newman criticized the uncontroversial nature of the characters and remarked, "After a while, these sections feel like texts designed to promote multicultural understanding in a middle school." Each resident is motivated by a common core of human emotions but fails to truly stand out as a fully fleshed-out human being.

Ultimately, *The Book of Unknown Americans* tells the story both of an immigrant community and of the United States as a nation of people with diverse paths, although the novel succeeds and resonates most strongly when it remains focused on its core plotline. It is the story of the small worlds of two families that offers insight into the national and global communities. As Arturo Rivera testifies about his origin story, after his marriage to Alma at a young age, people told them that they were naive and did not know the ways of the world. However, he counters, they did know: "Because the world to us was each other. And then we had Maribel. And our world grew larger."

Even with all the bad things that have occurred to his family in the United States, even with the dangers and prejudices that he has faced, Arturo's final testimonial also emphasizes the fact that, ultimately, this story is not just about the points of origin and life journeys of all these immigrants; it is also about their destination. Reflecting on his time in the United States, he expresses happiness and satisfaction. Looking ahead to a day when he will return to Mexico and tell his friends and families of his experiences in the United States, he closes the book with a promise—"I will tell them all the ways I loved this country"—highlighting the idea that immigrant life is about both the experiences of the past and the transformation of the self in the present.

*Julia A. Sienkewicz*

## Review Sources

Arana, Marie. Rev. of *The Book of Unknown Americans*, by Cristina Henríquez. *Washington Post*. Washington Post, 24 June 2014. Web. 8 Dec. 2014.

Rev. of *The Book of Unknown Americans*, by Cristina Henríquez. *Kirkus Reviews* 1 May 2014: 16. Print.

Castillo, Ana. "Americanos." Rev. of *The Book of Unknown Americans*, by Cristina Henríquez. *New York Times Book Review* 6 July 2014: 8. Print.

Kakutani, Michiko. "Homesick Strangers among Us." Rev. of *The Book of Unknown Americans*, by Cristina Henríquez. *New York Times*. New York Times, 10 July 2014. Web. 8 Dec. 2014.

Newman, Sandra. Rev. of *The Book of Unknown Americans*, by Cristina Henríquez. *Guardian*. Guardian News and Media, 19 July 2014. Web. 8 Dec. 2014.

# Boy, Snow, Bird

**Author:** Helen Oyeyemi (b. 1984)
**Publisher:** Riverhead Books (New York).
  320 pp.
**Type of work:** Novel
**Time:** The 1940s through the 1960s
**Locales:** New York City; Flax Hill, Massachusetts

(Courtesy of Riverhead Books)

Boy, Snow, Bird *is a fantasy novel about several generations of women living in a family with hidden sociological secrets.*

**Principal characters:**
BOY NOVAK, a young white woman
ARTURO WHITMAN, her husband, a widowed
  jeweler and former professor
SNOW WHITMAN, the light-skinned daughter
  of Arturo Whitman and his former wife, Julia
BIRD WHITMAN, the daughter of Boy Novak and Arturo Whitman

Nigerian British author Helen Oyeyemi's fifth novel, *Boy, Snow, Bird* (2014), is a quasi-magical exploration of race, femininity, and female relationships, told through a clever reimagining of the Snow White fairy tale set in 1950s New England. Oyeyemi's previous four novels also incorporated topics of race, gender, and family; with *Boy, Snow, Bird*, she continues to explore many of the same cultural issues, but the decision to situate her surreal-yet-realistic 1950s New England within a mythological fairy-tale setting gives the book a fresh and unique impact. Critics have praised *Boy, Snow, Bird*, with some calling it Oyeyemi's finest book and a prime example of modern emotional fantasy writing.

The first character introduced in *Boy, Snow, Bird* is a young white woman named Boy Novak, who lives with her father in New York's Lower East Side. Boy's unusual name ties into issues explored later in the book, but it also provides a bizarre fable-like aspect to the character from the opening sentences. Her father, who is not named and is referred to only once as "Papa" and thereafter as "the rat catcher" (a reference to his career), is brutal and violent. His violence is revealed through the way he treats his captured rats, allowing them to starve and thus to eat each other, and through his abusive behavior toward Boy. He hits her regularly, for a variety of reasons. As she says, "He'd hit me when I didn't flinch at the raising of his arm and he'd hit me when I cowered."

Boy lives in poverty, though she describes her father as making plenty of money. She has sharp, angular features, striking flaxen hair, black eyes, and white skin. She is not every boy's taste, but when they do like her, they become obsessed with her. She has one love, a local boy named Charlie, but her father violently disapproves. When she cannot take her father's abuse anymore, Boy flees New York, catching a bus from the Port Authority station to the farthest point on one line: Flax Hill, Massachusetts.

Flax Hill is a surreal landscape of artisans, a town specializing in the type of industry that exists primarily in fairy tales. According to Boy, everyone in Flax Hill makes beautiful things. She remains in Flax Hill, though she is uncertain as to why. She goes through a series of jobs before ending up working at a bookstore, where she comes under the mentorship of the store's kindly owner, Mrs. Fletcher, and develops a small circle of close friends.

In time, Boy enters into a romantic relationship with Arturo Whitman, a former professor from Boston who has come to Flax Hill to work as a jeweler. Arturo has a daughter, Snow Whitman, whose mother, Julia, was an opera singer who died shortly

© Piotr Cieplak

*Helen Oyeyemi is a Nigerian-born British novelist whose first novel,* Icarus Girl, *was published in 2005. Her novel* White Is for Witching *(2009) won a 2010 Somerset Maugham Award, and she was included in* Granta *magazine's 2013 list of the best young British novelists.*

after Snow's birth. The young Snow Whitman pines for a real mother. In addition to the obvious Snow White reference, the fairy-tale allusions are liberally sprinkled throughout the text. Thinking about Arturo's former wife, Boy muses that she looked like a "bashful Rapunzel," and she compares her own life experiences to situations in *Alice's Adventures in Wonderland* (1865). Boy becomes fascinated with Snow Whitman, whose every word and movement seem to have layers of symbolic meaning; she describes the girl as a "medieval swan maiden" with black-on-black hair and the pinkest of lips, and as looking like a character in a "Technicolor tapestry."

The issue of race is introduced via Boy's relationship with three black children who skip school each day to spend their time reading in Mrs. Fletcher's bookshop instead. Mrs. Fletcher allows this, as the local school for black children is inadequate. Boy's relationship with the three children—Sidonie, Phoebe, and Kazim—is the first foray into the topic of race in Flax Hill, an undercurrent that gradually becomes one of the novel's primary themes. The depictions of race lines, generational transmission of racial identity, and parent-child relationships within racially divided communities reflect the realities of the United States in the 1950s, but Flax Hill is also a fantasy land where these aspects of life are given surreal reflections through the characters, who are part realistic and part mythological archetype.

Boy is not passionate about Arturo Whitman, and she develops far more affection for Snow, partially due to the kinship that develops between the two motherless women. Even though Boy is an adult and Snow a child, both characters seem to sit in midway between the two states of being, neither children nor adults. Boy agrees to marry Arturo, accepting an engagement bracelet of a white-gold snake that is described as very "wicked stepmother" by Boy's friend Mia. Some of Boy's friends disapprove of the engagement, including her childhood sweetheart, Charlie, who visits and attempts to talk Boy out of the decision. As Boy and Arturo move closer to marriage, Boy also meets and develops relationships with Arturo's parents, Olivia and Gerald, and his sister Viv. Olivia Whitman becomes another central character in the narrative; she is depicted as a complex woman with tantalizing mysteries in her past, as revealed through the way other townsfolk depict her.

After her wedding, Boy receives congratulatory flowers from someone named Clara, who claims to be Snow's aunt. Arturo tells Boy that Clara is his elder sister who was banished from the family for behavioral problems. When Boy asks Mrs. Fletcher, she receives another story, though still vague, that Olivia Whitman sent Clara away from the family. The dark secrets lying behind the Whitman family's façade are not revealed until Boy bears Arturo's child, a revelatory event that causes Boy to reexamine everything she thought she knew about Arturo, Olivia, Snow, and the entire Whitman family.

Reviewers have differed on whether or not to reveal the twist that leads into the second and third parts of the book. At the end of the first part, Snow is sent away to live with Clara in Boston, just as Clara herself was once sent away by her own mother to live with relatives; the second part of the book is told through the eyes of Bird Whitman, Arturo and Boy's daughter, and takes place largely during her early teenager years. Bird discovers a series of letters written to her and her mother by Snow and begins a secret correspondence. The growing epistolary relationship between the two half sisters is one of the most moving and overtly magical aspects of the book, leaving readers to wonder if the strange things described by the two girls are metaphorical or real. Boy, who has become the wicked stepmother as a result of her banishment of Snow, has apparently refused to answer any of Snow's correspondence, and this relationship lends a tragic and emotionally resonance to the book's second act.

The third and final section returns to Boy as the narrator and sees the entire family reunited. The painful decisions of the family's mothers, first Olivia and then Boy, are given new meaning in a second, carefully imagined plot twist that brings new poignancy to Boy's behavior and the pain of her tortured past. In the final part of the book, the secrets of the Whitman family fade into the background as the story becomes a reflection on the lives of women, motherhood, friendship, love, and shame, and readers will wonder whether or not Boy will achieve redemption. Oyeyemi's ability to twist the narrative with revelations that cause readers to revisit past sections keeps the story riveting until the thought-provoking and moving conclusion.

Oyeyemi wrote her first novel, *The Icarus Girl* (2005), while she was still in college, and many of the articles written about her career have focused on her youth and her rapid rise to literary stardom. During her short but productive career, Oyeyemi has written extensively about race and womanhood, often enhanced by supernatural themes. Her 2007 novel, *The Opposite House*, which was inspired by a blend of Cuban and Yoruba mythology, and *White Is for Witching* (2009), about a family living in a haunted house, both use mythology, superstition, magic, and surreal elements to explore deeper themes involving family and interpersonal relationships. In her reflective 2011 novel, *Mr. Fox*, inspired by the French story of Bluebeard, Oyeyemi writes stories within stories, again using fantastic elements to delve into themes of love, relationships, and the role of fantasy in life.

The social and interpersonal themes explored in *Boy, Snow, Bird* resonate deeply, and the fairy-tale framing is clever without sacrificing integrity. *New York Times* reviewer Porochista Khakpour praised Oyeyemi's style as "always singular, like the voice-over of a fever dream"; Miriam Krule, reviewing the book for *Slate*, called it a "stunning and enchanting fairy tale." Whether *Boy, Snow, Bird* is viewed as an allegorical fairy tale or as a realistic historical novel, the result is a finely crafted and highly emotional drama that recalls the best of both genres and demonstrates Oyeyemi's deepening skill.

*Micah L. Issitt*

## Review Sources

Charles, Ron. Rev. of *Boy, Snow, Bird*, by Helen Oyeyemi. *Washington Post*. Washington Post, 25 Feb. 2014. Web. 21 Jan. 2015.

Clark, Alex. "Helen Oyeyemi Plays with Myth and Fairytale." Rev. of *Boy, Snow, Bird*, by Helen Oyeyemi. *Guardian*. Guardian News and Media, 22 Mar. 2014. Web. 21 Jan. 2015.

Khakpour, Porochista. "White Lies." Rev. of *Boy, Snow, Bird*, by Helen Oyeyemi. *New York Times Book Review* 2 Mar. 2014: 1. Print.

Krule, Miriam. "Snow Whitman." Rev. of *Boy, Snow, Bird*, by Helen Oyeyemi. *Slate*. Slate Group, 6 Mar. 2014. Web. 21 Jan. 2015.

# A Brief History of Seven Killings

**Author:** Marlon James (b. 1970)
**Publisher:** Riverhead Books (New York). 704 pp.
**Type of work:** Novel
**Time:** 1976–91
**Locales:** Kingston, Jamaica; Montego Bay, Jamaica; Miami, Florida; New York City

*Set in the Jamaica and United States of the 1970s through the 1990s,* A Brief History of Seven Killings *chronicles an assassination attempt on a reggae singer and the ultimate fates of his would-be assassins.*

(Courtesy of Riverhead Books)

**Principal characters:**
THE SINGER, an internationally renowned Jamaican reggae singer
PAPA-LO, leader of Kingston's Copenhagen City neighborhood
JOSEY WALES, his second-in-command, later leader of Copenhagen City
BAM-BAM, a Copenhagen City gang member
DEMUS, a Copenhagen City gang member
WEEPER, a Copenhagen City gang member, later leader of Josey's operations in New York
LUIS HERNÁN RODRIGO DE LAS CASAS, a.k.a. DOCTOR LOVE, a Cuban counterrevolutionary and explosives expert
LOUIS JOHNSON, a CIA operative working with the Copenhagen City gang
NINA BURGESS, a.k.a. KIM CLARKE, DORCAS PALMER, and MILLICENT SEGREE, a middle-class Jamaican woman and onetime lover of the Singer
ALEX PIERCE, an American journalist for Rolling Stone
BARRY DIFLORIO, the CIA station chief for Jamaica
SIR ARTHUR GEORGE JENNINGS, a ghost
TRISTAN PHILLIPS, a prison inmate and former New York gang member
JOHN-JOHN K, a hitman

The 1970s were a volatile decade in Jamaica, as rival political parties with opposing ideologies vied for control and foreign countries such as the United States turned the nation into yet another Cold War battleground. One of the most publicized events of that era, both within and outside of Jamaica, was the attempted assassination of the internationally famous reggae musician Bob Marley. On December 3, 1976, two days before Marley was set to perform in the government-sponsored Smile Jamaica concert, a group of gunmen entered his home in Kingston and opened fire. Marley, his wife, and his manager were seriously injured, but all three recovered, and Marley performed two days later as planned.

In *A Brief History of Seven Killings* (2014), Jamaican-born author Marlon James presents a fictionalized version of this assassination attempt on Marley, who in the novel is referred to only as "the Singer." The novel begins by documenting the events leading up to the assassination attempt and the motives behind it, but the bulk of the text focuses on its long fallout and the lingering effects of the incident on the intended victim, the would-be perpetrators, and various bystanders and others who become unknowingly involved. At the same time, the novel recounts the story of Jamaica's development during a tumultuous period marked by national unrest and international interference as well as the international expansion of Jamaican influence, both through cultural exchange in the form of the Singer and through the spread of Jamaican gang activity into US cities such as Miami and New York.

At the start of the novel, the poor neighborhoods of West Kingston are far from peaceful, with rival gangs clashing frequently. The gang based in the neighborhood of Copenhagen City, led by a don known as Papa-Lo, is affiliated with the conservative Jamaica Labour Party (JLP), the rival of the ruling party, the more socialist People's National Party (PNP). As some of Kingston's other neighborhoods are controlled by the PNP, gang clashes are often motivated in part by political factors. The political parties themselves are well aware of the gangs' loyalties and at times effectively use the gangs as unofficial militias.

Despite Papa-Lo's efforts to maintain control over Copenhagen City, he is undermined by his second-in-command, Josey Wales, who has been meeting with several individuals intent on using the Copenhagen City gang for their own ends, among them CIA officer Louis Johnson and anticommunist Cuban explosive expert Luis Hernán Rodrigo de las Casas, known as Doctor Love. Working without the authorization of his station chief, Barry Diflorio, Johnson provides the gang members with weapons, while Doctor Love trains them in the use of explosives. These individuals and others have a vested interest in aiding the JLP, as they fear that the PNP will lead Jamaica to communism. They therefore seek to destabilize the ruling party, using whatever means necessary.

As the headliner of the upcoming Smile Jamaica concert, which has been sponsored by the Jamaican government, the Singer is considered by some to be too close to the PNP and thus a danger, despite his positive relationship with the JLP-affiliated Papa-Lo. On December 3, 1976, Josey leads a group of gunmen, including the gang members Bam-Bam, Demus, and Weeper, to the Singer's home and attempts to kill him by shooting him in the chest. Portions of the event are witnessed by Alex Pierce, an American journalist who is trying to meet with the Singer, and Nina Burgess, a Jamaican woman who once slept with the Singer and now seeks his help in securing documents that will allow her to leave Jamaica. Josey spots Nina outside of the Singer's home, so, fearing for her life, she flees first to Montego Bay and then to the United States, taking on a number of assumed names and fabricated identities along the way.

As with the real attempt on Marley's life, the assassination attempt fails to kill or silence the Singer. While some of the would-be assassins, particularly Josey, prosper following the event, others are not as lucky. Over the next decades, the majority of the gunmen are killed, either by individuals suspecting their involvement in the attack or by their fellow conspirators. Josey becomes the leader of Copenhagen City after Papa-Lo's death, which he may have played a role in arranging, and he expands the gang's influence beyond Jamaica and into the United States, charging Weeper with running his operations in New York. The aftermath of the assassination attempt continues into the early 1990s, shaping the lives and deaths of the remaining conspirators. Even the two witnesses, Alex and Nina, are haunted by their memories of

(© Piotr Cieplak)

*Marlon James is the author of* John Crow's Devil *(2005) and* The Book of Night Women *(2009). He is a professor of English at Macalester College in Saint Paul, Minnesota.*

what they saw; Alex has worked for years to determine what really transpired that night in 1976, and Nina has moved from place to place and switched from identity to identity in an attempt to distance herself from her past. When the era of the gunmen comes to an end, Nina is finally free, but Alex learns that the influence of the conspirators will never truly fade.

A complex and layered novel, *A Brief History of Seven Killings* is told from more than a dozen different first-person perspectives. This structure allows the story to be told from all directions, allowing readers to piece together the narrative's events from the fragments each character gives them. Often, the question of which character knows what proves essential to the story, and the narrative structure calls attention to the secrets and schemes that fuel much of the novel's action. In his acknowledgements, James notes that he initially struggled with deciding which perspective to tell the story from until a friend suggested that the novel may not be only one person's story. Indeed, it is a story about not only the attempt on the Singer's life and the rise of Josey Wales but also the effects of political strife and foreign meddling on the people of Jamaica. The many characters are needed to provide a full picture of this life, for, as Nina mentions in her first chapter, "everybody lives in their own Jamaica." These multiple perspectives provide insight while also sometimes obscuring the narrative through their unreliability; Nina, for instance, takes on several new identities after fleeing Kingston and does her best to obscure the connections between each new identity and her old ones, although she is never truly able to escape her past selves. Some of the more unusual perspectives allow James to hint at future events long before they occur. For example, the ghost Arthur George Jennings, who narrates several chapters, seems somewhat unstuck in time and is therefore able to provide foreshadowing that living characters could not.

James's striking use of language plays a crucial role in differentiating the various narrators from one another and demonstrating how they construct their own identities. Nina's voice changes somewhat with each identity she takes on, while the extracts from magazine articles included in some of Alex's chapters provide a contrast between his narrative and spoken voices and his journalistic one. At times, characters use their spoken voices to ensure that they are perceived in certain ways, changing their language when advantageous. Josey, for example, has no trouble understanding American English or Cuban Spanish but feigns a degree of ignorance when speaking to individuals whom he hopes will continue to underestimate him. Nina likewise tailors her language to her circumstances, engaging in situational code-switching; she does not typically narrate or speak in Jamaican Patois but switches to it when necessary. These details lend complexity to the characters and further demonstrate the individuality of the Jamaican experience that Nina identifies shortly after her introduction. Another particularly effective use of language occurs in chapters narrated by characters who are under the influence of drugs, as with Demus and Bam-Bam in the chapters describing the assassination attempt, or are dying. Their muddled thinking and fear are palpable, and James's tendency to use unusual structures for such chapters or end them abruptly further enhances the immediacy of the narrative.

*A Brief History of Seven Killings* received largely positive reviews, with many critics praising the depth and scope of the novel as well as its numerous complex characters. In his review for the *Washington Post*, critic John Domini called the novel a "fascinating tangle of the naked and the dead," comparing its narrative structure to a "crazy-quilt," and expressed particular appreciation for the character of Nina, whom he cited as an "outstanding example" of James's dedication to his characters. *Telegraph* reviewer Nicholas Blincoe similarly praised James's portrayal of Nina, whose voice he describes as a "real achievement." Critics compared the novel to works by such authors as James Ellroy, William Faulkner, and David Foster Wallace, particularly in regard to its many narrators and its frequent changes in tone.

Although critical response was generally positive, some critics objected to the novel's overwhelming, ever-present violence. In her review for the *Independent*, Hannah McGill argued that the novel's violence and negativity are "perversely deadening" and at times make it difficult for the reader to care about the characters. Blincoe also argues that James's decision to use fictionalized names for real-life figures while recounting historical events somewhat hinders the politically charged aspects of the narrative. Nevertheless, *A Brief History of Seven Killings* is an intensely political novel that not only chronicles the aftermath of one particular event in Jamaican history but also documents the extensive impact of foreign interference on a postcolonial nation, its residents, and its diaspora.

*Joy Crelin*

**Review Sources**

Blincoe, Nicholas. "Vivid and Powerful." Rev. of *A Brief History of Seven Killings*, by Marlon James. *Telegraph*. Telegraph Media Group, 14 Nov. 2014. Web. 15 Dec. 2014.

Rev. of *A Brief History of Seven Killings*, by Marlon James. *Publishers Weekly* 14 July 2014: 47. Print.

Domini, John. "*A Brief History of Seven Killings* Cuts a Swath across Jamaican History." Rev. of *A Brief History of Seven Killings*, by Marlon James. *Washington Post*. Washington Post, 1 Oct. 2014. Web. 15 Dec. 2014.

Kellogg, Carolyn. "Marlon James' Views of a Crime in *A Brief History of Seven Killings*." Rev. of *A Brief History of Seven Killings*, by Marlon James. *Los Angeles Times*. Los Angeles Times, 3 Oct. 2014. Web. 15 Dec. 2014.

Lazar, Zachary. "The Harder They Come." Rev. of *A Brief History of Seven Killings*, by Marlon James. *New York Times Book Review* 26 Oct. 2014: 12. Print.

McGill, Hannah. "Jamaica's Violent Underbelly." Rev. of *A Brief History of Seven Killings*, by Marlon James. *Independent*. Independent.co.uk, 23 Oct. 2014. Web. 15 Dec. 2014.

# Brown Girl Dreaming

**Author:** Jacqueline Woodson (b. 1963)
**Publisher:** Nancy Paulsen Books (New York). 337 pp.
**Type of work:** Memoir, poetry
**Time:** The 1960s and 1970s
**Locales:** Ohio, South Carolina, New York

(Courtesy of Nancy Paulsen Books)

*In this literary memoir, author Jacqueline Woodson uses free verse to chronicle her experiences growing up as an African American in the 1960s and 1970s and the joy she began to take in the act of writing.*

In *Brown Girl Dreaming* (2014), award-winning author Jacqueline Woodson employs free-verse poetry to paint a self-portrait of her childhood and young adulthood in Ohio, South Carolina, and New York. Grouped into five chronological sections, the poems generally range from one to two pages in length, each capturing a moment or memory that builds an overall picture over time.

The author begins in part 1, titled "I Am Born," with a factual account of her birth on February 12, 1963. Woodson immediately identifies the period in history into which she was born, a time when the United States was fraught with tensions "between Black and White." She notes that her great-great-grandparents were slaves and that, although she was born in the northern state of Ohio, the South is an unmistakable part of her identity. Woodson acknowledges that the accounts of her earliest days are by necessity based on her family's memories rather than her own, noting in a poem titled "Other People's Memory" that the time of her birth has been variously described to her as morning, afternoon, or evening, depending on which family member tells the story. She relates how her father, Jack Austin Woodson, wanted to name her simply "Jack" after himself, but her mother, Mary Anne Irby, got her own way by the simple act of writing the name "Jacqueline" on the hospital forms once Jack had left the hospital. The idea that words can create, confirm, or disprove reality is further explored in a poem titled "The Woodsons of Ohio," in which the author notes that her father's family traces their lineage back to a man named Thomas Woodson, whom the family believes was a descendent of Thomas Jefferson and Sally Hemings. The poem subtly acknowledges the controversy surrounding this claim, but it also seems to indicate that Woodson considers the family's oral stories and handwritten records in family Bibles as strong evidence.

Part 2, "The Stories of South Carolina Run Like Rivers," comprises roughly one hundred pages that detail Woodson's childhood after her mother and father separated and her mother moved one-year-old Jackie and her two older siblings to South Carolina to stay with their maternal grandparents. The family immediately had to adjust to a far more hostile environment, taking care not to offend Caucasians by challenging them or even just looking them in the eye. Woodson describes her grandfather's somewhat unusual position of authority as a foreman at a printing press, noting that his white subordinates do not know how to react to having a black supervisor. Woodson's grandmother, in the meantime, does "daywork," which means riding a bus to the wealthier Caucasian neighborhoods to clean houses. She tells her grandchildren that she is not ashamed of the work, but she does it so that they will never have to.

Although Woodson never forgets her Ohio origins, the fact that she and her siblings were so young when their mother moved to South Carolina meant that the southern state quickly became the only home the children really knew. In fact, only Woodson's brother, Hope, who was three years old at the time of their parents' separation, has any real memories of their father. The children's grandparents become de facto parents, particularly when their mother travels to New York to look for a job and a home. When she eventually returns to retrieve her children, she has had another baby, a boy named Roman, who joins Hope, Odella (called Dell), and Jackie.

Part 3, "Followed the Sky's Mirrored Constellation to Freedom," begins with Woodson's first impressions of New York as a cold, gray, treeless void. The family settles near the children's aunt Caroline "Kay" Irby and quickly become part of a community of southern transplants. Poems such as "Herzl Street" evoke Woodson's memories of Saturday night gatherings for food and conversation, while others pieces memorialize individuals, particularly Aunt Kay, who died after falling down a flight of stairs. Another significant event in this period is the arrival of a blank notebook from an unremembered source. The relevant poem, titled simply "Composition Notebook," describes the author's joy at experiencing the smell, feel, and look of the blank white pages, even though she is not yet old enough to write herself. One of the volume's most moving poems, titled "On Paper" and quoted in full below, commemorates the moment when Woodson realized the potential of the written word:

> The first time I write my full name
> *Jacqueline Amanda Woodson*
> without anybody's help
> on a clean white page in my composition notebook, I know
> if I wanted to
> I could write anything.
> Letters becoming words, words gathering meaning, becoming
> thoughts outside my head
> becoming sentences
> written by
>
> *Jacqueline Amanda Woodson*

In spite of this early attraction to writing, however, Woodson experienced some difficulty learning to read. In the poem "Gifted," she compares herself to her sister, Dell, who has always excelled in school. Although "Gifted" is a simple poem, Woodson's choice of imagery is striking: she imagines her "gifted" sister as being surrounded by piles of presents, while she herself struggles to catch and hold words in her hands like dandelion seeds and then blow them away at a pace matching that of her fellow students. A later poem in the same section mentions that Woodson's uncle, Robert Irby, taught them to wish on dandelion puffs, leading the reader to realize that later events in Woodson's life infused earlier memories with increasingly sophisticated imagery.

(© Marty Umans)

In the fourth section of the book, titled "Deep in My Heart, I Do Believe," Woodson describes her first best friend, a girl from Puerto Rico named Maria. Additional poems deal with Woodson's continuing academic struggles, juxtaposed with her growing awareness of her special relationship with words. A striking series of eight poems in a row address her Uncle Robert's incarceration, first at Rikers Island and then at a prison in upstate New York. The fifth and last section of the book, titled "Ready to Change the World," begins immediately after the death of Woodson's grandfather, whom she had called "Daddy" due to his paternal role in her life during her time in South Carolina. Now a widow, Woodson's grandmother leaves South Carolina and moves in with the family in New York. Uncle Robert is released from prison and very interested in the continuing civil rights movement, and Woodson herself seems poised for the changes that will come as racial tensions continue to swirl all around her.

Although *Brown Girl Dreaming* is arranged chronologically, Woodson skillfully weaves ongoing themes throughout the different sections. As noted above, much of the volume is occupied with the civil rights movement, beginning in part 2, when Woodson becomes aware of the protest marches and sit-ins that have been taking place for years in South Carolina and elsewhere. One poem, titled "The Training," explains how the protestors attend sessions to learn how to remain nonviolent no matter how much they are provoked, adding a valuable historical side note to this volume that goes beyond Woodson's own experiences. Later, in part 4, Woodson notes during a summer visit back to South Carolina that her grandmother still sits at the back of the bus and will not eat in restaurants in spite of the changed laws, because she still lives in that small town and cannot afford to cause trouble.

Similarly, Woodson continually revisits the topic of learning to read. She is frustrated when teachers contrast her reading difficulties with her sister's seemingly effortless academic achievements, and also when she is told that the books she chooses are too babyish. Woodson learns best by repetition, and she is convinced that her slow study is what led to her discovery in a picture book of "brown people, more / brown people than I'd ever seen / in a book before." Oscar Wilde's short story "The Selfish Giant" (1888) represents another important influence in Woodson's life. Noticing her student's extreme interest in the story, the teacher asks Woodson to read it aloud in front of the class, but by this point Woodson knows it so well that she dramatically recites it from memory instead. Her teacher tells her that her performance was brilliant, and Woodson finally realizes that words will be her special talent in life. Soon after, Woodson creates her first homemade book about butterflies, a significant enough event that it is depicted in two different poems, "The Butterfly Poems" and "First Book."

Another way Woodson ties the poems into a cohesive narrative is by creating numbered miniseries of poems that are sprinkled throughout the book at various intervals. One series of ten numbered poems, all but one of which are seventeen-syllable haiku, is titled "How to Listen." This series spans all five sections of the book, portraying quiet moments when Woodson pauses to take a take a breath and observe what is happening around her. As such, they give the reader the same opportunity to pause and reflect. Other miniseries are smaller, such as the two poems that make up "After Greenville" and the two titled simply "Writing."

Another topic addressed throughout the book is religion. Woodson's maternal grandmother, Georgiana Scott Irby, was a Jehovah's Witness, and during the period when Woodson's mother was in New York, Georgiana insisted that the children be instructed in her faith. A poem in part 2 titled "What God Knows" explains that the children's grandfather, Gunnar Irby, does not share his wife's beliefs, telling the children that he does not need their prayers because he works hard and treats people well. In part 3, the children continue their religious education in New York because Mary Anne promised Georgiana they would, although Mary Anne herself does not accompany the children to church. In "Because We're Witnesses," Woodson enumerates the events in which they cannot participate as Jehovah's Witnesses, including Halloween, Christmas, and birthday celebrations, as well as activities from which they will later be precluded as adults, such as voting and going to war. Later, Woodson tries to puzzle out what it means when her Uncle Robert emerges from prison, now converted to the Islamic faith. In "I Believe," she itemizes many of the seemingly contradictory things in which she believes, such as the Bible and the Qur'an, and both passive and active resistance.

The last poem in the book, "Each World," discusses Woodson's realization that writing identifies possibilities, allowing the writer to create and imagine herself in different worlds and roles. In the last several stanzas, she lists all the worlds that are contained within herself:

> Ohio and Greenville
> Woodson and Irby
> Gunnar's child and Jack's daughter
> Jehovah's Witness and nonbeliever
> listener and writer
> Jackie and Jacqueline—

gather into one world
called You

where You decide

what each world
and each story
and each ending

will finally be.

This poem neatly summarizes Woodson's sense of how many different elements from not just her own life but also her family's and friends' lives came together to create the person and writer she was meant to become. It also represents a fitting end to this memoir, which employs striking language and imagery to create a beautiful portrait of an extraordinary life.

*Amy Sisson*

## Review Sources

Rev. of *Brown Girl Dreaming*, by Jacqueline Woodson. *Publishers Weekly* 26 May 2014: 63. Print.

Cart, Michael. Rev. of *Brown Girl Dreaming*, by Jacqueline Woodson. *Booklist* 1 Aug. 2014: 60+. Print.

Chambers, Veronica. "Where We Enter." Rev. of *Brown Girl Dreaming*, by Jacqueline Woodson. *New York Times Book Review* 24 Aug. 2014: 14. Print.

LaRocco, D. Maria. Rev. of *Brown Girl Dreaming*, by Jacqueline Woodson. *School Library Journal* July 2014: 126. Print.

Parravano, Martha V. Rev. of *Brown Girl Dreaming*, by Jacqueline Woodson. *Horn Book Magazine* Sept.–Oct. 2014: 126. Print.

Scattergood, Augusta. "*Brown Girl Dreaming* Blends History and Personal Memories into Lovely Verse." Rev. of *Brown Girl Dreaming*, by Jacqueline Woodson. *Christian Science Monitor*. Christian Science Monitor, 19 Sept. 2014. Web. 21 Jan. 2015.

# California

**Author:** Edan Lepucki
**Publisher:** Little, Brown (New York). 400
   pp.
**Type of work:** Novel
**Time:** Near future
**Locale:** California

California *is a dystopian novel about a couple living amid the ruins of California after
a vague environmental collapse leads to the
seeming end of the national government.*

**Principal characters:**
FRIDA ELLIS, former baker who lives in the
   apocalyptic ruins of the California wilderness and wants to find a community
   in which she can raise her child
CALVIN FRIEDMAN, her husband, a survivalist
   who travels with her to find a community to join outside of Los Angeles after she
   becomes pregnant with his child
ANIKA, member of the settlement who becomes her friend and knows about the secrets in the settlement's past
MICAH, her brother, whose mysterious past provides a new understanding of the communities that she and Cal encounter in California

(Courtesy of Little, Brown and Company)

Most reviews of Edan Lepucki's debut novel, *California*, noted that the novel would
not have been likely to receive national attention if not for Stephen Colbert, host of
the popular satirical news program *The Colbert Report*. Colbert mentioned *California*
at the crux of a segment criticizing web retailer Amazon regarding a dispute between
Amazon and the publishing house Hachette over e-book prices. In his criticism of
Amazon, Colbert asked his viewers to purchase copies of *California* (published by
a Hachette subsidiary) from Amazon rival Powell's Books. Though the two companies eventually reached an agreement, the Colbert "bump" hurt Amazon's sales and
transformed what would likely have been a somewhat humble debut into a national
bestseller. Some of the reviewers writing about *California* noted that Colbert's recom-
mendation was a mixed blessing: while Lepucki enjoyed massive sales, her book was
also subject to criticism far beyond the level that it may otherwise have merited.

   Lepucki's *California* is set in the eponymous state, in the near future after an un-
specified series of catastrophes has led to the collapse or at least withdrawal of government. Essentially, *California* is a dystopian story, and so reviewers analyzed the book
in comparison to the history of the genre, in which authors generally use an imagined future to explore the eventual outcome of the current progression of sociological,

technological, or environmental patterns. Books like Cormack McCarthy's *The Road* and George Orwell's *Nineteen Eighty-Four* are often cited as among the best examples of this genre from a literary standpoint. Dystopian future societies have also become a popular setting for young adult fiction, including the internationally popular *Divergent* and *Hunger Games* franchises, and some literary critics have become increasingly dismissive of dystopian fiction as a genre that appeals primarily to young or unsophisticated readers. There are many different types of dystopian fiction, with some authors using extreme future environments to make points about the nature of humanity or human societies, while others use dystopia as a way to explore issues like the potential consequences of war, environmental exploitation, or technological dependence. Lepucki's dystopia in *California* is not complex, and the author does not explore the scientific, sociological, or environmental issues that might have contributed to her imagined future. Lepucki only hints at these issues, while the story focuses squarely on human relationships and provides an interesting commentary on the balance between freedom and security.

In Lepucki's future, American society has devolved. The wealthy elite live in protected areas called "Communities," a familiar dystopian theme that serves to accentuate deepening class divisions in Western society. Lepucki alludes to environmental catastrophe through descriptions of storms and dramatic weather patterns, but these are not specifically explored in terms of how they represent or contribute to the broken-down state of society. Humans in the future California live in wasteland cities where homeless people abound, or they live in one of the protected Communities, or they live in the wilderness, organizing themselves into commune-like societies amid the forests and fields. Readers hoping to understand Lepucki's future will find themselves frustrated, as the dystopia the author foresees is clearly a very recent phenomenon and yet has evolved considerably given the breath of time that has passed from the present to the imagined future. Lepucki's main characters, a twenty-something married couple named Frida Ellis and Calvin Friedman, both had jobs during this social collapse. Frida remembers purchasing supplies from the stores going out of business as society was seemingly falling apart around them. In these memories of the bygone era, Frida notes that she purchased things with gold, a nod to the popular conspiratorial predictions that foresee the collapse of representational money and the need to switch to currency with "real" value.

Frida is the primary narrator of the story. She is a young woman, and is still clinging to physical objects that represent the safety and security she felt in her life before the collapse. Not only is she clinging to them, but she keeps a set of objects symbolizing that old life, artifacts of the precollapse society. Now, she and her husband Cal live in the wilderness outside of Los Angeles, where Cal, thanks to his survivalist skills, plants crops and snares animals for food. This fare is supplemented by visits from traders, who barter with the wilderness people. Frida trades her last cashmere sweater to one of the traders, who has a cart pulled by a mule, another animal that has seemingly survived the environmental catastrophe that ended society.

Frida and Cal spend much of their time having sex. In the first chapter, Frida notes that sex has "replaced the Internet, reading, going out to dinner, shopping," and editorializes this by saying that "the universe had righted itself, maybe." The couple's recreational sex eventually leads to Frida becoming pregnant. This is something that she wants, to give their lives more meaning and significance, but it deepens her desire to return to living in a community, with friends, neighbors, and conveniences. Frida is not cut out for the wild life, though Cal is far happier that they are living on their own. Out of love for Frida, Cal agrees to leave their modest

*Edan Lepucki is staff writer for* The Millions. *A graduate of the Iowa Writers' Workshop, Lepucki has published a novella,* If You're Not Yet Like Me *(2010), and her short fiction has appeared in* Meridian, McSweeny's, *the* Los Angeles Times Magazine, *and other publications.* California *is her first novel.*

home and traverse the wilds in search of a community. This journey covers the middle portion of the book. Along the way, Lepucki deepens Frida and Cal's characters by revealing memories and secrets that both are holding back from one another. In addition, the story of Frida's brother Micah, whose fate is initially mysterious, becomes a major plot device. The character is first introduced through Cal's memories of him, a rebellious student who made Cal feel culturally impoverished when they first met. The collapse pushed Micah toward more and more violent expressions of revolutionary ideology, but his ultimate fate is left unexplained until toward the end of the novel.

As the story develops, Frida and Cal encounter some of the archetypal groups that inhabit the apocalyptic wastelands. There is, for instance, a mysterious and purportedly dangerous group known as the Spikes, who erect large and wasteful metal monuments as a warning to intruders to their territory. Eventually, they come to a place known as the Land, which is an emerging community in which the residents have created the semblance of a social, cooperative society. However, there are secrets within the Land as well, including a mysterious relationship with a revolutionary organization known as "the Group," the revelation of which brings the story of Frida's brother Micah to conclusion. In the Land, there are no children, despite the fact that pregnancies have occurred, and Cal and Frida must therefore struggle with whether or not to reveal her pregnancy, which could possibly affect whether or not the couple is allowed to remain in the community, a decision arrived at by a vote among the community members.

Lepucki's *California* is a divided narrative, the most gripping part of which is the author's examination of the marriage between Frida and Cal, a discussion that contains interesting reflections on the nature of honesty and sacrifice in relationships. This theme is juxtaposed with the broader social drama of Lepucki's apocalyptic vision, and can therefore be compared to the author's examination of broader societal issues. For instance, through her characters' experiences, Lepucki explores the themes of safety and security, reflecting on how much a normal person would be willing to sacrifice for the ability to return to the comforts of affluence. In the end, Cal and Frida wind up living in The Pines, a strange Orwellian community that has the outward veil of 1950s social structure, but hides deep secrets.

Critics saw flaws in Lepucki's *California*, though most were eager to forgive these shortcomings as a mark of the author's inexperience. The fact that *California* was unexpectedly thrust onto the best-seller list, and therefore received far more attention from critics that the book would otherwise have earned, was acknowledged by many reviewers in their assessment of the book's plot and Lepucki's writing style. In the *New York Times*, novelist Jeff VanderMeer, who has written several superior works of dystopian fiction, referred to the book's adventure theme as "awkward and poorly written" and questioned the motivations and internal consistency of Cal and Frida's characters. Critic Amity Gaige, writing in the *Guardian*, felt the book was a mix of good and bad with "evocative scene and sentences," contrasting with "moments of retrospection or unhurried conversation that seem unlikely or disappointingly timed." Despite most critics finding faults, Lepucki's debut was also described as "powerful" and "promising." Ultimately, the dystopia in Lepucki's *California* does not seem particularly plausible or prescient, but the author's skill is in her earnest attempt to define a relationship within this bizarre cultural landscape. The best parts of the novel urge readers to care for the relationships within the story, even if they are unmoved by the collapsing society that exists around them.

*Micah L. Issitt*

**Review Sources**

Allfrey, Ellah. "Post-Apocalyptic World Falls Flat in 'California'." Rev. of *California*, by Edan Lepucki. *NPR Books*. National Public Radio, 7 July 2014. Web. 25 Jan. 2015.

Gaige, Amity. Rev. of *California*, by Edan Lepucki. *Guardian*. Guardian News and Media, 4 Sept. 2014. Web. 25 Jan. 2015.

Simon, Clea. Rev. of *California,* by Edan Lepucki. *Boston Globe*. Boston Globe Media Partners, 17 July 2014. Web. 25 Jan. 2015.

VanderMeer, Jeff. "Escape from L.A." Rev. of *California*, by Edan Lepucki. *New York Times*. New York Times, 3 July 2014 Web. 25 Jan. 2015.

Waclawiak, Karolina. "A Grave New World Awaits in Edan Lepucki's 'California.'" Rev. of *California*, by Edan Lepucki. *Los Angeles Times*. Tribune Publishing, 10 July 2014. Web. 25 Jan. 2015.

# Can't and Won't

**Author:** Lydia Davis
**Publisher:** Farrar, Straus and Giroux (New York). 304 pp.
**Type of work:** Short fiction

Can't and Won't *is Lydia Davis's first collection of short stories since her anthology* The Collected Stories of Lydia Davis *was published in 2009.*

In a profile of Lydia Davis for *New Yorker* magazine, Dana Goodyear described her as a "writer's writer's writer," an appellation that amounts, Goodyear wrote, to "dismissal by hyperbole." Davis, a poet, short-story writer, and novelist, has been working and publishing for more than thirty years. Her devoted fans include writers Rick Moody, Ali Smith, Miranda July, and Jonathan Franzen, who compared her to nineteenth-century French literary virtuoso Marcel Proust. Materially, the two writers could not be more different; Proust is famous for his dense sentences, with observations and reminiscences that run one to another without stopping, while Davis is an artist of economy. Her stories, called "short-short stories" by her fans and criticized as poems masquerading as short stories by her less-than-fans, are sometimes only one sentence long. Here, in its entirety, is the story "Old Woman, Old Fish" from *Can't and Won't* (2014), her latest collection of stories: "The fish that has been sitting in my stomach all afternoon was so old by the time I cooked and ate it, no wonder I am uncomfortable—an old woman digesting an old fish."

In 2009, Davis published *The Collected Stories of Lydia Davis*, an anthology of all her short stories to date; combined, they amounted to a little over seven hundred pages. Served up in bulk, her scrappy stories take on a peculiar "heft," Goodyear wrote. That year, Davis was belatedly lauded in the popular press; in 2013, she received the prestigious Man Booker International Prize. *Can't and Won't* is her first book since *Collected Stories*, though she released a translation of Gustave Flaubert's *Madame Bovary* (1856) in 2010. The full title of the collection is an excerpt from one of its stories: ". . . because, they said, I was lazy. What they meant by lazy was that I used too many contractions: for instance, I would not write out in full the words cannot and will not, but instead contracted them to *can't and won't*." The ellipses mask the beginning of the story, which reads: "I was recently denied a writing prize."

The title story comes relatively early in the collection. It is funny, given the strange mechanics of doling out literary prizes, but also surprising. It is tempting to transpose Davis onto the narrator of the story—most of her stories spring from an unidentified point of view—and wonder, when was the last time Lydia Davis was denied a writing prize? (Davis mentioned in a 2014 interview with NPR's Rachel Martin that the title story is based on a dream.) As a collection, *Can't and Won't* is oddly defiant and just as "uneven" as Arno Hofstadter of the *American Reader* suggests that it is. Dwight Garner, one of the *New York Times'* primary book critics, cited a friend who compared Davis's stories to mosquitoes: "Some you swat away, he says. Others draw blood."

*Can't and Won't* also contains an uncharacteristic strain of bitterness. In "Not Interested," an unnamed first-person narrator muses that picking up sticks in the backyard would be preferable to reading a particular book. In fact, when the narrator really thinks about it, she is bored even by the prospect of picking up sticks and also dreaming (*Can't and Won't* contains a number of dreams). But then again, the narrator thinks, perhaps she is just bored by new books, both good and bad: "I feel like saying: Please spare me your imagination, I'm so tired of your vivid imagination, let someone else enjoy it." Very few people have not had the experience of picking up a book only to put it down before finishing it, but Davis's dismissal invites negative connotations; it makes one defensive, throwing up a wall between writer and reader that Davis is usually so skilled at tearing down.

The characters in *Can't and Won't*, like just about everybody else in the world, like to complain. In one story, "I'm Pretty Comfortable, but I Could Be a Little More Comfortable," Davis expertly captures a series of thoughts, including "I'm hungry," "I'm cold sitting in the car," and "The back of my neck feels prickly." The story is witty and observant but also indicative of something less palatable in Davis's subject matter. Other micro-discomforts include "This pesto is hard to blend" and "I ordered an oat bran raisin muffin lightly toasted, but it wasn't lightly toasted." Like a number of other stories, "I'm Pretty Comfortable" evokes a very specific kind of person, and though Davis intends some jabs at the most comfortable class, her commentary itself sometimes becomes tedious. One story is about a too-expensive tin of peppermint candies, another is about which stories the narrator does and does not want to read in the *Times Literary Supplement*, and another is about how a woman does not like the composer George Frederic Handel as much as her husband. "The Cows," a sustained observation of a neighbor's trio of unremarkable cows, is a more successful commentary on perspective and finding profundity in life's mundane details. The cows, Davis writes, "do not know the words *person, neighbor, watch*, or even *cow*."

*Lydia Davis is a celebrated short-story writer, poet, translator, and novelist. She is the winner of a 2003 MacArthur Fellowship and the 2013 Man Booker International Prize.*

One of the most successful stories in *Can't and Won't* is called "The Landing." The story, as Davis writes in the first sentence, is about a "strange experience on an airplane." The narrator is traveling on an airplane when the pilot announces that there is something wrong with one of the plane's wings and that he will have to land it at a very high speed, which could cause the entire plane to crash or catch fire. The passengers have an hour to process the news. The steward is very calm, but the character of the plane and the people in it is very noticeably altered. Davis is at her best here, juggling large emotion and quotidian detail, capturing the exact moment when the public face of things falls away to reveal the fragility of every moment. At dinner that night, after the plane has been successfully landed, the narrator says, "I was looking into the face of a very small fried egg, a quail egg, on my plate, and it occurred to me that if the outcome had been different, the egg would at this very moment still have been looking up at someone, but at someone else, not me."

*Can't and Won't* is also peppered with dreams—dreamt by Davis herself and other dreams dreamt by close friends, she writes in the book's acknowledgements—as well as anecdotes translated from Flaubert's letters and his diary. It is brave to put one's own writing alongside that of Flaubert, but Davis's choice to include the anecdotes is in keeping with a definition of story best explained by author Philip Pullman in his *Fairy Tales from the Brothers Grimm: A New English Version* (2012). To tell a story, Pullman writes, is inherently to make it your own; in other words, the tale is in the teller. In *Can't and Won't*, Davis is the detective as well, having unearthed these gems from Flaubert's mountains of correspondence. In some cases, she connects disparate anecdotes that fit together in character or chronology; in others, her telling of the anecdotes and her presentation of them as stand-alone stories is its own form of artistry. One story, "The Visit to the Dentist," is only a few paragraphs long, yet virtuosic in its vastness. In it, Flaubert visits the dentist to have a tooth pulled. He crosses the town square where, when he was six or seven years old, he witnessed the aftermath of an execution while coming home from school, seeing blood on the guillotine and on the stones. He thinks about how he dreads having his tooth pulled just as, undoubtedly, some poor soul walked the same path dreading his own execution. In a few words, Flaubert traverses many years and embodies several people. "When I fell asleep [that night], I dreamed about the guillotine; the strange thing was that my little niece, who sleeps downstairs, also dreamed about a guillotine, though I hadn't said anything to her about it," he writes. "I wonder if thoughts are fluid, and flow downward, from one person to another, within the same house."

Davis's prose is delicate but not brittle. Her writing is unadorned and arresting in a way that is reminiscent of Flaubert, whose pristine sentences were grounded in his observations of the everyday. He once told his protégé Guy de Maupassant, "There is a part of everything which is unexplored, because we are accustomed to using our eyes only in association with the memory of what people before us have thought of the thing we are looking at. . . .Even the smallest thing has something in it which is unknown. We must find it." Davis brings her sensitivity and economy of style to the search.

*Molly Hagan*

## Review Sources

Garner, Dwight. "A Bowl of Berries Left to Dry in the Sun." Rev. of *Can't and Won't*, by Lydia Davis. *New York Times*. New York Times, 1 Apr. 2014. Web. 29 Jan. 2015.

Hofstadter, Arno. Rev. of *Can't and Won't*, by Lydia Davis. *American Reader*. Amer. Reader, 8 Apr. 2014. Web. 29 Jan. 2015.

Orner, Peter. "Illuminations." Rev. of *Can't and Won't*, by Lydia Davis. *New York Times Book Review* 6 Apr. 2014: 17. Print.

Schama, Chloe. "Lydia Davis Is the Perfect Writer for the Twitter Era." Rev. of *Can't and Won't*, by Lydia Davis. *New Republic*. New Republic, 7 Apr. 2014. Web. 29 Jan. 2015.

Taylor, Justin. "Wry and Dry: Reading the New Lydia Davis Book as Chinese Buffet." Rev. of *Can't and Won't*, by Lydia Davis. *New York Observer*. Observer Media, 13 Mar. 2014. Web. 29 Jan. 2015.

# Can't We Talk about Something More Pleasant?
## A Memoir

**Author:** Roz Chast (b. 1954)
**Publisher:** Bloomsbury (New York). Illustrated. 240 pp.
**Type of work:** Autobiography, graphic novel, memoir
**Time:** 2001–14
**Locale:** Flatbush, New York; suburban Connecticut

Can't We Talk about Something More Pleasant? *is a graphic memoir about a grown child caring for aging, eccentric parents.*

**Principal personages:**
Roz Chast, the author and narrator
Elizabeth Chast, her mother
George Chast, her father
Goodie, a private nurse

(Courtesy of Bloomsbury Publishing)

It is hard to conceive of a better title than *Can't We Talk about Something More Pleasant?* (2014) for a graphic memoir about dying parents. After all, talking about death is difficult even in the abstract. However, longtime *New Yorker* cartoonist Roz Chast refuses to take her title's admonition to heart. The brilliance of what Chast has done in her memoir lies in how she not only talks about death but shares her personal story of the death of her parents. Through humor and tenderness, Chast both processes the nature of her ordeal and offers a cautionary tale for readers who have yet to have "the talk" with their aging parents. It is of no surprise that, even as a graphic novel, *Can't We Talk about Something More Pleasant?* was shortlisted for the 2014 National Book Award, making Chast the first cartoonist to be a finalist in the adult nonfiction category.

In 2013, Katy Butler broke open a nationwide discussion of how medicine and a culture of death denial can take its toll on caring for aging parents in her book *Knocking on Heaven's Door: The Path to a Better Way of Death.* Butler is known for her narrative nonfiction and investigative journalism, and her memoir is a dense, heartbreakingly honest exposé of what can go wrong with medical care of the elderly at the end of life. In contrast, *Can't We Talk about Something More Pleasant?* is an almost cringe-inducingly intimate portrayal of Chast's relationship with her parents as they approach death. Chast sticks to her signature medium of cartoons to tell her story, her familiar wit turned just as often on herself as on her admittedly eccentric (read: batty) parents.

Chast's memoir focuses on the last decades on her parents' life, but it also includes plenty of family history, allowing the reader a window into both how Chast grew up and how her parents' lives evolved into one of solitary codependence. Chast uses her scratchy line drawings to describe how her parents, both children of Russian immigrants who settled in Brooklyn, essentially grew into doing everything together from the fifth grade forward. In one panel, Chast muses, "Maybe they believed that if they just held on to each other, really tightly, for eternity, nothing would ever change."

Chast's relationship with her parents growing up was tumultuous and stressful, and she distanced herself from them, despite becoming "more and more aware that at some point, we were all going to have to deal with this *aging* thing." Her parents were older when they had her. But they had led independent, functional lives, and she felt safe slipping into denial—"they weren't asking for help, and I wasn't volunteering"—and moving with her young family to the suburbs, leaving her seventy-eight-year-old parents to their lives in Brooklyn; they visited her, but Chast did not visit them for another eleven years.

Thus begins the first chapter, aptly titled "The Beginning of the End." In this and the following seventeen short chapters, Chast uses cartoon sketches, family photos, and text, including some of her mother's original poetry, to describe the saga of being a long-distance caretaker for her parents. Although she never strays from her personal story, she includes details that are helpful for anyone in a similar situation. While not everyone who reads this will have a neurotic father and an overbearing mother, the universal themes of aging, debilitation, and death will be relevant to everyone. That Chast manages to cover such topics with not only grace but also humor is a marvel.

Throughout the memoir, Chast's honesty renders the work extremely relatable. Readers with elderly parents will most likely nod in agreement as Chast describes her near-constant worrying once she realizes the extent of her parents' decline. Upon visiting their apartment after her eleven-year hiatus, she is forced to acknowledge that her parents are "moving into the part of old age that was scarier, harder to talk about, and not a part of this culture."

That the natural decline that comes with aging is not a part of our culture is precisely why this book is so important. By presenting the material in graphics, Chast takes what would normally be thought of as a morbid or taboo subject and makes it lighter. By making fun of herself and her stresses and failures as a caretaker, she makes the point that there is no such thing as the perfect way to deal with aging and decline. By breaking the memoir up into short chapters of cartoon panels, she reassures readers that the material will make them laugh, even at its grimmest. And it does. Though her humor can be self-deprecating, wry, or dry, Chast manages not to take her experiences too seriously while always staying on the mark. When she decides to call in an elder attorney, she depicts the "elder lawyer" as the Grim Reaper with a scythe in one hand and bag of money in the other, but in following panels she shows how the consultation led to a discussion in which her parents were convinced to write basic advanced directives and give Chast power of attorney.

Throughout her story, Chast is as quick to examine her own faults as she is her parents' quirks, and willing to admit to her fears and worries. The combination of her candor and humor results in an intensely personal memoir that is engaging and informative. In telling her story, Chast seems to cover nearly everything someone caring for an elder would need to know: the difficulties of keeping her parents' apartment clean, their hoarding, moving her parents into an assisted living facility near her family, her father's decline into dementia, palliative care, do-not-resuscitate orders and how to enforce them, caring for a grieving parent, home health aides, incontinence, hospice care, trying to reconcile with her mother, and the expense of it all, both financially and emotionally. And she does so without sentimentality. "Mostly people are glad that I've said it was really hard, and really messy," she told Emma Brockes in an interview published on the *Guardian* website on June 14, 2014. "I wanted to write about the entire experience, including the parts that were gross, and funny, and including my mixed feelings about my parents. I didn't want to write with a fake, rosy glow."

*Roz Chast is the author of seven graphic books. As a cartoonist, her work has been regularly published in the* New Yorker *since 1978 and has graced its cover six times.*

Chast insists that she has no real advice to offer other people going through a similar experience. In interviews she is hard on herself, especially with regard to her worries about spending all her parents' savings, leaving her nothing left to inherit. She said to Brockes, "It's a terrible, terrible thing and you look at yourself in the mirror and think: I'm a worm. I'm a lowly, sh——ty, crappy, horrible worm to be thinking this." But she recognizes it as just another part of the experience she was dealt and something that every child caring for elderly parents thinks about, even if they do not admit it.

It is clear that the experience of making this memoir was in part cathartic. Never close with her mother, Chast was often outright terrified of her, and her struggles increased after her father passed away. Unable to provide the care her mother needs, she hires a private nurse, Goodie, who actually manages to bond with her domineering mother. This leaves Chast feeling guilty, relieved, jealous, and grateful, emotions to which she dedicates one panel each. Just before her mother's death, Chast even attempts to find peace with her mother, telling her she wishes things had been different growing up. Her mother shuts down the conversation, and Chast leaves the visit sobbing. Reflecting on the experience, Chast recognizes that closure is not always an option. She also realizes that while she could not fix her relationship with her mother, she does have a wonderful relationship with her own children, something that makes her both grateful for her experience as a mother and sad that her own mother never got to experience the same joy.

For people familiar with Chast's work, the themes of anxiety, angst, and dysfunctional family relationships are not new. But in *Can't We Talk about Something More Pleasant?*, Chast manages to provide a broader context for those themes by painting a very personal family portrait. Her portrayal of her experience is powerfully intimate and unexpected for the genre she chose. Few cartoonists are able to maintain both a distinctive style and a distinctive voice while still being so transparent. Chast's work often feels like being let in on a secret, and it is no surprise that her memoir comes across almost as a diary.

As her mother's decline worsens, Chast enrolls her in twenty-four-hour hospice, only to visit one day and find her sitting on the couch, fully dressed and eating a tuna sandwich. "I knew," writes Chast, "that her retreat from the abyss should have filled me with joy, or at least relief. However, what I felt when I saw her was closer to: 'Where, in the five Stages of Death, is Eat Tuna Sandwich?!?!?'" Nearly a year later, when her mother finally does die, Chast arrives minutes later and sits with the body. Not knowing what else to do, she draws several portraits of her mother's body. Chast includes these intimate portraits as a final gift to her readers. Unlike the cartoon panels that fill her story, these drawings are stark and raw, a visceral reminder that it is, in fact, of the utmost importance to talk about the things that are less pleasant.

*Michelle Acciavatti*

**Review Sources**

Cooke, Rachel. "Roz Chast's Grimly Hilarious Family Memoir." Rev. of *Can't We Talk about Something More Pleasant?*, by Roz Chast. *Guardian*. Guardian News and Media, 13 July 2014. Web. 30 Oct. 2014.

McAlpin, Heller. Rev. of *Can't We Talk about Something More Pleasant?*, by Roz Chast. *SF Gate*. Hearst Communications, 28 May 2014. Web. 30 Oct. 2014

Witchel, Alex. "Drawn from Life." Rev. of *Can't We Talk about Something More Pleasant?*, by Roz Chast. *New York Times*. New York Times, 30 May 2014. Web. 30 Oct. 2014.

# The Children Act

**Author:** Ian McEwan (b. 1948)
**Publisher:** Doubleday (New York). 221 pp.
**Type of work:** Novel
**Time:** Present day
**Locale:** London

*Ian McEwan's latest novel explores science, faith, and good judgment through the eyes of a High Court judge in London.*

**Principal characters:**
FIONA MAYE, a High Court judge who presides over cases in family court
JACK MAYE, a pseudo-bohemian university professor and Fiona's husband
ADAM HENRY, a precocious seventeen-year-old leukemia patient and budding poet

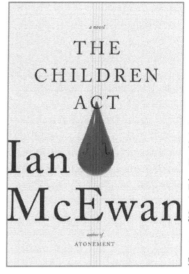

THE CHILDREN ACT

Ian McEwan

*author of* ATONEMENT

(Courtesy of Nan A. Talese/Doubleday)

Fiona Maye is a fifty-nine-year-old judge at the High Court of Justice of England and Wales, presiding over cases in family court in London. She is an ideal judge, equanimous and eloquent; like Aaron Sorkin's fictional President Jed Bartlet in the American television series *The West Wing*, Fiona is constructed as the judge one would want to oversee one's own divorce settlement or child-custody battle. "Among fellow judges," McEwan writes, "Fiona Maye was praised, even in her absence, for crisp prose, almost ironic, almost warm, and for the compact terms in which she laid out a dispute." In a trial involving two "unequally Orthodox" Jewish parents, for example, Fiona rules in favor of the less Orthodox wife, a woman with wild red hair, who left her conservative Haredi sect in North London to take a job as a primary school teacher. The educational future of the couple's two daughters, Rachel and Nora, is the object of the dispute. Should they receive a traditional, gender-segregated Haredi education, one in which they would only attend school until their mid-teens, or should they attend the coeducational Jewish school that their mother prefers? This case, like so many others Fiona hears, is about much more than it seems. "At stake was the entire context of the girls' growing up," McEwan writes. "It was a fight for their souls."

Fiona's decision in the Haredi case, outlined in the first pages of *The Children Act* (2014), is significant because in it, she outlines her definition of the term "welfare." Citing past rulings, Fiona writes that a child's welfare includes much more than the financial status of his or her parents or a determination of his or her present physical comfort. The term is actually much broader; it is "inseparable" from a child's well-being and "development as a person." Regardless of religious beliefs or customs, on which the court takes no position, Fiona rules that to deprive the girls of a social upbringing through which they might meet people of different beliefs and be given more opportunities to take control their own destinies is fundamentally against their welfare. They will live with their mother and attend the coed school.

Of course, not all of Fiona's cases are so clear-cut. A particular case, one that she reluctantly admits has had a disastrous effect on her emotional and sexual relationship with her husband, involves conjoined twins

*Ian McEwan is an award-winning English novelist and short-story writer. His best-known works include the short-story collection* First Love, Last Rites *(1975) and the novels* The Child in Time *(1987),* Atonement *(2001), and* Amsterdam *(1998), which won the Man Booker Prize. He lives in London.*

attached in such a way that both cannot survive. The Catholic parents refuse to agree to any operation that might kill one of the twins, so Fiona must decide which one, if either, will be given a chance at life. Fiona is celebrated for her nuanced decision in the case, but her own actions haunt her, and her personal life suffers.

As the book opens, Jack, Fiona's university professor husband, seeks her blessing to begin an affair with a much younger coworker. The request completely derails Fiona. Married for more than thirty years, she and Jack have had a happy and, until recently, sexually satisfying relationship. They have no children and have managed to keep their romance alive through spontaneous European vacations and an enviable social life. But it is clear that something is wrong, although Fiona cannot put her finger on what, and even if she could, her unshakably professional mien keeps her from sharing her doubts with Jack.

This is Fiona's emotional state when she receives a call late one Sunday night from her assistant. A seventeen-year-old leukemia patient, just a few months shy of his eighteenth birthday, is refusing a blood transfusion on religious grounds, and the hospital has asked the court to intervene. As horrible as it may sound, Fiona is somewhat relieved to take on the case. Work allows her to forget about her husband's possible infidelity—and the fact that he appears to have moved out of their cozy London apartment. Still, her marital trouble has her behaving just a little more recklessly than usual, and in an unorthodox but not unprecedented decision, she asks to travel to the hospital to speak with the boy, Adam, before making her ruling. The meeting sparks a chain of events that will bring Fiona and Adam together again later and change their lives forever.

This dramatic setup for Ian McEwan's *The Children Act*, his thirteenth novel, is a tall order for a book that is just over two hundred pages in length, but McEwan is a masterful dramatist. In another author's hands, *The Children Act* might seem overwrought or didactic, pitting faith against science in a clunky, overtly symbolic courtroom drama. But McEwan manages to avoid most of the pitfalls over which his story might have stumbled. Reviewers have praised the novel's flawless exterior: its expertly woven plot and its well-researched and emotionally articulate prose. McEwan is mindful of, and deeply familiar with, his subject matter, and he spends an astonishing though not unwelcome amount of time describing Fiona's cases with an "efficiency and elegance so alien to legal writing," according to Ron Charles of the *Washington Post*. A first-time reader, or someone who has never heard of the famous author, might be surprised to learn that McEwan is not actually a judge or, at the very least, a long-time lawyer himself.

Still, the novel is far from perfect. Many readers, though not wanting to put the book down, will all the while oscillate between like and dislike. Is this a novel that can be reduced to a good or a bad rating? Can it be simply liked? More immediately, is it a novel at all, or, as Deborah Friedell of the *New York Times* suggests, is it more of a novel-length allegory? Adam is a pitch-perfect portrait of melodramatic youth, a precocious poet in the mold of a young Percy Bysshe Shelley, but is too much weight given to his tortured yearnings? This is a more fruitful question, and one McEwan may very well have intended the reader to ask. How mutually beneficial could Fiona and Adam's relationship actually be? Lastly, what about Fiona herself? One cannot help but feel that once the plot is set in motion, it leaps to its own inevitable conclusions that strike a discordant note through the book as a whole. It would be too reductive to say that Fiona fits the mold of a frosty career woman who just needs to learn to emote, but the novel cuts a bit close to that trope.

Additionally, disturbing—though very small—conundrums plague *The Children Act*. Fiona encounters, on at least two occasions, clients who were falsely accused of rape. The information is meant as a small footnote, evidence for a subplot that questions the law's treatment of young and poor or middle-class boys. But the information, meant to endear the young men to the reader as innocent victims, strikes a sour note. How could McEwan have misjudged his audience so much to include such a loaded detail? He is doubtless aware that a not-insignificant proportion of his readers will have been directly or indirectly affected by rape—and not rape that was all made up (to win money to buy an Xbox, as one of Fiona's colleagues laments). It would seem less important to point out these small details if the novel were not about ethics, judgment, and the fundamentals of right and wrong.

More broadly, *The Children Act* asks a lot of hairy questions about fairness and Shakespeare's "infinite variety," as Fiona thinks of it. In the Haredi case—indeed, in all cases involving religious customs and secular institutions—Fiona invokes the words of Lord Justice James Munby, a real-life High Court judge: "The infinite variety of the human condition precludes arbitrary definition." In other words, what is right in one circumstance is not always right in another, and vice versa. As a judge, Fiona balks at the thought of such chaos, but to the reader, the notion provides hearty food for thought.

Much hay has been made about the fact that Adam Henry, the boy in the case, is a Jehovah's Witness. McEwan, a close friend of the late Christopher Hitchens, is well known for his atheist views. Hitchens, an eloquent and lively intellectual, was a leader in the adversarial New Atheism movement, but McEwan does not display any of his friend's arguments here. By examining the case from the perspective of the law, McEwan renders Adam's actual religion a moot point. Adam might have been a member of the Haredi sect from the beginning of the novel, if an Orthodox Jewish belief had fit the premise. This was a wise decision on McEwan's part; by imploding any expectation of a science-versus-religion debate, he reaches a more interesting plane of thought. Should one believe that blood transfusions are a sin? To the court, it does not matter. What matters, in *The Children Act*, is an issue that is much more difficult to determine: the welfare of human beings as they strive to do what is right.

*Molly Hagan*

## Review Sources

Charles, Ron. "*The Children Act*, by Ian McEwan, Puts Beliefs of Jehovah's Witnesses on Trial." Rev. of *The Children Act*, by Ian McEwan. *Washington Post*. Washington Post, 2 Sept. 2014. Web. 26 Nov. 2014.

Friedell, Deborah. "The Body's Temple." Rev. of *The Children Act*, by Ian McEwan. *New York Times Book Review* 14 Sept. 2014: 11. Print.

Hadley, Tessa. "The Intricate Workings of Institutionalised Power." Rev. of *The Children Act*, by Ian McEwan. *Guardian*. Guardian News and Media, 11 Sept. 2014. Web. 26 Nov. 2014.

Kakutani, Michiko. "Cast Adrift in a Realm of Choices: In Ian McEwan's *The Children Act*, Medicine Meets Religion." Rev. of *The Children Act*, by Ian McEwan. *New York Times*. New York Times, 14 Sept. 2014. Web. 26 Nov. 2014.

Wolitzer, Meg. "Legal Dilemmas Become Human Drama in Ian McEwan's Latest." Rev. of *The Children Act*, by Ian McEwan. *NPR*. Natl. Public Radio, 5 Sept. 2014. Web. 24 Nov. 2014.

# Citizen
## An American Lyric

**Author:** Claudia Rankine (b. 1963)
**Publisher:** Graywolf Press (Minneapolis).
160 pp.
**Type of work:** Poetry, essays
**Time:** 1960s–present
**Locale:** United States

(Courtesy of Graywolf Press)

*Citizen is an innovative collection of prose poems, essays, and scripts for situational videos. It includes artwork alongside anecdotes and reflections, often dealing with racial discrimination in the United States.*

**Principal personages:**
JAMES CRAIG ANDERSON, an African American man killed by white youths
JORDAN RUSSELL DAVIS, an African American teenager killed by a white man
MARK DUGGAN, a black British man killed by police in England
JENA SIX, six black teenagers prosecuted for beating a white teenager
TRAYVON MARTIN, an African American teenager killed by a Hispanic neighborhood watchman
SERENA WILLIAMS, an African American professional female tennis player

Claudia Rankine has had a long and impressive career, and her latest book, *Citizen: An American Lyric,* will only add to her prominent position as one of America's most widely praised poets and most honored literary figures. A graduate of Williams College with an MFA from Columbia University, she has edited numerous important anthologies and is the author of commissioned plays and several books of poetry. She has won various significant awards and was named a chancellor of the American Academy of Poetry in 2013. She has taught at some of the best universities in the United States, and her latest, highly innovative book was one of five finalists for the 2014 National Book Award for Poetry.

*Citizen's* first section—consisting, like most of the rest of the volume, of untitled prose poems—seems openly autobiographical. It deals with the constant, unrelenting difficulties of trying to live and thrive as a black person in the United States. The speaker's memory beginning on page 5, for instance, recalls a nun (presumably white) at a private Catholic school committing an act of racism toward the speaker in her youth. (This story is followed by a photograph showing white houses in a suburban neighborhood with a street sign astonishingly indicating the location as "Jim Crow Rd.")

On page seven, the speaker remembers a white friend who confused the speaker's name with that of her black housekeeper. The anecdote on the next page seems to have nothing to do with race. It does, however, explore a theme that pervades *Citizen*: close attention to possible insults inflicted by others—"What did he just say? Did she really just say that? Did I hear what I think I heard? Did that just come out of my mouth, his mouth, your mouth?" As these quoted sentences show, Rankine's phrasing is almost always exceptionally clear, colloquial, and striking.

The speaker of the first section of the volume is confronted by one astonishingly insensitive person after another. At the beginning of the section, the speaker is driving, when the passenger, an academic (presumably white), tells the speaker that "his dean is making him hire a person of color when there are so many great writers out there." Later, the speaker feels as if she is suffering from "John Henryism," a term coined to describe "people exposed to stresses stemming from racism." On the next page, a young girl and her mother (presumably white) seem uncomfortable sitting next to the speaker on a plane. Next, during the speaker's visit to a college, a female lunch companion makes an insensitive comment about affirmative action. On page fourteen, a general meditation on how it feels to be black in the United States is offered, while the next page includes a long anecdote about the racial profiling of one of the speaker's black friends. Other parts of the first section deal with racism at a Starbucks, on a subway platform, and at an insensitive therapist's office. The first section paints the speaker's life—one described in crisp, vivid language—as exceptionally sad. She encounters racists and racism everywhere.

Section 2 offers an extended, essaylike meditation on the racism encountered on the tennis court by Serena Williams. Even John McEnroe—known as an ill-mannered and foul-mouthed player during his professional tennis days—felt moved to tell Williams that he thought she was being treated unfairly by judges who seemed determined to rule against her and by fans who considered her sometimes rude and embarrassing. Rankine implies that Williams, who is admittedly vocal on the court and sometimes disparaging toward officials, has been mistreated, or at least misunderstood, because of her race.

Section 3 includes more anecdotes about the racism suffered by the speaker. On page 41, a friend uses slang in a way that insults her. Also within this section, a co-worker calls her by another person's name and an office manager is surprised to discover that the speaker, with whom he has been dealing over the phone, is black. On page 45, a "woman with multiple degrees" says, "I didn't know black women could get cancer." More racist insults pile up, typically one per page, so that eventually one wonders how the speaker can endure a life this painful. This is a life of consistent, persistent psychological suffering.

In section 4, race recedes momentarily as the book's chief focus and is temporarily replaced by other sources of pain and discomfort, such as body aches, bad memories, headaches, more slights, more insults, and more unfairness. One notices, especially in this section, how skillfully Rankine echoes ideas and phrasing from earlier in the book. Indeed, this volume exhibits much unity of theme, style, imagery, and tone. It is a relatively long book for a modern volume of poetry (even prose poetry), but it works as a single, coherent unit. Often the text feels not so much like a series of isolated prose lyrics but an extended meditation on the speaker's life and times, somewhat in the manner of William Wordsworth's *The Prelude* (1850).

The long poem that opens section 5 seems more abstract and experimental than much of the preceding writing in *Citizen*, thus demonstrating the commitment to innovation that is one of the most impressive aspects of this volume. By the end of this section, however, the familiar theme of loutish behavior by others reappears, and one senses again the speaker's repeated sufferings. Some readers may be reminded of the autobiographical writings of Zitkala-Ša, another important American woman of color, especially the latter's "The School Days of an Indian Girl," which Rankine's book resembles both in topic and in tone. In contrast, some readers may be struck by the differences between Rankine's volume and those of Zora Neale

(Courtesy of John Luucas)

*Claudia Rankine is the author of five books of poetry.* Citizen: An American Lyric *was short-listed for the 2014 National Book Award in Poetry. She is the recipient of numerous prizes and has taught at various universities, including Pomona College in California.*

Hurston, for example, whom Rankine cites approvingly. Anyone planning to teach Rankine's volume (or read it in a book club) may want to consider pairing it, for purposes of comparison and contrast, with Hurston's famous essay "How It Feels to Be Colored Me."

*Citizen* eventually moves outward from the chiefly single speaker of the book's first half to a broader concern with other victims of racial discrimination. Here again Rankin's interest in formal innovation is clear: the individual pieces of this section often consist of "script[s] for situation video[s]," which have been "created in collaboration with John Lucas." These scripts focus on such topics as Hurricane Katrina, Trayvon Martin, James Craig Anderson, Jordan Russell Davis, the Jena Six, Mark Duggan, the policy of stop-and-frisk, the presidency of Barack Obama, and the corruption of the American justice system. This section provides further examples of how the entire book is enlivened and diversified by the inclusion of works of art, usually paintings (but also various other kinds of visual effects).

Section 7 returns to a more personal focus. Familiar themes reappear: aches, pains, slights, insults, evidence of broader racism, and a final anecdote about the way the speaker has been slighted by yet another person. Throughout, *Citizen* plays persistently ironic variations on its seemingly simple title: the speaker of these prose poems feels, in many ways, significantly disenfranchised, significantly put out, put upon, and put in her place. For many readers this book will confirm all their worst suspicions about race relations in the United States, not just in the past but, sadly, in the present as well. It will suggest to them that although at least fifty years have gone by since the glory days of the civil rights movement, racism is still very much part of American society. The election of an African American president, the numerous achievements of and recognition won by Rankine, and even the publication of this handsome, haunting book, with its vivid, memorable phrasing, will seem to many insignificant compared to the suffering, pain, petty insults, and violent deaths this book records.

Reviewers have been unstinting in their praise of *Citizen*, with one writer rightly comparing it, both in substance and in form (if not in tone), to Walt Whitman's *Leaves of Grass* (1855). Her book could easily be recommended to anyone who wants to learn how to communicate effectively in crisp, lucid language. This is an eminently readable book—one printed on heavy, glossy paper that does full justice to all the artwork, making the volume itself feel nearly as substantial in weight as it seems thematically. Clearly, Rankine speaks powerfully to many contemporary readers, and her book, in addition to its obvious strengths as a piece of writing, will certainly have historical value as a reflection of the state of contemporary American culture.

*Robert C. Evans*

**Review Sources**

Chiasson, Dan. "Color Codes: A Poet Examines Race in America." Rev. of *Citizen: An American Lyric*, by Claudia Rankine. *New Yorker*. Condé Nast, 27 Oct. 2014. Web. 23 Dec. 2014.

Farmer, Jonathan. "Blackness Visible." Rev. of *Citizen: An American Lyric*, by Claudia Rankine. *Slate*. Slate Group, 9 Oct. 2014. Web. 23 Dec. 2014.

Lee, Felicia R. "A Poetry Personal and Political: Claudine Rankine on 'Citizen' and Racial Politics." Rev. of *Citizen: An American Lyric*, by Claudine Rankine. *New York Times*. New York Times, 29 Nov. 2014 Web. 23 Dec. 2014.

Ulin, David L. "Poet Claudia Rankine Ruminates on the Body Politic in 'Citizen.'" *Los Angeles Times*. Los Angeles Times, 9 Oct. 2014. Web. 23 Dec. 2014.

# Colorless Tsukuru Tazaki and His Years of Pilgrimage

**Author:** Haruki Murakami (b. 1949)
**First published:** Shikisai o motanai Tazaki Tsukuru to, kare no junrei no toshi, 2013, in Japan
**Translated from:** the Japanese by Philip Gabriel
**Publisher:** Alfred A. Knopf (New York). 400 pp.
**Type of work:** Novel
**Time:** From twenty years ago to the present day
**Locale:** Tokyo, Japan

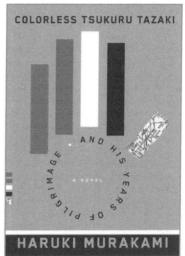

(Courtesy of Knopf)

*Haruki Murakami's* Colorless Tsukuru Tazaki and His Years of Pilgrimage *is a moving fictional portrait of a young man's isolation, which he cannot move beyond unless he is willing to revisit the relationships of his past.*

**Principal characters:**
TSUKURU TAZAKI, a train station engineer with a profound fear of abandonment
SARA KIMOTO, his current girlfriend
YUZUKI "SHIRO" SHIRANE, his former friend
ERI "KURO" KURONO HAATAINEN, his former friend
YOSHIO "AO" OUMI, his former friend
KEI "AKA" AKAMATSU, his former friend
FUMIAKI HAIDA, a university student who briefly befriends him

In *Colorless Tsukuru Tazaki and His Years of Pilgrimage* (2014), Tsukuru Tazaki is an unmarried man in his thirties who works in Tokyo as an engineer overseeing the construction and renovation of train stations. Although he has had a few fairly serious girlfriends over the years, he cannot seem to find meaning in these associations until he meets Sara Kimoto. Sara tells Tsukuru, however, that she senses some kind of emotional blockage in him that will likely impede their relationship. Tsukuru reveals that sixteen years earlier, in the summer of his sophomore year in college, his four closest friends abruptly cut off all communication with him without any explanation. His sense of abandonment was so great that he became obsessed with death for months afterward, and even though he eventually recovered, he found that he had permanently changed, both physically and emotionally.

Initially, Tsukuru's reaction to this desertion by his high school friends may seem overly dramatic, but the author quickly makes clear that these were no ordinary adolescent friendships. Tsukuru and his friends had formed an unusually tight-knit group

after working together on a volunteer project in their hometown of Nagoya, and they
quickly became inseparable, despite their
very different personalities. Tsukuru explains
to Sara that Shiro, Kuro, Ao, and Aka nicknamed themselves after the colors that make
up part of their last names, which mean, respectively, "white root," "black field," "blue
sea," and "red pine." Shiro was a talented pi-

*Haruki Murakami's work has been translated from Japanese into more than fifty languages. In 2009, he won the Jerusalem Prize, which is awarded to writers whose work addresses the themes of freedom, society, and government.* Colorless Tsukuru Tazaki and His Years of Pilgrimage *is his thirteenth novel.*

anist and passionate animal lover, Kuro was a literature buff with a quick wit, Ao was
an enthusiastic athlete, and Aka was academically gifted. From the beginning, Tsukuru
felt himself to be dull in comparison with his friends, having no particular passion in
life other than an attraction to train stations. He has always found it significant that his
was the only name in the group unrelated to color, and his friends teased him good-
naturedly about this, not realizing that he was taking his apparent "colorlessness" to
heart. Years later, Tsukuru's insecurity and lack of self-esteem are exacerbated when
he tentatively makes a new friend in Tokyo named Haida, only to once again be abandoned without explanation. It is not in his nature to be angry with his friends, however;
he assumes that the fault lies within him, believing himself to be an empty vessel with
nothing to offer in a relationship.

Although Tsukuru does not completely recover from the pain caused by his friends,
he has since managed to focus on his work and his simple daily routines. When he
meets Sara in the present day, he is immediately attracted to her, but he is chagrined to
learn that she does not believe he is emotionally present during their lovemaking. Sara
manages to elicit from Tsukuru the story about his friends' desertion and immediately
concludes that he must track them down and demand an explanation for their actions.
At first reluctant, Tsukuru eventually agrees to let Sara find out his friends' current
whereabouts. A few days later, he is stunned to learn that Shiro is dead, although Sara
will not reveal any details. Kuro has married and moved to Finland, but Ao and Aka
are still in Nagoya, so Tsukuru seeks them out first. Though pleased to find that they
are willing to speak with him, he is utterly shocked when he discovers that sixteen
years earlier, Shiro told the group that Tsukuru had raped her. Upon hearing this, Tsukuru decides to travel to Finland to find Kuro, in the hope that Shiro, who later became
the victim of an unsolved murder, may have revealed to Kuro why she made such an
accusation when she and Tsukuru never had sexual contact of any kind.

To Tsukuru's profound relief, all three of his surviving friends have long since realized that he would never have committed such a violent act, but they also know they
have traveled down paths from which they cannot return. The concept of choices and
consequences is a common theme in Murakami's work, and he takes it further here by
exploring the degrees of difference between passive desire, active intention, and actual
deed. For instance, Tsukuru has had vivid erotic dreams about Shiro and Kuro almost
from the beginning of the group's friendship, which is not surprising considering their
youth and constant proximity to one another. The dreams seem completely normal
until one night, long after the group's break with Tsukuru, when his new friend Haida

spends the night at Tsukuru's apartment. This time, the dream about Shiro and Kuro seems so real that he wonders if it is actually happening. Even more perplexing is that fact that the encounter also involves Haida, whose presence seems to fill the bedroom even though Tsukuru knows him to be asleep in the next room. Years later, when Tsukuru discusses Shiro's accusation and her eventual death with Kuro, he speculates whether he might be responsible for these events, even if he was not physically present when they happened. As in Murakami's best-selling three-part novel *1Q84* (2009–10; English translation, 2011), the author seems to suggest that unconsummated desire may have unexpected consequences, even if only in an alternate reality or within the human psyche, for which both parties must ultimately acknowledge responsibility.

Another significant theme in this novel is the importance, whether real or imagined, of names. Tsukuru means "to make things," which is fitting in that he helps make the train stations that are essential to modern Japanese society. Tsukuru is pleased to learn that Kuro is now also a maker of things; she has become a fairly accomplished potter, and in fact she met her Finnish husband while he was in Japan studying pottery mak-ing. The most striking use of this device, however, lies in the association of names with colors. In addition to the original group, Tsukuru's new friend's name, Haida, means "gray field," leading Tsukuru to reflect on the differences between black and white and his simultaneous but unrequited attraction to Kuro (black) and Shiro (white). When Tsukuru locates Kuro in Finland, she insists that he refer to both her and Shiro by their real names, in part because they all became different people once the group went their separate ways. Notably, Sara's name is completely unrelated to any color, perhaps suggesting that she will be the one to help Tsukuru finally let go of the idea that he is colorless.

In terms of imagery, much emphasis is placed throughout the novel on hands and fingers. When Tsukuru has the disquieting dream about Shiro, Kuro, and Haida, he notes that both women's hands move simultaneously over his skin like sightless crea-tures. Later, when Tsukuru meets with Ao in Nagoya, Ao reflects that the group of friends used to be like the five fingers of a hand, functioning best in concert and mak-ing up for each other's shortcomings. Still later, Tsukuru has a conversation with two colleagues in which he learns that vestigial sixth fingers are more common than he knew. The men wonder why the trait has not become even more widespread and con-clude that five just happens to be the ideal number of fingers for what a hand needs to accomplish.

Unsurprisingly in light of Tsukuru's profession, train stations also appear through-out the novel, both literally and figuratively. Tsukuru often goes to stations simply to observe the trains arriving and departing, which has a soothing, hypnotic effect on him. When he returns to Japan from Finland, finally somewhat at peace with his past, he tries to express his feelings to Sara, noting that he can only prepare for a meaning-ful relationship by building a station in his psyche in order to give the trains a place at which they can arrive.

Some readers may note that several seemingly important plot elements remain un-resolved. Unlike with the original group of friends, no firm explanation is given for why Haida also breaks off contact with Tsukuru. In addition, during the course of their friendship, Haida relates a complicated story to Tsukuru about an encounter his father had years prior with a pianist who claimed to possess a mysterious token of death. For years afterward, Tsukuru continues to ponder the significance of this tale, but its meaning is never made clear. Similarly, when Tsukuru reconnects with his friends, there is much discussion about Aka's status as the owner of a corporate training company; all of the surviving friends, including Tsukuru, express their distaste for Aka's current occupation, but it is not entirely clear why, unless the point is simply that people make unexpected choices in life. Tsukuru and Sara's relationship is also left on a rather ambiguous note. Nonetheless, by the novel's end, Tsukuru has undeniably experienced a significant and compelling transformation, finally becoming willing to take an emotional risk that would have been unthinkable before he confronted his past.

*Amy Sisson*

## Review Sources

Rev. of *Colorless Tsukuru Tazaki and His Years of Pilgrimage*, by Haruki Murakami. *Publishers Weekly* 28 Apr. 2014: 105. Print.

Hartnett, Kevin. "*Colorless Tsukuru Tazaki and His Years of Pilgrimage* Is Straightforward and Un-Murakami-like." Rev. of *Colorless Tsukuru Tazaki and His Years of Pilgrimage*, by Haruki Murakami. *Christian Science Monitor*. Christian Science Monitor, 12 Aug. 2014. Web. 30 Oct. 2014.

Hong, Terry. Rev. of *Colorless Tsukuru Tazaki and His Years of Pilgrimage*, by Haruki Murakami. *Library Journal* 15 June 2014: 87. Print.

Ott, Bill. Rev. of *Colorless Tsukuru Tazaki and His Years of Pilgrimage*, by Haruki Murakami. *Booklist* 1 Aug. 2014: 31–32. Print.

Rich, Nathaniel. "The Mystery of Murakami." Rev. of *Colorless Tsukuru Tazaki and His Years of Pilgrimage*, by Haruki Murakami. *Atlantic* Sept. 2014: 38–40. Print.

Sniderman, Andrew Stobo. Rev. of *Colorless Tsukuru Tazaki and His Years of Pilgrimage*, by Haruki Murakami. *Maclean's* 18 Aug. 2014: 54–55. Print.

# Console Wars
## Sega, Nintendo, and the Battle That Defined a Generation

**Author:** Blake J. Harris (b. 1982)
**Publisher:** HarperCollins (New York). 576 pp.
**Type of work:** History, media, technology
**Time:** 1990–96
**Locales:** United States, Japan

(Courtesy of Harper Collins/It Books)

Console Wars *follows the six-year tenure of Tom Kalinske as president and CEO of Sega of America, during which time he helped Sega break Nintendo's stranglehold on the video-game market and shaped the future of the industry for a decade to come.*

**Principal personages:**

TOM KALINSKE, CEO and president of Sega of America, 1990–96; a former Mattel executive

HAYAO NAKAYAMA, president of Sega Enterprises, Ltd., 1984–99, who selected him to take on Nintendo

MINORU ARAKAWA, founder and president of Nintendo of America until 2002

HOWARD LINCOLN, senior vice president and general counsel of Nintendo, 1983–94; chair of Nintendo of America, 1994–2000

The video-game industry of the 1990s was a cultural force to be reckoned with. Nintendo's near-total hegemony via the Nintendo Entertainment System (NES) and its portly plumber mascot, Mario, reached its climax in the early 1990s at about the time Sega debuted its Genesis gaming console and new mascot, Sonic the Hedgehog. In grand capitalistic tradition, virtual battle lines were drawn among gaming consumers who would declare their loyalty to either the Nintendo system or the Sega system but never both. Thus, the war of the consoles was created and became the basis of writer-filmmaker Blake J. Harris's first book, *Console Wars*.

As one would expect, there is a wealth of corporate intrigue, deceit, high-tech innovation, and dramatic reversals of fortune to recount in a book that chronicles the early years of the video-game industry, which remains relatively untouched ground. Several critics express disappointment with the book, however, explaining that the dance that Harris does in presenting both a novelesque narrative amid a retelling of real-life accounts of corporate rivalry in popular history fails to deliver on the promise of the book's premise and subject matter.

Harris builds his account around one man, Tom Kalinske, and his eventful tenure as president and CEO of Sega of America. Kalinske gained fame in the toy industry

during the 1980s when he was instrumental in reviving sales for American toy manufacturer Mattel and its Barbie and Hot Wheels lines and later with the launch of the
smash-hit He-Man Masters of the Universe line of action figures.

Kalinske was hand-picked by Hayao Nakayama, then president of a struggling
Sega, to take over Sega of America and shake things up. Harris tells the story of corporate intrigue and scrappy underdogs and includes all the ingredients of a boilerplate
corporate thriller. The problem many critics have found, however, is that that *Console
Wars* is not fiction. It is not simply a thriller or a novel but ostensibly an account of
events that actually happened. Narrative nonfiction, particularly the historical variety,
requires a delicate touch: it must tell a good story without overstepping the bounds of
what the author can reasonably know lest it lose its credibility. Unfortunately, Harris
crosses the line from reasonable extrapolation to outright fabrication within the first
few pages of his book, and acknowledges as much with a note at the front of the book
that states that "details of settings and description have been altered, reconstructed, or
imagined" with Harris's "best judgment" in determining what should be adjusted or
completely made up.

From the first interaction between Kalinske and Nakayama, Harris insists on writing extensive dialogue for every character, which, as reviewer Chris Suellentrop for
the *New York Times* notes, often comes across as "stilted and phony." The decision to
fabricate dialogue based on interviews and best guesses is a risky one for a nonfiction
writer, but it can be forgiven if the dialogue adds something to the narrative in terms of
drama or characterization. Critics have generally found this not to be the case in *Console Wars*. Though almost every character has dialogue, there is almost no distinction
between the personalities of the various players.

Harris also describes every character with a level of personal familiarity that strains
believability. Nintendo lawyer Howard Lincoln is "elegant, imposing." Trip Hawkins,
founder of game-development company Electronic Arts, is "brilliant but mercurial."
Strategically applied bits of detail are the lifeblood of nonfiction, but they must be
grounded in reality and be used sparingly.

When the book does enter into fascinating territory—for instance, deals and betrayals between Nintendo, Sega, and Sony that would eventually lead to the birth of the
Sony PlayStation and the death of Sega—it is hard to appreciate the drama because
doubts about the reality of what the reader is being told permeate every line of text.
As Frank Cifaldi for the video-game blog *Kotaku* wrote in a May 14, 2014, review, "I
can't shake the feeling that despite the book having more than 200 interview subjects,
I'm missing another side of the story."

There is no shortage of interesting anecdotes and revelations in *Console Wars*. For
instance, Sonic the Hedgehog, familiar as a cute blue cartoon with a smirk, was originally conceived by Sega of Japan with fangs and wearing a leather jacket and having a
busty girlfriend. However, Harris ends up with a book that, in the words of *Telegraph*
reviewer Tim Martin, "feels hideously false." The Sonic-with-fangs image is intriguing, especially when one factors in the cultural divide between Japan and America, but
the entire anecdote is cast into doubt by the simple fact that readers have nothing more
than Harris's word to go on.

Harris's credibility is further strained by the baffling lack of criticism in his book. The people and companies Harris chronicles are guilty of all sorts of shady business practices, from Nintendo's borderline monopolistic business practices to high-stakes business betrayals to unrepentantly manipulative marketing aimed at children. Yet every person on either side of the Sega/Nintendo divide is portrayed as some kind of hero, their rivalry a noble war between honorable competitors. The closest Harris comes to ethical or philosophical nuance is when in the wake of his first major successes with Sega, Kalinske pauses to consider the implications of increased violence in video games. But this is quickly written off so that Kalinske can get back to battling Nintendo.

Similarly, Harris never lays out a case as to why the Sega/Nintendo/Sony rivalries are important. Perhaps this is due to Harris's intended readership. As he explained to Dave Tach for Polygon, "My ideal reader is my grandmother who is somebody who knows nothing about video games." Additionally, it is taken as a given that the origins of various video-game systems and the backroom antics of the companies that make them are a subject worthy of the reader's attention. One could argue that the massive size of the modern video-game industry, which is expected to exceed $13 billion in annual revenue by the end of 2015, is a good reason to pay attention to its history, but this basic point never seems to be made in Harris's book.

(© Katie Wanner)

*Console Wars is Blake J. Harris's first book. He is coproducing a documentary and feature-film adaptation of it for Sony Pictures. Prior to becoming a full-time writer and film producer, he was a commodities trader.*

The inescapable impression is that Harris is too much of a video-game fan and too close to his sources to provide a balanced account of what transpired; some ethical nuance and introspection would have bolstered the author's credibility and added dimension to a story that feels performed by cardboard cut-outs rather than actual people with flaws. As Suellentrop notes, Harris seems "too beholden to his sources" with Tom Kalinske rarely stumbling professionally, making a mistake, or acting "out of spite or anger." Furthermore, Harris tends to blame Sega's Japanese partners for the company's problems, while the American side of Sega is routinely absolved of any fault.

The problems with the book's credibility could be at least partially overlooked if the narrative of corporate espionage was better written. Unfortunately, Harris's account of an admittedly dramatic era in the video-game industry can at times be boring. Further, there is an overuse of clichés and failed attempts at humor or linguistic playfulness, as in the confusing mixed metaphor, "Getting straight answers out of [Sega president] Nakayama was like catching a shadow and pulling its teeth with a needle from a haystack."

Despite the book's problematic writing and lack of journalistic rigor, not all critics were completely put off by *Console Wars*. The technology-oriented magazine *Wired*, for example, published a May 13, 2014 review by Chris Kohler that praises Harris's "extensive access" and the "amount of research and dedication" to the topic. Cifaldi also praised *Console Wars* and expressed his belief that the book's "previously undisclosed information" would excite even "the most seasoned video game history buff" and that it is a worthy addition to the small-but-growing library of video-game industry histories, such as David Shef's *Game Over* (1994). Although Stephen T. Watson for the *Buffalo News* had several criticisms of the book, he ended his review thanking Harris for taking him back in time when "the only thing that mattered was getting to the next level."

Many critics commented that Harris's writing style and the novelesque feel of the prose would make, as Marc Levinson for the *Wall Street Journal* wrote, a better "screenplay than a credible work of nonfiction." In fact, Harris is codirecting a feature film and documentary based on the book. The film rights were bought by Sony Pictures before *Console Wars* was even published, and they have hired Seth Rogen and Evan Goldberg to adapt the screenplay and direct the film.

*Kenrick Vezina*

## Review Sources

Kohler, Chris. "The Untold Story of How Sega Nearly Won the Console Wars." Rev. of *Console Wars: Sega, Nintendo, and the Battle That Defined a Generation*, by Blake J. Harris. *Wired*. Condé Nast, 13 May 2014. Web. 12 Jan. 2015.

Levinson, Marc. Rev. of *Console Wars: Sega, Nintendo, and the Battle That Defined a Generation*, by Blake J. Harris. *Wall Street Journal*. Dow Jones, 23 May 2014. Web. 12 Jan. 2015.

Martin, Tim. "'Console Wars' by Blake Harris Feels Hideously False." Rev. of *Console Wars: Sega, Nintendo, and the Battle That Defined a Generation*, by Blake J. Harris. *Telegraph*. Telegraph Media Group, 2 Aug. 2014. Web. 12 Jan. 2015

Suellentrop, Chris. "Sega and Nintendo Wage Battle That Was No Game." Rev. of *Console Wars: Sega, Nintendo, and the Battle That Defined a Generation*, by Blake J. Harris. *New York Times*. New York Times, 18 May 2014. Web. 12 Jan. 2015.

Tach, Dave. "Why a Sega Kid Wrote 'Console Wars' for His Grandmother Based on 'Game of Thrones.'" Rev. of *Console Wars: Sega, Nintendo, and the Battle That Defined a Generation*, by Blake J. Harris. *Polygon*. VOX Media, 7 June 2014. Web. 28 Feb. 2015.

Watson, Stephen T. "Behind the Scenes at Nintendo, Sega in 'Console Wars.'" Rev. of *Console Wars: Sega, Nintendo, and the Battle That Defined a Generation*, by Blake J. Harris. *Buffalo News*. Buffalo News, 6 July 2014. Web. 28 Feb. 2015.

# Consumed

**Author:** David Cronenberg (b. 1943)
**Publisher:** Scribner (New York). 320 pp.
**Type of work:** Novel
**Time:** The early twenty-first century
**Locales:** France; Budapest, Hungary; To-kyo, Japan

*In filmmaker David Cronenberg's debut nov-el,* Consumed, *a couple of freelance cyber-journalists investigate a murder case that in-volves disease, cannibalism, and conspiracy.*

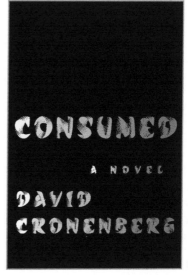

(Courtesy of Scribner)

**Principal characters:**

CÉLESTINE AROSTEGUY, a French philosopher who dies and is partially eaten

ARISTIDE AROSTEGUY, her husband, the French philosopher suspected of murder-ing and eating her

NAOMI SEBERG, an Internet journalist specializing in sensational crime, death, and bizarre subjects who is first drawn to the death of Célestine

NATHAN MATH, Naomi's romantic partner, a freelance photojournalist specializing on interesting medical conditions and aspiring to publish in the *New Yorker*

Celebrated film director David Cronenberg's debut novel *Consumed* centers on themes similar to those the director has explored in many of his films, including sexual devi-ancy, technology, human connectivity, and the relationship between media and mod-ern relationships. Cronenberg's experience in storytelling through films results in a highly descriptive writing style, and the author demonstrates a keen ability to delve into descriptions of the bizarre and grotesque with stunning realism. Cronenberg's de-but has other levels as well. It is a modern cyber noir, following amateur photo-sleuths as they stumble through a murder investigation, and an interesting documentation of the increasing tendency to intermix personal relationships with communication via Skype, e-mail, and text messaging. Cronenberg's novel is relatively simple in plot but complex in both characterization and descriptive detail, and his fascination with strange sexual, mechanical, and technological obsessions provides a fruitful landscape for a mystery that operates on multiple levels.

The central characters in Cronenberg's *Consumed* are the modern journalists Na-than Math and Naomi Seberg. As the narrative unfolds, told largely through Nathan and Naomi's observations, Cronenberg depicts them as a romantic couple, though much of their interaction takes place via telephone, Skype, and text messaging rath-er than in person. Nathan Math is a freelance photojournalist, fascinated by medical oddities and searching for one great story that will propel him from selling photos to second-rate magazines to the *New Yorker* medical annals. When the story begins, Cronenberg finds Nathan in Hungary conducting a bizarre interview with Dr. Zoltán Molnár, an imposter who has been conducting an experimental breast cancer treatment on a Slovenian woman, Dunja, and invites Nathan to photograph his procedure.

While Nathan is in Budapest, Naomi finds herself investigating the case of Célestine Arosteguy's death. A well-known celebrity philosopher, with avant-garde tastes and a passion for bizarre sex, Célestine is depicted as the American fantasy of an aging French postfeminist sex symbol. Through Naomi's descriptions, the reader learns that Célestine has died under mysterious circumstances and that some feel her husband, fellow philosopher Aristide Arosteguy, is the one responsible. Aristide has disappeared, and Naomi is in France attempting to get a meeting with him. It does not take long for Cronenberg's characteristic interest in explicit sexuality to overwhelm the novel. Within the first two chapters, both Nathan and Naomi have been wrapped up in seductive or overtly sexual encounters. Cronenberg's taste for the unusual is also on full display as Nathan's sexual interlude with Dunja features a pair of irradiated breasts and a discussion of the sexual appeal of death and cancer, and Naomi deals with sexual advances from a man with a strange, real-life disease that causes his penis to bend at a near right angle.

While most reviewers praised Cronenberg's skill with language and characterization, some reviewers noted that Cronenberg's world occasionally strains believability. Seemingly every character in *Consumed* is an intellectual, well versed in the Western canon of art, thought, and philosophy. Every person hides some deformity, obsession, or dark desire, and every encounter and conversation seems to be intended to delve into deeper philosophical or social issues. There is a complete lack of the normal in *Consumed*, which both plunges readers into his bizarre noir-erotica and simultaneously leaves the landscape bare, without the banal reflections that makes unusual things stand out from the background. Within the first few chapters, Cronenberg's characters discuss communism, sexuality, technological eroticism, and death. These are the kinds of questions that arise continually in conversations in which individual characters at times seem like vehicles for the artist's musings, rather than real people.

As the story progresses, Nathan and Naomi are predictably drawn together, their separate investigations converging on the same subject, the enigmatic sixty-something Arosteguys. As this occurs, Cronenberg's plot hinges on coincidence bordering on fatalism, thus giving the gritty crime drama a touch of magical realism or surrealism. Early in the novel, the behavior of his primary protagonists, Nathan and Naomi, also seems puzzling. Through a series of distant cybercommunications, readers learn that they love each other very much, and yet their love for one another is presented through conversation but not demonstrated through their behavior. When Nathan contracts an

> *David Cronenberg is a Canadian director who has directed more than two dozen feature-length films as well as shorts and television episodes. His films have won a variety of film society and festival awards, including an award at the Cannes Film Festival. He has also won two best director awards from the National Society of Film Critics. Consumed is Cronenberg's first novel.*

unusual venereal disease and then passes it on to Naomi, she is angry but accepting. The disease becomes a plot device, as Nathan tracks down the scientist who named and diagnosed it, and this eventually leads him back to Naomi. Both characters make decisions that seem childish, ill informed, compulsive, and simplistic, although, through conversations and their respective internal monologues, Cronenberg makes it clear that his heroes are intensely intelligent. The discussions of sex and perversion and the intertwined scenes that merge consumerism, eroticism, and fetishism are so pervasive that the interactions between Nathan and Naomi occasionally seem inhuman. Admiring reviewers saw this as part of Cronenberg's style and praised his unflinching ability to meld grotesque imagery with sexual and even romantic symbolism and sentiment.

As *Consumed* reaches the middle chapters, the mystery component of the story becomes a more important focus in the story. Repeatedly, Cronenberg utilizes the familiar cliffhanger plot device when moving from chapter to chapter, thus pulling readers deeper into the mystery. Unexpectedly, what begins as an examination of consumerism, art, sexuality, and eroticism takes on a political dimension as the protagonists become involved in a bizarre North Korean complication involving political subterfuge, communism, and cannibalism. Another motif involving entomology, larvae, and parasitism is also developed, seemingly drawing on various instinctively troubling images, which are then folded into the overarching sexually suggestive themes. Cronenberg's *Consumed* does not provide readers with a surprising "reveal" or "twist" to the mystery, and as readers learn what really happened to Célestine Arosteguy, it is clear that the relationships between the characters and their sometimes disjointed discussions of broader philosophical issues are the true focus of the story.

Reviewers were largely positive in writing about Cronenberg's debut novel, with some comparing his writing favorably to his most acclaimed films. In *Slate*, reviewer Karina Longworth compared the book to Cronenberg's 1982 film *Videodrome*, one of the artist's earliest films, and argued that Cronenberg has become an important pioneer of a visual (and now literary) genre that can be characterized as "body horror" or "embodiment dysmorphia." The theme of embodiment is discussed directly in the novel, especially in the way that Nathan and especially Naomi use technology to effect physical disembodiment and erect barriers between them and others in their environments. In the *New York Times*, reviewer Jonathan Lethem praised Cronenberg's "clinical curiosity" but remarked that the characters of Nathan and Naomi at times appear flat as Cronenberg does not allow them room to express any moral judgment regarding the behavior of any of the book's other characters, even when these characters engage in behavior that is morally ambiguous, if not objectionable. Writing for the *Independent*, reviewer Hannah McGill also noted Cronenberg's lack of character depth but praised his use of language, his absurd humor (as she sees it), and his skill in exploring the way that technology affects human relationships. In McGill's opinion, the book demonstrates how people's increasing interest in technological modes of connectivity comes from the human desire to "connect and create" and is not simply the result of an increasingly cynical and disconnected social landscape.

Fans of Cronenberg's films will find many of the director's characteristic themes and methods on display in *Consumed*. During his fifty years as a director, Cronenberg has often demonstrated his interest in exploring the confluence of culture, technology, and sexuality. He has also produced graphic and unsettling visions of horror and mutilation, such as *Scanners* (1981) and his adaptation of *The Fly* (1986). His 1996 film *Crash*, which received a special jury prize at that year's Cannes Film Festival, helped the director to achieve broader recognition as a leading modern filmmaker. In the 2000s, Cronenberg directed some of his most critically acclaimed and popular films, including the crime dramas *A History of Violence* (2005) and *Eastern Promises* (2007). Cronenberg's *Consumed* makes unflinching use of graphic sexuality and violence, and while the novel may prove too graphic or disturbing for some readers, it is fitting addition to the artist's canon and provides a fast-paced and gripping example of modern noir literature.

*Micah L. Issitt*

**Review Sources**

Lethem, Jonathan. "All Atwitter." Rev. of *Consumed*, by David Cronenberg. *New York Times*. New York Times, 26 Sept. 2014. Web. 6 Jan. 2015.

Longworth, Karina. "Bibliodrome" Rev. of *Consumed*, by David Cronenberg. *Slate*. Slate Group, 2014. Web. 6 Jan. 2015.

McGill, Hannan. "The Sunny Side of Geeky Perverts." Rev. of *Consumed*, by David Cronenberg. *Independent*. Independent Print, 16 Oct. 2014. Web. 6 Jan. 2015.

Poole, Steven. Rev. of *Consumed,* by David Cronenberg. *Guardian*. Guardian News and Media, 8 Oct. 2014. Web. 6 Jan. 2015.

Vishnevetsky, Ignatiy. Rev. of *Consumed*, by David Cronenberg. *Chicago Tribune*. Tribune Media, 24 Oct. 2014. Web. 6 Jan. 2015.

# Cubed
## A Secret History of the Workplace

**Author:** Nikil Saval
**Publisher:** Doubleday (New York). 368 pp.
**Type of work:** History
**Time:** 1600s to the present

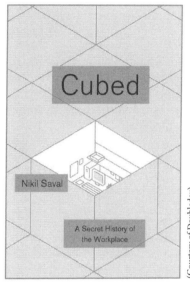

(Courtesy of Doubleday)

*Cubed examines the inextricable link between the growth of offices as places of business and the current condition of the white-collar worker. It traces the history of the office from its inception through the offices of the twenty-first century, ultimately questioning the meaning and role of work in contemporary society.*

At the most basic level, *Cubed: A Secret History of the Workplace* (2014) tells the story of the rise of the office worker in clear writing, based on exacting research. The paperwork once largely associated with the office can trace its origins back to the clerks of the 1700s, while the more modern concept of the office space itself can be attributed to the countinghouses that grew out of mercantile businesses in the nineteenth century. The first dramatic increase in clerical work came about as a result of the industrialization of Great Britain and the United States. The greater outputs by factories called for more paperwork, and clerks were employed because of their ability to produce this paperwork. Some would pass their days writing copies of important documents. Soon others would perform the role of bookkeeper. Rather than employing one partner and one clerk in a small space, the push was on to have many workers in a larger space.

From the new importance of clerks grew the need to "dress the part," leading to businesses such as Brooks Brothers. Soon there would be calls for shorter working days in order to have time for self-improvement. The white-collar worker was in much demand. The annual salary paid to these workers after a few years of service was higher than a blue-collar worker could ever hope to achieve.

*Cubed* goes on to document the advent of female workers and their role in the new workplaces. It follows the rise of the cubicle and gives recognition to architects such as Frank Lloyd Wright and Louis Sullivan, who strove to adapt the factory mentality to the office setting, making it palatable for those who labored within its walls. It traces the history of nonmanual labor through the era of time-management studies, the tumultuous 1980s, and the first decades of the twenty-first century, documenting the growth of freelance workers who call home or cafés their places of work.

In the introduction to *Cubed*, author Nikil Saval writes, "This book is inspired by and is an homage to C. Wright Mills's *White Collar,* a dyspeptic and classic work about the nonmanual worker at mid-century. Though I don't discuss this book in detail, its influence and ideas are everywhere." Since Saval makes it clear that Mills's book is essential to an understanding of his own work, it is worth the time to gain an understanding of *White Collar* (1951). At the same time, though Saval invokes Mills's name from the beginning, Jill Lepore, in her review for the *New Yorker*, is correct in pointing out that while Mills's approach was sociological, Saval has instead taken a primarily historical view.

According to Lepore, Mills found that those in the white-collar crowd "were so profoundly alienated from everything that mattered that they had no past, no politics, and no culture, and were so numbed by the paper-clipped pointlessness of their days that they had been anesthetized to their own alienation." Saval comments on this detachment as well, attributing a great deal of it to the delusional belief that, à la Horatio Alger, any man can make his way to the top with enough hard work. He notes that the first, smaller offices that involved employees working alongside employers fostered this outlook, frequently referenced in the book as a kind of cube-to-corner-office mentality, which has somehow persisted despite changes in the office setting. According to Saval, even as this career growth becomes less and less likely with the advent of the new office and workplace structures, white-collar workers hold it as a sacred tenet.

Saval's thorough examination of the social history of white-collar workers also makes reference to Herman Melville's "Bartleby, the Scrivener" (1853). In this short story, Bartleby joins his fellow clerks in working their lives away in a dimly lit, cramped countinghouse. All goes well until the boss asks Bartleby to do something other than write. He asks Bartleby to help compare two copies of a document. Bartleby does not flatly refuse; instead, he says, "I would prefer not to." Saval cites this well-known story as an example of the perverted atmosphere that has categorized the office and its workers from its very beginning, illustrated by Bartleby's hesitant behavior at a time when a clerk was considered "an unfamiliar figure, an inexplicable phenomenon" who did not fit into the familiar agricultural or factory roles. That identity crisis has only persisted as the office has continued to take on various forms over the decades.

In addition, Saval explores the connection between the workplace and the work itself. Putting the discussion into context with specific examples, he argues that while some companies may have begun to explore different office-building designs and services—including such corporations as the Larkin Company, which offered classes and a company newspaper for employees—the "monotony" that characterizes the work itself does not change. Saval links this reality once again to the industrial attitude engrained in early American culture that emphasized hierarchical routine as the best method for productivity. Ironically, the cubicle design itself started as an optimistic idea to make workers feel less like "a cog in a machine" and get them moving around, known as the Action Office. However, as Saval chronicles, this ambitious concept quickly succumbed to the old industrial mindset as well, easily morphing into the plain-walled cubes designed for maximum capacity found in the majority of contemporary offices.

Ultimately, Saval's work goes beyond a detailed history of work and the workplace. His book questions the enduring ethos and presumptions that underlie the very existence of the office and the work environments that have evolved as a consequence. Even the notion of freelance workers who consider themselves liberated from the corporate grind fall under his gaze. Will they ever join tighter in protest for better wages, or will they pursue their own self-interests while believing they are indeed free of the tyranny of the workplace?

This interesting question brings *Cubed* beyond a place in the history-of-the-workplace or the what-the-workplace-means-to-society genre and into a place of its own. Saval questions the ability of the white-collar worker to continue as the definition of the workplace changes, especially since the freelance life is a solitary one. He concludes that in some ways, shared workplaces for freelance workers are a form of social home for those who work away from an office. The difference here is that the workers are not united because they share a common employer; they are united because they share a common interest in or need for human interaction. If the modern office has moved beyond fulfilling that need and has instead become a place where workers labor in cubicles, cut off from one another and discouraged from any form of social interaction, what reason is there to show up in these offices in droves to live a life that is devoid of meaning?

The first step toward this dystopian view of the office was taken when artisans separated from their work and became shopkeepers who handled wares created by others. The next step was taken when businesses grew in complexity due to the advent of the railroad and the telephone, so that a partner could not realistically manage the day-to-day business with the help of only one or two trusted clerks. More clerks were needed, as well as bookkeepers, secretaries, and managers to oversee those workers. The net result was the specialization in tasks with attendant education for those positions, whether they be bookkeeper, accountant, secretary, marketing professional, or salesperson. Each step took the individual further away from a time when one's work had meaning and was worthy of the time invested in that work. What if the white-collar worker who designs buildings finds that work to be satisfying at a deeper level than "mere work"? What if the editors toiling in a café find the process of honing a piece for publication as integral to their happiness as the artisans of an earlier age found their process of creation?

*Nikil Saval worked as an editorial assistant at publishing companies before becoming an editor for the print and digital magazine* n+1. Cubed *is his first book.*

In the final analysis, *Cubed* is not only an impressive work with significant insights and a depth of research supporting the organized telling of a complicated history; it is also an invitation to question the very nature of work as it has come to be understood in the twenty-first century. It is understandable, based on the convoluted examples of the transformative yet paradoxically stagnant nature of the office and its workers presented and analyzed over many years, that Saval cannot offer a concrete solution to what he depicts as a flawed structure. Though this means that the book does not have a clear ending, as Richard Sennett notes in his review for the *New York Times*, at least "it is an honest one." With such a large percentage of the working world still confined to cubicles, critics agree that Saval has proved that it is worthwhile to consider where the office came from if there is ever going to be any hope for a satisfying alternative, whether devised by employers or by the workers themselves.

*Gina Hagler*

**Review Sources**

Filler, Martin. "The Road to the Zombie Office." Rev. of *Cubed: A Secret History of the Workplace*, by Nikil Saval. *New York Review of Books*. NYREV, 19 June 2014. Web. 24 Feb. 2015.

Howard, Jennifer. Rev. of *Cubed: A Secret History of the Workplace*, by Nikil Saval. *Washington Post*. Washington Post, 30 May 2014. Web. 24 Feb. 2015.

Lapidos, Juliet. "Why Do Our Offices Make Us So Miserable?" Rev. of *Cubed: A Secret History of the Workplace*, by Nikil Saval. *New Republic*. New Republic, 20 Apr. 2014. Web. 24 Feb. 2015.

Leith, Sam. Rev. of *Cubed: A Secret History of the Workplace*, by Nikil Saval. *Guardian*. Guardian News and Media, 3 July 2014. Web. 24 Feb. 2015.

Lepore, Jill. "Away from My Desk." Rev. of *Cubed: A Secret History of the Workplace*, by Nikil Saval. *New Yorker*. Condé Nast, 12 May 2014. Web. 24 Feb. 2015.

Sennett, Richard. "Office Max." Rev. of *Cubed: A Secret History of the Workplace*, by Nikil Saval. *New York Times Book Review* 15 June 2014: 11. Print.

# Deep Down Dark
## The Untold Stories of 33 Men Buried in a Chilean Mine and the Miracle That Set Them Free

**Author:** Héctor Tobar (b. 1963)
**Publisher:** Farrar, Straus and Giroux (New York). 320 pp.
**Type of work:** Current affairs
**Time:** 2010
**Locale:** San José Mine; Copiapó, Chile

Deep Down Dark *tells the exclusive story of the thirty-three men trapped 2,300 feet below ground for sixty-nine days after the collapse of the San José Mine in the Atacama Desert near Copiapó, Chile, on August 5, 2010.*

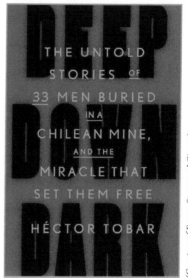

(Courtesy of Farrar, Straus and Giroux)

**Principal personages:**
MARÍO SEPÚLVEDA, a trapped miner who becomes a leader of the group.
MARÍA SEGOVIA, sister of trapped miner Darío Segovia; helps lead the victims' families
LUIS URZÚA, shift supervisor among the trapped miners
EDISON PEÑA, a trapped miner who becomes popular in the media
VÍCTOR SEGOVIA, a trapped miner who records events in a journal

On August 5, 2010, thirty-three men were trapped 2,300 feet underground when the San José Mine in Copiapó, Chile, collapsed. The owners of the mine had not kept the mine up to safety standards, and, the miners found themselves with grossly inadequate food and supplies. Even the chimneys that might have served as escape routes were of no use because they were not equipped with the required ladders. The men spent sixty-nine days below ground, the first seventeen of those without any contact from the outside world. While they were trapped and awaiting rescue, the thirty-three men pledged that they would not tell their stories individually. Instead, they would tell their story as a group, splitting any profits to be made from their miraculous story equally.

The miners collectively chose Pulitzer Prize–winning journalist Héctor Tobar to tell their story, and in May 2011, about seven months after the rescue, they met with him for the first time. While researching the story, Tobar would make five trips to Chile for hours of exclusive interviews with the miners and their families. *Deep Down Dark* is the book that resulted, and it presents the definitive account of "The 33," as the group became known.

In *Deep Down Dark*, Tobar begins by showing the miners each preparing for that fateful day, some leaving behind families they would not see again for weeks. The present-tense narration heightens the drama, effectively building tension despite the fact that the outcome is known in advance. The language used to describe the actual experience of the collapse is vivid, capturing the sense of terror as enormous slabs of rock fall and block the mine's only exit. The collapse, however, is only the beginning; the real story unfolds as the survivors take stock of and react to their situation.

*Héctor Tobar is an author and journalist whose work includes the nonfiction book* Translation Nation *(2005) and the novels* The Tattooed Soldier *(1998) and* The Barbarian Nurseries *(2011). He shares a 1993 Pulitzer Prize for coverage of the 1992 riots in Los Angeles.*

The first weeks are filled with a fear of being left to die in the dark. The men wonder how long it will take, how quickly they'll run out of food. The horrifying sound of further collapses is interspersed with deathly silence. Even when they hear what they hope is rescue drilling, the sound moves closer and closer only to turn away from reaching them. Each time the men are left to wonder if this was the last rescue effort, a maddening prospect.

The dynamics among the men are the heart of the story. The shift supervisor steps back, feeling his skills are inadequate for the problems they face, leaving the group leaderless until others step into certain roles. Among them are Mario Sepúlveda, who leads prayers and takes control of rationing the limited provisions, and Víctor Zamora, who relieves stress through humor. Still, tensions quickly erupt in the close confines of the mine, revealing the truly human side of the situation. Tobar shares some of the entries Víctor Segovia made in his journal, entries that include not only comments on his companions, but also notes on what they are doing to survive. This knowledge of the men's routines while trapped, before the possibility of rescue was a fact, establishes the sense of desperation felt by those living underground while sealed off from the outside world.

Tobar describes the hot, utterly dark living conditions a half mile underground. Again, differences in personalities become quickly apparent. Some men actively attempt to escape or send some signal to the surface that they are alive. Others prefer to conserve their strength and limited food supply and simply wait. Some men sleep in the Refuge, the area where provisions are stored, while others choose to sleep in the trucks some distance away. The reader learns to recognize each man by the short bit of biography that is given: the man with a wife and a girlfriend up top, the man who is awaiting the birth of a child, the man who was in the mine for the very first time, and so on. Each of these brief descriptions also serves to give the reader an emotional connection to each of the men, illustrating what they were like before they descended into the mine that day and how the experience changes them.

Tobar also provides the reader with a thorough view of the events outside the mine. A tent community is created just outside the mine compound's gates, where the families of the miners wait to learn whether their loved ones are dead or alive. Many of the families traveled hundreds of miles and are determined to stay until the fate of the men is learned; the community gains the name "Camp Hope." They are there so long that eventually school classes are held for the children. María Segovia becomes the "mayor" of the town through her natural leadership in insisting that everything must be done to save her brother, Darío, and the others. From even before it is known if the men are alive until the moment they are freed, she does not let up her pressure on mine or government officials. Ultimately, Chile's minister of mines takes to joining her for tea and frank discussion.

Tobar paints a full picture of the politics of the situation as well. The miners find themselves in their predicament due to the lack of effective oversight of the mine. The operators have shirked their responsibility to keep up with the latest safety requirements, and the accident ignites a storm of negative media attention. Government officials, too, are criticized for their role in the collapse. But the story turns positive as seemingly all of Chile rallies to overcome the challenges of the rescue effort and prevent a national tragedy. The minister of mining, Laurence Golborne, is involved from the start. Once he receives positive press, other government officials, including the president of Chile, make sure to be on site.

There is an international component to the rescue as well, with drilling equipment and expertise offered by countries with those capabilities and media attention from around the world. Despite the cooperation, it takes enormous resources and an excruciating seventeen days just to make contact with the trapped miners. Even NASA takes on an advisory role, and consults on how to communicate with and send supplies to the men once it is established that they are alive. Various experts debate on decisions ranging from how to introduce solid foods to how much and how soon to expose the men directly to the media. And it is when the miners are given access to the media frenzy aboveground that they decide the only way to settle their fights over the rights to their own story is to commit to telling it as one.

Keeping track of the stories of thirty-three men is a daunting task. Tobar not only gives each miner a shorthand identity for the reader to recognize, he interweaves each man's experience in order to give the reader a comprehensive experience of the ordeal. Each day of captivity scratches away at the bravado and fortitude of the men, even after the threat of starvation is removed and they are provided access to luxuries like television. Some turn to religion. Some turn inward. Some work hard to do whatever is necessary, while others sit defeated and overwhelmed. The psychological damage lasts well after the rescue, too, and Tobar is careful to explore the lingering effects of the trauma on some of the miners.

The main emotional tide of the book is so closely focused on the time spent in the claustrophobic confines of the mine during those days when contact with the surface was uncertain that when the men are finally taken above ground and reunited with their families, it is almost anticlimactic. The part of the story that defies expectation is that all thirty-three men managed to survive the fungus that grew on them, the incessant darkness and noise of tumbling rock that surrounded them, the gnawing uncertainty about their survival, and the inadequate nutrition they received. Equally miraculous is the ability of the drillers to reach the exact point they aimed for while drilling through layers of rock with inaccurate maps.

In many ways, *Deep Down Dark* tells a story with an ending that is known by all. The media attention to the miners' plight meant that every detail was reported during the event, often many times over. Yet the reporting that was done at the time could not possibly tell the stories of the individual men and their collective experience while trapped below ground. Even in the limited interviews after their rescue, the miners gave no details about the days before contact with the surface. Because of the pact the men made and honored, Tobar's work is the only way to know what escaped the attention of live coverage of the accident and rescue. All of the events in the book are true, yet they are relayed to the reader in a narrative form. In this case, the narrative creates the tension that drives the reader through page after page, wondering along with the men when and if help will arrive.

*Deep Down Dark* was widely praised by critics as a worthy addition to the ranks of narrative nonfiction. Many reviewers noted the evenhanded way the book tells the story of each of the thirty-three men. As Noah Gallagher Shannon wrote in his review for the *Washington Post*, "There's no unified story of survival, Tobar seems to be saying, only each man's story." Others commented on the fascinating way in which Tobar explores the role of the media in the story, with the dilemma of being trapped with only a narrow connection to the outside world reflecting the ways in which modern media impacts the life of even the most insulated individuals. Critics also enjoyed Tobar's rich language and evocative description.

Ultimately, Tobar's work is the tale of gripping survival with a deeply human touch. Scott Wallace summed it up in his review for the Los Angeles Times: "Tobar delivers a masterful account of exile and human longing, of triumph in the face of all odds. Taut with suspense and moments of tenderness and replete with a cast of unforgettable characters, *Deep Down Dark* ranks with the best of adventure literature."

*Gina Hagler*

## Review Sources

McClelland, Mac. Rev. of *Deep Down Dark*, by Héctor Tobar. *New York Times*. New York Times, 20 Nov. 2014. Web. 18 Feb. 2015.

Shannon, Noah Gallagher. "Rev. of *Deep Down Dark*, by Héctor Tobar. *Washington Post*. Washington Post, 20 Nov. 2014. Web. 18 Feb. 2015.

Smith, Wendy. Rev. of *Deep Down Dark*, by Héctor Tobar. *Boston Globe*. Globe Media Partners, 20 Oct. 2014. Web. 18 Feb. 2015.

Wallace, Scott. "Hector Tobar's 'Deep Down Dark' Chronicles Chile's Mine-Shaft Miracle." Rev of *Deep Down Dark*, by Héctor Tobar. *LA Times*. Los Angeles Times, 2 Oct. 2014. Web. 18 Feb. 2015.

# Dept. of Speculation

**Author:** Jenny Offill (b. 1968)
**Publisher:** Alfred A. Knopf (New York).
192 pp.
**Type of work:** Novel
**Time:** Present
**Locale:** Brooklyn, New York

*Jenny Offill's second novel—her first in fif-teen years—employs a breezy, yet arresting fragmented structure to illustrate love, mar-riage, parenthood, and infidelity.*

(Courtesy of Knopf)

**Principal characters:**
WIFE, the book's narrator and protagonist, a self-avowed "art monster" who eschews personal relationships in favor of writing but inevitably falls in love, marries, and has a daughter
HUSBAND, her husband, a sound artist who takes a better-paying job in advertising to support the family
DAUGHTER, their child, intelligent and beguiling

*Dept. of Speculation*, the sophomore novel by Jenny Offill, follows the shifting tides of an intimate relationship from courtship to early marriage to parenthood and through infidelity in "curious, often shimmering fragments of prose," as the novelist Roxane Gay wrote for the *New York Times*. The slim volume—only 192 pages—took Offill nearly a decade to write but moves with a swiftness that belies its arduous birth. Each paragraph, set apart from those that surround it, contributes to a larger tale about love, marriage, parenthood, and infidelity. If there is a larger plot (one kicks into gear near the end) it is disillusionment, or perhaps, coming to terms with the inevitable imper-fection, the innate unrealized-ness of career, family or simply being alive.

Offill published her first novel, *Last Things*, a coming-of-age tale, in 1999. The book was well-received, and in her own life, Offill married and had a daughter. She began writing a second book—what would become *Dept. of Speculation*—shortly af-ter her first. In its earliest iteration, the novel, composed in a more traditional, linear structure, was about a second marriage and was told from the points of view of a daughter and the second wife. Later, Offill told Angela Ashman in a January 29, 2014, interview for the *Village Voice*, that though she is admittedly a "really slow writer," she could not figure out why her second novel just "wouldn't catch fire." It was not until Offill began taking notes for the book on index cards that she discovered the novel's true structure: disparate moments coalescing and transforming to capture a life in the process of being lived. In one of the book's first fragments, Offill describes this form perfectly while talking about memory. "Memories are microscopic," she writes. "Tiny particles that swarm together and apart. Little people, Edison called them. Entities."

*Dept. of Speculation*, which features an unnamed writer protagonist a bit like Offill herself, opens as the narrator has just finished her well-received first novel. Her voice immediately establishes itself as sardonic and occasionally bleak, if only winkingly so, as if to assure the reader that she understands the inherent absurdity of everything. Still, she recounts her early years (likely her mid-to-late-twenties, though this is never made explicit) with a tender, and perhaps longing, sense of her own earnestness. Later, when she is older, more cynical, and even unhappy, she is still acutely aware of unexpected moments of joy, most of which comes from her daughter. In the beginning, the young narrator vows to become an "art monster." She places a sticky note above her writing desk that reads, "WORK NOT LOVE!" Still, inevitably, she does fall in love. The man is a sound artist, and when she meets him he is recording soundscapes of New York City. (The novel is set in Brooklyn; the borough and New York City as a whole are integral to the story.) Their courtship, at least as it appears in Offill's prose, is a short one. He proposes in the gem room at the natural history museum.

As their relationship changes from the particular intoxication of early love ("You called me. I called you. *Come over, come over*, we said.") to the easy intimacy of marriage ("My husband clears the table.") to his ultimate betrayal ("The husband and wife walk in the other direction."), Offill's pronouns change. The effect is surprisingly visceral, though its focus on the husband, particularly at the end, comes at the expense of the couple's daughter who, as Gay rightly noted, is the book's most interesting character. She is born after Offill's narrator suffers a miscarriage. In some ways, the birth of the child renders her child-like as well, and the now-transformed earnestness of her youth returns to her. Early in the novel, the narrator orders a steak at a fancy restaurant in Paris. It arrives raw and she is unable to eat it. Embarrassed, she hollows out a bread roll, stuffs the meat inside and secrets the rolls in her purse. She is surprised when she leaves the restaurant and no one stops her at the door. After her daughter is born, she writes: "I remember the first time I said the word to a stranger. 'It's for my daughter,' I said. My heart was beating too fast, as if I might be arrested."

Her feelings toward her child are expansive and complex. In their totality they form a genuinely stunning portrait of motherhood. The girl herself, as Gay notes, is "precocious without being cloying, moderate with her affection, deliberate in her ways." Like her mother might have been, the unnamed baby is born "at war with the world," Offill writes, but as she grows, makes peace with it as she discovers the fluorescent lights at the Rite-Aid drugstore, the sound of a garden hose, and balls of all shapes and sizes, including the moon. Both husband and wife delight in the child's budding personality. As with all new parents, her every discovery and game delights them. Describing the child as a toddler, Offill writes, "'Babies, babies,' she mutters darkly as she covers [her stuffed animals] with white napkins. 'Civil War Battlefield,' we call it."

Fragments with the daughter are surprising, funny, and occasionally poignant. In one, when the girl is six, she writes a note back to her mother scrawled over the one that the narrator has placed in her lunchbox. "Stop writing I love you," it says. The narrator compares the sudden and overwhelming feeling the note gives her to a sudden break-up. Comparatively, the fragments involving the husband are less evocative. He is nice. He is from Ohio. He fixes things when they are broken. He appears in one dimension, it is only the narrator's feelings *about* him that are complex. When he cheats on her, she is genuinely blindsided, and though readers may care little about the man, the emotional fallout from the revelation is described in terms that are occasionally stunningly truthful. The wife's deep hurt and anger are as cutting as they are impotent. She looks to yoga, half-heartedly contemplates contacting an old boyfriend, and then gets a new haircut and a new outfit to visit her husband at his office. Her rage has no outlet until she asks to see the other woman in front of her husband's workplace. It is the only scene that rejects the fragmented structure of the novel; it takes place over the course of three pages in continuing sequence. The clichéd nature of the meeting infuriates her—"She

(© Michael Lionstar)

*Jenny Offill's first novel,* Last Things, *was published to critical acclaim in 1999. Dept.* of Speculation, *published fifteen years later, is her second novel. The* New York Times *named it one of their top ten books of 2014.*

would not have let one of her students write the scene this way," she begins. She rages in the pouring rain. She kicks a newspaper stand and screams at her husband to present the other woman to her. She tells the woman things, but we do not know what. Offill seems to realize that this detail in unimportant. But the novel has some difficulty absorbing such a large plot point into its fragile structure. Offill lets the affair take center stage (as, it must be supposed, such a life-changing incident naturally would) but at the expense of the delicate observations she has so carefully laid out. The pronouns shift with the husband's infidelity, but so does the book itself; it becomes a different novel, one that seems bent on providing some kind of finite resolution.

    Throughout the book, Offill's narrator works as a college writing professor and also as a ghostwriter for a pompous almost-astronaut and businessman who wants to write a book about the history of the space program. The novel already includes random tidbits (see the Edison anecdote above), but the jobs allows her to draw upon a wealth of scientific facts and, of course, the story of Carl Sagan, the astrophysicist and beloved host of the television program *Cosmos*, and his extramarital affair with Ann Druyan, who would become his second wife. Thus, personal observations are suffused with odd bits of trivia—about Buddhism, about the Voyager spacecraft, about poets and proverbs. Some, within the cascading nature of the novel's prose, hit their mark, while others are vaguely irritating, as if, Gay noted, simply invoking a subject's breadth is enough to lend emotional weight the narrative itself. *Dept. of Speculation* is a pleasingly breezy work of literary fiction, which is not to say that it is not intermittently brilliant, some fragments landing squarely in the solar plexus. But Offill is at her best when she allows herself to find something startling in the most ordinary observations. Her narrator, for instance, is an unmistakable member a very specific, yuppyish class of Brooklynites that she distances herself from and embraces in equal measure. In one fragment she writes: "How has she become one of those people who wears yoga pants all day? She used to make fun of those people. . . . The truth about getting older is that there are fewer and fewer things to make fun of until finally there is nothing you are sure you will never be."

*Molly Hagan*

## Review Sources

Blair, Elaine. "The Smallest Possible Disaster." Rev. of *Dept. of Speculation*, by Jenny Offill. *New York Review of Books*. NYREV, 24 Apr. 2014. Web. 7 Jan. 2015.

Gay, Roxane. "Bridled Vows." Rev. of *Dept. of Speculation*, by Jenny Offill. *New York Times*. New York Times, 7 Feb. 2014. Web. 7 Jan. 2015.

Wolitzer, Meg. "'Speculation' Shows Good Stories Come in Small Packages, Too." Rev. of *Dept. of Speculation*, by Jenny Offill. *All Things Considered*. NPR, 23 Jan. 2014. Web. 5 Feb. 2015.

Wood, James. "Mother Courage." Rev. of *Dept. of Speculation*, by Jenny Offill. *New Yorker*. Condé Nast, 31 Mar. 2014. Web. 7 Jan. 2015.

# The Dog

**Author:** Joseph O'Neill (b. 1964)
**Publisher:** Pantheon Books (New York).
256 pp.
**Type of work:** Novel
**Time:** 2007 to the present
**Locale:** New York City; Dubai

*In Joseph O'Neill's strange yet affecting new novel, an unnamed New York lawyer struggles with persistent guilt as he navigates the ambiguities of Dubai.*

**Principle characters:**

UNNAMED PROTAGONIST also known as X, a New York City lawyer who takes a position working for the billionaire family of an old college buddy in Dubai

OLLIE CHRISTAKOS, his friend

TED WILSON, also known as THE MAN FROM ATLANTIS, his fellow American expatriate and a scuba diver

EDDIE BATROS, the narrator's old college buddy, a Lebanese billionaire

SANDRO BATROS, Eddie's older brother

ALAIN BATROS, Sandro's teenage son

JENN, the narrator's ex-girlfriend

(Courtesy of Pantheon)

A coastal city located in the United Arab Emirates, Dubai rises like a mirage out of the Middle Eastern desert. Dubai is home to the tallest skyscraper in the world, the Burj Khalifa, and also to one of the world's largest shopping malls, the Mall of the Emirates, which contains an indoor ski center called Ski Dubai. Off of the coast floats "The World," a man-made archipelago constructed to look like a map of the earth. Dubai is a city of extremes: extreme heat, extreme pleasure, and wealth beyond one's wildest imagination. "The city that launched a thousand magazine features was presented to Westerners as many things: Rich, strange, tacky, threatening," Daniel Brook wrote in his 2013 book *A History of Future Cities*, excerpted on the website *Next City*. "But most of all, it was presented as new." New as in clean and untainted, but also "new" as in a place where it is impossible to leave one's mark, to give any indication at all that one has been there. Nobody is more familiar with this concept of newness as it applies to Dubai than Joseph O'Neill's nameless narrator, X, in his arresting new novel, *The Dog*.

O'Neill, an Irish Turkish novelist, won the PEN/Faulkner Award for his first novel *Netherland* (2008) in 2009. If *Netherland* was a rich construction of "nowness" for the early aughts, *The Dog* could be its neurotic counterpart, taking place in the constant present of the pre-recession years. Life is one long upswing for the high-rise residents of Privilege Bay, among them the "Uncompromising Few" at the Situation high-rise apartment building, the "Dreamers of New Dreams" at the Aspiration, and the "Pioneers of Luxury" at the Statement. O'Neill's narrator, a lawyer from New York City, joins the ranks of the Uncompromising Few after accepting a position as a trustee for the extremely wealthy Batros family. He went to college with Eddie Batros, who now oversees a global conglomerate with his father. The details of the enterprise are sketchy, but O'Neill's narrator trusts Eddie on the basis of one fondly remembered study abroad trip to Dublin.

In early 2007, the two men reunite and Eddie puts him in touch with his older brother in Dubai. Sandro Batros is blustery, stupid, and obese. He lacks the charm of his father and the intelligence of his younger brother—the Batroses require someone to look after the family finances, but also to keep Sandro (and his money-grubbing wife) in check. The narrator warms to the idea of leaving New York City, a place in which he no longer counts a single human attachment. Thus—though not without tribulations— the narrator breaks free from the man he once was, rising, ghostlike from the ashes of a nasty breakup and becoming conversant in the language of luxury. He is given a fresh start, but loses his identity in the process.

O'Neill's protagonist, who is referred to as X, which stands for the first letter of his first given name (an "unutterable" word, X says, after a Swiss great uncle), is an extremely verbose narrator. To successfully convey X's perturbed and culpable state of mind, O'Neill has strategically crafted a defined voice for his antiheroic main character. In his review of the book for the *New York Times*, Lawrence Osborne described the story as "narrated in a deliberately pedantic and exasperated voice." At the same time, the extent of the application of this narrative technique throughout the book has drawn criticism from some reviewers who feel that it becomes too tedious. X's prose is peppered with legalese and extended parentheticals. He speaks and thinks like a man on trial. In his asides, he strains to absolve himself of guilt—for watching Internet porn, for relying on Dubai's underpaid server class, or for breaking up with his New York girlfriend, Jenn, when they were trying to have a baby. At his job, he orders a set of custom-made stamps that say something to the effect that while he has, in fact, signed said legal document, he is not bound by what it says. Osborne wrote, "'The Dog' is an enactment of the Western mind's obsessive moral legalism and guilt-parsing, while trying constantly to get the guilt off its shoulders."

(Courtesy of the author)

*Joseph O'Neill is a writer of Irish Turkish descent. His first novel,* Netherland, *won the 2009 PEN/Faulkner Award for fiction. Raised in Holland, O'Neill and his family reside in New York City.*

Perhaps, but it would be fair to say that X possesses that very American trait in excess. In one passage, he vows to never form a serious romantic relationship ever again. In the place of romance he has, he reasons, a luxury massage chair—the coveted Pasha Royale X400™—and a personalized escort service. "This must be doable," X proclaims. "It may be that most lives add up, in the end, to the sum of the mistakes that cannot be corrected. But I have to believe there's a way for everyman (the masculine includes the feminine) to avoid the following epitaph: Here lies [everyman]. On balance, he did harm." In Charles Dickens's *A Christmas Carol*, Ebeneezer Scrooge's dead partner, Jacob Marley, is forced to wander the earth as a spirit clad in chains, each link forged by an ill deed he committed in life. X does his best to shed his own chains not in action, but in labyrinthine passages that double back on themselves, modifying and digressing before evaporating altogether.

X's guiltless foil is a man named Ted Wilson, a fellow American expat who is known among divers as the "Man from Atlantis." X, and his only friend, Ollie Christakos, are also divers. X enjoys the weightlessness of the deep sea diving. In *The Dog*'s opening sentence, he muses:

> Perhaps because of my growing sense of the inefficiency of life lived on land and in air, of my growing sense that the accumulation of experience amounts, when all is said and done and pondered, simply to extra weight, so that one ends up dragging oneself around as if imprisoned in one of those Winnie the Pooh suits of explorers of the deep, I took up diving.

X and Ollie enjoy the solitude of diving together. Ted, on the other hand, dives alone—which is incredibly dangerous—flitting in and out of the waves with the ease of his namesake, an aquatic superhero. In the book's first pages, Ollie catches a glimpse of Ted and speaks of the sighting as if he had seen a rare animal or the Loch Ness monster. X reports that there is even a website that tracks sightings of Ted.

Ted, as X says early on, is equally at home in the water (if not more so) as he is on land. His aquatic affinities are mirrored in his personal life—or lives, as readers later learn. When Ted goes missing, it is discovered that he has been leading a double life. This accusation is never proven, though Ted's life is the source of much speculation in the book. In fact, as X writes almost enviously, "It's one thing to offer intrusive conjecture about a person's recreational activities, another thing to place a person into a machine for grinding by crushing. This happened to Ted Wilson. He was discussed into dust." Regardless, Ted's successful disappearing act absolves him from the deeds he committed as the person he once was; X has moved halfway around the world to escape his past, but he is not so lucky.

The dynamic between the two men is another one of the book's riffs on authenticity and reality. Dubai is perhaps one of the most inauthentic (and surreal) places on the planet—in league with Las Vegas or Disney World—with its man-made islands and ski slopes. Very little that exists in the city is organic to the landscape, just as almost no one who lives in Dubai is actually from Dubai. Near the book's end, X takes Alain

Batros, Sandro's spoiled teenage son who has been forced to work as X's useless intern, on a field trip to a museum called the Al Fahidi Fort. The fort was built in the late eighteenth century and is officially known as the oldest structure in Dubai. This fact is telling, given the region's ancient history.

The fort, X says, is the "real deal, if by realness we mean oldness." Approaching the façade, X imagines Arab warriors emerging from the desert sand on horseback. "What can I say about what happens next?" he writes, woefully. Instead of living history, X and his charge are confronted by a flock of stuffed flamingos hanging from the ceiling, a strange and ill-sized diorama on par with the out-of-date window scenes of ancient peoples at the American Natural History Museum in New York City, valuable more for their kitsch than their accuracy. Another display features an ancient pearl diver reaching for an ancient seabed. X hesitates, trying to reconcile Dubai's claim that the city was once the pearl-diving capital of the world with the fact that, in his own diving excursions, he has never seen a single oyster. "I'm minded to say something to the kid about the historic context of this diver," X explains. "It's a lost cause, however, because one doesn't know what the cause is. Who can really know what actually happened and what one is to make of it all?"

*Molly Hagan*

## Review Sources

Acker Shah, Jennifer. "The Abracadabrapolis." Rev. of *The Dog*, by Joseph O'Neill. *Slate*. Slate, 10 Sept. 2014. 28 Jan. 2015.

Forbes, Malcolm. "'The Dog,' by Joseph O'Neill: Review." Rev. of *The Dog*, by Joseph O'Neill. *San Francisco Chronicle*. Hearst Communications, 22 Dec. 2014. Web. 28 Jan. 2015.

McAlpin, Heller. 'The Dog': Dubious Dealings in Dubai." Rev. of *The Dog*, by Joseph O'Neill. *NPR*. Natl. Public Radio, 13 Sept. 2014. Web. 28 Jan. 2015.

Osborne, Lawrence. "Time Out Dubai." Rev. of *The Dog*, by Joseph O'Neill. *New York Times Sunday Book Review*. New York Times, 4 Sept. 2014. Web. 28 Jan. 2015.

# Duty
## Memoirs of a Secretary at War

**Author:** Robert M. Gates
**Publisher:** Alfred A. Knopf (New York).
618 pp.
**Type of work:** Political memoir
**Time:** Fall 2005 to summer 2011
**Locale:** Washington, DC

Duty *presents an insider's look at the Department of Defense under two different presidents, from different parties, during a time of constant international conflict. American troops were at war in either Iraq or Afghanistan (and at times both) during Robert Gates's entire tenure as secretary of defense.*

**Principal personages:**
ROBERT M. GATES, US secretary of defense
from December 2006 to July 2011
GEORGE W. BUSH, forty-third president of the United States
DICK CHENEY, vice president under Bush
BARACK OBAMA, forty-fourth president of the United States
JOE BIDEN, vice president under Obama
HILLARY CLINTON, secretary of state during Obama's first administration

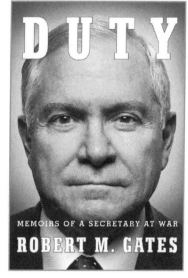

(Courtesy of Knopf)

Robert M. Gates is the only secretary of defense to be asked to stay on in that position by an incoming administration—a fact made more remarkable because the outgoing president was of one party and the incoming administration of another. Gates joined the administration of George W. Bush in December 2006, and when Barack Obama was elected in November 2008, Obama asked Gates to stay on and be a part of his administration. Gates left Obama's cabinet in July 2011. This insider memoir is especially significant because Gates served two presidents who were very different, and Obama was still in office when this book was published. Before serving as secretary of defense, Gates had served in various capacities in six previous presidential administrations, going back to Richard Nixon's presidency—usually dealing with foreign policy, national security, or intelligence issues. Because Gates pulled no punches when describing his problems and disagreements with those with whom he worked, this book was greeted with much interest by journalists, historians, political scientists, and pundits when it appeared early in 2014.

After the terrorist attacks on the United States on September 11, 2001, President George W. Bush launched a war against Iraq, which was thought to be one of the major sponsors of terrorism against the Western world. While the military defeat of the Iraqi army was accomplished quickly, many Americans became disillusioned with the war as the mission turned into a long-term occupation and an exercise in "nation building." In response to public backlash against the war, Bush's first secretary of defense, Donald Rumsfeld, resigned, and Bush asked Gates to consider taking the job. Although Gates was happy in his position as president of Texas A & M University, he believed—as the book title suggests—he had a duty to respond if US military personnel were fighting and the president requested him to lead the Department of Defense.

In his four-and-a-half years as secretary of defense, Gates was primarily occupied with the ongoing wars in Iraq and Afghanistan, and he notes in his introduction that these conflicts are what the bulk of this book covers. Iraq was the primary focus during his time serving under Bush, and Afghanistan during his time in Obama's cabinet. Gates repeatedly emphasizes his determination to do what was right for the US troops fighting in these wars—seeing they had the proper supplies, dealing with the problems of extended tours and numerous rotations overseas for career personnel, and ensuring proper care for wounded veterans. He found that in pursing these matters, he was often at war with the entrenched civilian bureaucracy of the Pentagon. Gates argues that both the high-ranking military officers and the highly placed civilian employees in the Defense Department are often so intent on fighting the next war—planning for and trying to secure funding for advanced weapon systems that might be needed in a major powers conflict in the future—that they ignore the immediate needs of the troops fighting a different kind of war in the present. In this context, he describes his efforts to get a new type of vehicle supplied to the frontline troops fighting in Iraq—the mine resistant ambush protected (MRAP) vehicle. Although prototypes had been developed for this vehicle, Gates found it difficult to persuade either civilian bureaucrats or high-ranking military officers of the pressing need for it. Bucking the bureaucracy, Gates pushed to see that thousands of these vehicles were produced as soon as possible and sent to the troops who needed them.

Gates also often found himself fighting Congress. During Bush's presidency, Democrats in Congress wanted to end the war in Iraq and often tried to block bills to fund the effort. On the other hand, no matter how antiwar any member of Congress, from either party, might appear to be, the defense industries in his or her home state or congressional district are nevertheless sacrosanct and off-limits for any proposed cuts. Besides fighting the members of Congress who opposed particular policy decisions or the funding of certain programs, Gates was also frustrated with the dysfunctional nature of Congress during the highly partisan years during which he served. In his six years in office, he notes, Congress never passed a budget, so the funding for the Pentagon was pieced together a bit at a time by the continuing resolutions Congress used to fund the government.

Although Iraq and Afghanistan were two different kinds of wars with varied issues involved, Gates came into the Bush cabinet at a time when an increase in the number of US forces in Iraq was being debated (and was eventually adopted), and in the early part of Obama's administration, President Obama became convinced, against his own preferences, that a temporary increase in the US military presence in Afghanistan was also needed. Gates chronicles in detail the debates within the White House, and between the White House and the military, that went into both of these decisions.

Little of what Gates describes here is truly surprising—most readers probably take it for granted that getting entrenched bureaucracies to think differently, or to act at all, is a monumental task. Likewise, the fact that a department secretary would have disagreements with Congress is also largely to be expected. What is perhaps most valuable in Gates's memoir is the rare chance of seeing a cabinet secretary working with two very different presidents—men with different personalities, different political philosophies, and different political constituencies. Gates was at times at odds with both presidents. Because of his background working in several Republican White Houses, including President George H. W. Bush's administration, Gates admits that he was more often in agreement with George W. Bush and had more clashes with Obama. Yet his memoir is not simply an exercise in describing how the Republicans were generally right and the Democrats usually wrong. Gates critically analyzes the strengths and weaknesses of both presidents, and says both Bush and Obama always treated him professionally and courteously, even when they disagreed with him. Neither ever made opposition on issues into a personal matter. Somewhat surprisingly, Gates also notes that he was often in agreement with Hillary Clinton, who served as secretary of state under Obama. In the Bush administration, Gates notes that he, Secretary of State Condoleezza Rice, and National Security director Stephen Hadley often made common cause, supporting Bush's ideas, with Vice President Cheney being the "outlier" who advanced contrary opinions.

Even before Obama won the Democratic nomination in 2008, there were rumors that whether a Republican or Democrat won the election that year, Gates might be asked to remain in his position, to provide some sense of continuity in the handling of the wars in Iraq and Afghanistan. Gates denies any desire to stay on and says that his strategy was to make it so clear he was ready to leave that no one would conceive of asking him to stay. But when Obama did make the offer, the same sense of duty that compelled Gates to take the job in the first place impelled him to accept.

*Robert M. Gates served under eight US presidents, most notably as CIA head under George H. W. Bush and secretary of defense under George W. Bush and Barack Obama. He published a memoir of his earlier career in 1996:* From the Shadows: The Ultimate Insider's Story of Five Presidents and How They Won the Cold War.

Although the wars in Iraq and Afghanistan constituted the greatest crises that Gates faced in his time at the Pentagon, other issues also demanded much attention. Obama was determined to end the military's ban on homosexuals openly serving in the armed forces, and while Gates agreed with him on this issue, most of the military leadership did not. Gates faced a serious battle in convincing the chiefs of staff and other high-ranking officers that the change was a wise one. Since Obama came into office in the midst of a serious economic downturn, budgetary issues were also a constant battle for Gates. He was repeatedly asked to find more cuts in the Pentagon's budget even while the nation was at war. Several times Gates also refers to the ongoing nature of modern international crises—they are never permanently settled. While the United States has never gotten into an open military conflict with Iran, every president since Jimmy Carter has had to deal with that nation in a near-crisis mode. While the Cold War has ended, concern about Russia's intentions and the relationship between Moscow and Ukraine or Georgia remains. International defense and foreign policy issues do not come and go, Gates says—they come and stay.

Critical reception of *Duty* has been mixed. Memoirs of officials involved in positions of great responsibility in times of crisis and controversy will always be suspected of a self-serving intent to justify the author's actions. Many critics have noted that Gates criticizes both Bush, with whom he more often agreed, and Obama, with whom he had more disagreements. Yet he praises both on some matters, and seems to be judicious in his criticism. Gates expresses throughout the book that his love and concern for the men and women who fought for the United States were virtually the only things that kept him going in this job, and few reviewers seem to doubt the sincerity of these feelings. Parts of the book seem repetitive—and sometimes the same events are described in more than one context—but the repetitiveness and the wearisome rendition of endless cycles of meetings and briefings and reports may actually capture something about the nature of bureaucratic work, even for those at the level of cabinet secretary. Some have noted that a tell-all book of this nature may mean that Gates is unlikely to be called upon to serve in any future administration, but the reader gets the distinct impression that Gates is certainly not anxious to reenter the fray.

*Mark S. Joy, PhD*

**Review Sources**

Bose, Meena. Rev. of *Duty: Memoirs of a Secretary at War*, by Robert M. Gates. *Presidential Studies Quarterly* (2014): 563–64. Print.

Herman, Arthur. "Two Leaders Judged." Rev. of *Duty: Memoirs of a Secretary at War*, by Robert M. Gates. *Commentary* 137.4 (2014): 52–4. Print.

Jervis, Robert. "Serving or Self-Serving? A Review Essay of Robert Gates's Memoir." Rev. of *Duty: Memoirs of a Secretary at War*, by Robert M. Gates. *Political Science Quarterly* 129.2 (2014): 319–31. Print.

Wolfe, Alan. "Defensive Secretary." Rev. of *Duty: Memoirs of a Secretary at War*, by Robert M. Gates. *Commonweal* 141.10 (2014): 20–2. Print.

# Elephant Company
## The Inspiring Story of an Unlikely Hero and the Animals Who Helped Him Save Lives in World War II

**Author:** Vicki Constantine Croke
**Publisher:** Random House (New York). 368 pp.
**Type of work:** History, biography
**Time:** 1920–58
**Locales:** Europe, Asia

Elephant Company *is the true story of Billy Williams, an English officer with a gift for handling elephants who trained the giant animals to save lives in Burma during World War II.*

**Principal personages:**
JAMES HOWARD WILLIAMS, a British soldier, also known as "Elephant Bill"
SUSAN ROWLAND, his wife
BANDOOLA, his elephant companion

(Courtesy of Random House)

Author Vicki Constantine Croke has built her career around writing about animals and human-animal interactions. Hailing from Massachusetts, she is a journalist and author who writes animal-related stories for public radio, magazines, and newspapers, including the *Boston Globe*, where she wrote the Animal Beat column for thirteen years. In *Elephant Company: The Inspiring Story of an Unlikely Hero and the Animals Who Helped Him Save Lives in World War II* (2014), Croke turns her journalistic lens toward the story of British soldier and onetime media sensation Lieutenant Colonel James Howard Williams, colorfully known as "Elephant Bill," who became internationally famous after World War II for assembling a team of elephants to help evacuate prisoners of war from Japanese-occupied Burma.

On one level, *Elephant Company* is an intimate biography of Williams, describing his lifelong passion for wildlife and his almost spiritual approach to working with animals, especially elephants. Simultaneously, the book also gives readers detailed information about Burma during World War II, the Japanese occupation, and the life and culture of the elephant handlers and trainers who worked in the lumber industry before and during the war. Through the story of Williams and his Burmese elephant brigade, *Elephant Company* also provides an informative introduction to the more unusual aspects of elephant biology and behavior. The book reveals, for instance, that elephants have an uncanny sense of smell and a highly complex social dynamic, made more complex by the intense hormonal and behavioral changes that they undergo as part of their breeding cycle. In telling Williams's story, Croke also builds recognition for the unique characters of the individual elephants, who seamlessly become the book's other protagonists.

The book's brief introduction describes how Williams became an international hero following the end of World War II, after his story was retold in the London *Times* and the *New York Times* and profiles of his life and experiences during the war were published in magazines such as *Life* and the *New Yorker*. Had Williams's story occurred in the twenty-first century, his seemingly preternatural ability to understand elephant behavior and bond with elephants would most likely have earned him the title of "elephant whisperer," and reviewers of Croke's book were quick to assign Williams this label.

Croke's introduction provides more significant insight, however, in profiling Williams. He is portrayed and described as brave and sensitive, with ahead-of-his-time attitudes concerning the value of living and bonding with animals. According to Croke, elephants became Williams's obsession and shaped the way he approached his life, including his relationships with other humans and the courtship of his wife, Susan. Williams, Croke writes, made elephants his religion, and receiving the nickname "Elephant

(© Christen Goguen)

*Vicki Constantine Croke is an author and journalist known for writing about animal behavior and human-animal interactions. She is the author of* The Modern Ark *(1997), about the history of zoological parks around the world, and* The Lady and the Panda *(2006), about the first panda brought to the United States. Croke has also written articles about animal issues for the* New York Times, *the* Boston Herald, Popular Science, Discover, *and the* Washington Post.

Bill" was, for him, like being christened with a new name that acknowledged the life transformation that was facilitated by his experiences with his elephant companions.

Croke takes a more or less chronological approach to Williams's life and work, but she begins with a nonchronological retelling of one of his most harrowing experiences. Having fallen gravely ill in the jungles of Burma, Williams had to rely on his bond with an elephant named Bandoola to survive and make it out of the jungle. This opening chapter introduces readers to the environment where the essence of Williams's heroic transformation takes place, as well as to his relationship with Bandoola, one of the central characters in his drama. By placing the first chapter at the peak of Williams's most dramatic moment, Croke draws readers into the aspects of his life and experiences that are most extraordinary. She then takes readers back in time and tells the story of Williams's early life and how he first developed his passion for animal behavior.

Williams was the son of a mining engineer, originally from the English town of Cornwall. He studied mining as a youth, but he was drawn to forestry and wildlife from a young age, and many of his formative experiences involved befriending animals; as a child, he had a pet donkey named Prince who became one of his most intimate friends. Williams enlisted in the British army during World War I and served in the Devonshire Regiment in the Middle East. It was in Afghanistan that he became a military animal handler, working with camels and mules. While with the camel regiment, he developed a transformative relationship with a camel named Frying Pan, an experience that demonstrated to him the depth that was possible in a relationship between a human and an animal.

Just before his discharge from the army, Williams was invited by a friend in his regiment to travel to the British-controlled colony of Burma, where elephants were being used by the Bombay Burmah Trading Corporation to facilitate the harvesting of teak from the jungles in order to sell to lumber companies. Bombay Burmah had lost many of their animal handlers and forestry experts during the war, and the company's managers were searching for strong, morally upstanding men to take on the role. Although he did not have any experience working with elephants, Williams was fascinated by the idea. In 1920, he left England for the Burmese coast.

It is ironic that Williams, who is remembered as an early advocate of ecological responsibility and a more nuanced and sensitive approach to the treatment of animals during training, would be introduced to elephant handling through the ecologically devastating British lumber industry of the 1920s. Williams worked along the Upper Chindwin River, where elephants were vital to the hauling of teak logs, which would then be floated downstream to collection areas in the Burmese capital of Rangoon. Because teak is extremely water resistant, it was an important import for Britain and the country's naval industry.

Croke's story follows Williams as he learns about elephants from the other elephant handlers in the Bombay Burmah Company. Training elephants to work in the lumber industry is shown to be a cruel business. Wild elephants were often "broken" through a process called "kheddaring," where violence and abuse were used to frighten the captured elephants into obeying any command given by their handlers. Later, when Williams met Bandoola, the elephant who would become his closest friend, he learned that captive-born elephants are capable of being trained using positive reinforcement and food. Williams preferred this kinder approach and built his own training school for elephants, using only gentleness, respect, and positive reinforcement to teach them. Croke also uses this opportunity to introduce, in vivid detail, the surreal culture of expatriate British citizens living in a remote British colony yet maintaining their traditional British habits, customs, and activities amid a harsh environment of parasites and tropical diseases.

In December 1941, the Japanese invaded and then occupied Burma as part of their early Asian campaign of World War II. The Allied forces failed to halt their advance, and soon the lives of the natives and the British citizens were in peril as the Japanese army marched across the jungle. Thousands of refugees died from starvation and disease. Others were captured and killed by Japanese soldiers. Williams took part in the independent efforts of the Bombay Burmah Company to evacuate British women and children in the absence of help from the British armed forces. They used elephants as a makeshift evacuation force in areas where traditional vehicles were not available or were unable to navigate.

Williams then joined the Eastern Army and became an elephant adviser and specialist in the Elephant Company of the Royal Indian Engineers. These events in Croke's book read like a military adventure, as Williams and his comrades, both elephant and human, risk their lives to save hundreds of refugees and work tirelessly ahead of Allied soldiers and behind enemy lines in order to rescue prisoners and others marooned in the jungles. As the Japanese began capturing elephants, Williams engaged in harrowing missions to recapture them from enemy forces. Under Williams's leadership, the elephants in his company built bridges to aid in evacuation operations and engaged in a dangerous trek across the Burmese border, all the while pursued by Japanese soldiers. Williams's relationship with the heroic elephant Bandoola is one of the central themes of the book, and Croke does an admirable job transforming the charismatic elephant into a gripping character.

Croke's *Elephant Company* is not the first literary treatment of Williams's unconventional life and heroic exploits during the war. After arriving back in England a national hero, Williams wrote his own memoir, the best-selling *Elephant Bill* (1950). He followed this with a series of other books, several of which also touched on his experiences with the elephants of Burma. After Williams died in 1958, his widow, Susan Rowland Williams, wrote *The Footprints of Elephant Bill* (1962) about her husband and his philosophy of life. *Elephant Company* approaches the Elephant Bill story from slightly different angle, however, since Croke had access to Williams's archives of unpublished diaries and letters. It was from these primary sources that she was able to build an intimate portrait of Williams with insights not entirely covered in the other books, while her own expertise allowed her to blend his story with an insightful examination of animal behavior.

*Micah L. Issitt*

## Review Sources

Gruen, Sara. "Unlikely Warriors." Rev. of *Elephant Company: The Inspiring Story of an Unlikely Hero and the Animals Who Helped Him Save Lives in World War II*, by Vicki Constantine Croke. *New York Times*. New York Times, 10 July 2014. Web. 27 Oct. 2014.

Price, Matthew. Rev. of *Elephant Company: The Inspiring Story of an Unlikely Hero and the Animals Who Helped Him Save Lives in World War II*, by Vicki Constantine Croke. *Boston Globe*. Boston Globe Media Partners, 12 July 2014. Web. 27 Oct. 2014.

Wyatt, Neal. "World War II Reading." Rev. of *Elephant Company: The Inspiring Story of an Unlikely Hero and the Animals Who Helped Him Save Lives in World War II*, by Vicki Constantine Croke. *Library Journal*. Library Journal, 28 July 2014. Web. 31 Oct. 2014.

# The Empathy Exams

**Author:** Leslie Jamison (b. 1983)
**Publisher:** Graywolf Press (New York). 226 pp.
**Type of work:** Essays

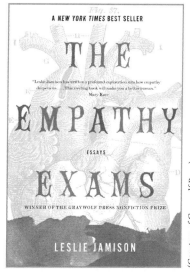

*Leslie Jamison's collection of eleven literary essays is largely about the complexity of identifying with the pain of others.*

Leslie Jamison's book of eleven essays, *The Empathy Exams*, has been called "extraordinary," "dazzling," and "gutsy" by reviewers. Although barely out of her twenties, she has been compared to Virginia Woolf, Joan Didion, and Susan Sontag. Jamison holds degrees from Harvard University and the Iowa Writers' Workshop, and is working on a PhD in English at Yale University. Her first book, a novel entitled *The Gin Closet*, came out in 2010 to decent reviews. But her real forte may very well be the literary essay—as much narrative as discursive analysis.

Jamison ponders the meaning and significance of experiences that highlight empathy, the human ability to identify with others, although she often seems more concerned with the pain, especially woman's pain, than the empathy such pain might elicit. As is true of any good essayist, Jamison is sometimes participant, sometimes observer, of the human encounters that bring her essays into focus. Her subjects range from her role as an actor paid by medical schools to pretend certain illnesses to train doctors to have more empathy to her assistance in her brother's participation in an extreme marathon in a rural area of Tennessee. She writes about getting punched in the face by a mugger in Nicaragua and falling from a rope in the jungles of Costa Rica. She describes reporting on a conference for those who have contracted a rare physical or psychological disease and worrying that she will catch it.

Jamison is not unaware that her fascination with pain and suffering experienced both by herself and by others makes her, as Olivia Laing notes in her review in the *New York Times*, walk a tightrope between voyeurism and narcissism. However, Jamison is, if nothing else, honest and clear-eyed in her willingness to expose her own weaknesses and imaginatively zero in on the suffering of others.

The title essay is the best in the collection, not only because it effectively introduces the problem of empathy on which the essays focus, but also because the situation it describes centers on Jamison as both an observer and a participant. Even as she inhabits the world of the sufferer, she watches the doctors who try to understand that pain and feel it themselves. Jamison argues that empathy requires inquiry as much as imagination, for it necessitates recognizing that the pain someone suffers has a complex network of connections beyond what one can actually see. But what makes the essay compelling is not just the metaphor of playing the role of one in pain, but also Jamison's delineation of her own unwanted pregnancy and how she feels about what she decides to do about it.

Jamison says that when bad things happen to other people she imagines them happening to herself, but she is not sure whether that is empathy or theft. For example, when her brother develops Bell's palsy, a condition that leaves part of his face paralyzed, she becomes obsessed with it, trying to imagine how it would be to move through the world with an unfamiliar face. She decides this is not really empathy for she does not transfer herself into the country of the other so much as import the other's problems into her own world.

The essay "Devil's Bait" explores the curious situation of people who believe that they have fibers or insects emerging from the skin, a condition first identified and named Morgellons in 2001. The problem the disease raises about empathy is that the experts are convinced that it is not a disease but a delusion, whereas the only ones who are convinced that it is "real" are those who suffer from it. The essay explores the human need to justify what might be psychological by convincing others that it is physical; indeed victims of Morgellons would prefer that it be a physical disease than a psychological delusion.

The fact that 70 percent of Morgellons patients are women only adds to doctors' suspicion that the condition is so-called female stuff, a kind of hysteria. Once again, Jamison relates this to her own experience, for she says the disease crystallizes something she has always felt—that there is something wrong about her body. She says "Morgies" are emblems of how difficult it is for us to feel comfortable in our own skin. And of course, she has an experience of her own that seems somehow similar. While Jamison was in Bolivia, a botfly larva infested her ankle. Back in the United States, she hurriedly went to the emergency room when she saw the worm emerge from her ankle, but she had difficulty convincing the doctors that what she saw actually happened. Her fear that there might be another worm still inside was worse than the actual worm. What she says she came to understand is that the distinction between real and unreal is the difference between suffering produced by something outside the self and something inside.

In her essay "Morphology of the Hit," Jamison draws on Russian formalist Vladimir Propp's *Morphology of the Folktale*, which she discovered in graduate school, to try to come to terms with a mugger attack in Nicaragua. By looking back at her experience as if it were a text, she tries to give the experience of being hit a form, and thus significance—which, in a way, is what she does in all the essays in this collection.

The weakest pieces in the book are the six short meditations in "Pain Tours I" and "Pain Tours II." These include essays on trying to identify with miners near the highest city in the world in Bolivia, the reality television show *Intervention*, and taking a gang tour in Los Angeles. Other pieces are a rumination about Frida Kahlo, who wore plaster corsets for most of her life because of a weak spine; a meditation about Joan Didion's 1983 book on civil war in Central America; and a lyrical piece on James Agee's *Let Us Now Praise Famous Men*.

"The Immortal Horizon" is about an ultra-marathon in northern Tennessee started in 1977 as a grueling exercise in pain attempted by only a few and finished by hardly anyone. Jamison's brother Julian, for whom she is the support person for the race, says he wants to run a hundred miles when no one knows he is running. Why people would choose such torture and pain is the question that Jamison pursues here. The answer she comes up with is that people do it because it hurts so much and they are still willing to do it. Ultimately, she says it is a commitment to something that resists labels.

*Leslie Jamison published her first book, a novel called* The Gin Closet, *in 2010. Her collection of essays,* The Empathy Exams, *won the 2011 Graywolf Press Nonfiction Prize.*

"In Defense of Saccharin (e)" depends largely on Jamison's citing a number of authors and philosophers who have commented on sentimentality; for example, Oscar Wilde, who defined a sentimentalist as someone who wants the luxury of an emotion without having to pay for it. Jamison argues that artificial sweeteners have the same intensity as sentimentality—they are sweeter than sugar, but without calories, offering the shell of sugar without its substance. She goes on to explore how artificial sweeteners are a symbol of sentimentality, for both describe a sweet emotion or taste that feels undeserved, therefore, unreal. However, Jamison wonders if antisentimentality is genuine, suggesting it is a kind of self-righteousness by way of dismissal. She wants to make a case at least for the value of the moment when one falls into sentimentality and then feels its flatness. Maybe, she says, if saccharine provides a fictional oversimplification of feeling, then perhaps its value is in the moment of unmasking, when one emerges from being enthralled by it.

In "Fog Count," Jamison visits a prison in Fayetteville, West Virginia, to see Charlie Engle, who she met at the ultramarathon in Tennessee, and with whom she has been corresponding for nine months. What she wants to know is what happens when you confine a man whose whole life is motion, running. She says Engle's story is the story of a system that strip-mined the American housing market. Jamison sees herself as a tourist—unsure if she is really entering Engle's world or simply shopping around its environs. She wants to know what incarceration is really like. Yet she knows there comes that inevitable point in time when she can go, and he cannot.

"Lost Boys" is about the 1993 death of three young boys in West Memphis, Arkansas, for which three teenage boys were brought to trial for murders called satanic rituals. Or, more properly, the essay is about the trilogy of films called *Paradise Lost*, which deals with the trials, the appeals, and the years in jail, until the young men were released on appeal in 2011. Jamison says she watched these films as a teenager and got angry, but she admits she likes who she was when she watched the films because of her empathy with the accused boys and her rage at what she saw as injustice.

"Grand Unified Theory of Female Pain," the final essay in the collection, opens with references to literary women: Miss Havisham from *Great Expectations*, Anna Karenina, Mina Harker from *Dracula*, and Sylvia Plath. The essay is about the idea of the "wounded woman," whom Jamison says we have romanticized and idealized, believing that pain is a prerequisite to the female consciousness. The issue this raises is that women's pain is often thought somehow unreal, that is, psychosomatic, emotional, or psychological. The essay is divided up into brief discussions of different "wounds": her own cutting, Ann Carson's poem "The Glass Essay," Stephen King's *Carrie*, and the TV show *Girls,* among others.

Jamison also writes to several of her favorite women, asking them to tell her about their thoughts on female pain. From their comments, she concludes we are both revolted by female pain and attracted to it, proud and ashamed. She says she wants this essay to be a manifesto against the accusation of wallowing in pain. She concludes by admitting that the wounded woman is called a stereotype and sometimes is, but she insists sometimes the woman is truly in pain and the possibility of obsessing about pain is no reason to stop representing it. Pain that is called trite is still pain, and to claim pain is a cliché is just an alibi that allows us to close our hearts. Jamison insists that she wants our hearts to be open.

Indeed, Jamison's desire that our hearts remain open to the pain of others is a fitting coda to this collection, which thoughtfully and honestly examines the complexity of what is perhaps the most difficult, yet most essential human ability: empathy.

*Charles E. May*

**Review Sources**

Rev. of *The Empathy Exams*, by Leslie Jamison. *Kirkus Reviews* 82 (2014): 4. Print.

Garner, Dwight. "Contemplating Other People's Pain." Rev. of *The Empathy Exams*, by Leslie Jamison. *New York Times* 28 Mar. 2014: C23. Print.

Greenberg, Gary. "We, Not Me." Rev. of *The Empathy Exams*, by Leslie Jamison. *American Scholar* 83 (2014): 114–15. Print.

Laing, Olivia. "Never Hurts to Ask." Rev. of *The Empathy Exams*, by Leslie Jamison. *New York Times* 6 Apr. 2014: BR 26. Print.

Seaman, Donna. Rev. of *The Empathy Exams*, by Leslie Jamison. *Booklist* 110 (2014): 13. Print.

Warnica, Richard. Rev. of *The Empathy Exam*, by Leslie Jamison. *Maclean's* 127 (2014): 61–62. Print.

# Euphoria

**Author:** Lily King (b. 1963)
**Publisher:** Atlantic Monthly (New York).
256 pp.
**Type of work:** Novel
**Time:** 1932–33; 1971
**Locales:** Sepik River, Territory of New
Guinea (now Papua New Guinea); New
York City

*In* Euphoria, *Lily King tells of a love triangle
between three Western anthropologists deep
in the Territory of New Guinea in the early
1930s. The main characters are based on
real people, among them famed American
anthropologist Margaret Mead, but* Euphoria *creates for them a fictional ending that
differs from the historical reality.*

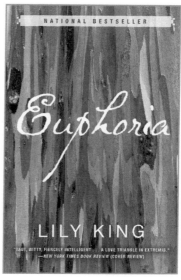

(Courtesy of Atlantic Monthly Press)

## Principal characters:

ELINOR "NELL" STONE, an American anthropologist studying indigenous tribes in the
Territory of New Guinea
SCHUYLER "FEN" FENWICK, her husband, an Australian anthropologist
ANDREW "ANDY" BANKSON, an English anthropologist in love with her
XAMBUN, a member of New Guinea's fictional Tam tribe
MALUN, Xambun's mother

In Lily King's *Euphoria* (2014), three young Western anthropologists deep in the
jungle of New Guinea battle their affections and disaffections for each other, which
threaten to overshadow their professional work. Elinor "Nell" Stone is an American
anthropologist who has enjoyed great popular success with her book on the children of
a tribe from the Solomon Islands in the South Seas. She is married to the somber Australian anthropologist Schuyler "Fen" Fenwick, a relationship that appears to be on
the rocks. On Christmas Eve 1932, English anthropologist Andrew "Andy" Bankson,
lonely for professional company, meets Nell and Fen at a government outpost. Andy
invites the couple to study a New Guinea tribe of his choosing near the Kiona people
he is studying. Nell and Fen agree, and Andy takes them down the Middle Sepik River
to their new destination on his motorized canoe. It does not take long for conflict to
break out among the three, for both romantic and professional reasons.

Thematically, *Euphoria* seeks to combine a passionate love-triangle story with an
intellectual reflection on the origins of Western anthropology. As King readily acknowledges, her three principal characters are based on three real Western anthropologists.
Nell Stone is modeled after pioneering American anthropologist Margaret Mead, the

most famous of the three; her husband, Fen, is based on Mead's own second husband, New Zealander anthropologist Reo Fortune; and Andy Bankson is based on the English anthropologist Gregory Bateson. However, the specific interactions and eventual fate of King's characters move them increasingly into the realm of the fictional. In *Euphoria*, their triangular affair comes to a conclusion of the author's own creative design.

Basing differently named fictional characters on thinly disguised historical personages is an accepted narrative device in historical fiction. In her acknowledgements at the end of *Euphoria*, King states, "I have borrowed from the lives and experiences of these three people, but have told a different story." This is certainly true, as many of the novel's details and the creative, fictional outcome of *Euphoria* are of King's own devising.

At the end of the novel, King acknowledges as well that *Euphoria* "was initially inspired by a moment described in Jane Howard's 1984 biography *Margaret Mead: A Life*." She elaborated on this in an interview with Alexis Burling in the April 14, 2014, issue of *Publishers Weekly*, relating that she came across Howard's book in a bookstore in Maine and was particularly struck by the chapter in which Mead, then thirty-one, met Bateson while in New Guinea with Fortune. Although the chapter was brief, it gave her the idea for the story that would become *Euphoria*.

(© Laura Lewis)

*Lily King's first novel,* The Pleasing Hour *(1999), won the Barnes & Noble Discover Great New Writers Award. The English Teacher (2005) earned the Maine Literary Award, and* Father of the Rain *(2010) won both the Maine Literary Award and the New England Book Award for fiction.* Euphoria, *King's fourth novel, received the inaugural Kirkus Prize.*

Indeed, many events during the time King's Nell, Fen, and Andy spend together, from Christmas Eve 1932 to March 1933, are based closely on the interactions of Mead, Fortune, and Bateson at this time, as told in chapter 11 of Howard's *Margaret Mead*. In addition, the story of Nell and Fen's prior adventure in New Guinea, dated from July 1931 to December 1932 in the novel, is inspired by chapter 10 of Howard's work, which describes Mead and Fortune's research in New Guinea from September 1931 to December 1932. Thinly veiled events and circumstances from this time are used in *Euphoria* to flesh out Nell and Fen's memories and discussions.

King's plot structure for the first four chapters of *Euphoria* mirrors the narrative strategy employed in Howard's relevant chapter. In *Margaret Mead*, Howard describes how Mead and Fortune meet Bateson at a Christmas Eve party in 1932 and proceeds to give background information about Bateson's past and character; *Euphoria* does the same. The novel moves from an omniscient narration that brings Nell and Fen to the party to Andy's first-person narration of his past. Andy's account closely mirrors

Bateson's past, although a fictional recent suicide attempt distinguishes King's character from the historical figure.

Generally, the events surrounding the trio's meeting and time together along the Middle Sepik River in the Territory of New Guinea rather closely follows the description and background of the historical meeting related by Howard's biography. Some passages in both texts appear very, very close. For instance, of the babies of the fictional tribe of the Mumbanyo, Nell says that they "plunk them in stiff baskets and close the lid, and when the baby cries they scratch the basket. That's their most tender gesture." Similarly, Howard's biography includes Mead's observation that among the tribe of the Mundugumor, "babies were carried around in harsh, stiff, opaque baskets. . . . Nobody cuddled or comforted them when they cried."

An author of historical fiction can certainly work with her historical material in a creative way and incorporate historical facts as described by historians as well. King clearly acknowledges that she was inspired by Howard's biography. It is interesting, though, how much of the backstory of the characters, the setting, and the circumstances of their meeting are transferred very closely from the historical events as described by Howard. This material is used well by King to fill many pages of *Euphoria* and contributes powerfully to bringing to life three characters who, in the end, follow distinctly different paths than their historical counterparts.

Unfortunately, when King did not rely on Howard's biography or other acknowledged sources, significant factual errors slipped into the text. In an early electronic version of *Euphoria*, published in May 2014 ahead of the June hardcover release, chapter 1 features Nell and Fen's observation of "a sloth hanging like a melting sack from a tree" along the Sepik; in the tribal village where Andy Bankson lives, he witnesses "monkeys caterwauling on high branches"; and on Lake Tam, where Nell and Fen conduct their work and are joined by Andy, they hear the "greeet greeet greeet of the monkeys." King even invents a proverb for her isolated New Guinea tribe: "Not even a monkey walks alone." The problem, which one astute reader almost immediately pointed out in an online review, is that there are neither sloths nor monkeys in New Guinea. In the hard-copy version, "sloth" has been replaced by "quoll," a native marsupial, and mentions of monkeys have been either removed or replaced with "possum," a mammal indigenous to parts of New Guinea.

Despite perhaps relying overmuch on its key source and generating a few factual errors of its own, *Euphoria* manages to tell an engaging story about three young Western social scientists struggling with their romantic feelings—and emerging repulsions—for one another in a deeply foreign environment. Nell, Fen, and Andy are all carried along on a wave of professional optimism; they sincerely believe that their research of indigenous tribes on the island of New Guinea will provide beneficial knowledge to all of humanity, and it is this mindset that gives rise to King's title. Nell is the first to point out to Andy that a strange elation can capture scientists: "It's that moment about two months in [your local research], when you think you've finally got a handle on the place. . . . It's a delusion. . . . It's the briefest, purest euphoria." Later, Andy, too, will experience the kind of euphoria that comes from seeming to be on the brink of understanding an alien culture. This shared experience links him emotionally with Nell, with whom he has fallen hopelessly in love despite her marriage to Fen. *Euphoria* uses its rich historical background very well to construct a compelling story of a love triangle. Mead and Fortune's marriage was indeed falling apart during this time, and Mead did become interested in Bateson romantically. However, in *Euphoria*, things move much more quickly than they did in history.

In *Euphoria*, Nell Stone is the character in the middle. She is falling out of love with her husband, Fen, and in love with the engaging Andy. Perhaps to shine a sympathetic light on Nell's turn from one lover to another, Fen is made into a dark antagonist, and as the novel moves toward its climax, he becomes increasingly evil. At the outset, Fen has eaten human meat along with local cannibals, confessing, "It does taste like old pig." He breaks Nell's glasses and her typewriter and exhibits a self-involved lack of concern for her well-being in their sexual relationship, demonstrated in starkly described sex scenes. He calls Andy a "deviant," a pejorative term for "homosexual." Yet when Andy suffers a fever, Fen shaves Andy and kisses him, indicating Fen's own hypocrisy—or, perhaps, repressed sexuality. Topping it off, he manipulates an indigenous man, Xambun, into raiding a local village to steal an artistically carved flute so he can sell it to a Western museum. Andy, on the other hand, emerges as an admirer of Nell's anthropological approach. Unlike Fen, who is jealous of Nell's success, Andy feels inspired by Nell's rapport with the indigenous people, such as Malun, the mother of Xambun. As King guides *Euphoria* to its climax, the characters increasingly diverge from the historical personages on which they are based. This is most obvious in the case of Fen, who becomes a vicious caricature of his historical base, Reo Fortune, while Andy becomes all-understanding and virtuous. Where Fen is evil, Andy is good.

The conclusion of *Euphoria* may appear somewhat unsatisfactory to some readers. It feels as though King sacrificed the complexities of her historical models to provide a rather neat, clear-cut ending. Tragedy occurs, and in a final scene set in New York City in 1971, it is revealed that evil has met with poetic justice. The novel ends with a deliberate pull at readers' heartstrings—a typical strategy for novels, of course, but when compared to the more ambiguous historical figures who gave their background and story to many of *Euphoria*'s pages, the ending appears somewhat too neat and reductive. In the end, readers must decide if this telling of "a different story" is literarily satisfactory for them.

Ultimately, *Euphoria* stands out as a remarkable historical novel that dares to hew very close to its key source. As a novel, it tells a tale that becomes strikingly different from the events that occurred in reality. King transfers her characters out of historical models to give them a new life and alternate ending. Overall, the story may captivate readers who enjoy being dropped into a fascinating, challenging, exotic world and are unbothered by artistic license or deviations from factual historical events.

*R. C. Lutz*

**Review Sources**

Beck, Evelyn. Rev. of *Euphoria*, by Lily King. *Library Journal* 15 May 2014: 69. Print.

Dickie, Elizabeth. Rev. of *Euphoria*, by Lily King. *Booklist* 15 Apr. 2014: 24. Print.

Eakin, Emily. "The Way She Saw It." Rev. of *Euphoria*, by Lily King. *New York Times Book Review* 8 June 2014: 1+. Print.

Rev. of *Euphoria*, by Lily King. *Publishers Weekly* 14 Apr. 2014: 30–31. Print.

# Every Day Is for the Thief

**Author:** Teju Cole (b. 1975)
**First published:** 2007, in Nigeria
**Publisher:** Random House (New York). 176 pp.
**Type of work:** Novella
**Time:** 2005
**Locale:** Lagos, Nigeria

*Teju Cole's first book is a novella that follows a young American medical student who returns to his home city of Lagos, Nigeria.*

(Courtesy of Random House)

Teju Cole is an American journalist and short-story writer who was raised in Nigeria. His widely acclaimed American debut novel, *Open City* (2011), follows a half-Nigerian, half-German medical student named Julius as he wanders about New York City. Yet although the book earned Cole the 2012 Hemingway Foundation/PEN Award, which recognizes outstanding debut book-length works of fiction, *Open City* was not, in fact, Cole's first published book; that distinction belongs to the novella *Every Day Is for the Thief*, first published in Nigeria in 2007. In 2014, the novella, in which a young medical student returns to the Nigerian city where he grew up, was published in the United States for the first time.

 *Open City* and *Every Day Is for the Thief* are remarkably similar in terms of style, structure, and the difficulty of classifying them in terms of genre. *Every Day Is for the Thief* is composed of vignettes and photographs taken by Cole himself and reads like an autobiography—though he told Audie Cornish for National Public Radio's (NPR) *All Things Considered* that the narrator is "crankier" than he is. The book captures Lagos in all of its vibrancy and lawlessness. Like the best travelogues, *Every Day Is for the Thief* identifies the truth of a city, even if, according to Cole, it does not accurately identify its geography. (In an interview with Matthew Kassel for the *New York Observer*, in reference to his depiction of an alleyway of carpenters building coffins, Cole admitted, "I really thought when I was writing it that a lot of that stuff was true. But I've been back a couple of times to look, and I can't find it.")

 *Every Day Is for the Thief* begins at the Nigerian consulate in New York City, where Cole's unnamed narrator, a dual American and Nigerian citizen, encounters the first of countless bribes while renewing his Nigerian passport. He bemoans his fellow Nigerians' "casual complicity" in their country's "informal economy." Corruption is rampant and pervasive in Nigeria, a nation that has suffered under colonial and military rulers for years. While quick to defend the creativity, ingenuity, and ultimately humanity of its people, the narrator is frustrated by the lack of progress in the country. The stagnation is self-perpetuating, Cole writes:

> The systems that could lift the majority out of poverty are undercut at every turn. Precisely because everyone takes a shortcut, nothing works and, for this reason, the only way to get anything done is to take another shortcut. The advantage in these situations goes to the highest bidders, those individuals most willing to pay money or to test the limits of the law.

As the narrator observes, the armed police in Lagos make (or made, at least in 2006–7, when the book was written) the equivalent of less than $100 a month, which forces them to depend on bribes to survive. The narrator recalls the story of family friend who worked as an immigration officer. The man refused to take bribes at his new rural post, but his honorable stance cost his colleagues money, so they requested he be transferred to a different location to deprive someone else of their pay.

The same culture of necessary lawlessness in Nigeria is referenced in the book's title, taken from a Yoruba proverb that says, "Every day is for the thief, but one day is for the owner." Hustlers like the "the yahoo boys" are all too familiar with the edict; in one of the book's most fascinating vignettes, the narrator happens upon a group of men at an Internet café who are arduously typing out scam letters to con wealthy (or elderly) foreigners. Watching the university-aged boys type the letters "by the hunt and peck method," he likens the experience to "discover[ing] the source of the Nile or the Niger."

The unwieldy nature of public life in Lagos, Nigeria's most populous city, contributes to the narrator's heightened sense of being. In one vignette, he tries to hold two essential truths about the city at once: Lagosians are family oriented, often fervently religious, and, on the surface, happy; yet many Lagosians have known tremendous grief as a result of arbitrary acts of violence. At a wedding engagement ceremony with his cousins, the narrator sees a woman who is friends with his aunt. He watches her, smiling and greeting guests, while his cousins tell him about how her husband was horrifically murdered by armed robbers in 1998. Armed home invasions were common

*Teju Cole is an American writer who was raised in Nigeria. His second novel,* Open City *(2011), won the Hemingway Foundation/PEN Award, the Internationaler Literaturpreis, the Rosenthal Family Foundation Award for Fiction from the American Academy of Arts and Letters, and the New York City Book Award.*

in the 1990s, and the narrator recalls hiding in the bathroom with his family while robbers tried to break down the front door. Yet looking at the woman, he "can see nothing that looks like grief and nothing that looks like the terrible humiliation in the story. . . . It is a great and painful wonder to me, just at that moment, that there is no trace of it on her face, no visible mark, seven years on."

On the other side of this extraordinary resilience is fear. "The barely concealed panic that taints so many interactions here is due precisely to the fact that nobody is in control, no one is ultimately responsible for anything at all," the narrator says. This panic is assuaged by the embrace of superstitious and spiritual beliefs, particularly evangelical Christianity in the south and extreme Islam in the north. The narrator reports that shortly before his visit to Nigeria, the country was named the world's most religious country, its people the happiest, and its government the third most corrupt, an unusual combination of superlatives that is evident in Nigerian culture. There is tremendous pressure to say that one is happy, to express optimism or expect miracles.

In another vignette, the narrator visits a marketplace, a gathering of goods and people that he refers to as "the essence of the city." He haggles with a man who is surprised when he starts speaking Yoruba. Embarrassed, the seller tells the narrator that he thought that he was an *oyinbo*, a white man, but more specifically, a foreigner. The narrator is irritated; when he lived in Lagos, he was never called *oyinbo*. It is one of the many instances in which the narrator must reckon with his role as both a visitor and a native.

On the same excursion, the narrator describes the capture and brutal murder of a young thief. While this particular incident happened six weeks ago, he weaves together memories of similar incidents to tell the tale. The eleven-year-old boy was accused of stealing a baby and was subsequently beaten and set on fire. A videotape of the murder circulated, sparked outrage, and then disappeared from the public consciousness. The vignette, which concludes with the image of a bumper sticker praising the benevolence of God, illustrates the random cruelty of life—or rather, how quickly the tide of violence can rise up and overtake one's life.

Like the author, Cole's narrator is also a photographer, at least in the sense that he carries a camera with him everywhere he goes, though photography is not his profession. Cole's own photos appear throughout the book. Most are voyeuristic, often street scenes shot from balconies or bus seats. Some are blurry or off-center, as if Cole had only time to raise the camera to his eyes and click before hastily pulling it back down again. In the book's last vignette—the one with the coffin-making carpenters—the narrator thinks, "I want to take the little camera out of my pocket and capture the scene. But I am afraid. Afraid that the carpenters, rapt in their meditative task, will look up at me; afraid that I will bind to film what is intended only for memory, what is meant only for a sidelong glance followed by forgetting." The images are compelling in their own right and are particularly striking in juxtaposition with Cole's semi-fictional narrative; they are the souvenirs of a place where truthfulness means many things, the ephemera of a city in constant transformation.

*Molly Hagan*

## Review Sources

Garner, Dwight. "It's Home, Malevolent Yet Oddly Captivating." Rev. of *Every Day Is for the Thief*, by Teju Cole. *New York Times*. New York Times, 25 Mar. 2014. Web. 6 Feb. 2015.

White, Duncan. Rev. of *Every Day Is for the Thief*, by Teju Cole. *Telegraph.* Telegraph Media Group, 2 June 2014. Web. 6 Feb. 2015.

Wolitzer, Meg. "In *Every Day Is for the Thief*, Cole Chronicles a City's Reality." Rev. of *Every Day Is for the Thief*, by Teju Cole. *NPR.* Natl. Public Radio, 26 Apr. 2014. Web. 6 Feb. 2015.

# Everything I Never Told You

**Author:** Celeste Ng (b. 1980)
**Publisher:** Penguin (New York). 304 pp.
**Type of work:** Novel
**Time:** 1938–77
**Locale:** Middlewood, Ohio; Cambridge, Massachusetts; Toledo, Ohio; Iowa; Virginia

*Celeste Ng's strong debut novel,* Everything I Never Told You, *looks unflinchingly at the secrets, the dynamics, and the history of a mixed Asian and European American family whose surviving members try to discover why the elder daughter, Lydia Lee, died at sixteen.*

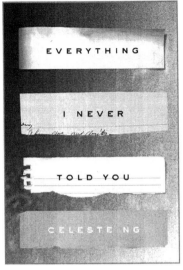

(Courtesy of Penguin)

**Principal characters:**
LYDIA ELIZABETH LEE, a Chinese European American sixteen-year-old who drowns, the result of an apparent suicide
MARILYN LEE, née Walker, her mother
JAMES LEE, her father
NATHAN "NATH" LEE, her brother and the oldest of the three Lee children
HANNAH LEE, her sister and the youngest of the Lee children
JACK WOLFF, her friend
LOUISA CHEN, James's teaching assistant
OFFICER FISKE, a police officer who investigates Lydia's initial disappearance
DR. JANET WOLFF, Jack's divorced mother

*Everything I Never Told You* (2014) opens with two short, powerful sentences—"Lydia is dead. But they don't know this yet"—that set the tone and theme for Celeste Ng's debut novel. It is a book about family secrets, family dynamics, and the difficulty of really knowing one's sibling, child, spouse, parent, or any other human being. To tell her story, Ng successfully combines an omniscient narrator with episodes told from the multiple points of view of all five members of the Lee family. At the center of the novel is the unexpected, inexplicable death of the sixteen-year-old Lydia Elizabeth Lee.

In the beginning of the book, Ng shows how suddenly and profoundly ordinary family life can be shattered by sudden tragedy. At six thirty on a Tuesday morning in May 1977, Lydia's father, mother, and two siblings do not suspect anything is wrong or different in their lives, and her father, James, leaves for work. It is the youngest daughter, eleven-year-old Hannah, who first notices Lydia's absence from the family breakfast table. Ng's inclusion of seemingly small and unimportant details such as this provides clues to future events in the novel; here, she signals that Hannah will prove to be the most observant of the Lee family.

Alarmed, Lydia's mother, Marilyn, discovers that her room is empty and she cannot be found anywhere in the house or the garage. The son, Nathan "Nath" Lee, a high school senior about to graduate, quietly tells Hannah that he heard Lydia's radio play until eleven thirty last night. Trying to maintain normalcy, Marilyn sends Nath and Hannah to school. She calls Lydia's school and learns that she is not in class. She then calls James at the college where he teaches.

As is often and effectively the case throughout *Everything I Never Told You*, an incident in the novel is used to segue into another character's point of view. Here, the point of view switches to the still-unsuspecting James Lee at his desk, worrying about his students' lack of interest. He is forty-five, tenured, an American-born Chinese man. He recalls that even some of the staff at his college occasionally mistake him for a visitor from Asia.

This memory introduces a key theme of Ng's debut novel: the still-pervasive lack of cultural acceptance and understanding of Asian Americans in the United States in the 1970s. Incidents ranging such seemingly innocuous mistakes to more vicious racial taunting, such as other children making slit-eyed grimaces at members of the Lee family, ring true for the period. Even James's teaching assistant, twenty-three-year-old Chinese graduate student Louisa Chen, was surprised when she looked at James's family picture and exclaimed, "Your wife's—not Chinese?" Alongside the questions surrounding Lydia's death, the novel also presents many of the various challenges of being an Asian European American family during the period.

Reunited at home, the four Lee family members talk to the police, and Officer Fiske tells them that "most missing-girl cases" end quickly when the "girls come home by themselves." Ng's novel drops a few more clues about the Lees. Officer Fiske remembers that in 1966, James reported Marilyn missing, but James insists now that this was just "a misunderstanding." Asked to provide a recent photo of Lydia, he finds one from Christmas 1976 that shows her in a sullen mood. James chooses instead a photo from her sixteenth birthday a week ago, in which, Nath muses, Lydia "looks like a model in a magazine ad." Already there are many questions about who Lydia really is. These questions mount until Lydia herself is given a voice later in the novel, leading to a surprise ending.

Quickly, the novel reveals that different family members have different information or lack of information about Lydia. Her parents believe she was a popular girl, but Nath knows she was without close friends. He suspects his classmate Jack Wolff of some foul play. Ever since Jack humiliated Nath in front of other kids when Marilyn disappeared back in 1966, Nath has considered Jack his sworn enemy. The son of a divorced physician who works night shifts at the local hospital, Jack appears to be the exact opposite of Nath. Nath is studious; Jack struggles at school. Nath is gentle; Jack is reputedly a rebel who smokes and ravishes one high school girl after another in his steel-gray Volkswagen Beetle. Nath recollects that Lydia has become friends with Jack this spring. While telling her parents she was studying with girlfriends, a lie upheld by Nath, Lydia spent hours with Jack in his car. In a move indicative of how little the

Lees talk to each other about important things, Nath withholds this observation from his parents to avoid recriminations about covering up for Lydia.

Hannah is also keeping secrets. In her bed later, she remembers how she heard the front door closing during the night, looked out her bedroom window, and saw Lydia walking across the front lawn. Hannah decides not to tell her parents and Nath about this for fear of being blamed for letting Lydia walk out at night. This sets a pattern of characters keeping secrets so that the puzzle of Lydia's death cannot be solved by them together.

The next day, a loose rowboat is discovered on the local lake. The police call James, who states that Lydia could not and did not want to swim. On Thursday morning, the police find Lydia's body in the lake, and the information gap between the reader and the rest of the Lee family has been closed.

From this point, the reader is spellbound as the possible reasons for Lydia's death are probed. The police find no evidence of foul play and rule the death a suicide. James flees from the unthinkable and into an affair with the welcoming Louisa Chen. Marilyn is convinced it was an outside killer. Nath suspects Jack. Hannah tries and fails to comprehend what went on in Lydia's mind on the day of her death.

Intrinsically linked to Lydia's death is her family's history. At its core, the novel shows, are the diametrically opposed desires of James and Marilyn: "Because more than anything, [Marilyn] had wanted to stand out; because more than anything, [James] had wanted to blend in." When they met in 1957, Marilyn Walker was a student at Radcliffe College, studying to become a doctor in direct opposition to the wishes of her mother, who wanted Marilyn to create a comfortable family home that would be pleasing to her husband-to-be; James Lee was finishing his PhD in American history at nearby Harvard University. James was born in California to a Chinese American family, and, like his parents, he desperately wanted to fit into the mainstream American society that rejected him. Marilyn meets James when taking his new class on the American cowboy. She kisses him during his first office hours, and they quickly fall in love.

*Celeste Ng earned her master of fine arts degree in creative writing from the University of Michigan in 2006. Her short story "What Passes Over" won a Hopwood Award for graduate short fiction the same year, and another story, "Girls, at Play," won a 2012 Pushcart Prize.* Everything I Never Told You *is her first novel.*

*Everything I Never Told You* suggests that James sees in Marilyn the all-American girl he desired for so long, while Marilyn sees loving James as a chance for further rebellion. Their plans for James to teach at Harvard while Marilyn attends medical school are dashed: James is not hired because he is not "the right fit," despite being academically the best candidate, and Marilyn finds out that she is pregnant. James accepts an offer at a small college in Ohio, and Marilyn accompanies him as his wife, forgoing medical school. At their wedding in June 1958, Marilyn's mother tells her that it is wrong to marry James. She never speaks to her daughter again.

Other flashbacks reveal the details of the first Lee family crisis and its possible link to Lydia's death. After Nath and Lydia are born, Marilyn feels unfulfilled and discontent with her life. When her mother dies in spring 1966, she realizes that her mother's vision was to exist to please a man. Marilyn resolves never to become like her mother, and shortly after the funeral service, she leaves her family without notice and enrolls at a community college near Toledo, Ohio, where she plans to take the courses she needs to complete the undergraduate work that was interrupted years before. Two months later, Marilyn learns that she is pregnant again. At the hospital, she gives her husband's phone number, and he shows up to drive her home.

Apparently reunited, the Lee family tries to cover up this fissure in silence. However, Marilyn unconsciously repeats with Lydia the same mistake her mother made. Marilyn wants Lydia to live her own dream of becoming a doctor, and she takes control of Lydia's life. Meanwhile, James pressures Lydia to be popular, expressing his own frustration with the racism he has faced since childhood.

As the novel moves ahead, it becomes plausible that the conflicting desires of mother and father may have driven a young teenager to suicidal despair. There may also have been problems with Jack Wolff, with whom the previously compliant Lydia had gradually begun to rebel. This is revealed when the point of view shifts to Lydia's own thoughts, which carry Ng's novel to a surprise ending that is well prepared through multiple clues.

Celeste Ng's *Everything I Never Told You* is a powerful debut novel with complex characters and a moving evocation of past times. It is a sad yet very moving novel that explores the question of to what extent one person can ever truly know the mind and heart of a loved one.

*R. C. Lutz*

## Review Sources

Chee, Alexander. "The Leftovers." Rev. of *Everything I Never Told You*, by Celeste Ng. *New York Times Book Review* 17 Aug. 2014: 16. Print.

Haggas, Carol. Rev. of *Everything I Never Told You*, by Celeste Ng. *Booklist* 15 May 2014: 13. Print.

Hong, Terry. Rev. of *Everything I Never Told You*, by Celeste Ng. *Library Journal* 1 May 2014: 69. Print.

Ross, Michele. "Celeste Ng Tells the Story of an Ohio Family Touched by Tragedy in Her Haunting Debut, *Everything I Never Told You*." Rev. of *Everything I Never Told You*, by Celeste Ng. *Cleveland.com*. Plain Dealer, 10 July 2014. Web. 25 Nov. 2014.

Tobar, Hector. "*Everything I Never Told You* a Moving Tale of a Dysfunctional Family." Rev. of *Everything I Never Told You*, by Celeste Ng. *Los Angeles Times*. Los Angeles Times, 4 July 2014. Web. 25 Nov. 2014.

# Factory Man
## How One Furniture Maker Battled Offshoring, Stayed Local—and Helped Save an American Town

**Author:** Beth Macy
**Publisher:** Little, Brown (New York). Illustrated. 464 pp.
**Type of work:** Biography, economics
**Time:** 1902–Present
**Locales:** Bassett, Virginia; Galax, Virginia; Dalian, China

(Courtesy of Little, Brown and Company)

*Beth Macy's* Factory Man *chronicles the rise of the Bassett family's furniture companies and John D. Bassett III's struggle to protect his business and employees in the face of globalization.*

**Principal personages:**
JOHN D. BASSETT III, head of the Vaughan-Bassett Furniture Company
JOHN DAVID "J. D." BASSETT, his grandfather, a cofounder of the Bassett Furniture Company
CHARLES COLUMBUS "C. C." BASSETT, his great-uncle, a cofounder of Bassett Furniture
JOHN D. "DOUG" BASSETT, his father, a onetime head of Bassett Furniture
JOHN EDWIN "ED" BASSETT, his cousin-once-removed, a onetime head of Bassett Furniture
BOB SPILMAN, his brother-in-law, onetime head of Bassett Furniture
ROB SPILMAN, his nephew, CEO of Bassett Furniture beginning in 2000
LARRY MOH, the Chinese-born founder of Universal Furniture
HE YUNFENG, a Chinese businessman seeking to build a furniture empire

As its title suggests, *Factory Man: How One Furniture Maker Battled Offshoring, Stayed Local—and Helped Save an American Town* tells the story of the eponymous factory man's struggles to preserve his business and employees' livelihoods despite challenges brought about by globalization. At heart, though, the book is the deeply personal story of a family and two towns as well as the broader tale of the furniture-manufacturing industry in the United States. In *Factory Man*, Beth Macy presents a sweeping historical epic that extends over more than a century and spans the globe, from the unincorporated communities of Virginia to the isolated factory towns of northern China.

The entwined stories of the Bassetts and the towns in which they lived and operated their factories begin as far back as the late eighteenth century, when Nathaniel

Bassett was deeded nearly eight hundred acres of land in what is now Henry County, in southern Virginia. The family continued to amass property and wealth over the decades, but the Civil War put an end to much of their

*Beth Macy is an award-winning journalist. She is the daughter of a factory worker, and* Factory Man *is her first book.*

aristocratic way of life. After the war, Nathaniel Bassett's great-great-grandson John David "J. D." Bassett opened a store and post office on the family's land, which soon became known as the unincorporated community of Bassett. Intent on expanding his business, J. D. Bassett opened a sawmill and arranged a lucrative lumber deal with the Norfolk and Western Railway, which he persuaded to run its new line through his property. After the railroad was built, he began to sell his lumber to furniture companies in northern cities such as Grand Rapids, Michigan; however, he was not satisfied merely to sell materials to other companies. In 1902, J. D. Bassett and his brother Charles Columbus "C. C." Bassett, along with their partners, founded the Bassett Furniture Company. Soon, Bassett Furniture was turning the ample hardwoods found on Bassett land into ornate bedroom furniture and shipping the inventory throughout the United States and Canada.

Over the decades, Bassett Furniture expanded in a multitude of new directions, producing furniture beyond bedroom sets and providing seed money to independent companies that nevertheless remained deeply tied to Bassett, largely through family relationships. One such company was the Galax, Virginia–based Vaughan-Bassett, founded in 1919 by Bunyan Vaughan, whose brother, T. G. Vaughan, was married to J. D. Bassett's daughter Blanche. Meanwhile, the main Bassett Furniture Company remained under the family's tight control, passing from J. D. to his son John D. "Doug" Bassett in 1960. In the mid-1960s, however, the line of succession became a source of significant conflict within the Bassett family. Dying of cancer, Doug Bassett named C. C. Bassett's son, John Edwin "Ed" Bassett, chair of the company's board, but contrary to expectations, he did not name his son, John D. Bassett III, as Ed Bassett's second in command and heir to the company's leadership. Rather, he gave the position to son-in-law Bob Spilman. This decision would shape the fate not only of John D. Bassett III (whom Macy frequently refers to as JBIII) but also Bassett Furniture and the American furniture-making industry.

John D. Bassett III and Spilman clashed frequently, and in the early 1970s, after buying and merging two furniture factories in Mount Airy, North Carolina, Spilman sent Bassett to the newly formed National Mount Airy Furniture Company. Macy suggests that Spilman intended for Bassett to fail in North Carolina, but he instead succeeded in turning National Mount Airy into a profitable manufacturer of high-end furniture. Upon his return to Virginia, however, Bassett found that there was still no room for him among the leadership of Bassett Furniture. In 1982, tensions came to a head—possibly in the form of a Bassett-Spilman fistfight—and by the end of the year, Bassett resigned from his family's company and took a position with Vaughan-Bassett in Galax. As plant manager—and later as president and chief executive officer—Bassett worked to revitalize the flagging company, introducing new product lines and opening new factories and subsidiary companies.

Meanwhile, however, new competitors in Asia were beginning to have a significant effect on the American furniture industry. In the 1970s, a Chinese-born American named Larry Moh had joined forces with his brothers-in-law to determine how to manufacture furniture in Asia. The partners soon discovered how to use cheap rubberwood lumber to produce furniture similar in style to that made from Virginian hardwoods. Their company, Universal Furniture, soon became a major force in Asia, and other furniture companies followed suit. Because of the availability of cheap materials and labor, Chinese companies began selling to American furniture retailers at far lower prices than American manufacturers could manage. However, the lower cost of wood and labor proved to be only one of the reasons for the low wholesale prices. As Bassett discovered in the early 2000s, some Chinese companies, particularly the furniture empire headed by businessman He YunFeng, were selling furniture to retailers at wholesale prices that were less than the cost of materials in an attempt to take over the market and put American manufacturers out of business. Macy notes that this practice, known as "dumping," is considered illegal by the World Trade Organization when it results in the closure of factories and unemployment of large numbers of workers.

Seeking to protect his company and employees, Bassett embarked on a crusade against the companies engaged in dumping. Trade organizations and the US government eventually concluded that the companies had engaged in illegal dumping and required the companies in question to pay duties on goods exported to the United States. A portion of the funds collected was granted to the American furniture manufacturers harmed by the years of dumping, including Vaughan-Bassett. Although the government's decision did not save all of the struggling furniture companies, and some Chinese companies evaded punishment by opening new factories in countries such as Vietnam, Bassett's struggle against illegal trade practices can ultimately be considered a successful one. By the 2014 publication of *Factory Man*, both Bassett Furniture and Vaughan-Bassett remained in business, and Vaughan-Bassett proudly proclaimed that all of its furniture was crafted in the United States.

Macy concludes *Factory Man* with a collection of historical photographs as well as extensive notes and a Bassett family tree—the latter an essential resource in a work that covers more than one hundred years and several generations of the Bassett family. The inclusion of notes and photographs underscores Macy's exhaustive research, which gives the book more personal flavor than one might expect from a work of business history. To present a thorough portrait of the Bassett family, Macy conducted interviews not only with the famously reticent Bassetts and their extended family, but also with current and former factory workers and townspeople, as well as members of the furniture industry and government officials with whom the Bassetts interacted. The members of the Bassett family presented in the book are, for the most part, three-dimensional and lifelike, with both admirable strengths and serious personal flaws. Bob Spilman, John D. Bassett III's primary rival at Bassett Furniture, is portrayed more negatively, as are Chinese factory owners such as He YunFeng and the various individuals who opposed Bassett's antidumping crusade. As the book is ultimately about Bassett and is overall sympathetic to his perspective, however, that is perhaps to be expected.

In keeping with the findings of her research, Macy does not hesitate to describe the sneaky and often completely dishonest business practices in which some of the Bassetts engaged, which included deliberately driving Michigan furniture factories out of business, poaching workers from rival companies, and producing knockoffs of other manufacturers' popular pieces. Indeed, some readers may find a hint of a double standard in the book, as Chinese factory owners' practices are deemed unfair while those carried out by the Virginia factory owners against their rivals are treated as simply part of business. Macy likewise acknowledges the uncomfortable legacy of the family's slaveholding past and the company's unfair treatment of African American workers for much of the twentieth century, although she argues that while Bassett Furniture hired black workers for worse jobs and at lower wages than white workers, the company at least *hired* black workers, unlike many of its rivals. Macy's multifaceted portrayal of the Bassetts does at times backfire and may cause some readers to question the accuracy of some family members' perspectives. Similarly, her inclusion of certain rumors—such as that John D. Bassett III and Spilman came to blows and that at least one Bassett man fathered a child with an African American servant under questionable circumstances—raises questions that will likely never be answered.

Reviews of *Factory Man* were largely positive, with critics praising Macy's extensive research and committed depiction of the struggles faced by many American factory workers. In a review for the *New York Times*, Mimi Swartz wrote that Macy "makes a complex, now universal story understandable" and that her "passion and enthusiasm are palpable on every page." Writing for *SFGate*, Lucas Mann echoed those sentiments, noting that as both a dedicated reporter and the daughter of a factory worker, Macy is uniquely positioned to tell the stories of the Bassett family and their employees with candor and understanding. Although the majority of critics praised the book, some identified problematic elements in Macy's—and, by extension, Bassett's—argument. Writing for the *Wall Street Journal*, Mark Levinson commented that although he found the book well crafted and engaging, he was skeptical about Macy's assertion that Chinese competition was the primary cause of the factory closures. He noted that a lack of innovation in both furniture design and manufacturing practices on the part of "executives in a sheltered industry" played just as damaging a role as globalization. However, Levinson added that Bassett should not be included among those executives. Indeed, throughout *Factory Man*, Macy demonstrates that it was Bassett's willingness to take the initiative that enabled his company to survive and thrive amid ever-increasing global challenges.

*Joy Crelin*

**Review Sources**

Rev. of *Factory Man*, by Beth Macy. *Kirkus*. Kirkus, 15 June 2014. Web. 30 Jan. 2015.

Levinson, Marc. "Book Review: 'Factory Man' by Beth Macy." Rev. of *Factory Man*, by Beth Macy. *Wall Street Journal*. Dow Jones, 18 July 2014. Web. 30 Jan. 2015.

Mann, Lucas. "'Factory Man,' by Beth Macy." Rev. of *Factory Man*, by Beth Macy. *SFGate*. San Francisco Chronicle, 31 July 2014. Web. 30 Jan. 2015.

Pike, Earl. "'Factory Man' Is Beth Macy's Boisterous Account of a US Furniture Business Battling the Tide of Globalization." Rev. of *Factory Man*, by Beth Macy. *Cleveland.com*. Northeast Ohio Media Group, 4 Sept. 2014. Web. 30 Jan. 2015.

Swartz, Mimi. "Still Made in the USA: 'Factory Man,' by Beth Macy.'" Rev. of *Factory Man*, by Beth Macy. *New York Times*. New York Times, 15 Aug. 2014. Web. 30 Jan. 2015.

Weinberg, Steve. "Business Book Review: 'Factory Man: How One Furniture Maker Battled Offshoring, Stayed Local—and Helped Save an American Town,' by Beth Macy." *Dallas Morning News*. Dallas Morning News, 19 July 2014. Web. 30 Jan. 2015.

# Faithful and Virtuous Night

**Author:** Louise Glück (b. 1943)
**Publisher:** Farrar, Straus and Giroux (New
York). 80 pp.
**Type of work:** Poetry

Faithful and Virtuous Night, *the latest collection of poems (interspersed with short
prose poems) by distinguished poet Louise
Glück, won the 2014 National Book Award
for poetry.*

(Courtesy of Farrar, Straus and Giroux)

Louise Glück's latest book of poems, *Faithful and Virtuous Night* (2014), which won
the 2014 National Book Award for poetry,
follows hard upon the 2012 publication of
her impressive collection *Poems 1962–2012.*
That book showed the full range and evolution of Glück's talents, whereas the latest
volume, with fewer pages, offers a more limited sense of her achievement. The poems
in this book are often long and occasionally somewhat prosaic. The shorter poems are
often the most effective, but there is much writing of all sorts to admire.

A brief prose poem titled "A Work of Fiction" exemplifies many of the strengths (as
well as one or two of the weaknesses) of Glück's newest volume. The first thing one
notices about this poem, as well as about practically every other piece in this latest collection, is how immediately accessible Glück's writing can be. The phrasing is clear to
the point of sometimes sounding undistinguished (as in "a wave of sorrow enveloped
me"). But at a time when some poets seem to prize being as puzzling and indecipher-
able as possible, Glück is refreshingly lucid. In this poem, the speaker describes an
experience that almost all readers have had, and thus this poem is one to which most
of Glück's readers can instantly relate. Unlike some of the longer works in *Faithful
and Virtuous Night*, which are probably most meaningful to the author herself, poems
such as "A Work of Fiction" are of almost archetypal significance, especially when
one considers the possibility that this poem is not simply about the end of a book but
about the inevitable end of life, both for the speaker and for everyone. There is, indeed,
an elegiac tone in many of the poems in this collection, as if Glück were looking back
over her own life and anticipating closure.

In "A Work of Fiction," practically everything works. The imagery of light and
darkness; the symbolism of walking "out into the night" (with its clever use of preposi-
tions); the striking simile about the cigarette; and, especially, the wonderful wordplay
involved in the reference to the "cigarette glowing and growing small," with the sudden surprise of the final brief word. All these aspects of the poem help make this an
immensely memorable piece. The repetition of the word "brief" adds to the overall

sense of impermanence and mutability, while the balance of the final sentence brings the text to a polished, artful conclusion. Lamenting different kinds of endings, Glück here creates something genuinely, enduringly beautiful out of evanescence and loss.

*Faithful and Virtuous Night* opens powerfully, with a splendid poem titled "Parable." Here and in many of the texts in this volume, Glück writes in ways that are somehow utterly clear while also sounding vaguely mysterious. Sometimes, when reading her poems, one has the sense that one is reading a superb prose translation of verse originally written in another language, as in "Parable." The effects are delicate and their impact difficult to explain, but one way to appreciate the excellence of the phrasing is to pick out a phrase that sounds out of place, such as "arguments going back and forth." Those words sound merely prosaic; they might have been written by anyone. Most of the other phrasing, however, sounds somehow distinctive, which partly results from the unusual syntax—subjects and verbs are delayed in a poetic technique known as "inversion." Thus one line appears as, "each / further issue we debated equally fully," instead of the more normal, more mundane "we debated each further issue equally fully"; or, similarly, the words "many times this happened" instead of "this happened many times." Yet syntactical balance also contributes to the phrasing's impact, as in "less flexible and more resigned"

> *Louise Glück is one of America's most distinguished and most honored poets. She teaches at Yale University and is the author of numerous books of poetry, including* Poems 1962–2012 *(2012), which exemplifies her long career as a writer.*

or in "where the snow had been, many flowers appeared," as well as in the next line, which is also distinguished by its use of alliteration and assonance. All in all, phrasing like this sounds close enough to colloquial English to be completely comprehensible but also different enough to sound alluring and intriguing. Many passages in *Faithful and Virtuous Night* are effective and affecting in just these ways.

Similarly powerful is the next poem, titled "An Adventure," which contains a number of especially memorable or even haunting moments, such as these: "As we had all been flesh together, / now we were mist," and "We had escaped from death— / or was this the view from the precipice?" In poems such as this, one senses that Glück is grappling with issues of broad, deep human importance, especially issues of the purpose of life and the fear of approaching death. In her best poems, there is often a sharpness and precision of observation that is instantly striking. It is hard to imagine a more vivid opening than these first lines of the poem titled "The Past":

> Small light in the sky appearing
> suddenly between
> two pine boughs, their fine needles
> now etched onto the radiant surface
> and above this
> high, feathery heaven—

Smell the air. That is the smell of the white pine,
most intense when the wind blows through it . . . .


Here, as in much of her poetry, Glück captures universal sensual, emotional experiences to which readers can all relate, rendered on paper so memorably. *Faithful and Virtuous Night* is full of passages like these—passages that stick in the mind for reasons almost too subtle to explain. In the passage just quoted one notes the appearance of "suddenly" (Glück is an expert at knowing when to insert line breaks); the echo of "pine" by "fine"; the alliteration of "high" and "heaven"; and the superbly metaphorical "feathery." Meanwhile, the abrupt command of "Smell the air" typifies the effect of directly addressing readers that Glück uses often in this book. Here as in many other poems, she creates the sense that the reader is there with the speaker. In this way, Glück implies a real desire to communicate with her readers, to involve them. She does not deliberately puzzle her readers or push them away.

If *Faithful and Virtuous Night* ever does seem somewhat uninvolving—and sometimes it moves in that direction—that is because it occasionally seems too generic. Sometimes the speaker seems to be relaying memories that, however important they may seem and be to that speaker, are not made as vivid and memorable on the page for readers as they could have been. Thus the title poem, which begins with intriguing wordplay and a striking image, can eventually seem to drag on a bit too long. The memorable phrasing of the opening lines eventually gives way to passages such as this:

I picked up *My First Reader*, which appeared to be
a story about two children—I could not read the words.

On page three, a dog appeared.
On page five, there was a ball—one of the children
threw it higher than seemed possible, whereupon
the dog floated into the sky to join the ball.
That seemed to be the story.


There is little about the actual language here that draws one's attention or makes one want to reread to discover why and how the phrasing is so striking. By this point the interest in the poem has become mainly an interest in narrative and character rather than in language.

In general, the best poems in *Faithful and Virtuous Night* are those that do not go on for page after page. Many readers will feel that Glück is most effective when she is least concerned with a speaker's private experiences. Her best poems tend to be the ones with the most mythic resonances. Often these are the brief prose poems, printed as solid paragraphs (as in "A Work of Fiction"). They appear at regular intervals, giving the book a structure and rhythm in which seemingly autobiographical works (often long and apparently private) alternate with works of more general significance (often short and more symbolic). The entire book closes with one of these prose poems titled "The Couple in the Park," which is memorable in every way, especially for its evocative final line: "This must explain the puzzling music coming from the trees."

*Robert C. Evans, PhD*

**Review Sources**

Campion, Peter. "Acquainted with the Dark." Rev. of *Faithful and Virtuous Night*, by Louise Glück. *New York Times*. New York Times, 26 Sept. 2014. Web. 20 Jan. 2015.

Chiasson, Dan. "A View from the Mountain." Rev. of *Faithful and Virtuous Night*, by Louise Glück. *New Yorker*. Condé Nast, 10 Oct. 2014. Web. 20 Jan. 2015.

Rev. of *Faithful and Virtuous Night*, by Louise Glück. *Publishers Weekly* 21 July 2014: 161. Print.

Quinn, Annalisa. "The Ecstatic Blankness of Poet Louise Glück. Rev. of *Faithful and Virtuous Night*, by Louise Glück. *NPR Books*. NPR, 11 Sept. 2014. Web. 20 Jan. 2015.

# Family Life

**Author:** Akhil Sharma (b. 1971)
**Publisher:** W. W. Norton & Company (New
York). 224 pp.
**Type of work:** Novel
**Time:** 1970s–2000s
**Locale:** Delhi, India; Queens, New York

Family Life *tells the story of the Mishra fam-*
*ily, Indian immigrants who find a new life*
*in the United States in the late 1970s. The*
*Mishra parents invest their desires for suc-*
*cess in their sons, Ajay and Birju, while try-*
*ing to achieve the American dream, but in*
*the process they are met with tragedy. The*
*novel follows the family through the turmoil*
*and readjustment caused by this tragedy.*

(Courtesy of W. W. Norton & Company)

**Principal characters:**
AJAY MISHRA, the youngest son of the Mishras and the narrator of the novel
BIRJU MISHRA, his older brother
MR. MISHRA, their father
MRS. MISHRA, their mother

*Family Life* Akhil Sharma is a novel about an Indian family that immigrates to the
United States in the late 1970s. It is semiautobiographical, with the base of the story
drawn from Sharma's life, yet the events have been changed or embellished to create a
compelling drama. Written in the first-person, it is told from the point of view of eight-
year-old Ajay, who is the younger of the two Mishra sons, the oldest being Birju. Their
father had left India for the United States by himself because of a prosperous job. The
two boys and their mother stayed in India to wait for their father to bring them with
him. Finally, he is able to fly the rest of his family to the United States, where they
live in the Queens borough of New York City. In the beginning, the Mishras are met
with relatively good luck and fortune but then fall into hardships. Birju quickly adapts
to their new life and excels at school, while Ajay struggles to feel at home in Queens.

The boys' parents had high expectations when they immigrated to the United
States. The Mishras pinned most of their hopes for future success on Birju, whom
they see as having very high potential, especially academically. Birju is a brilliant
scholar who is focused and, even at an early age, fairly centered. Unfortunately, these
ambitions are suddenly cut when their son is met with a tragic, disabling accident.
Shortly after Birju is accepted to the Bronx High School of Science, he hits his head
in a swimming pool and slips underwater, unconscious, for three minutes before he is
rescued. Unfortunately, he is left with permanent brain damage. This event changes

the lives of the Mishras, as they must concentrate their efforts on Birju's health. They get a new home, where they hire live-in help for Birju. During this difficult time, their father starts to drink heavily due to the stress of Birju's condition and his increasing depression. Their mother takes up a minimum-wage job in a garment factory for extra income. Ajay starts to see how much his father has changed as he disappears into alcohol and depression. He says that "he now seemed mysterious, like he was a different person, someone who looked like my father but was not the same man."

Ajay takes his frustrations out on his incapacitated older brother, calling him "smelly" and "fatty" as he lies comatose. Birju will never walk again for the rest of his life. He is blind, laying in bed and regulated by heavy doses of medicine that do little to improve his condition. The family is crippled with sadness. Ajay tells his father that he is sad, and his father responds by saying, "I want to hang myself every day." Ajay's mother is obsessed with trying to revive Birju. They pray every day for his recovery, while tears stream down their faces. The feelings of loss, isolation, and alienation exacted by the family's tragedy uncover what appears to be empty striving for a successful material life.

Regardless of the stress and uncertainty, Ajay still loves his brother. He sometimes acts as if Birju can hear him. For instance, he crawls into bed with him to complain about high school anxieties. Ajay and his mother also try to make light of the situation by teasing Birju with playful name-calling, pretending that he is coherent and responsive.

Ajay is eventually left to take over as the family's ticket to future success. At the same time, he is left to feel a mix of resentment and guilt, making his parents proud while retaining his sanity. He eventually attends Princeton University and goes on to become a banker, while honing his writing skills.

Ultimately, *Family Life* is the story of a boy growing up in a foreign land in the shadow of an older brother who has stopped growing and maturing. It is also the story of what such damage can cause, devastating a family that strives for success and perfection; how they react to the stress of loss; and how they interact with the Indian community that supports them.

The Mishras become close to the other Indian immigrant families that live in their neighborhood. The family's relationship with them becomes complex—a mix of support and competition. The other families are also striving to achieve the American dream but they retain their customs and superstitions from India. For instance, Mrs. Mishra is devoted to the welfare of Birju, which the community thinks is saintly. The Indian parents send their children to her so that she can bless them before their tests.

Sharma captures, knowingly and with sympathy, the shifting moods of Ajay as the reader follows him into manhood. Ajay struggles with a life of absolute freedom and the guilt of needing to help his family in order to cope with the tragedy of his elder brother. He feels deeply the anger and despair of his parents, who vested Birju with their hopes for success. The reader feels along with Ajay his rage for not living up to their expectations that he will become the success story they yearn for. Ajay also struggles with racism and feeling alienated from his peers. He laments that he and his family are not white, which he feels would make it all the more easy for them to succeed in America.

Akhil Sharma's writing is elegant, without pretension or unnecessary flair. Sharma writes with a sparse, flattened tone reminiscent of American author Ernest Hemingway, whom Sharma has named as a profound influence. His style, with his attention to character development instead of detailed prose, emphasizes the sense of loss and frustration that overcomes the Mishra family.

In an interview with Philip Maughan for the *New Statesman*, Akhil Sharma discussed his writing style and how this was a painstaking project for him. It took him thirteen years to write *Family Life*, which he laments might not have been "the right investment"

(© Ben Miller)

*Akhil Sharma is the author of* An Obedient Father *(2001), which was published to great acclaim and won the PEN/Hemingway Award and Whiting Writers' Award in 2001.* Family Life *is his second novel.*

of his time. But, for him it was cathartic—a way to deal with what was a traumatic event in his childhood.

Sharma found it difficult to write in the first person with a child as the narrator. Sharma says that the danger of having a child as a narrator is that they cannot adeptly process the meaning of things. Yet he succeeds with telling his story with clarity, depth, and feeling through the child protagonist by minimizing details and describing the character's actions in detail.

*Family Life* is reminiscent of three fairly recent novels with similar plots. Indian author Jerry Pinto's novel *Em and The Big Hoom* (2012) is about an Indian family that is coping with mental illness in the family. *We Are Not Ourselves* (2014) by American author Matthew Thomas is about three generations of an Irish American family who are struggling with mental illness and the expectations of the American dream. *The Namesake* (2003), by Jhumpa Lahiri, shares the Indian immigration theme of Sharma's novel, where the children of immigrants become the promise of success and the fulfillment of the American dream. The parallels to these novels are starkly similar—with the anticipations of success and the reality of tragic disappointment when faced with harsh reality.

*Family Life* has been met with mostly positive acclaim. A reviewer for *Kirkus* called it a "moving story of displacement and of the inevitable adjustments one must make when life circumstances change." Kirsty Gunn, writing for the *Guardian*, hailed the novel as a masterpiece with a clear writing style: "Sharma's plain style, its gaps and fissures and mighty sense of lack, is both proof of the inability of words to render grief and a demonstration that they can do exactly that. . . . Sharma's simple words tell in order that they might show," she wrote. Sharma relies on simplicity and a sparse narrative to tell his story to great effect.

*Richard Joseph Stein*

**Review Sources**

Deraniyagala, Sonali. "The Repercussions." Rev. of *Family Life*, by Akhil Sharma. *Sunday Book Review*. New York Times, 3 Apr. 2014. Web. 27 Feb. 2015.

Rev. of *Family Life*, by Akhil Sharma. *Kirkus*. Kirkus, 7 Apr. 2014. Web. 27 Feb. 2015.

Rev. of *Family Life*, by Akhil Sharma. *Publishers Weekly*. PWxyz, n.d. Web. 27 Feb. 2015.

Gunn, Kirsty. "An Unhappy Emigration." Rev. of *Family Life*, by Akhil Sharma. *Guardian*. Guardian News and Media, 10 May 2014. Web. 27 Feb. 2015.

Maughan, Philip. "The Son Also Rises: Family Life by Akhil Sharma." Rev. of *Family Life*, by Akhil Sharma. *New Statesman*. New Statesman, 15 May 2014. Web. 27 Feb. 2015.

Seervai, Shanoor. "'A Love Letter to My Mother:' Akhil Sharma on His Novel And His Family." Rev. of *Family Life*, by Akhil Sharma. *Wall Street Journal*. Dow Jones, 25 Jan. 2015. Web. 27 Feb. 2015.

Sharma, Akhil. "A Novel Like a Rocket." Rev. of *Family Life*, by Akhil Sharma. *New Yorker*. Condé Nast, 7 Apr. 2014. Web. 27 Feb. 2015.

# The Feel Trio

**Author:** Fred Moten (b. 1962)
**Publisher:** Letter Machine Editions (Tucson). 93 pp.
**Type of work:** Poetry

The Feel Trio *is an avant-garde collection of prose poems, often elliptical in phrasing, syntax, and meaning. The collection was one of five finalists for the 2014 National Book Award in Poetry.*

(Courtesy of Letter Machine Editions)

Many general readers may not know what to make of the first several lines of Fred Moten's latest book of poetry *The Feel Trio*. They might note the anaphora (the repetition of words at the beginning of sentences or verse) in the first two lines of the second poem: "welcome to what we took from is the state. / welcome to kill you, bird. the welcome state," or the repetition of sound in the words "hurt," "world," and "bird" or the colloquial "been lost" in the next two lines: "and its hurt world, where you been lost and tied, / bird. it's some hot water on the second floor." They may see that the next line, "and the altar on the bottom is an order pair," could connect to the line before because "altar" in this line seems to echo the sound of "water" in the previous line, and "the bottom" contrasts in meaning with "the second floor." Finally, in reading the sixth line, "of lemon chocolate on the curb. get jumped in.," a general reader may take note of the detailed reference to "lemon chocolate on the curb" and the abruptness of the final three-word phrase in that line, which seems especially striking because it is so short after the long phrases that preceded it. Despite these observations, what, one may wonder, is Moten's message? Is there a message in these lines? Does his choice of words combine to become anything, or are they simply random choices and are therefore *meant* to be random?

It is certain that Moten is not aiming to communicate in any clear or obvious fashion. This is a poem in the avant-garde tradition of Gertrude Stein, Hart Crane, or Ezra Pound's *The Cantos*. Part of the point of such poetry is to call attention to the peculiarity of the speaker in the poem and of the writer and to make both figures seem uncommon, intriguing, fascinating, perhaps even exasperating. It is in many ways poetry as self-display yet displays nothing clearly.

If one turns to another page of *The Feel Trio*, one reads these first few lines of another poem:

the violence of the coping strata is specific and seasoned. we give
sh—— away to hurt people and build poor shelters that move and
wrap around. we love to hold the continual failure in one another,
till new things come from that like bullets that catch bullets for
butter and chocolate.

Again, many readers will not be sure how to react to poetry such as this. That, of
course, is part of such poetry's function: to puzzle, to confuse, to make one unsure
(perhaps unsure even about what poetry now *is*). Is the quoted phrasing rhythmic or
musical or striking in its sound effects? Poetry used to be associated with language of
that sort, and perhaps one can detect such language here. After all, it can be argued that
both assonance and alliteration appear in the first quoted sentence and that verbs are
strongly, even rhythmically, emphasized in the sentence that follows. Anaphora and
alliteration appear in "we give" and "we love"; internal rhyme appears in "come" and
"from"; and there may even be some alliterative wordplay on "bullets" and "butter."
But what, if anything, does such poetry *say*? What meanings does it communicate,
what emotions does it stir, what rich significance does it possess and convey? Perhaps
such questions would seem, to Moten's admirers, misguided and naïve.

Yet reactions like this to writing like this are hardly new. Take, for example, part of
the rejection letter Stein received from publisher Arthur Fifield in 1912 for one of her
repetitious manuscripts:

I am only one, only one, only one. Only one being, one at the same time. . . . Being only
one, having only one pair of eyes, having only one time, having only one life, I cannot
read your M.S. three or four times. Not even one time. Only one look, only one look is
enough.

So the issues raised by work like Fred Moten's are not unique to Fred Moten's work.
They are, instead, issues raised by much contemporary poetry, often the poetry that is
short-listed for major prizes, such as the National Book Award. In fact, Moten's *The
Feel Trio* was one of the top five contenders for that award in 2014.

Around the time that Fifield wrote to Stein, the great split began to occur in modern
poetry, pitting work like Stein's, Crane's, and Pound's (which struck many readers
as arcane, esoteric, and baffling) against poetry that was far more accessible to most
general readers (without being merely simplistic), such as the works of William Carlos
Williams or, later, Philip Larkin, among others. The split is probably even older when
one thinks of some of the nonlyrical verse of William Blake, as opposed to his highly
accessible and much-beloved lyrics.

If one sets Fred Moten's book side by side with other poetry finalists for the 2014
award, the effect is notable. All the writers except Moten are fairly accessible to the
general reader, and some of them are even more so to a great degree. Fanny Howe's
*Second Childhood* is sometimes elliptical. Claudia Rankine's *Citizen: An American*

*Lyric* is almost entirely and absolutely lucid. Maureen N. McLane's *This Blue* is richly playful but almost always instantly intelligible. Louise Glück's *Faithful and Virtuous Night*, which was the winner of the 2014 award, represents the kind of poetry that most readers are likely to find appealing on many different levels. Here, for instance, are the first few lines of one of Glück's poems in the collection: "It came to me one night as I was falling asleep / that I had finished with those amorous adventures / to which I had long been a slave." Everything here will strike many readers as relevant to their own lives and experience: the situation, the thought, and above all the clarity of phrasing and syntax, which appeals because it is so obviously an effort to communicate genuinely.

Fred Moten has chosen a different style, as here: "I pray to the elegant string. of off-handed evenness, / the window is a soma you talk through. what music / you'll become and the beautiful cars you'll drive!" Lines like these excite some readers. Poet and book reviewer Patrick James Dunagan, for instance, wrote for the *Rumpus* that in *The Feel Trio*, Moten's "references are contemporary as well as historical, steeped in jazz and black history, representing a cultural lexicon of the utmost accomplished chops filled with slang, humor, and critical acumen." Likewise, poet CM Burroughs in the journal *Lana Turner* says of *The Feel Trio* that "with the same unbinding and idiosyncratic raveling that is crafted in jazz and the blues, Moten has made a speaking that reads as if filtered through one composer's confident score then replayed in various registers, instruments, and genres of sound." A reviewer for the online poetry blog *Galatea Resurrects* has written that *The Feel Trio* is "delightful and enjoyably challenging to read, because its author is delightful and often challenging to listen to, and because it moves just far enough beyond his other very fine books to challenge the world to give him the notice he has deserved all along."

Moten, then, does have passionate advocates. Still, it would splendid to read a future volume by him that made a more obvious effort to reach out to readers other than those who already admire what he is doing. Moten probably has much to share with people who would love to read him if he wrote more accessibly. One fears that in the long run it will be the poets who write as Glück, Howe, McLane, and Rankine do who will be read and reread, pondered, and remembered and that a potentially vital, valuable voice like Moten's will become even less accessible to future readers.

*Robert C. Evans*

© Kari Orvik, Tintype Studios

*Fred Moten teaches at the University of California, Riverside. He is the author of several books of poetry, including* Arkansas *(2000),* I ran from it but was still in it *(2007),* Hughson's Tavern *(2008), and* B Jenkins *(2010).*

## Review Sources

Burroughs, C. M. Rev. of *The Feel Trio*, by Fred Moten. *Lana Turner Journal.* N.p., 2014. Web. 9 Jan. 2015.

Rev. of *The Feel Trio*, by Fred Moten. *Galatea Resurrection.* Eileen R. Tabios, 7 Dec. 2014. Web. 23 Dec. 2014.

Dunagan, Patrick James. Rev. of *The Feel Trio*, by Fred Moten. *Rumpus.* The Rumpus, 30 May 2014. Web. 23 Dec. 2014.

Williams, Tyrone. "On the Lower Frequencies: The Variegated Spaces of Fred Moten and. . . ." Rev. of *The Feel Trio*, by Fred Moten. *Jacket2.* Jacket 2, Kelly Writers House, 12 Aug. 2014. Web. 23 Dec. 2014.

# The Fever

**Author:** Megan Abbott (b. 1971)
**Publisher:** Little, Brown (New York). 320
pp.
**Type of work:** Novel
**Time:** The present
**Locale:** Dryden, a small town

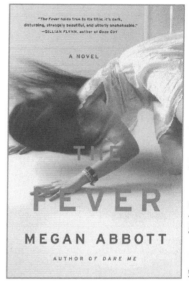

(Courtesy of Little, Brown and Company)

*The Fever chronicles the town of Dryden's descent into rumor, speculation, and panic when teenage girls begin to succumb to a mysterious illness.*

**Principal characters:**
DEENIE NASH, a sixteen-year-old girl whose
    friends begin to fall ill
TOM NASH, her father, a high school teacher
ELI NASH, her eighteen-year-old brother
LISE DANIELS, her friend and the first girl to
    become ill
GABBY BISHOP, her friend and the second girl affected
KIM COURT, Gabby's friend and the third girl affected
SKYE OSBOURNE, Gabby's friend

The seventh novel by award-winning writer Megan Abbott, *The Fever* (2014) explores what happens when a strange illness threatens the young women of a small town, weaving the tale through the perspectives of three of the town of Dryden's residents: sixteen-year-old Deenie Nash; her eighteen-year-old brother, Eli; and their father, Tom. Abbott's prose is at some points hauntingly descriptive and at other points maddeningly vague, in keeping with the often-unreliable nature of the novel's narrators. Indeed, the story is told as much through what the characters are thinking as through what they are trying to keep from thinking about. Published in July 2014, *The Fever* met with a largely positive critical response and was named one of the best books of the summer by numerous popular publications.

*The Fever* begins, in a section aptly titled "Before," with a scene that takes place sometime before the main events of the narrative. As Deenie and several other girls wait to receive their first shot in the three-shot human papillomavirus (HPV) vaccine regimen, conversation among the young women sheds light on one of the overarching elements of the novel. One girl says, "The first time, you can't believe how much it hurts." Another adds, "You're sore for a few days. They say by the third time, you don't even feel it." The girls are talking about receiving their vaccinations, but, as in many conversations in *The Fever*, the specter of sexual awakening lingers over the scene. It is no coincidence that the arrival of the mysterious illness that afflicts several of

Deenie's friends coincides with their sexual coming-of-age. The illness itself is frightening, but the townspeople's true fears seem to lie elsewhere, as indicated by the immediate rumors of pregnancy and sexually transmitted disease that spread when the first girl falls ill and the almost obsessive concern the town's parents have for their daughters' "fragile"—in the words of Deenie's father—

*Megan Abbott is the author of several acclaimed crime and mystery novels, including* Die a Little *(2005) and* Dare Me *(2012). Her novel* Queenpin *(2007) won the Mystery Writers of America's 2008 Edgar Award for best paperback original.*

bodies. Although as focused on a central mystery as Abbott's other novels, *The Fever* is ultimately the story of coming of age in a world where teenage girls are simultaneously the most endangered and the most dangerous people of all.

The day after Deenie loses her virginity to Sean Lurie, her coworker at the local pizza restaurant, her childhood friend Lise collapses in class, having a seizure for which there is no immediate, easy explanation. Perhaps even more frightening to Deenie is the way the seizure seems to reveal an inner darkness hidden deep within her friend. While Lise receives medical attention, a flood of questions begins: Is she pregnant? Has she been taking drugs? The situation is heightened when Lise has another seizure, followed by a cardiac event. While Lise lies comatose in the hospital, Deenie and Lise's friend Gabby becomes the second girl to fall ill, experiencing a seizure-like series of involuntary physical tics while onstage during an orchestra concert.

The people of Dryden and representatives from the local health department begin to suggest possible causes. Lise's mother believes the HPV vaccine to be responsible and convinces some of the local parents of her theory, while other parents and students attribute the illness to the sick girls' trip to an algae-infested lake in which a young boy had drowned a decade before. The legitimacy of those theories is called into question, however, when Gabby's friend Kim, who neither received the vaccine nor swam in the lake, becomes the third to fall ill. As other girls begin to exhibit similar symptoms, their parents and friends, as well as the growing number of outsiders intrigued by the illness, suggest additional possible causes: environmental contamination, a bizarre sexually transmitted disease, toxic shock syndrome, and even demonic possession.

Meanwhile, Deenie struggles with her guilt over remaining healthy while her closest friends fall sick; of her immediate social group, only she and Gabby's friend Skye remain unaffected. She feels perhaps even guiltier for having slept with Sean, with whom Lise was also involved—a betrayal she perceives as linked to Lise's collapse the day after the event. She does not reveal Lise's involvement with Sean to the reader until well into the novel, and that revelation underscores her unreliability as a narrator. Spurred on by her guilt, Deenie slowly unravels the mystery of what is happening to the girls of Dryden, eventually tracing the illness back to its source. In the end, the true nature of the illness for most of the girls leaves many of the people of Dryden unsatisfied. The series of events that led to Lise's collapse, however, is both unthinkable yet, in a realm as fraught with rumor and jealousy as high school, far easier to understand.

In many ways, *The Fever* combines three defining elements of Abbott's fiction: her genre influences, her tendency to draw from real-life events, and her focus on complex female characters. Although not focused on a murder or a disappearance, as were several of Abbott's earlier works, *The Fever* is at heart a mystery novel, and the question of what caused the illness plaguing the girls of Dryden remains of great importance throughout. In addition to noting its effectiveness as a mystery, reviewers commented on *The Fever*'s elements of horror, from the lake seemingly haunted by death and strange plant matter to the girls who seem, in their most ill moments, to resemble possessed young women in need of exorcism. However, such elements are just a small part of the novel's horror; the lake is eliminated as a suspect early on, and exorcism is only proposed as a serious solution by a lone commenter on one of the sick girls' YouTube videos. The true horror of *The Fever* is not supernatural but societal. The idea of demonic possession may send a chill down the reader's spine, but Abbott seems to argue that it is humankind, and the monsters humanity can conjure out of thin air, that is truly something to fear.

Much like Abbott's earlier novels *The Song Is You* (2007) and *Bury Me Deep* (2009), *The Fever* is based loosely on real-life events. In 2011 and 2012, a number of teenage girls in Le Roy, New York, a former industrial town about thirty miles south-west of Rochester, began to manifest a variety of physical and vocal tics. Some girls also experienced seizures or fainting spells. The tics eventually spread to a boy and an adult woman, but it remained primarily prevalent among young women. Authorities investigated a number of possible causes, among them environmental contamination from both a 1970 train derailment and the many factories that formerly operated in the town. The HPV vaccine and a potentially contaminated swimming hole also came under suspicion. Ultimately, however, doctors diagnosed the affected individuals with conversion disorder, in which stress—in this case possibly caused by family troubles, school pressures, and economic concerns—manifests in physical symptoms. As multiple people were affected, doctors also made a diagnosis of mass psychogenic illness (sometimes known as mass hysteria). In a June 2014 article for the *Huffington Post*, published shortly after the release of *The Fever*, Abbott comments that she was struck by the Le Roy case and immediately began writing *The Fever* after seeing videos of some of the affected girls, drawing from those true events to create her novel. She was particularly inspired by the role social media and technology played in publicizing— and possibly exacerbating—the situation in Le Roy. This element is readily noticeable in *The Fever*, in which rumors travel quickly via text message and the affected girls speak out about what is happening to them in videos posted to YouTube. Although Abbott's novel concludes with a realization far more dramatic than the ultimately mundane findings of the Le Roy investigators, her use of real-life inspiration lends *The Fever* a degree of authenticity that offsets the at-times-unbelievable events. Many critics praised Abbott's incorporation of real-life elements, although *New York Times* reviewer Hannah Tennant-Moore deemed the setting "exploitative."

Throughout her writing career, Abbot's books have focused primarily on women, and her two novels immediately preceding *The Fever*, *Dare Me* (2012) and *The End of Everything* (2011), specifically feature teenagers. As with those previous books, her portrayal of young women in *The Fever* was largely praised by critics, many of whom appreciated Abbott's ability to write about teen friendships and conflicts with a seriousness uncommon in much adult literature. In a review for the *Boston Globe*, crime novelist Clea Simon noted that in Abbott's hands, there is "nothing coy or quaint about women coming of age." Critics also praised the authenticity of the teenage characters. Novelist Steph Cha, in her review for the *Los Angeles Times*, wrote that Abbott "demonstrates an uncanny ear for the voice of youth," applauding the conversations and text messages throughout the book. Other readers, however, may find some of the dialogue and text messages—for instance, the rather clumsily brand-dropping text message "Have u heard of toxik shok? tampax can kill u"—to be less authentic than they would prefer.

Despite the novel's widespread critical acclaim, Abbott's portrayal of women in *The Fever* did receive some criticism. In her review for the *New York Times*, Tennant-Moore identified some elements of the novel as problematic, in particular pointing to the way in which the female characters seem to be punished for their sexuality while the male characters are not, bringing to mind the "pervasive depiction of lustful girls as hysterical and self-destructive, and lustful boys as simply normal." Indeed, some elements of the novel could be considered similarly troubling. Mothers are typically either absent or viewed by the characters as victims or hysterical conspiracy theorists. Deenie herself expresses a degree of internalized sexism, feeling disgusted by the girls her brother sleeps with but leaving Eli largely free from judgment; she alone bears the guilt for sleeping with Sean, who she knew was also involved with Lise, while not considering that he was an equal partner in that betrayal. The ultimate causes of the strange illness likewise tie into some unfortunate stereotypes about women. It is important, however, to avoid conflating the beliefs of the author with those of her characters. Patriarchal thinking does seem to be alive and well in *The Fever*; however, it seems likely that rather than endorsing such viewpoints, Abbott seeks to call attention to the destructive effects they can have on young women in Dryden and beyond.

*Joy Crelin*

**Review Sources**

Cha, Steph. "In Megan Abbott's *The Fever*, Teen Girls' Panic Is Contagious." *Los Angeles Times*. Los Angeles Times, 12 June 2014. Web. 30 Oct. 2014.

Rev. of *The Fever*, by Megan Abbott. *Kirkus Reviews* 5 May 2014: 116. Print.

Rev. of *The Fever*, by Megan Abbott. *Publishers Weekly* 28 Apr. 2014: 104–5. Print.

French, Liz. "Books for the Masses: Toxic Teens and Other Creatures." Rev. of *The Fever*, by Megan Abbott. *Library Journal* 1 July 2014: 30. Print.

Simon, Clea. Rev. of *The Fever*, by Megan Abbott. *Boston Globe*. Boston Globe Media Partners, 16 June 2014. Web. 30 Oct. 2014.

Tennant-Moore, Hannah. "The Awakening." Rev. of *The Fever*, by Megan Abbott. *New York Times Book Review* 29 June 2014: 9. Print.

# Fives and Twenty-Fives

**Author:** Michael Pitre
**Publisher:** Bloomsbury (New York). 400 pp.
**Type of work:** Novel
**Time:** 2006; 2011
**Locales:** Iraq; various locations in the United States and Middle East

*The story of the trials and tribulations of three veterans from a platoon responsible for repairing and clearing roads littered with bombs as they try to adjust to the civilian world while always being reminded of the war they experienced in Iraq.*

**Principal characters:**
PETER DONOVAN, the lieutenant who leads the platoon in charge of repairing Iraqi roads and clearing bombs found in potholes, later a college undergraduate
LESTER "DOC" PLEASANT, a Navy corpsman, the medic in his platoon
KATEB "DODGE" AL-HARIRI, an Iraqi interpreter in his platoon

(Courtesy of Bloomsbury Publishing)

War stories come in many forms. Some are tales of heroism in which seemingly ordinary men do extraordinary things, while others are polemics for peace in which warfare in general is considered an untenable condition that consumes innocent lives. Elements of truth can be found in both of these variations and in others not mentioned here. Many posit that no one can truly understand what a veteran goes through save for another veteran. A skilled storyteller cannot fully recreate the drama of combat without experiencing it. The sights, sounds, and emotions of those moments are so interconnected and complex that they often defy words. Still, this does not keep authors from trying to bridge the gap. The very best war stories transport readers to distant lands and convey much of the anxiety and fear of those moments under fire. They get readers close to the experience even if they fall short of fully explaining it.

Michael Pitre represents the ideal chronicler of war stories. A veteran of two tours of duty in Iraq as an officer in the US Marine Corps, Pitre knows firsthand the trials and tribulations of military service in a combat zone. His first novel, *Fives and Twenty-Fives* (2014), is no ordinary effort by an arm-chair author seeking to capture the mindset of a foreign world; it is a composite sketch of the people, places, and events that Pitre witnessed while serving his country. Although none of the stories he recounts took place as they are relayed, they provide snippets of life based on actual experiences of marines fighting a most unconventional of wars.

In a genre where superhuman actions abound, Pitre's cast of characters does not consist of conventional heroes. None of them is perfect and they are all real people, just like the men and women who have put on military uniforms throughout history. The characters do not consider themselves special, and each has a secret or a serious limitation that defines his experiences. Pitre's book also differs from the norm in that his story bounces from the present to the past as the book's three central characters, Lieutenant Peter Donovan, Corpsman Lester "Doc" Pleasant, and Iraqi interpreter Kateb "Dodge" al-Hariri try to make sense of their lives.

Readers meet these three main characters as they struggle to adjust to life outside of the military. Although each of them performed different roles during the war in Iraq, they were united by their shared experience. Even when those experiences led them to fight, in the end, they were bound by an affinity that people who go through traumatic experiences together share. As civilians, each of the characters struggles with the ghosts of the central event of their lives, illustrated by the juxtaposition of flashbacks to the war. Pitre captures the terrible toll that war takes upon the youth who are required to wage it. This novel is not a denunciation of war itself so much as it is a plea to take care of those who endure it. The representation of the Iraqi perspective, in the form of the intriguing and dynamic character of Dodge, also sets this war narrative apart from others in the genre, offering a glimpse into the darker and relatively untold story of those left behind in the true aftermath of the war.

The main figures in Pitre's account are not a combat unit, but a roadside repair platoon whose job entails keeping the roadways of Iraq free of mines and fully paved. Every day, new deadly traps are placed along the roadway in hopes of killing some Americans who might be passing by in a single blast or to cause a convoy to halt long enough for insurgents to launch an attack against them. The book's title derives from the rule of thumb embedded in the minds of every member of the platoon. When a roadside bomb is detected, the convoy stops and everyone scans five meters in all directions. A bomb located in the five-meter range has the explosive power to blast through a truck's frame, killing all onboard. After tending to the security of the fives, the convoy dismounts to investigate a twenty-five-meter perimeter around the disturbance in the ground that prompted the unit to halt in the first place. A bomb inside this range would kill those detached to fix the potholes that litter the landscape and always contain a bomb.

The story Pitre shares is thus not of a unit engaged in sustained firefights with the enemy; it follows a group whose job seems that it should be a bit more removed from the blatant fear of combat, but considering the nature of the war in Iraq, is anything but. Every pothole, every stretch of broken earth along a roadway brings with it possible death. A steady and demoralizing stream of casualties afflicts the unit, and tensions are always high. Constant vigilance is the most critical consideration, and it is something that is difficult to maintain in the monotonous desert landscape that surrounds them. The line between friend and foe is almost always blurry. Pitre captures the travails of combat in Iraq in which every situation is fraught with danger, and he describes these events in a straightforward and detailed manner that successfully conveys the reality and gravity of the situation, rather than sacrificing this authenticity for dramatic effect.

(© Aubrey Edwards)

*Michael Pitre served two tours of duty in Iraq as an officer in the US Marine Corps.* Fives and Twenty-Fives *is his first novel.*

Pitre also shares some of the memories that afflict combat veterans when they return to the civilian world. Even for those who escape without physical scars, there are always emotional ones simmering just below the surface. To watch a fellow marine die or suffer injury before one's eyes has a devastating psychological impact. So does the experience of coming in contact with close-quarter explosions. At no point does Pitre browbeat readers with platitudes about the need to look after returning veterans. He provides an understated narrative that leaves little doubt that the way service personnel are treated while in the military and are often abandoned when they are released is nothing short of tragic, leading to the destruction of many young lives.

When the parades, the waving flags, and the admiration of one's neighbors begin to diminish, military veterans are left with their memories. What they have seen and what they have experienced simply cannot be understood by those who were not there. At the beginning of the novel, former marine officer Donovan seems to have a lot going for him after having left Iraq. A student at Tulane University working toward a master of business administration degree, he is, on the surface, living the dream so carefully spelled out by recruiters: serve one's country, get the GI Bill, go to college, and live a successful life. What the recruiters often do not share is that with that commitment comes the likelihood that even after the guns have fallen silent, the emotional and physical scars of those hours locked in mortal peril remain. Outwardly, Donovan is a typical undergraduate. He looks the part to be sure, but he is not anything like those who surround him. Try as he might, he struggles to pay attention, to fit in, and to find love. He is not ready to fully commit. The war still haunts his thoughts, and it seems that it always will.

Pitre's marines are outwardly tough, if inwardly insecure. The officers and noncommissioned officers are acutely aware that everything they do is being judged by the marines under their command, and as such, they recognize that they must never show fear, never show uncertainty. To convince men to do things that they would never do under normal circumstances is the epitome of leadership. Not everyone who rides along with the marines exhibits these traits or is even a marine, however. Navy corpsmen serve as medical attendants attached to marine units. When these units are in danger, it is often the corpsman who steps in to perform a life-saving role. In Pitre's book, Corpsman Pleasant does not get lost in the bravado of the Marine Corps—he finds solace in his medicine bag through the abuse of pain killers. It starts off simply enough: a roadside blast, a loss of life, and a neophyte corpsman facing his first casualties. However, that singular event sends him into a downward spiral from which he loses his position in the military and spends a very tenuous existence in the civilian world battling his addictions. Like Donovan, Pleasant finds the transition back to the civilian world anything but easy.

Pleasant's closest compatriot in Iraq is not an American; it is the Iraqi interpreter, Dodge, whose story is extraordinarily complex. Reviewers have unanimously agreed that Dodge, who is part of a wealthy family that was well appointed in Saddam Hussein's Iraq before the American invasion, is undeniably the most powerful of Pitre's trio of main characters. With his native land thrown into turmoil at the very moment he was enjoying the scholarly life of a college student in Baghdad, Dodge found his excellent command of the English language in demand in the US military. Of course, like many of the characters in Pitre's book, he carries with him a rather dark secret. When Dodge goes to work for the roadside-bomb unit, the reader eventually discovers that he is in many ways intimately connected to those who attempt to kill American soldiers every day. It is an ironic twist, yet one that illustrates the complexities of the Iraqi battlefield. Dodge has to keep his face covered on many occasions to avoid being recognized. His life seems to perpetually hang in the balance, and like all of the characters in the book, he struggles with his demons in his own way.

*Fives and Twenty-Fives* is a book worthy of picking up. Pitre has succeeded both in portraying the war in Iraq in a manner that does not glamorize combat but instead highlights the equally gritty, everyday work side of the conflict, as well as in telling the often-neglected story of the Iraqi people. It is an account that takes readers alongside boisterous marines, those who try to lead them, those who try to help them, and those who assume a mercenary role in an effort to survive in a war-torn country. In a world turned upside down by war and internal strife, the characters in this book look to each other when the moment of truth appears. Despite personal conflicts that simmer to the surface near the end of their deployment—conflicts that seem to make repair of the rift between them impossible—they once again seek each other out as they struggle to find their way in their postwar worlds.

*Keith M. Finley, PhD*

## Review Sources

Benedict, Helen. "Fives and Twenty-Fives Review—Michael Pitre's Riveting Iraq War Novel." Rev. of *Fives and Twenty-Fives*, by Michael Pitre. *Guardian*. Guardian News and Media, 2 Oct. 2014. Web. 17 Feb. 2015.

Rev. of *Fives and Twenty-Fives*, by Michael Pitre. *Publishers Weekly* 14 June 2014: 54. Print.

Kakutani, Michiko. "In Iraq, Dread Is in the Air." Rev. of *Fives and Twenty-Fives*, by Michael Pitre. *New York Times*. New York Times, 20 Aug. 2014. Web. 17 Feb. 2015.

Turrentine, Jeff. "Review: 'Fives and Twenty-Fives,' by Michael Pitre, a Tale of Dangerous Duty in Iraq." Rev. of *Fives and Twenty-Fives*, by Michael Pitre. *Washington Post*. Washington Post, 25 Aug. 2014. Web. 17 Feb. 2015.

# Flash Boys
## A Wall Street Revolt

**Author:** Michael Lewis (b.1960)
**Publisher:** W. W. Norton (New York). 288 pp.
**Type of work:** Current affairs, economics
**Time:** 2009–13
**Locale:** Financial district of New York City

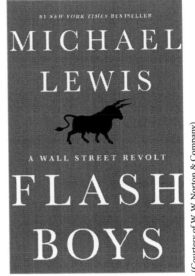

(Courtesy of W. W. Norton & Company)

*Alleging that high-speed stock traders use high-tech equipment and data lines to gain an advantage over other traders,* Flash Boys *has created a considerable stir among investors, the personnel of brokerage firms, and journalists who cover the financial world.*

**Principal personages:**
BRAD KATSUYAMA, a stock trader for the Royal Bank of Canada (RBC), the founder of Investor's Exchange
RONAN RYAN, his coworker at RBC and one of his sources
DAN SPIVEY, one of the founders of Spread Networks
SERGEY ALEYNIKOV, a Russian-born computer programmer

In *Flash Boys* (2014), author Michael Lewis delves into the arcane and little-understood internal workings of the United States' financial markets, as he has done in some of his previous works, such as *Moneyball* (2003) and *The Big Short* (2010). Lewis has a special talent for making subjects such as this understandable to nonspecialists and turning technical jargon and complicated story lines into enjoyable reading. The subject here is high-speed trading, in which, according to Lewis, stock traders use computer systems and data lines to gain a fraction of a second's advantage in knowing what bids and orders are being placed, allowing them to manipulate orders so as to make a tiny profit by buying stock at lower prices to fulfill buy orders that have just been placed. The profit on each share may be only a fraction of a cent, but spread over hundreds of daily trades of tens of thousands of shares, it can be a very lucrative enterprise. Since these high-speed traders make many such transactions every trading session, they are also high-frequency traders, although not all high-frequency traders are involved in the kind of high-speed trading that Lewis believes to be unethical.

After an introduction in which Lewis describes how he became interested in the subject, the main body of the book begins with an account of a project to lay cable for a high-speed data line from New Jersey to Chicago. The project is directed by Dan Spivey, one of the founders of Spread Networks. Although negotiations have to be held with many landowners and government entities for the right of way for this line, the builders try to keep the purpose of the line secret. They are attempting to lay a cable in the straightest, most direct route possible, because turns and angles in the line can slow down data transfer by fractions of a second. Eliminating those delays can be worth much to those traders who want the advantages that ultra-high-speed networks can give them. When the line is finally completed, large brokerages involved in high-speed trading pay millions of dollars for access to it. The line gives them very slight but valuable advantages in data-transmission speed over those using standard, slower lines. One customer actually asks Spread Networks if they can double the price of their service, presumably so that fewer competitors could afford to take advantage of it.

Readers soon learn that the popular perception of national stock exchanges, with brokers on the floor shouting buy and sell orders in a maddened frenzy, is badly outdated. Today there are numerous exchanges where stocks are traded, but the actual trading happens on computers, in a fraction of the time such transactions took when more direct human interaction was required. So the speed at which those computers can communicate, and even the physical proximity of the computers, becomes a valuable asset. One fascinating part of the book explores how small the variations in speed are that high-speed traders hope to exploit. Before anyone like Spread Networks was offering a specialized high-speed line, the data-transmission services provided by public telecom companies such as AT&T, Verizon, or Level 3 could vary, but only by a fraction of a second. To send data from New Jersey to Chicago might take 16 milliseconds one day and perhaps 17 milliseconds the next. Some traders find that a particular Verizon line is quicker—it takes only 14.65 milliseconds to send the data between the same two centers—and this difference of less than three-thousandths of a second is so valuable that the traders call this Verizon line the "Gold Route." At one point, Dan Spivey is concerned about the route his new data line is taking. The line has to cross a road to get to the right of way they have permission to use; this right-angle crossing is going to cost him one hundred nanoseconds, which troubles Spivey, even though a nanosecond is a billionth of a second.

Much of the book focuses on Brad Katsuyama, a Wall Street trader for the Royal Bank of Canada (RBC). In 2007 Katsuyama starts to notice that when he tries to place an order for a large block of stock, the shares available at the just-quoted asking price disappear in a fraction of a second, and available shares for purchase suddenly go up in price—"as if the stock market had read his mind," Lewis notes. Katsuyama begins to explore why this happens and can find no one who can explain it. Even the computer technicians within RBC seem baffled by the phenomenon. This leads him to dig deeper, and eventually he puts together a team of experienced traders and computer technicians who are able to understand what is happening and who then try to find ways to keep the high-speed traders from exploiting this advantage.

Eventually Katsuyama realizes he is going to have to find someone with experience in the world of high-speed, high-frequency trading who has "defected" or is willing to do so, because no one outside of this world seemed to be able to understand what is going on. One of the most important of his informers is Ronan Ryan, an Irish-born immigrant who becomes a much-sought-after technician on Wall Street. Working through several jobs at various telecommunications companies, Ryan eventually becomes one of the most knowledgeable people involved in the construction of the technology needed for high-speed trading networks. But he has always wanted to work on the financial side of Wall Street rather than in information technology, so Katsuyama is able to hire him away from a much-higher-paying position at Goldman Sachs by offering him a job as a stock trader. At RBC, Ryan becomes Kat-

*Michael Lewis's first book,* Liar's Poker *(1985), was about his experiences working at Salomon Brothers, a Wall Street investment firm. He has written several nonfiction best sellers, including* Moneyball *(2003),* The Blind Side *(2006),* The Big Short *(2010), and* Boomerang *(2011).*

suyama's "translator," explaining the technical side of what makes high-speed trading work and helping him find ways to work around the advantages these traders have.

The team Katsuyama puts together to build a system that can outwit the high-speed traders includes many individuals who fit the stereotypical perception of a computer geek—brilliant, yet with quirky personalities and somewhat lacking in social skills—yet Lewis's treatment of them is sympathetic, for he considers them the heroes of the story. Eventually Katsuyama and his team put together an RBC project named Thor that is designed to protect their customers from the advantages that high-speed traders have in the market. Later, Katsuyama and some of his team leave RBC to start their own small stock-market exchange, called Investor's Exchange or IEX, to offer similar protection to their clientele.

*Flash Boys* quickly became a best seller, and the book prompted much discussion among journalists who cover the financial world. Many small-scale investors believed that Lewis had shown that the stock markets are rigged in favor of the high-speed traders, and there were calls for government investigations and further regulation. Holly Bell, a professor of business at the University of Alaska Anchorage, wrote in a review in *Reason* in November 2014 that Lewis's suggestions of fraud were "gaining purchase" and that both the FBI and the New York state attorney general were investigating the practices of high-speed traders.

Lewis admits that what the high-speed traders are doing is legal at this time but argues that further regulation is needed. However, he admits that a previous attempt at regulation, the US Securities and Exchange Commission's Regulation National Market System rule of 2007, is what made the whole phenomenon of high-speed trading possible. What the high-speed traders are doing is similar to front running, which is an illegal practice in which brokers benefit from insider information from their own firm about what stocks are going to be acquired in large numbers. Technically, however, high-speed traders are not front running because they are getting their information by simply watching transactions on the open market.

Even those who agree with Lewis's basic contention have raised the question of just how important all of this is—how much are typical investors actually being hurt by the very small profits the high-speed traders make on any specific stock transaction? Some have suggested that the very fact that the RBC's Thor project or Katsuyama's Investor's Exchange can create a system to negate the high-speed traders' advantages is evidence that the financial markets self-regulate to correct perceived abuses. Critics have noted that Lewis's book lacks balance, as no one involved in high-speed trading is included to present their side of the story. As in many of Lewis's books, the characters he focuses on emerge as clear-cut heroes, fighting villains who are described just as starkly, with no murkiness or gray areas. Reality, of course, is rarely so neat and tidy.

*Mark S. Joy, PhD*

**Review Sources**

Bell, Holly. "High Frequency, Fat Target." Rev. of *Flash Boys: A Wall Street Revolt*, by Michael Lewis. *Reason* Nov. 2014: 73–75. Print.

Broughton, Philip Delves. Rev. of *Flash Boys: A Wall Street Revolt*, by Michael Lewis. *Wall Street Journal*. Dow Jones, 31 Mar. 2014. Web. 26 Nov. 2014.

Gapper, John. Rev. of *Flash Boys: A Wall Street Revolt*, by Michael Lewis. *FT.com*. Financial Times, 3 Apr. 2014. Web. 26 Nov. 2014.

Maslin, Janet. "Hobbling Wall Street Cowboys: *Flash Boys* by Michael Lewis, a Tale of High-Speed Trading." Rev. of *Flash Boys: A Wall Street Revolt*, by Michael Lewis. New *York Times*. New York Times, 31 Mar. 2014. Web. 26 Nov. 2014

# Flirting with French
## How a Language Charmed Me, Seduced Me & Nearly Broke My Heart

**Author:** William Alexander (b. 1953)
**Publisher:** Algonquin Books of Chapel Hill
(Chapel Hill, NC). 266 pp.
**Type of work:** Memoir
**Time:** 2010
**Locales:** United States; France

*In his third memoir, William Alexander details his obsession with learning to speak French like a native at the age of fifty-seven. He describes and despairs of various methods he tries to gain fluency.*

**Principal personages:**

BILL ALEXANDER, the narrator
ANNE ALEXANDER, his wife
KATIE, his daughter, who is studying French
in college
ZACH, his son
SYLVIE, his French pen pal

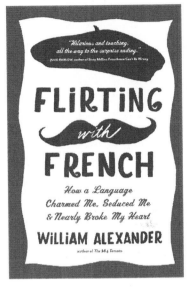

(Courtesy of Algonquin Books)

This memoir follows the style of William Alexander's previous two books, *The $64 Tomato* and *52 Loaves*. Each focuses on a different obsession of his: gardening, baking bread, and in this work, learning a language. Each book employs Alexander's wry, self-deprecating humor and easygoing tone. Each places his adventures in the context of something larger. In *Flirting with French*, readers learn not only about how we acquire language but also about the human heart and the physical difficulties one can suffer in aging. The subtitle, which can be taken at first as commentary, becomes more serious as readers accompany Alexander through several episodes of atrial fibrillation and resultant surgeries. That narrative is braided into the larger story of language learning and forms a minor thread on *coeur*, the French word for heart. *Coeur* is also the root of the word *courage*, a term that is dropped into the narrative at several points.

In his use of humor and the playful tone, as well as the use of himself as a do-it-yourself project of sorts, Alexander resembles his younger contemporary A. J. Jacobs. The latter focuses exclusively on himself in books such as *The Know-it-All* and *The Year of Living Biblically*, questing for intelligence and moral ground, while at the same time sharing enough additional information so that he is not perceived as hopelessly narcissistic.

France, and particularly Paris, has long fascinated Americans. Many contemporary writers have penned memoirs about visiting or living in France, such as Janice MacLeod's *Paris Letters*, Thad Carhart's *Piano Shop on the Left Bank*, and the works of Peter Mayle. However, few of these memoirs detail the author's struggles to acquire the language. Perhaps the most closely related work is Alice Kaplan's 1994 memoir *French Lessons.*

Each of Alexander's memoirs includes a reading list. *Flirting with French* has three pages of sources, primarily focusing on the

*William Alexander is director of technology at a psychiatric research institute in New York. He writes for* New York Times *op-ed pages, including an article on the benefits of failing at French, and has made guest appearances on National Public Radio.*

human brain, memory, and language. It is a curious list, composed mainly of books, but much of the material is dated. Memoir does not require a formal bibliography, of course; these works are not keyed to pages as they might be in a work of pure nonfiction. The list of sources almost makes the book feel as if, contrary to his tone, Alexander wishes to be seen as a serious scholar. However, if that was his intent, articles from 1981, 1989, and 2002 undermine credibility, as do books from the 1980s and 1990s.

During November 2014, *Flirting with French* took the number-eleven spot in a *New York Times* list of bestselling travel books. This seems an odd classification for the book, although one can consider the book a narrative of journeying through language learning. Its twenty-four chapters contain only two brief trips to France. The first journey is a ten-day cycling trip Alexander takes with his wife, Anne, three months after beginning his quest to speak French like a native. The second trip is a solo venture for a two-week total-immersion class at a top-rated language school, Millefeuille Provence.

Readers of Alexander's previous books will not be surprised to find him trying to speak French like a native. His first two books have a sort of foreshadowing of this outcome. Near the end of *The $64 Tomato*, Alexander and his wife get on a plane for Europe. In *52 Loaves*, they go to Paris so that Alexander can take a bread-baking course at the Ritz and then spend time at a French monastery baking bread. This memoir opens with his acknowledgement of loving France from the time he first arrived as a twenty-two-year-old with a backpack and through several subsequent visits with his wife and family.

Chapter titles rely heavily on popular culture, most often making puns by taking or remaking names of books or films: *A Room with a* Veau, *It's Complicated, Die Hard, Le Social Network,* and *Glazed and Confused.* Each chapter begins with an epigraph; although Alexander quotes dialogue from popular movies—such as *The Whore of Mensa, Die Hard,* and *The Matrix Reloaded*—he also includes references to Mark Twain and Julia Child. The chapters themselves vary in length; most weave information about language and brain development into the descriptions of Alexander's own experiences.

The book focuses on one year in Alexander's quest for the ability to speak French like a native, long after passing adolescence, considered by many experts the optimum age to do so. During that year he devotes more than nine hundred hours to studying the language, in addition to watching films and television shows in French. Persistence is Alexander's strong suit, as Jan Benzel mentions in her review for *New York Times,* "He hurls himself at French again and again almost like a cartoon character who, smacking up against a slammed door, slides to the floor in a puddle of humiliation."

The book can bog down in places for any reader not as besotted with French as Alexander is. In a chapter entitled "William the Tourist Meets William the Conqueror," one of the longest chapters in the book, Alexander concentrates more on the history of France and the development of the French language, rather than on the glories of the French countryside he and Anne bike through. Spending nearly half the chapter on the technical aspects of the language constitutes too much detail for many readers. Likewise, discussions of the ideas of Noam Chomsky or the linguistic regulatory powers of l'Académie française feel like so much static disrupting the broadcast of Alexander's trials, even though they clearly demonstrate his passion for language.

Readers may also weary of Alexander's complaints about the difficulties of learning French and of the structure of the language itself. He does make his case artfully and humorously, which is the saving grace, raising complaint to the level of art form. He complains about gendered nouns and numerals, the seeming illogic of decisions l'Académie française makes, and the difficulty of retaining vocabulary as he learns new words. At times, the reader wants to tell Alexander to quit whining and work on what he said he would do.

However, the title of the book may offer a clue, however subconsciously. Alexander is *flirting* with French; he is not setting up a serious relationship, despite the hours he logs in language study. The title may have been selected for its alliterative properties or to signal Alexander's frothy approach, but it seems to be the right term.

Alexander's self-mocking stories of his difficulties with the language are arguably the most enjoyable parts of the book. Most chapters contain at least one of these vignettes. For example, on the cycling trip, he seeks directions, showing the map to a man he does not realize is visually impaired and setting off confidently down the wrong road. In another chapter, he learns that getting the gender of a word correct has nothing to do with intuition, writing, "Faced with masculine breasts and feminine beards, masculine arms and feminine legs, a cup of hot water that, once you drop a teabag into *her* transgenders into *him*, English speakers look for some kind of logic in gender assignment. This is a mistake."

Simply trying to determine whether to address the person to whom you are speaking as *vous* or the less formal *tu* when speaking or writing French is a conundrum. Alexander agonizes over this kind of dilemma, finally creating a flowchart to help make the determination. Like much of the book, this flowchart is funny while being instructive; questions to be answered include, "Were you at Woodstock?" and "Is your spouse former president Jacques Chirac?" Despite Alexander's frustration with the French, who do not have a unique word for either "wife" or "daughter," his chart is not gender-neutral. The slant is definitely masculine, with a separate question to determine the right pronoun for a father-in-law, but not a mother-in-law, and a direct address that conjures up a male reader: "Do you feel lucky? Well, do you, punk?"

Alexander recalls his attempts with Rosetta Stone, Pimsleur audio, Fluenz French, two French pen pals, and immersion classes in both New York and France, in addition to watching television programs on TV5 Monde. Not every reviewer found Alexander's wide variety of language acquisition methods charming. As Claire Lundberg wrote for *Slate*, "I kept feeling that Alexander was holding French at arm's length in order to protect his idea of it, as if doing the hard work of learning the language might shatter the perfect picture of the country he'd created." This is a valid critique; for all his efforts, Alexander does not seem to approach his studies in any coherent way. In fact, it is Katie, Alexander's college-aged daughter, who demands that he begin learning to conjugate verbs, six months into his studies, and coaxes him into ten minutes of study each night. She also helps him identify gendered nouns by writing and posting color-coded sticky notes on objects in the kitchen.

The kitchen—and all it represents—is another source of French immersion for Alexander. He spends most of a day making authentic croissants before Katie arrives home for her break, adapting Julia Child's recipe, which he includes in the book. From his first trip to France, Alexander has been in love with French food and spends time detailing both ridiculous and sublime experiences in restaurants. "I'll have the ham in newspaper, and my son will have my daughter," he once ordered in a restaurant in Paris.

Despite all of these efforts, Alexander concludes near the end of the book that although he has learned a great deal of French, he has not learned French, certainly not at the level he had hoped to attain. He admits, "The truth is, not only have I failed to become fluent, or even conversant, in French, but I've failed spectacularly—more so than I ever imagined possible." It is this failure that ultimately makes the book so readable; Alexander is in his late fifties, trying to learn a difficult, albeit beautiful and romantic, language. The reader identifies with such a quixotic quest, cheers him on, laughing at the predicaments he encounters. Along the way, despite not becoming as proficient as he had hoped after thirteen months of study, Alexander demonstrates through brain scans taken before and after he began to study French that his brain has become healthier. Language study, he believes, is a fountain of youth for the brain.

In addition to having written his three books, Alexander maintains TheFrenchBlog. com, which he began soon after *Flirting with French* was published. The blog continues his commentary on and love for French language and culture. His readers will surely continue to follow his journey into all things French.

*Judy A. Johnson*

## Review Sources

Benzel, Jan. "Old Dog, New Trick: Flirting with French by William Alexander." Rev. of *Flirting with French*, by William Alexander. *New York Times*. New York Times, 3 Oct. 2014. Web. 8 Jan. 2015.

Rev. of *Flirting with French*, by William Alexander. *Kirkus Reviews* 82.16 (2014): 117. Print.

Latimer, Joanne. "How a Language Charmed Me, Seduced Me & Nearly Broke My Heart." *Maclean's* 127.40 (2014): 69–70. Print.

Lundberg, Claire. "Les Mots Justes." Rev. of *Flirting with French*, by William Alexander. *Slate*. Slate Group, 9 Sept. 2014. Web. 8 Jan. 2015.

# Florence Gordon

**Author:** Brian Morton (b.1955)
**Publisher:** Houghton Mifflin Harcourt (New
  York). 320 pp.
**Type of work:** Novel
**Time:** 2009
**Locale:** New York City

*Florence Gordon presents a portrait of the
titular protagonist, a longtime feminist intellectual who, though difficult and unlikeable,
is nonetheless memorable as an individual
who refuses to compromise principles in
the process of interacting with family and
friends and coping with newfound fame in
the twilight of her career.*

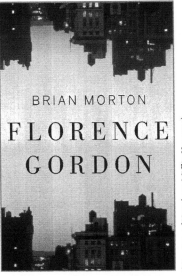

(Courtesy of Houghton Mifflin Harcourt)

**Principal characters:**

FLORENCE SILVERBLATT GORDON, a seventy-five-year-old intellectual Jewish feminist
  activist and essayist

DANIEL "THE PROFESSOR" GORDON, her forty-seven-year-old son, a police officer

JANINE GORDON, her forty-something daughter-in-law, a psychologist and devoted
  athlete

EMILY GORDON, her nineteen-year-old granddaughter and assistant, a vegan who attends Oberlin College

SAUL GORDON, her ex-husband, a teacher and long-unpublished writer who is jealous
  of her success

KEVIN CLEAVER, the young earring-wearing man who replaces her longtime editor
  when he retires

VANESSA, her psychotherapist friend

LEV, a warm and caring psychology lab director

The protagonist of *Florence Gordon* (2014) is the living embodiment of Welsh poet
Dylan Thomas's admonition not to "go gentle into that good night" but "rage, rage
against the dying of the light." A 1960s-era radical feminist, Florence has over the
years published a number of collections of intellectual essays that, while earning her
respect in various literary and social circles, have done little to expand her fame or
increase her income. Now in her mid-seventies, with her latest book of essays recently
published, Florence decides to write her memoirs, even as she contrarily wonders who
would be interested in her thoughts and experiences of the past. That past, she realizes,
has become increasingly irrelevant, since the feminist principles Florence and her ilk
espoused a half century earlier have greatly changed, and she is as out of touch with

contemporary ideas and goals as she considered the suffragists of the 1910s to be during her heyday in the 1960s.

An independent self-starter beholden to no one, Florence nonetheless receives a massive ego boost from a glowing article about her by a respected critic for the *New York Times Book Review*. Recognition in such a widely distributed venue thrusts Florence into the public spotlight, serves as the impetus for her to take off on her first-ever book tour (arranged by the younger, more marketing-oriented replacement for her gentlemanly longtime editor Edward, who has fallen ill), and acts as a catalyst for her to renew her efforts to complete her memoir. In an indelibly memorable scene, the irascible Florence walks out on a gathering of well-wishers at a surprise seventy-fifth birthday party thrown for her: she is not fond of surprises, she would rather be alone, and she has work to do. It is work, rather than human relationships, that has always sustained her and best engaged her mind.

Florence's plans are complicated not only by the additional demands on her time generated by the article but also by the presence in New York City of several family members and a coterie of admiring friends, who disrupt and distract Florence from her purposes. Most of the other characters, especially those related to Florence, exhibit to varying degrees the quick intelligence and deep-seated stubbornness for which she is noted. Like her, they are supposed to be communicators; like her, they sometimes choose not to communicate, keeping crucial information to themselves at critical junctures out of self-interest, spite, or pride. As much as the main characters enjoy talking and doing, they often leave important words unsaid and deeds undone.

As a teenager, Florence's only son, Daniel, wanted to be a writer like his parents. Instead, he joined the US Army, then became a police officer with the Seattle Police Department's crisis intervention unit, where he served for more than twenty years. On the job, he is treated less like a law enforcement officer and more like a social worker with a badge. Although Florence considers him a disappointment for his career choice, Daniel takes accumulated vacation time to be with his wife, daughter, and mother in New York. There, he experiences a bout of anxiety and suffers a mild heart attack that requires a short stay in a hospital. For reasons of his own, Daniel neglects to inform anyone in his family about his hospitalization.

Daniel's wife, Janice, also has a secret. In New York to attend a psychology seminar, she is attracted to the seminar's director, Lev, primarily out of curiosity for something other than routine. Lev is a warmhearted, overweight slob, physically unlike Janice's well-built husband but interested enough to give her the undivided attention she does not receive at home. She has a one-time sexual encounter with Lev—Daniel witnesses the two holding hands in a restaurant prior to their assignation, which triggers his panic attack—and afterward never mentions her infidelity to her husband. But Daniel senses what has happened, and in an especially telling scene at a public gathering, he subtly uses his commanding physical presence to back Lev into a corner to demonstrate his dominance over his presumed rival.

Florence's whiny ex-husband, Saul, bitter about his former wife's fame, dissembles constantly. On the one hand, his pride demands that he lie about his teaching prowess and the demand for his writing, although he has fallen into financial hardship and lives in a run-down neighborhood; on the other hand, necessity causes him to beg Florence to use her influence to help him land steady work.

Perhaps the most interesting secondary character is Emily Gordon, Janice and Daniel's nineteen-year-old daughter, who is taking a break from Oberlin College, significantly the first institution of higher learning in the United States to admit female students. Highly intelligent like the rest of the family, Emily serves as a bridge between the liberated twentieth-century woman as represented by Florence and the independent twenty-first-century woman, who is conversant and comfortable with modern technology such as Facebook and Twitter. Emily, like her mother and father, also withholds information: she has surrendered her virginity and taken Ecstasy for the first time during a weekend with her needy boyfriend, aspiring toy designer Justin. Afterward, immune to his pleas, she dumps Justin and keeps mum about her sexual and pharmacological awakening. Emily volunteers to become a research assistant for

(© David Kumin)

*Brian Morton teaches at his alma mater, Sarah Lawrence College, and at New York University. A 2001 Guggenheim Fellow, he also received the American Academy of Arts and Letters Award. His second novel,* Starting Out in the Evening *(1998), won the Koret Jewish Book Award for Fiction and was adapted for film in 2007.* Florence Gordon *is his fifth novel.*

Florence, whose sudden recognition demands more of her time. Though Florence initially has only contempt for her naïve granddaughter, Emily proves to be a match for her, with a good mind and a sharp tongue, and the two women grudgingly begin to bond, going so far as to attend a protest together.

Florence, too, hides something from her family. For the past several years, she has experienced restlessness in her hands, and one of her feet sometimes flops beyond her control. After a series of long-delayed medical tests, she learns she has a debilitating illness. Rather than rely upon her family for comfort and care, Florence makes her own plans to deal with the affliction.

A quiet novel of ideas rather than complex plot or dynamic action, *Florence Gordon* deals with many of the same issues and themes found in author Brian Morton's earlier work. Like *The Dylanist* (1991), which centers on a group of aging progressives and communists, *Florence Gordon* concerns someone removed from the mainstream of American society who clings to a personalized political and social philosophy forged in the past while ignoring or overlooking changes wrought by the passage of time. As in Morton's *Starting Out in the Evening* (1998) and *Breakable You* (2006), one major thread is the contrast between the idealism of youth and the rigidity of old age, particularly the internal or external compromises that must be made when the mentalities of the young and the elderly clash. The motif here extends from the concerns of the elderly (dignity, honor, legacy)—illustrated best through Florence's humorous, touching, and ultimately futile effort to convince Mount Kisco Jewish Senior Center's crotchety, unkempt, and incontinent Yetta Berman of the advantages of adult diapers—through the considerations of the middle-aged (material comfort, status, security) to the interests of the young (image, popularity, connection). *Florence Gordon* continues Morton's examination of the conflict in the attempt to balance critical and commercial success and highlights the importance of small, everyday decisions that greatly affect characters' lives, two threads that also underscore Morton's *A Window across the River* (2003).

As in all of Morton's long fiction, New York City and its environs provide a familiar base, a colorful backdrop, and a fertile ground to mine for material. The author uses elements of the metropolis sparingly for crisply sketched images, descriptions of singular individuals plucked from among the city's teeming, ethnically diverse masses that act as exemplars of human behavior, and opportunities to put sardonic, sharply observed comments in the mouths and minds of his characters. As in his other novels, Morton includes dozens of relevant literary and historical allusions, from Mary Wollstonecraft and Elizabeth Cady Stanton to Gloria Steinem and *Middlemarch* (1871–72), that emphasize the radical feminist foundation upon which *Florence Gordon* is built.

The multitude of references to social reformers, activists, writers, essayists, and philosophers (and, in Janine's case, to psychologists and psychiatrists) slows an already-leisurely narrative, particularly for those who wish to further explore the allusions, the better to appreciate the author's skill in presenting a unified, well-organized concept built around a fictional icon of the genuine American feminist movement. However, in compensation, Morton's prose style is extremely reader friendly, with a succession of short chapters comprising brief paragraphs of concise sentences that work well to present an unforgettable portrait of a unique character.

*Jack Ewing*

**Review Sources**

Rev. of *Florence Gordon*, by Brian Morton. *Kirkus Reviews* 15 June 2014: 20. Print.
Rev. of *Florence Gordon*, by Brian Morton. *Publishers Weekly* 2 June 2014: 34. Print.
Wilkinson, Joanne. Rev. of *Florence Gordon*, by Brian Morton. *Booklist* Aug. 2014: 33. Print.

# The Forgers

**Author:** Bradford Morrow (b. 1951)
**Publisher:** Mysterious (New York). 256 pp.
**Type of work:** Novel
**Time:** The present
**Locales:** New York City; Kenmare, Ireland

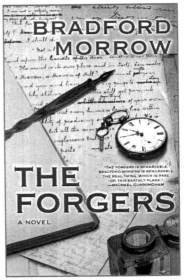

(Courtesy of Mysterious Press)

*Bradford Morrow's seventh novel is presented as a murder mystery, with a brutally maimed victim on page 1. The Forgers is also the story of a convicted fabricator of literary relics who proves himself a loving son and husband, ruthlessly honest about himself but not always a reliable narrator.*

**Principal characters:**

WILL, the narrator, a reformed forger of
  literary memorabilia
MEGHAN DIEHL, his girlfriend and eventual
  wife, the owner of a used-book shop
ADAM DIEHL, Meghan's older brother, a collector of rare books, manuscripts, and
  autographs, as well as a suspected forger
HENRY SLADER, another forger, Will's nemesis
ATTICUS MOORE, Will's friend, a dealer in rare books

As a college student, Bradford Morrow was befriended by the owner of a used-book store in Boulder, Colorado, and also became a bibliophile. He has collected rare books ever since and has himself befriended many specialists in this rarefied field, several of whom have written friendly comments about his new mystery novel. *The Forgers* (2014) tells the story of three men convicted or suspected of literary forgery—not on the grand scale of a new Shakespeare play or a Churchill diary, but forgery of book inscriptions, letters, and manuscripts that could reshape scholarly opinion while commanding considerable prices at book auctions.

Novels about forgery usually focus on the high-stakes game of art forgery, treated, for example, by Robertson Davies in *What's Bred in the Bone* (1985). Bradford focuses on literary forgery. Although one character mentions the forgery of whole printed editions, famously carried out over many years by the nineteenth-century bibliophile T. J. Wise, the real focus is on inscriptions added to increase the value of an already-valuable book or on letters or diaries that conceivably could have been written by a celebrated author. Forgeries are, by nature, different from hoaxes such as the Hitler-Tagenbücher (Hitler Diaries), "discovered" in 1983 and subsequently revealed to have been produced by a con man in Stuttgart who had copied material from various sources into notebooks using postwar paper and ink and then sold the collection for millions of dollars. Forgeries like the inscriptions treated here are produced meticulously on paper that is either authentically old or chemically treated to appear appropriately aged. The forgers of these documents regard themselves as literary figures of a sort, both scholars and artists.

The novel's first-person narrator is a convicted felon named Will—he gives only his first name, and only in one of the many flashbacks as he tells his tale. Will has gone straight and has remained friends with former customers by swearing that he will never resume his nefarious trade. Over the course of his narrative, he explains how he learned the technique and its appeal from his parents, a beloved mother who taught him calligraphy before her early death and an admired but largely absent father who collected rare books and inspired a love of Sir Arthur Conan Doyle and the Sherlock Holmes mysteries.

When his father buys a pen once used by Doyle, Will feels the urgent need to channel the author, whose signature he once copied for his mother, and to write something that Doyle might have written himself. With no

(credit: Jessamine Chan)

*Although murder figures centrally in several of Bradford Morrow's seven novels, including* Giovanni's Gift *(1997) and* The Diviner's Tale *(2011), his fiction covers a wide range of American life. He has written illustrated books, edited anthologies of poetry and gothic fiction, and received many awards as a writer and editor, including the 1998 Arts and Letters Award in literature from the American Academy of Arts and Letters. He teaches literature at Bard College.*

interest in college or a career, he realizes that he can support himself by purchasing rare books and reselling them, salting legitimately rare items with a few of his newly forged "finds." All goes reasonably well, and he lives a simple but comfortable life until he receives a letter threatening to expose his fraud. The letter is signed "Henry James" and written in a good facsimile of the long-dead novelist's handwriting on what could easily pass as a piece of his embossed stationery.

Will suspects that the letter and its increasingly threatening sequels come from a bibliophile named Adam Diehl, whom he knows from rare-book auctions at New York's vast Park Avenue Armory. That is where he also met Diehl's sister, Meghan, with whom he has become romantically involved. He has identified Diehl as the source of a forged manuscript that he once bought from his late father's favorite dealer, Atticus Moore. Will is only somewhat surprised when police come to his door with a confession written and signed in his own handwriting. He shows them the letters from Henry James, which they take in evidence, but he is unable to convince anyone that he has been set up. He refunds buyers of the forgeries traced to him and does prison time and community service. When he gets out, he swears never to resume his former line of work. Though he realizes its addictive attraction, he is resolute because he wants to keep his friends in the book business and, more important, his former girlfriend. Will feels certain that Meghan is the only woman who has truly loved him since his mother died.

Meghan and Will grow closer after her brother dies a gruesome death, savagely attacked in their childhood home. On a vacation in Ireland, Will proposes marriage, and the couple settle down to a peaceful life together. However, the threatening letters resume, and Will's sense of guilt returns with them. Faced with a very live blackmailer, Will suggests a complete change of scene. The newlyweds relocate to Kenmare, the small Irish town where he proposed marriage, and their life takes a happy turn, even though Will grows increasingly paranoid. Before long, the letters resume, bearing new threats from the talented forger whom Will regards as his doppelgänger and nemesis. Only after a final confrontation with the murderous double do the police close in.

The police solve the murder case toward the end, and readers who have not already solved it soon will. Things never were as they seemed, Will realizes, as he sits down to write his narrative—a story that he intends first of all as a memoir for the daughter he has had with Meghan.

As a murder mystery, *The Forgers* breaks all the rules, but then it never really sets out to follow them. It is a postmodern mystery where the emphasis is less on the crime than on the passions that led to it, less on the solution than on the emotions of those it has touched. Even the most dogged detective on the case of Adam Diehl's murder seems to work by fits and starts, and one even has to wonder about the victim's name: What's the deal? The narrator's nemesis, Henry Slader, has a name very like that of John Shade, the hack poet in Vladimir Nabokov's very postmodern novel *Pale Fire* (1962), and it plays on the past tense of the verb "slay." Also, like the narrator of Nabokov's *Lolita* (1955), Will seems much less interested in what he has done than in the cruel mistress that made him do the terrible deed; he likewise is more concerned still with his nemesis, Slader, the Quilty to his Humbert Humbert.

As a narrator, Will seems a very postmodern type, as interested in the words he uses and the paper he writes them on as he is in the story that he is telling—or, perhaps, postponing. His narrative voice is pleasant enough and occasionally quite stylist: "I sensed his eyes betrayed a subtle recognition of me. The unmodulated tone of his voice, flat as a folio's flyleaf, was unreadable. I have always been far better at interpreting inanimate manuscripts than living voices and the looks on people's faces."

In an interview with Pam Lambert for the September 15, 2014, issue of *Publishers Weekly*, Morrow remarked that he is drawn to morally conflicted characters who "deceive themselves even as they're deceiving others so that they can excuse themselves." When such a character tells his story, as Will does, the narrator can be justly deemed unreliable.

In a larger sense, the novel is a meditation on the nature of fiction itself. Fiction is by definition a fabrication, something made up, though it often follows familiar conventions, like the Harlequin romance or the police procedural. A major author can write, as James Joyce's autobiographical hero Stephen Dedalus does near the end of *A Portrait of the Artist as a Young Man* (1914), that he wants "to forge in the smithy of my soul the uncreated conscience of my race." There is not the slightest hint of forgery in Joyce's novel, but there is an element of deception that enters in novels like André Gide's *Les faux monnayeurs* (1925; *The Counterfeiters*, 1927), where the coinage of counterfeit currency becomes a metaphor for differences between the literary original and the copy. Especially toward the end of his narrative, Will realizes that he is a kind of forgery himself, forged in a sense by the authors who have inspired him to imitate their writing. And in a kind of echo of his beginnings, *The Forgers* ends with the narrator training the daughter he has named after his mother—training her in the art of calligraphy, for which she shows both interest and talent. Who knows what she will do in time?

The mystery novel is a good vehicle for teaching the details of a subject. The reader learns about it along with the detective, from whose point of view the story is often told. This novel lacks the drive toward detection, for the narrator knows all about forgery before the action begins. Will records many details for the benefit of his reader; however, he withholds other details that would satisfy the curious reader but would turn the literary novel into the true confession. He may have a confession to make, but he makes the reader guess what it would be.

Early reviews praised the novel's atmospherics, especially its details about the market for rare books and manuscripts. Some noted the rather slow development of the mystery plot and the large number of red herrings, both of which prove necessary for the first-person narrative. Scott Adlerberg's review in the *Los Angeles Review of Books* suggests that the novel itself is a fake—"an inauthentic mystery"—because it lacks the narrative drive of a good whodunit. Nevertheless, for all its false starts and obfuscations, *The Forgers* presents the sympathetic and amazing yet surprisingly credible story of a man who has nearly mastered the art of deception.

*Thomas Willard*

**Review Sources**

Adlerberg, Scott. "Fake Mysteries." Rev. of *The Forgers*, by Bradford Morrow. *Los Angeles Review of Books*. Los Angeles Review of Books, 1 Nov. 2014. Web. 26 Nov. 2014.

Rev. of *The Forgers*, by Bradford Morrow. *Kirkus Reviews* 1 Sept. 2014: 28. Print.

Rev. of *The Forgers*, by Bradford Morrow. *Publishers Weekly* 1 Sept. 2014: 45. Print.

Wells, Susanne. Rev. of *The Forgers*, by Bradford Morrow. *Library Journal* 1 Aug. 2014: 86. Print.

# Fourteen Stories, None of Them Are Yours

**Author:** Luke B. Goebel (b. 1980)
**Publisher:** University of Alabama Press (Tuscaloosa, AL). 184 pp.
**Type of work:** Novel
**Time:** 2000–2013
**Locales:** East Texas; Coastal California; Oregon; Arizona; New York City; rural Ohio

*Luke Goebel's postmodern narrative presents an antihero who has lost his beloved older brother to death and his cherished girlfriend to another man. The plot is nonlinear, and the style self-referential, full of wordplay and narrative trickery.*

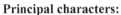

(Courtesy of Fiction Collective 2)

**Principal characters:**
H. Roc, also known as THE KID, the narrator, a thirty-three-year-old white male
CARL, his older brother, a biker with a heart of gold
CATHERINE, his lost love
COACH, his old writing teacher
JULIE TOWNLOVE, his nickname for the girlfriends of his youth
THE APACHE, an older worker at his mother's ranch resort in Arizona
MAESA, a waitress in New York City whom he abandons

Readers who enjoy postmodern fiction can take great delight in Luke B. Goebel's debut novel, *Fourteen Stories, None of Them Are Yours*. The title itself is tongue-in-cheek: there are actually only thirteen stories in the book strung together to make up this novel, although perhaps the fourteenth story is the novel itself. Goebel's text is not for readers who dislike postmodernism and its associated narrative techniques.

However, both kinds of readers can appreciate Goebel's narrative honesty. Right from the beginning, in the title story, or first chapter, called "Insides," Goebel makes clear that his text works with narrative indeterminacy, textual self-references, direct asides to the reader by the narrator, nonlinear plots, and creative play with nonstandard words, grammar, and syntax. This works very well to present a stylistically innovative text. With its references to the narrator's past experimentation with peyote, and elements of the road novel later on, a reader may consider Goebel's novel a postmodern version of Hunter S. Thompson's classic *Fear and Loathing in Las Vegas* (1971) for the twenty-first century.

In "Insides," the narrator has checked himself into a hospital to find the source of his inexplicable pain. While he undergoes preparations for a CT scan, he feels like "I'm a living thing in a hospital on my back." In a disjointed narrative process, he remembers his childhood growing up a rich boy in Ohio and the recent breakup with his girlfriend, Catherine. Some of his disorientation the narrator blames on the aftereffects of having taken peyote with a group of American Indians in Mendocino, California, some years ago. There is a first reference to the narrator's beloved older brother Carl. In bits and pieces, the reader learns the narrator is over thirty years old by now and was in jail once when he was younger and in rehabilitation multiple times. He is sober by now. "Insides" works well to introduce the reader to the novel's style and its major theme of loss. The reflection on loss is triggered first by the narrator's loss of Catherine and is reinforced later by his loss of Carl.

The next segment, "The Adventures of Eagle Feather," takes place before Carl died and before the narrator became Catherine's boyfriend. Yet the narrator addresses the reader directly in brackets from the point of the novel's present, which is revealed to be fall of 2013 later on. In his mock-authorial asides, a typical postmodernist technique, the narrator confesses that "writing this book isn't smart." Back with Carl in Oregon, he finds an eagle feather he wants to give to his creative writing professor, who is also Catherine's teacher. He is called Coach later in the novel and figures throughout as a self-acknowledged ambiguous father figure. Back in Oregon, the narrator wanted to become "an Indian Kid, a great white Indian peyote writer." In the novel's present, the narrator feels he has "done the white man peyote walk for seven years plus" after eating peyote in Mendocino.

This self-expressed desire of a white character/author to be someone else may remind the reader of this trend among earlier white writers like Normal Mailer. In his essay "The White Negro: Superficial Reflections on the Hipster" (1957), Mailer expressed admiration for the urban African American alternative lifestyle he and other European Americans sought to emulate in the late 1950s. For Goebel's narrator, this desire comes with a postmodern self-awareness of the impossibility of this wish. The narrator lets it be known throughout his narrative that his idea of American Indian culture and character is culturally constructed by himself from a white point of view. The narrator's "true Injun" is a fictional construct and not to be mistaken for any authentic vision or description. As such, the narrator deludes himself self-consciously. He invites the readers to be aware also of the delusional nature of his narrative construction of his fictional American Indians.

In the third story, "Drunk and Naked as He Was," Goebel's narrator applies the same idea of literary misconstruction of a cultural character by turning to the quintessential American cultural icon, the cowboy. For reasons unstated, the narrator feels "IT WAS TIME to play the cowboy." To do this, he moves from New York City to East Texas. There, he rents a ranch and buys a puppy for 150 dollars. Had he not bought it, its owners would have sent it to the pound to be euthanized. The narrator and readers share the sense of the outlandishly ridiculous nature of this situation and his approach to it, as well as the narrator's silent despair about his quest to create a satisfactory identity for himself.

It is in the fourth story, "Boot of the Boot," that the major plot elements leading to the theme of postmodern reflection on the nature of loss are finally expressed. This is done via a disjointed narrative that is the trademark of Goebel's experimental fiction.

The narrator explains that the story is what he wrote several months after he moved to Texas, when Catherine left him for a Spanish man while she was alone in Europe. The narrator calls his rival "Manuelo," a version of the much more common Spanish first name Manuel. Manuelo may be the man's real name, or a deliberate, pejorative slight by the spurned narrator. To add to his grief, the narrator states unequivocally for the first time that his older brother Carl has died. There is personal poignancy added when the narrator states, "He died at 33, year I am now." This double loss inspires and propels the narrator to tell his story in a fashion made to resemble the rumination of a grieving man suffering flashbacks from peyote use. Goebel's writing captures this intentionally disjointed style very successfully.

(credit: Marie Goebel)

*Luke B. Goebel was awarded Fiction Collective Two's Ronald Sukenick Innovative Fiction Prize. The prize supported publication of his first novel,* Fourteen Stories, None of Them Are Yours: A Novel.

After another chapter highlighting the narrator's loss of Carl, the sixth story or chapter, "Tough Beauty," offers postmodern fireworks to the reader. The narrator gives himself the clearly fake and ironic name of H. Roc. In his late brother's huge 1988 motor coach recreational vehicle (RV) that is twenty-five years old now, he gets ready to drive up coastal California from San Diego. Suddenly, he flashes back to his time with Julie Townlove. He tells his readers: "Julie Townlove I made up as a symbol of my youth . . . . Back when a joint in the park meant, dynamite, women galore." She is a composite character representing all his girlfriends from his past rolled into one.

While with Julie, H. Roc recalls taking peyote before the narrative becomes completely surreal. Like a tall tale, not to be taken for truth, the narrator relates how he shot dead Julie's American Indian lover with a bow and arrow, joined the United States Army, fought in Afghanistan, and was discharged for mental instability. Back in his RV in the present, the narrator calls America "a great land that is going away but still has a chance."

The subsequent seven stories or chapters in *Fourteen Stories* continue to explore the issues introduced so far in postmodern style. In "Apache," the young narrator seeks to prove his manhood by horseracing an old worker, whom the narrator assumes is an Apache, at his mother's Arizona ranch resort. The narrator wants to earn being called the Kid. This exploration of manhood in America reads like a postmodern version of a classic Hemingway tale. "Out There" continues the story of the narrator's road trip up the California coast in his late brother's RV. While driving, the narrator remembers in a wonderful syncretistic simile Carl's "Christ-like Buddha nature." He remembers an episode from his pre-Catherine phase in New York City, when he was in love with Maesa, a young waitress who still grieves for the mother she lost to illness when she was fourteen and for the father who left the family long ago. The narrator decides to leave Maesa as he does not want her to put him into a parental role. A reader may sense that even in a postmodern novel, poetic justice is delivered when the narrator is left by Catherine later on and suffers greatly for it.

In the final, thirteenth story, "Chores," the narrator seeks to obtain some measure of grace and inner closure by trying to connect with Carl's spirit and honor his memory. He does so in a matter that is both profound and reverential even though it does not appear to be so at first glance. It is also a close-cutting commentary on the idea of American manhood at the turn of the twenty-first century.

With all its disjointed time lines, the narrator's authorial interjections in his own stories, and his recollections of drug visions, Goebel's plot for *Fourteen Stories* is remarkably internally consistent. Once a reader has puzzled out all the plot details strewn over the thirteen chapters, the emerging picture is recognizably sound and solid. Internal consistency, not necessarily to be expected, far outweighs slight inconsistencies.

Goebel's debut novel is honestly straightforward in announcing its literary techniques from the first page on. In this, his narrative works far better than a novel like Lionel Shriver's *Big Brother* (2013), for example. Unlike *Big Brother*, which masquerades as traditional realism for hundreds of pages only to spring a postmodern ending on readers, Goebel's *Fourteen Stories, None of Them Are Yours* delivers what it sets out to do as a brilliant piece of innovative and experimental, postmodern American writing.

*R. C. Lutz*

## Review Sources

Rev. of *Fourteen Stories, None of Them Are Yours*, by Luke B. Goebel. *Kirkus Reviews* 15 Sept. 2014: 243. Print.

Pactor, Marcus. Rev. of *Fourteen Stories, None of Them Are Yours*, by Luke B. Goebel. *Green Mountains Review* 27.2 (2014): 149–152. *Literary Reference Center*. Web. 18 Feb. 2015.

Sheppard, Gary. Rev. of *Fourteen Stories, None of Them Are Yours*, by Luke B. Goebel. *Southeast Review*. Southeast Review, 2015. Web. 1 Feb. 2015.

# Fourth of July Creek

**Author:** Smith Henderson (b. 1973)
**Publisher:** HarperCollins (New York). 470 pp.
**Type of work:** Novel
**Time:** 1979–81
**Locale:** Montana

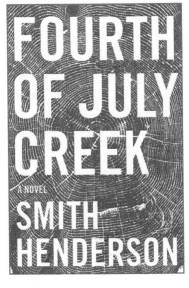

(Courtesy of Ecco)

Fourth of July Creek *is a novel about a social worker in rural Montana who becomes involved with a family of survivalists living in the Montana woods.*

**Principal characters:**
PETE SNOW, a social worker living in rural Montana
BENJAMIN PEARL, an eleven-year-old boy
JEREMIAH PEARL, Benjamin's father, a paranoid antigovernment survivalist
RACHEL SNOW, Pete's estranged daughter who has run away from home

Debut novelist Smith Henderson was a Phillip Roth resident in creative writing at Bucknell University in 2011–12 and won the 2011 PEN Emerging Writers Award for fiction before publishing his first novel, *Fourth of July Creek* (2014), which he has said in interviews was the product of more than ten years of planning. Hailing from Montana, he drew on his personal knowledge of the scenery and ambience of the state to craft a vivid portrait of rural landscapes, ranging from small, neon-lit strips and dying towns to lush wildernesses in which people who shun society choose to hide. Critics have compared Henderson's writing to that of William Faulkner and Cormac McCarthy, especially with regard to his atypical temporal structure and the poetic quality of his prose. Henderson also won widespread praise from critics for the originality of his story and his complex, emotionally nuanced characters.

The primary character in *Fourth of July Creek* is social worker Pete Snow, whom the reader finds living and working in rural Montana after the collapse of his marriage and family. The details of Pete's marriage and his troubled relationship with his daughter, Rachel, are revealed in bits and pieces throughout the novel. When Pete first appears, he has been called out by the police to the home of one of the families he works with. This first case involves a mother who shot her son with his own air rifle because he was leaping up and down on the carport's corrugated roof, threatening to cave it in and potentially damage his mother's car. Pete describes the mother to the police as a "disaster" who spends most of her disability check on drugs and obstinately refuses to follow Pete's advice on caring for her children. The son is a recreational "gas huffer" whom Pete describes as smelling of Cheetos and semen. It is not a pretty picture, and this disturbing portrait of dwindling lives in a rural wasteland is the reader's introduction to Pete's working life. Here, drugs and children are easily abused, and the populace is wary of therapy, government intervention (except in the form of disability assistance), and fancy theories about psychological disorders. Pete says, "The cranks and drunks up here took to Jesus (in jail, if it pleases the court) and worried creases into the spine of the good book, consulting it like the I Ching or a Ouija board."

*Fourth of July Creek* contains many unsettling descriptions of the cases that fall under Pete's jurisdiction in the bleak communities of rural Montana. It is clear from

(Credit: Rebecca Calavan)

*Advertising writer Smith Henderson won the 2011 PEN Emerging Writers Award in fiction for his short stories, which have been published in* American Short Fiction, Witness, *and the* New Orleans Review. Fourth of July Creek *is his first novel.*

the outset that Pete cares deeply about the children he is tasked with protecting. He has become cynical and damaged by the futility of his task and the seemingly endless parade of broken individuals he sees on a daily basis, but underneath his frustration, he is a compassionate, caring individual whose heart aches for the children (and sometimes the parents) caught up in nightmare lives, their situations further complicated by the failures of the social-services system to genuinely help individuals escape from the downward spiral of poverty, abuse, and depression.

The crux of the plot begins when Pete is called out to a school in Tenmile, the little town that forms the heart of his route, because the teachers have discovered a strange, extremely smelly child wandering the school. None of the teachers or students have ever seen the child, whose name, it turns out, is Benjamin Pearl. Pete learns that Ben, an eleven-year-old who looks more like eight or nine, has never been to school and apparently lives in the wilderness. After buying the boy some new clothes and a meal, Pete takes him home and meets the child's father, a frightening, cloudy figure named Jeremiah Pearl. Jeremiah holds Pete at gunpoint and refuses to let Ben keep the clothing Pete has bought for him, saying he would rather put a bullet in his own son's brain than allow him to be corrupted by the system.

The encounter with the Pearls fades into the background for several chapters as the narrative delves further into Pete's life, gradually revealing, through memories and flashbacks, how his current situation took shape. It becomes clear that Pete's wife, Debbie, was unfaithful to him, and though they attempted to reconcile, Pete was unable to come to grips with this betrayal, leading to the collapse of their marriage. To Henderson's credit, his exploration of Pete's faults and failings compromise the reader's fondness for Pete and his status as the story's "hero," but in a way that ultimately serves to make him seem all the more real and complex as a person. Pete's own family dramas seem like something from one of his case files, though perhaps not quite as drenched in poverty and hopelessness. In the sections of the book exploring Pete's relationship with his daughter, Henderson chose to alternate his narrative style, switching at times to present tense, a second-person voice, or even a question-and-answer format. Though initially confusing, this narrative shift makes it clear that the passages are a departure from the primary story arc.

Gradually, the case of Jeremiah Pearl comes back into the narrative. The reader learns that Jeremiah has been making what is called "broken money"—essentially punching holes and scratching phrases into US coins as a form of artistic rebellion. This habit of collecting and defacing currency brings new depth to the character, whose first introduction made him seem like a dangerously unstable monster. "He says we're at war," a pawn broker tells Pete, describing Jeremiah as a man obsessed with a host of conspiracy theories, including distrust of the monetary system that underlies the modern world. This special variety of paranoid conspiracy theory is called "hysterical numismatics." Having become curious about Jeremiah, Pete attempts to learn more about him by interviewing residents of Tenmile who know or have had occasion to meet the man. He discovers that in addition to his rebellious artistry, Jeremiah is obsessed with theories about the fictional Zionist Occupational Government, a series of conspiratorial ideas first created during World War II, based on the belief that a Jewish Zionist group has taken control of various national governments.

Once Pete begins taking a serious interest in the Pearl family, Henderson's novel takes on a new dimension, becoming a blend of sociological exploration and noir mystery. Each new interview, with bar owners, marijuana growers, and other denizens of Tenmile, gives Pete new pieces he uses to reconstruct Jeremiah's history. There is a sense of building dread as well, as many of the witnesses' comments and Pete's own reflections indicate that Jeremiah's currency-defacing artistic projects may soon attract the attention of the federal authorities. Pete comes to believe that Jeremiah sees himself as a revolutionary on course for a devastating confrontation with the government. As his investigation proceeds, interspersed with chapters that gradually dig deeper into Pete's own past and family, Pete begins to uncover a new mystery, the hints of what transformed Jeremiah Pearl from a seemingly normal man into a paranoid zealot hiding out with his half-wild son in the Montana wilderness.

Part of the appeal of *Fourth of July Creek* is the author's skill with character development. Over the course of the book, readers develop a view of Pete that is highly layered and complex. At his best, he is heroic, affectionate, supportive, and nurturing; at his worst, he is selfish, self-destructive, petty, and even violent. Pete becomes an interesting vehicle for the exploration of a dark, at-times hopeless world, described with considerable poetry. At times, the darker aspects of Pete's life mirror the bleak hopelessness he uncovers in his job, while at other times he is a beacon within the world, a caring figure heroically straining to keep lost children from falling into the abyss. In crafting the character of Jeremiah, whose life is revealed substantially through the stories told by others, Henderson accomplishes an enviable feat by creating a character who initially inspires revulsion but slowly becomes resistant to easy categorization. By the end of the book, Jeremiah Pearl has become a fascinating and tragic figure, and Pete finds himself searching for a way to help the man and his son.

Critics gave *Fourth of July Creek* positive reviews, with some hailing it as one of the best books of 2014. In the *New York Times*, critic Jonathan Miles highlighted

Henderson's use of characteristic styles used by Cormack McCarthy and, before him, William Faulkner, including the use of coined words, temporal and narrative confusion, and "wandering pronouns." Reviewing the book for the *Guardian*, Jeff VanderMeer said that Henderson had come "within shouting distance of writing a great American novel" and praised the richness of his language and characters. Critic Amy Gentry, writing in the *Chicago Tribune*, had a slightly more critical take; while she enjoyed the writing style and saw the appeal of what she called "social work noir," she also felt that Henderson's female characters lacked agency and fullness. In general, though critics found scattered flaws in Henderson's debut, reviewers praised the book as an example of great American literature from an author at the beginning of a promising career.

*Micah L. Issitt*

**Review Sources**

Charles, Ron. Rev. of *Fourth of July Creek*, by Smith Henderson. *Washington Post*. Washington Post, 3 June 2014. Web. 6 Feb. 2015.

Gentry, Amy. Rev. of *Fourth of July Creek*, by Smith Henderson. *Chicago Tribune*. Tribune Interactive, 6 June 2014. Web. 6 Feb. 2015.

"Lost in the Woods." Rev. of *Fourth of July Creek*, by Smith Henderson. *Economist*. Economist Newspaper, 14 June 2014. Web. 6 Feb. 2015.

Miles, Jonathan. "Independence Days." Rev. of *Fourth of July Creek*, by Smith Henderson. *New York Times Book Review* 6 July 2014: 15. Print.

VanderMeer, Jeff. Rev. of *Fourth of July Creek*, by Smith Henderson. *Guardian*. Guardian News and Media, 10 July 2014. Web. 6 Feb. 2015.

# Frog Music

**Author:** Emma Donoghue (b. 1969)
**Publisher:** Little, Brown (New York). 416 pp.
**Type of work:** Novel
**Time:** Summer 1876
**Locale:** San Francisco, California, and environs

*A murder mystery based on actual events and real people,* Frog Music *paints a vibrant picture of boomtown San Francisco while attempting to solve the murder of a young female cross-dresser during the smallpox-plagued summer of 1876.*

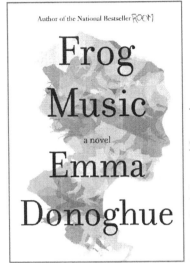

(Courtesy of Little, Brown and Company)

**Principal characters:**

BLANCHE BEUNON, an attractive, French-born former circus equestrian, now a popular erotic dancer, occasional prostitute, and property owner

JEANNE "JENNY" BONNET, her friend and confidant, a fellow French native who dresses like a man, rides a bicycle, packs a pistol, and picks fights

ARTHUR PIERRE LOUIS DENEVE, her lover and pimp, a darkly handsome, arrogant former circus aerialist

ERNEST GIRARD, Arthur's tall, pale, cruel protégé who emulates his mentor in all things

P'TIT ARTHUR, Blanche and Arthur's unwanted one-year-old son who was sent to a home for abandoned children

CARTWRIGHT, a diminutive albino reporter for the *San Francisco Chronicle*

DETECTIVE BOHEN, a tough, no-nonsense lawman who investigates Jenny's murder

As Blanche Beunon, the protagonist of Irish author Emma Donoghue's historical novel *Frog Music* (2014), bends to untangle a shoelace, a shotgun blast explodes through the window of her rented room at San Miguel Station outside San Francisco. The lethal pellets whistle over her head, striking and killing her companion, Jenny Bonnet. Even as she grieves the shocking, sudden loss of her friend, Blanche wonders: Was Jenny the intended target, or did she unintentionally thwart her own murder thanks to a stubborn knot?

The circumstances surrounding Jenny's murder propel much of the narrative as the novel travels by small, sometimes awkward increments backward and forward in time. The story is told through Blanche's eyes as she, the most amateur of sleuths, gathers clues in an attempt to piece together who killed Jenny and why. By the end of the first chapter, Donoghue has established a number of the same themes that informed much of her earlier work, chief among these the exploration of female sexuality. Donoghue, who declared her homosexuality at an early age, previously dealt with lesbianism in the novels *Stir Fry* (1994), *Hood* (1995), and *Landing* (2007). In addition, *Frog Music* is not the first of Donoghue's novels to fictionalize sordid historical events; *Slammerkin* (2000) and *The Sealed Letter* (2008) are both tales of a criminal nature that take place in times gone by. *Frog Music* brings all of these elements together in a colorful tale that illustrates what a properly motivated, strong-willed woman can accomplish when she sets her mind to it.

Flashbacks to a month before the murder focus on Blanche's occupation as an exotic dancer and singer at the House of Mirrors in Chinatown, where she has become the main attraction, despite having only recently arrived in town. After the show, as is her habit, she sleeps with a wealthy trick at a nearby hotel. As Blanche leaves the hotel for the apartment building she has purchased, she is run down by a person on a penny-farthing bicycle. At first glance, the bicycle rider appears to be a man, but "he" is really a woman, Jenny, dressed in men's clothing.

Jenny offers to buy Blanche a drink as an apology for bruising her. The two women converse in a tavern and begin to bond despite the disparities in their personalities and lifestyles. Jenny exhibits an uncanny knack for making keen observations and asking direct questions, though she is notably tight-lipped when it comes to her own personal history. Blanche, who has many acquaintances but no true friends, is drawn to Jenny's bold mien and wry wit. It is revealed that Jenny, who has lived in San Francisco since she was a small child, earns a living by catching frogs for restaurants. She has been arrested and imprisoned several times for cross-dressing and is well known throughout the city. Because Jenny has no proper home, Blanche invites her to sleep on the couch of her apartment for the night.

Soon afterward, the men in Blanche's life—Arthur Deneve, her well-dressed pimp and lover, and Ernest Girard, Arthur's close friend—enter after their nightly carousing. The three principals have known each other for nearly a decade, having performed together at a circus in France. Now, the two men do nothing but drink, gamble, and engage in shady transactions, all while living off Blanche's earnings. Arthur and Ernest banter insultingly with Jenny, who shrugs off their nasty comments. Jenny spots a photograph of P'tit Arthur and asks about the small child, stirring Blanche's dormant maternal instincts. P'tit has, since birth, been housed for a weekly fee at an unknown facility for unwanted children. Blanche decides to find her son and care for him herself. She eventually locates the house where P'tit is being kept in squalor amid dozens of other infants and rescues him. Though she has no mothering skills, Blanche does the best she can to provide for her child, and she begins to build a relationship with her son.

Both Jenny and Blanche are fitting additions to Donoghue's roster of resourceful, multifaceted female characters. Blanche—who, according to Ron Charles's review for the *Washington Post*, "isn't a whore with a heart of gold so much as a woman with a heart of many alloys"—could be compared to the mother in Donoghue's 2010 bestseller *Room*. Both are women trying to do the best they can for their children despite adverse circumstances.

Arthur, now sick with smallpox, chides Blanche for paying more attention to P'tit than to her occupation. Soon after his recovery, Arthur and Ernest bring a wealthy American to the apartment and insist that Blanche sleep with him. Outraged—she always enjoys sex, but she insists on choosing her own partners—Blanche flees, leaving most of her money, her possessions, and her child behind. She runs into Jenny, and the two women spend the night at various public houses. When they finally return to the apartment, it is deserted. Blanche and Jenny scour the city and eventually find Arthur and Ernest gambling. Blanche begs for the return of her child, but Arthur uses him as a bargaining chip, demanding Blanche return to the apartment to work. Blanche refuses, and together, she and Jenny take a buggy out of town, seeking respite from the heat and the smallpox epidemic and craving time and space to resolve Blanche's intolerable situation. A few days later, Jenny is killed.

At the scene of the crime, Detective Bohen of the San Francisco Police investigates, and the city coroner's assistants come to take away Jenny's body for autopsy. A reporter, Cartwright, arrives to interview Blanche for his newspaper, and she blurts out that Arthur and Ernest were probably behind the murder. After all, she reasons, who else does she know who would have cause to kill either her or Jenny?

Later, Blanche returns to San Francisco and cautiously approaches her apartment building in case Arthur or Ernest is lying in wait, ready to kill her too. She buys a newspaper, from which she discovers new facts about her late friend and learns that Arthur has left town. Emboldened by the news, Blanche makes her way up to her apartment, only to find it stripped. All the furniture is gone, her cache of money is missing, and worst of all, the deed to her building, once hidden behind a picture frame, has vanished. Within minutes, a Chinese former resident arrives to tell her that Arthur has sold the apartment to him and that she must leave, as he is converting the building into a boarding house for fellow Asians.

*Emma Donoghue has published eight novels, several short-story collections, stage and radio plays, screenplays, and three full-length nonfiction works since 1993. Her novel* Hood *(1995) won the Stonewall Book Award,* The Sealed Letter *(2008) won the Lambda Literary Award for Lesbian Fiction, and* Room *(2010) won the Rogers Writers' Trust Fiction Prize.*

While Blanche stands stunned, Ernest arrives to confirm that Arthur has gone. He demands that Blanche clear Arthur's name in the matter of Jenny's death. If she does not, he threatens, she will never see P'tit again. Blanche deduces that at least P'tit is still alive, and Ernest knows where he is. Over the remainder of the novel, Jenny's murder case plays itself out as Blanche grapples with Ernest for the return of her child.

As both a fictional account of historical events and an intimate portrait of nonmainstream female characters under duress, *Frog Music* has much to recommend it. Donoghue is particularly skilled at depicting the bustling, ethnically diverse San Francisco of 1876 and making the reader feel a part of the action as Blanche strides resolutely along the city's sordid streets. For fans of the crime genre, however, the mystery surrounding the death of Jenny Bonnet falls short. Though the author provides a plausible, if improbable, solution to an unsolved crime more than a century old, it seems to be more of a narrative convenience than the result of shrewd investigation. Throughout, Donoghue fails to meaningfully or engagingly elaborate on a story that, by her own admission, already lacks substantial source material. The depth and strength of her characters are often overshadowed by shortcomings in narrative. In a review for the *New York Times*, Patrick McGrath wrote of the book's colorful characters, burdened by a dragging plot: "The reader stops caring, and all the roistering hilarity in the world can't mask the novel's lack of narrative energy."

Donoghue supplements the story with a number of extra sections. She performed a great deal of research in the course of writing the novel, and in an afterword, she provides data about the real people on whom the story was based and gives additional information about the city of San Francisco during the time period. In a section titled "Song Notes," Donoghue includes facts about the many tunes that are excerpted throughout the novel. Finally, there is a glossary of the multitude of French terms, many of them rude, that the four principal characters use in the course of conversation.

*Jack Ewing*

**Review Sources**

Charles, Ron. Rev. of *Frog Music*, by Emma Donoghue. *Washington Post*. Washington Post, 25 Mar. 2014. Web. 20 Oct. 2014.

Holt, Karen. "Once upon a Time in the West." Rev. of *Frog Music*, by Emma Donoghue. *O: The Oprah Magazine* Apr. 2014: 98. Print.

McGrath, Patrick. "Gomorrah by the Bay." Rev. of *Frog Music*, by Emma Donoghue. *New York Times Book Review* 4 May 2014: 14. Print.

# Geek Sublime
## The Beauty of Code, the Code of Beauty

**Author:** Vikram Chandra (b. 1961)
**Publisher:** Graywolf Press (Minneapolis).
Illustrated. 256 pp.
**Type of work:** Literary history; memoir;
technology

*In* Geek Sublime: The Beauty of Code, the
Code of Beauty, *Vikram Chandra shares
insights into the nature of art and beauty
through discussions of programming languages, Indian poetry, and his own experiences as a writer.*

(Courtesy of Graywolf Press)

Part memoir, part literary and technological
history, and part philosophical treatise, *Geek
Sublime: The Beauty of Code, the Code of
Beauty* is a complex work that combines its
many seemingly disparate topics into a cohesive discussion of the nature of beauty.
As both a computer programmer and a critically acclaimed novelist, author Vikram
Chandra is in the unique position of being able to comment on both fields and compare them from the perspective of an insider rather than an outside observer or critic.
Through his detailed discussions of the evolution of programming languages and the
literary qualities of Indian poetry, Chandra provides a solid introduction to the fields of
literature and computer science that is fueled by his deep personal connection to both.

Chandra begins *Geek Sublime* with a chapter that sets the stage for the book's
central questions, documenting the tendency among computer programmers to equate
code to art. He notes that one of the primary connections between programming and
the literary arts is both fields' shared emphasis on language, particularly in regard to
expressing ideas with clarity and precision. Language serves practical purposes in
both writing and coding, he points out, but it is also used for aesthetic purposes—to
create beauty. Both code and literature can be described as beautiful; however, the
qualities that make them so can be immensely different.

After putting forth the seemingly simple yet truly complex questions that form
the basis of the book, Chandra goes on to introduce *Geek Sublime*'s autobiographical elements. Born in India in 1961, Chandra began writing as a child and later attended college in the United States, where he studied creative writing and eventually
enrolled in Columbia University's film school. While at Columbia, he found a job
that introduced him to personal computers. Chandra soon developed an interest in
coding, which he parlayed into a career as a freelance programmer and consultant. He
pursued his programming career in conjunction with his career as a writer and teacher

of creative writing, publishing his first novel, *Red Earth and Pouring Rain*, in 1995. This dual career prompted Chandra to think about coding and literature and the ways in which they are similar and different. While writing his novel, he became particularly interested in considering the similarities and differences between computer code and Sanskrit literature, which is an extremely broad body of text assembled over thousands of years and, like code, follows a set of complex grammatical rules.

Throughout the remainder of *Geek Sublime*, Chandra writes at length about both topics. In the chapter titled "The Language of Logic," he provides an overview of how computers work, noting that even technology professionals well versed in operating computers often do not have a complete understanding of how such machines function.

*Vikram Chandra is the author of several books, including the critically acclaimed novels* Red Earth and Pouring Rain *(1995) and* Sacred Games *(2006).*

Chandra explains that computers function using logic gates, which accept inputs and produce outputs based on certain operators, such as AND, OR, NOT, and XOR, the last of which Chandra likens to "either-or." These logic gates follow the rules of Boolean algebra proposed by the nineteenth-century British mathematician and logician George Boole. To help his readers gain a better understanding of these concepts, Chandra includes illustrations of logic gates and fragments of computer code throughout the chapter. He goes on to trace the evolution of computer code, from binary to machine code to Fortran, demonstrating code's tendency to become more readable by human programmers over time.

The evolution of programming languages and the programs in which people write code has often been a source of conflict within programming culture, and Chandra calls attention to this conflict, which has often been manifested in disputes about what constitutes "real" programming and who counts as a "real" programmer. He notes that women have often been excluded from the ranks of "real" programmers despite their long history in the field; the nineteenth-century British mathematician Ada Lovelace, a woman, is commonly considered to have been the world's first computer programmer, and programming was often considered women's work during the early days of modern computing. Because of the male-dominated culture of American programming and the overall societal message that math and science are not for girls, Chandra argues, the number of women pursuing computer-related careers in the United States fell dramatically throughout the twentieth century. He contrasts this with the situation in India, where there are significantly more women working in computer technology. However, issues of gender inequality remain and must continue to be addressed.

From his discussion of programming culture, Chandra segues back into his career as a writer, which led him to investigate the question of what makes a poem beautiful. To answer this question, he began an investigation into Indian poetry, especially works originally composed in Sanskrit, and determined that various qualities of Indian literature seemed particularly relevant to his question. One of the most important of those qualities is *rasa*, literally "taste" or "juice," which Chandra defines as "the aestheticized satisfaction or 'sentiment' of tasting artificially induced emotions"—that is, the feeling of satisfaction experienced by the readers when the writer has, through the power of words, made them feel an emotion that they otherwise would not have felt. *Rasa*, according to Chandra, is perhaps the most important element that contributes to what the ninth-century Indian philosopher Anandavardhana called *dhvani*, or "the soul of poetry." Chandra also cites the importance of *samskaras* and *vasanas*, "'latent impressions' left by one's experience and past lives" that poetry enables to manifest. Art, then, has a unique ability to evoke deep, multilayered emotions and in turn to inspire a sense of satisfaction about such emotions.

Ultimately, Chandra concludes that computer code does not have the same ability; any emotions inspired by code will likely be based on the functions that code serves and how well it performs such functions. Code can be beautiful, in the sense that it can be as elegant and precise as any poem, but it does not have the soul found in other forms of literary art. At the same time, Chandra notes that by focusing solely on the elegance and aesthetic beauty of code, programmers are doing themselves a disservice. Code may not be able to evoke *rasa* and thus may not truly qualify as art, but it has the remarkable ability to "materialize logic," an ability that Chandra argues deserves just as much recognition.

In the United Kingdom, *Geek Sublime* was published with the subtitle "Writing Fiction, Coding Software." Although that description captures the book's subject matter appropriately, the American subtitle, "The Beauty of Code, the Code of Beauty," more accurately conveys the book's overarching focus on the nature of beauty. *Geek Sublime* asks the difficult question of what makes something beautiful, applying this complex question to both code and literature. In both cases, precision and clarity of language and structure are of extreme importance; however, it is the ability of art to evoke feeling that seems to define beauty for Chandra. A particularly interesting example of the difference between code and literature arises from Chandra's description of a particularly sloppy, disorganized computer program as a "big ball of mud," which grows ever bigger as subsequent generations of programmers add to it and make changes, effectively contributing new layers of mud to the ball. The big ball of mud is messy and inefficient, something that arises out of necessity but is far from ideal. In a later discussion of art, however, Chandra remarks that "mud is where life begins." A certain degree of disorganization, which would be damaging to a computer program, gives art life; "the form of art rises from impurity, from dangerous chaos," Chandra writes.

In addition to his focus on the nature of beauty, Chandra takes some interesting side journeys, shedding light on aspects of programming history and Indian literary history of which many readers may be unaware. Particularly interesting are the parallels that can be drawn between the erasure of female programmers, who played a crucial role in the early decades of computer programming but were effectively eliminated from the historical record, and the suppression of work by certain female Indian poets, such as the eighteenth-century poet Muddupalani, whose frequently erotic work, and career as a whole, was suppressed following the British colonization of India. Chandra's discussion of the conflicts between computer programmers who assert the superiority of certain programming languages also seems to connect with his exploration of the conflicts between mainstream, Vedic Sanskrit writings and those from Tantric, Jain, or Buddhist viewpoints. Such conflicts are not confined to any one form of art, as Chandra makes very clear.

Reviews of *Geek Sublime* were generally quite positive and praised Chandra for creating a complex work that not only combines elements of two seemingly divergent fields but also merges the historical and the personal. In his review for the *Guardian*, Steven Poole praised Chandra's effective, coherent explanations of technical concepts; he also appreciated the book's discussion of the gender issues present in the programming world, which Chandra notes overwhelmingly values an abrasive brand of masculinity. James Gleick, writing for the *New York Times*, similarly praised Chandra for tackling the programming community's gender problem and especially took note of the parallels between the hypermasculine coding culture and the code of masculinity enforced by the British during their occupation of India. Reviewers did at times note that the book, as a complex work that combines multiple distinct topics into a single discussion, does take its time arriving at its central thesis; at the same time, as a reviewer for the *Economist* noted, "the wait is worth it." Chandra's investigation into the nature of beauty is one deeply rooted in history, and it is only by understanding the evolution of code and the soul of poetry that one can draw one's own conclusions.

*Joy Crelin*

## Review Sources

Rev. of *Geek Sublime*, by Vikram Chandra. *Kirkus*. Kirkus, 2 July 2014. Web. 26 Jan. 2015.

Rev. of *Geek Sublime*, by Vikram Chandra. *Publishers Weekly*. PWxyz, 2014. Web. 26 Jan. 2015.

Gleick, James. "A Unified Theory." Rev. of *Geek Sublime*, by Vikram Chandra. *Sunday Book Review*. New York Times, 22 Aug. 2014. Web. 26 Jan. 2015.

"Multilingual: Inspiration for Poetry and Logic." Rev. of *Geek Sublime*, by Vikram Chandra. *Economist*. Economist Newspaper, 8 Feb. 2014. Web. 26 Jan. 2015.

Pears, Iain. Rev. of *Geek Sublime*, by Vikram Chandra. *Telegraph*. Telegraph Media Group, 15 Feb. 2014. Web. 26 Jan. 2015.

Poole, Steven. "A Skeptical Take on Coding Culture." Rev. of *Geek Sublime*, by Vikram Chandra. *Guardian*. Guardian News and Media, 26 Feb. 2014. Web. 26 Jan. 2015.

# A Girl Is a Half-Formed Thing

**Author:** Eimear McBride
**First published:** 2013, in the United Kingdom
**Publisher:** Coffee House Press (Minneapolis). 227 pp.
**Type of work:** Novel
**Time:** Late twentieth century
**Locale:** Ireland

(Courtesy of Coffee House Press)

*Eimear McBride's wrenching debut novel explodes conventional language to convey the implosion of a girl's life.*

**Principal characters:**
THE GIRL, the narrator; an unnamed girl who comes of age in rural Ireland
YOU, her brother
MAMMY, their mother

If books came with warning labels, Eimear McBride's *A Girl Is a Half-Formed Thing* (2013) would surely have one. The novel is a stunning technical achievement in the vein of writers such as James Joyce and Samuel Beckett, but its content—McBride's "relentless examination of a teen-age girl's psychic and moral collapse," as James Wood described it in the *New Yorker*—is almost physically painful to read. In some ways, the book is anchored in McBride's own experience; her brother, like the narrator's, died of a brain tumor in his twenties, though she insists that the work is fundamentally separate from the story of her life.

Reviewers and McBride herself have described the book's prose as "challenging," which is likely why publishers were initially wary of accepting it. In the following excerpt, the narrator, who is no more than a toddler at the time, struggles to escape the bath her mother has drawn for her:

> Down those stairs fast as I can. Shampoo on my forehead. In my eyes. Nettle them. Mammy. Yelling Lady you come back or you'll get what for. A mad goat I'll be. Rubbing bubbles. Worse and worse and hotter like mints I'll turn my nose at. Always get me. In the hall. You by wormy bit of hair. Lug me rubbing ankle skin up the stairs. She in suddy ocean. You settle down. Quicker over the quicker's done. I am boldness incarnate, little madam little miss. Put back your head I'll wash it down and off your face.

McBride makes no distinction between dialogue and thought or dialogue and speaker. Her jagged prose rushes furiously forth, lifted by the momentum of the narrator's raw emotion. At the same time, particularly as the narrator ages, her words act as little shields, desperately trying to deflect the brutal blows of the life into which she has been thrown. McBride's vocabulary expands as the narrator gets older—the book's opening lines ("For you. You'll soon. You'll give her name. In the stitches of her skin she'll wear you say") are narrated from the womb—but the construction of the words does not change.

The narrator, who is known to readers only by what others call her—usually "the girl"—is born in rural Ireland. Her older brother was born with a brain tumor, resulting in mild intellectual disabilities and an increased susceptibility to head injuries. Her father left the family before she was even born, leaving her mother to raise the two children alone. Mammy, as the children call her, is vividly drawn, even when she appears in shadow, as in the above dialogue. Her frustrations as a single mother come to a head when her own father comes to visit. A wealthy, controlling, and pious man who looks like Clark Gable, he berates his daughter, calling her children heathens and effectively disowning her. The siblings' relationship with

PHOTO OF: Eimear McBride
AUTHOR OF: A Girl Is a Half-formed Thing
PUBLISHER: Coffee House Press
PHOTOGRAPHER CREDIT: Jemma Mickleburgh

(© Jemma Mickleburgh)

*Eimear McBride is an Irish writer who trained as an actor before writing her first novel.* A Girl Is a Half-formed Thing *won the Baileys Women's Prize for Fiction (formerly the Orange Prize), the Goldsmiths Prize, and the Desmond Elliot Prize, among others.*

their mother changes forever that day, after she beats them in a fury. Religion becomes the theme of the household, and the girl becomes fixated on sin.

The grandfather is only the first of several thoroughly horrible people to appear in the novel, which is one of the book's great flaws. A number of characters exist only as villains or bogeymen, out to hit the girl exactly where it will hurt the most, thus raising the book's great ethical conundrum. As the girl comes of age, she is raped by an uncle and, like many young victims of sexual assault, embraces sex as a way to address her pain. She serially sleeps with men throughout high school and college, during which time she is taken advantage of constantly and raped multiple times. As her life spirals out of control due to the illness of her brother, clearly the only person whom she has ever truly loved and who also loved her, she reignites her most destructive relationship while also seeking the company of a group of sinister men who hang out in the woods in her hometown. The book culminates in an episodic scene so implausible in its parade of horrors that the story's inevitable end comes as a welcome relief. Told this way, the girl is a victim before she is even born; it is her only name, existing "in the stitches of her skin" as she says in the book's first lines. Yet she is also complex and vividly real, which leads one to question the validity of her circumstances—could this really happen to a person? Is it possible for a life to be so horrific, so utterly lonely? But conversely, what does it say that, when being forced to share the body of this poor unloved girl, one draws back and protects oneself by saying, "This could not possibly be true"?

The narrator's complicated relationship with sex and sin begins even before her uncle rapes her, derived from the strict piety of the world in which she lives. This world bursts from the page with sparkling clarity, though ironically, it is unclear exactly when in time the action takes place. Certain clues, such as the brother's Walkman and his adeptness at video games, place the girl's teenage and college years in the 1980s, but the haziness on this point only reinforces the stifling timelessness of Irish Catholic tradition. The girl's yearning to break free of this world engenders some of the novel's best prose; Wood described it as "a visceral throb," with sentences that "run meanings together to produce a kind of compression in which words, freed from the tedious march of sequence, seem to want to merge with one another, as paint and musical notes can." He pointed to a passage in which the girl calls her terrible uncle, looking for comfort after being informed that her brother will not live much longer. "Can he see all about me patients miracling well?" she thinks, desperate to evoke from him some small comfort. The necessity of the words make them vital, a lifeline to which the narrator (and the reader) holds on for dear life.

*Molly Hagan*

## Review Sources

Charles, Ron. Rev. of *A Girl Is a Half-Formed Thing*, by Eimear McBride. *Washington Post*. Washington Post, 16 Sept. 2014. Web. 9 Feb. 2015.

Cohen, Joshua. "Bloody Hell." Rev. of *A Girl Is a Half-Formed Thing*, by Eimear McBride. *New York Times Book Review* 21 Sept. 2014: 12. Print.

Enright, Anne. Rev. of *A Girl Is a Half-Formed Thing*, by Eimear McBride. *Guardian*. Guardian News and Media, 20 Sept. 2013. Web. 9 Feb. 2015.

McAlpin, Heller. "Challenging, Shattering *Girl* Is No Half-Formed Thing." Rev. of *A Girl Is a Half-Formed Thing*, by Eimear McBride. *NPR*. Natl. Public Radio, 10 Sept. 2014. Web. 9 Feb. 2015.

Wood, James. "Useless Prayers." Rev. of *A Girl Is a Half-Formed Thing*, by Eimear McBride. *New Yorker*. Condé Nast, 29 Sept. 2014. Web. 9 Feb. 2015.

# The Good Spy
## The Life and Death of Robert Ames

**Author:** Kai Bird (b. 1951)
**Publisher:** Random House (New York). 448 pp.
**Type of work:** Biography
**Time:** 1934–83
**Locales:** United States; the Middle East

*The Good Spy follows the life and career of CIA officer Robert Ames, whose fruitful relationships with his Middle Eastern sources provided the US government with valuable insights into the Israeli-Palestinian conflict.*

(Courtesy of Crown Publishers)

**Principal personages:**
ROBERT AMES, a case officer and later national intelligence officer with the Central Intelligence Agency (CIA)
YVONNE AMES, his wife
MUSTAFA ZEIN, one of his sources, a well-connected Lebanese businessman
ALI HASSAN SALAMEH, another source, a high-ranking member of the Palestine Liberation Organization (PLO)
YASSER ARAFAT, the leader of the PLO

During the early 1960s, Robert Ames and his family lived in a three-bedroom house in the US consulate compound in Dhahran, Saudi Arabia. Although ostensibly working as a commercial officer, he was in fact a CIA case officer tasked with recruiting and managing sources in the area. Young Kai Bird, who lived across the street from Ames in Dhahran, believed Ames was a member of the US Foreign Service like his own father; only many years later did Bird learn the truth about his neighbor. Bird's personal connection to Ames, however tenuous, granted him an unprecedented degree of access when he began researching the man's life and career, allowing Bird to conduct interviews with Ames's friends and family, particularly Ames's wife, Yvonne, who remembered Bird decades after they shared a neighborhood.

Ames was born in Philadelphia in 1934 to Albert and Helen Ames. He and his two siblings grew up in a working-class household, and Ames excelled in both academics and basketball. He attended La Salle University on an athletic scholarship, graduating in 1956. Ames was drafted into the army later that year and was eventually assigned to a listening post in what is now Eritrea. There, he first began to study Arabic, a choice that would shape the direction of his CIA career. He returned to the United States when his tour of duty was complete and soon met a young secretary named Yvonne Blakely, whom he married in 1960. Ames initially hoped to work for the Foreign Service, but after failing the written exam, he applied for a position with the CIA and was quickly hired. New hires were required to undergo training both in Washington, where they learned the basics of recruiting and gathering information from sources, and at Virginia's Camp Peary. At Camp Peary, known as the Farm, Ames and his fellow trainees underwent paramilitary training and completed practical training in the recruitment and managing of assets.

*Kai Bird is the author of several biographies as well as the memoir* Crossing Mandelbaum Gate *(2010). He and co-author Martin J. Sherwin were awarded the Pulitzer Prize for the 2005 biography* American Prometheus: The Triumph and Tragedy of J. Robert Oppenheimer.

After completing his training, Ames was assigned to the CIA's Near East Division. In mid-1962 he was assigned to a post in Dhahran, where he and Yvonne lived across the street from Bird's family. After leaving Dhahran, the family lived Beirut, Lebanon. Ames was next posted to Aden, in the British protectorate of South Yemen, where he witnessed the violence of civil war firsthand as rival groups sought to overthrow the British colonial government and claim power for themselves. American relations with the new South Yemen government became strained after the nation achieved independence from Britain, and Ames was eventually forced to leave the country, settling again in Beirut.

It was in Beirut that Ames met American-educated Lebanese businessman Mustafa Zein, who would become a valuable source of information and a close friend for the rest of Ames's life. An extroverted and popular man, Zein was particularly helpful in introducing Ames to Middle Easterners who might not have sought him out on their own. By far the most significant introduction facilitated by Zein was to Ali Hassan Salameh, sometimes known as the Red Prince, a young Palestinian man who was a high-ranking member of the PLO and close to PLO leader Yasser Arafat. Prior to Ames and Salameh's first meeting in 1969, contact between the US government and Palestinian leaders had been effectively nonexistent, largely because the United States considered organizations such as the PLO to be terrorist groups. Salameh himself had been involved in a number of terrorist attacks, but Ames nevertheless believed he could be a valuable source of information. As a result of Ames's meetings with Salameh, the United States was able to maintain an unofficial channel of communication, known as a "back channel," with the PLO and Arafat, allowing the CIA to collect information about the activities of the PLO and rival groups and gain insight into the Palestinian perspective. Despite the extensive communication between Salameh and Ames, Salameh never became an official CIA asset, and the CIA was consequently unable to protect him from foreign intelligence services. In January 1979, Salameh was assassinated by the Mossad, the Israeli intelligence agency. Limited communication between the United States and the PLO continued, however.

Having been promoted to the position of national intelligence officer for the Near East and South Asia Division of the CIA's National Intelligence Council in 1978, Ames worked primarily out of the CIA's US headquarters during the late 1970s and early 1980s. On April 16, 1983, however, he traveled once again to the US embassy in Beirut. Two days later, a truck bomb exploded after driving into the first floor of the embassy. Ames and sixty-two other individuals were killed.

Ames's death stunned his family and friends. Bird suggests that in addition to its personal toll, Ames's death represented a significant setback in Israeli-Palestinian relations. He begins *The Good Spy* with a prologue focusing on the events of September 13, 1993, the day on which Israeli prime minister Yitzhak Rabin and Arafat signed a peace accord at the White House. This event, which in Bird's mind could not have occurred without Ames's work, is particularly notable not only for its political significance but also for one troubling omission: members of the CIA, which had played such a crucial role in the peace process, had not been invited. Instead, as Bird later learned from Frank Anderson, then the chief of the Near East and South Asia Division, more than two dozen CIA employees traveled to Arlington National Cemetery. There they paid tribute to Ames and several other CIA members who had died while working toward the same goals.

As the inclusion of this anecdote indicates, *The Good Spy* was meticulously researched and based not only on official accounts but also on the memories of those who worked with Ames and knew him best. Bird explains in his author's note that although he met with a CIA representative to discuss the declassification of documents pertaining to Ames, nothing ever came of that meeting, and he thus received no CIA assistance while writing the book. Instead, Bird drew heavily from Ames's letters home as well as the memories of his friends and family, particularly Yvonne, who had previously been reluctant to speak to interviewers about her late husband, and Zein, whose unpublished memoir proved a valuable source of details regarding his communication with Ames and Salameh. Bird also interviewed numerous retired CIA and Mossad officers, whose impressions of Ames are scattered throughout the book, and refers to those who preferred to remain anonymous by helpfully italicized pseudonyms. It is unfortunate that Bird was unable to access CIA documents related to Ames, as they may have been able to verify some of Bird's educated guesses regarding the government's knowledge and approval of Ames's back channel. Indeed, Bird's relatively frequent use of words and phrases such as "likely," "must have," and "perhaps" calls attention to the gaps in the narrative, those parts of Ames's life and career that remain classified. At the same time, a biography based on government files rather than personal anecdotes could easily lack the sense of humanity so evident in Bird's portrait of Ames. As a spy, he was politically significant but not flashy enough to impress a public more interested in the James Bond sort of espionage. As a husband, father, friend, and coworker, however, he was evidently extraordinary.

*The Good Spy* was widely praised by critics, who appreciated its in-depth look into the life and career of a man whose achievements were not widely known outside intelligence circles but whose work left an indelible mark on the CIA and American-Palestinian relations. Reviewers also praised Bird's detailed account of the state of US intelligence gathering in the Cold War–era Middle East, which chronicles the shift from technologically based spying to human intelligence gathering and back again. In addition to documenting Ames's career, Bird provides context for the events that take place and backstory for all the major players. In his review for the *New York Times*,

Dwight Garner writes that Bird "looks consistently backward . . . as well as forward" in order to clarify the significance of Ames's era in relation to the increasingly complex Middle East of the early twenty-first century.

Bird's writing is clear and usually concise, although *The Good Spy* does suffer from a degree of repetition that at times makes the book feel like a collection of biographical essays originally published separately rather than a single narrative. Critic James Mann, in his review for the *Washington Post*, specifically points to Bird's tendency to introduce particular figures and explain concepts multiple times. However, such repetition could be helpful for readers who are unfamiliar with the people and political groups involved and need some help keeping the players straight. Mann also notes that the book seems to lose focus after Ames's death. The penultimate chapter, "Beirut Destiny," chronicles the embassy bombing and its immediate aftermath; the book's final chapter, "The Enigma of Imad Mughniyeh," tackles the question of who was behind the attack. Bird supplies the names of several individuals who may have been involved, including the eponymous Mughniyeh, a Lebanese terrorist associated with the organizations that would become Hezbollah, and Ali Reza Asgari, an officer in Iran's Revolutionary Guard who defected to the United States in 2007. However, because many of the facts remain unclear, the chapter itself may leave some readers dissatisfied. Despite these occasional flaws, *The Good Spy* is ultimately an informative and engaging look at the United States' intelligence-gathering efforts during a turbulent and influential era in the Middle East and at a good spy who wanted to make a difference.

*Joy Crelin*

**Review Sources**

Drogin, Bob. "'Good Spy' Scrutinizes Middle East CIA Officer Robert Ames." Rev. of *The Good Spy: The Life and Death of Robert Ames*, by Kai Bird. *Los Angeles Times*. Los Angeles Times, 16 May 2014. Web. 17 Oct. 2014.

Gardner, Dwight. "A Life in the Shadows in the Cold War Mideast: Kai Bird's 'The Good Spy' Portrays Robert Ames." Rev. of *The Good Spy: The Life and Death of Robert Ames*, by Kai Bird. *New York Times* 15 May 2014: C4. Print.

Rev. of *The Good Spy: The Life and Death of Robert Ames*, by Kai Bird. *Kirkus* 1 Apr. 2014: 10. Print.

Rev. of *The Good Spy: The Life and Death of Robert Ames*, by Kai Bird. *Publishers Weekly* 10 Feb. 2014: 74. Print.

Mann, James. Rev. of *The Good Spy: The Life and Death of Robert Ames*, by Kai Bird. *Washington Post*. Washington Post, 23 May 2014. Web. 17 Oct. 2014.

Romeo, Nick. "'The Good Spy' by Kai Bird Makes the Case for a More Humane Form of Espionage." Rev. of *The Good Spy: The Life and Death of Robert Ames*, by Kai Bird. *Christian Science Monitor*. Christian Science Monitor, 20 May 2014. Web. 17 Oct. 2014.

# How Google Works

**Authors:** Eric Schmidt (b. 1955) and Jonathan Rosenberg (b. 1961)
**Publisher:** Grand Central (New York). Illustrated. 304 pp.
**Type of work:** Technology, business

*Veteran Google executives share the business principles that have made Google one of the world's most successful technology companies in* How Google Works.

(Courtesy of Grand Central Publishing)

In the years since its founding in 1998, technology giant Google has intrigued observers with its variety of products and reputation as an innovative and creative working environment. In *How Google Works*, veteran Google executives Eric Schmidt and Jonathan Rosenberg, writing with Google executive communications director Alan Eagle, share some of the business practices that have helped Google grow and expand into a broad range of industries. As Google's former chief executive officer (CEO) and former senior vice president of products, respectively, Schmidt and Rosenberg have unique insight into the inner workings of Google as well as firsthand knowledge of the mindsets of the company's founders, Larry Page and Sergey Brin. A foreword by cofounder Larry Page begins the book, signaling that any Google secrets given away in the following pages are shared with the blessing of the company's management.

The authors begin *How Google Works* with an introduction that chronicles the book's genesis in an in-house management seminar and goes on to outline the business practices they will discuss. In order to guide business owners through the growth of their companies, the book is divided into chapters concerning the steps a business owner might undertake, beginning with attracting the right personnel. At the most basic level, Schmidt and Rosenberg credit much of Google's success to the company's focus on hiring individuals whom they term "smart creatives." Smart creatives, the authors explain, are characterized by a willingness to try new things and take risks, a tendency to express opinions and engage in debate, and the possession of a well-rounded intellect that includes business and analytical intelligence as well as an understanding of user experience. Smart creatives also tend to be self-directed, independent, thorough, and communicative. Such individuals are often considered difficult to manage because of their independence and tendency to object to bad ideas, even when those ideas come from personnel much higher on the corporate ladder. For Google and companies hoping to duplicate its success, however, smart creatives are the ideal employees, and attracting them to the company must be a high priority.

In order to attract smart creatives, Schmidt and Rosenberg explain, a company must have a corporate culture that appeals to such workers and enables them to thrive. As an example, they share an anecdote about a group of Google employees who decided, on their own time and of their own volition, to improve the relevance of the advertisements shown to Google users. Without a company culture that allows employees to pursue projects independently—and one that encourages employees to want to spend their free time improving their company's products—such an event could never have happened. The idea of having an official company culture is neither a new one nor an uncommon one, but Schmidt and Rosenberg note that in many cases, a company's supposed culture consists only of a set of slogans that sound good but are ultimately meaningless. A company cannot succeed in creating a culture, they explain, unless it commits fully to its ideals. Elements of Google's culture that the authors cite as particularly effective are the company's commitment to removing bad apples from the workplace, its plan to create "a culture of Yes," and its most famous edict, "Don't be evil."

Just as a successful company culture requires true commitment to a set of values, so too must a company's strategy reflect its actual goals and activities, rather than a set-in-stone business plan. In their chapter on strategy, Schmidt and Rosenberg explain that while it is necessary to have a plan, the plan itself must be fluid, and those in charge must be willing to make changes and adapt whenever necessary. In particular, strategic plans must be able to be adjusted along with the growth of the company and its introduction of new products and ventures into new areas. The authors caution business owners to avoid making decisions based on market research; rather, technical insights should be at the core of each new product.

In order to ensure that the company will have technical insights in the first place, Schmidt and Rosenberg advise business owners to prioritize the hiring process and design it so that it enables the company to hire the best and brightest smart creatives. By putting in place a company culture in which smart creatives thrive, the company will have already set the stage for the hiring process, as smart creatives typically like to work with other smart creatives. At Google, the ideal candidate is capable of solving problems and learning new things, is knowledgeable about the role for which he or she is being hired; has a degree of leadership experience; and possesses a quality known as "Googleyness," which encompasses personal characteristics such as ambition and interpersonal skills. The hiring process typically involves multiple interviews and the input of a hiring committee, which makes the ultimate decision whether to hire an individual. This process, Schmidt and Rosenberg note, is consistent with Google's overall emphasis on making decisions based on solid data.

The ability to make decisions and form a consensus is essential in any company but especially in one designed for ongoing growth. As in the hiring process, business decisions must be based on data, and those proposing particular courses of action must support their proposals rather than rely on automatic support. The authors warn against blindly adhering to what they call the "Highest-Paid Person's Opinion," or "HiPPO." The best options are not always those of the high-ranking employees, and so all employees must be willing to assert themselves and dissent when necessary. Good communication is paramount in this respect. Schmidt and Rosenberg go on to explain the Google approach to communication, which focuses on direct and to-the-point messages sent only to the employees who need to receive them. Meetings should likewise be planned so that they accomplish their intended purpose without wasting time better spent innovating. It is the pursuit of innovation that must ultimately drive a company, and Schmidt and Rosenberg note the importance of culture and corporate strategy in creating an environment that fosters such attempts. They cite Google's much-publicized "20 percent time," in which employees are allowed to spend 20 percent of their working time on independent projects, as one major factor in Google's innovation attempts. Google's e-mail service, Gmail, is just one of the many former 20 percent projects that became official Google products. Schmidt and Rosenberg conclude by looking to the future and making predictions about the increased role of technology—particularly the Internet and mobile technology—in everyday life. They encourage business owners to consider what the future may bring and prepare accordingly.

*Eric Schmidt and Jonathan Rosenberg are former Google executives who now serve as executive chair and as adviser to the CEO, respectively. Alan Eagle is Google's director of executive communications.*

As Google insiders, Schmidt and Rosenberg provide a unique take on the traditional management book, basing their business recommendations not on their many years of experience at various companies but largely on their tenure at Google specifically. Because of this, *How Google Works* often seems best suited for companies similar in industry and organization to Google. However, many of their recommendations—particularly those related to the development of a productive corporate culture and the establishment of protocols for clear and concise communications—are relevant to companies in a broad range of industries. In addition to providing such insights, Schmidt and Rosenberg's inside view of Google gives the reader a closer look at some of the company's most famous employees. The authors detail not only the contributions of founders Page and Sergey Brin but also those of notable former Googlers such as Yahoo CEO Marissa Mayer and Facebook chief operating officer (COO) Sheryl Sandberg, whose names most readers will likely recognize.

Although the authors' insider perspective makes for an interesting read, it is at times somewhat problematic. The focus of the book is on how Google functions, and Schmidt and Rosenberg naturally have a degree of bias in favor of Google's business practices; the Google way seems to be the best way, at least in the eyes of the authors. Because of their status as current Google employees, and the fact that they cowrote the book with the head of Google's corporate communications, it sometimes feels as if the book is an extended advertisement for Google rather than a true guide for business owners. In addition, Schmidt and Rosenberg at times seem to reshape Google's history to better fit their book's thesis. In his review for the *Guardian*, Steven Poole wrote that "the alert reader will . . . perceive Google's history being massaged if not airbrushed." He goes on to note, for example, that although the authors write that Google's founders always intended to make money from advertisements, Page and

Brin actually expressed a negative view of advertisements in their early writings about the search engine. The authors acknowledge some of Google's failed products, such as Google Wave and Google Reader, but as Poole noticed, the reasons for the retirement of such products, some of which were quite popular, are not adequately explained. As critic Brad Stone points out in his review for the *New York Times*, Schmidt and Rosenberg likewise do not reflect on why they moved from high-ranking executive positions at Google to advisory roles, and this omission raises more questions than it answers.

Despite critical objections to certain aspects of the book, reviews of *How Google Works* nevertheless praised many of its elements. Schmidt and Rosenberg's discussion of Google's decision to enter the Chinese market and subsequent decision to leave the market in the wake of widespread censorship and attempts by Chinese hackers to break into Google systems, for instance, intrigued many critics. This discussion, which is included in the chapter on decision making and consensus, exemplifies the key Google principle of considering multiple perspectives and changing course when necessary. *Independent* reviewer Max Wallis dubbed this anecdote a "diamond" in the midst of "zirconia" and noted that although the book lacks depth in many areas, it is nevertheless an absorbing read, one that gives the reader "a blinking view of what it is to work at one of the world's most successful companies."

*Joy Crelin*

**Review Sources**

"Don't Be Modest: The Search Giant Shares Some of Its Business Methods." Rev. of *How Google Works*, by Eric Schmidt and Jonathan Rosenberg, with Alan Eagle. *Economist*. Economist Newspaper, 27 Sept. 2014. Web. 18 Jan. 2015.

Rev. of *How Google Works*, by Eric Schmidt and Jonathan Rosenberg, with Alan Eagle. *Kirkus*. Kirkus, 22 July 2014. Web. 18 Jan. 2015.

Poole, Steven. "*How Google Works* by Eric Schmidt and Jonathan Rosenberg—Review." *Guardian*. Guardian News and Media, 26 Sept. 2014. Web. 18 Jan. 2015.

Sinofsky, Steven. "Book Review: 'How Google Works' by Eric Schmidt and Jonathan Rosenberg." *Wall Street Journal*. Dow Jones, 3 Oct. 2014. Web. 18 Jan. 2015.

Stone, Brad. "'How Google Works,' by Eric Schmidt and Jonathan Rosenberg." *New York Times*. New York Times, 7 Nov. 2014. Web. 18 Jan. 2015.

Wallis, Max. "*How Google Works* by Eric Schmidt and Jonathan Rosenberg, Book Review." *Independent*. Independent.co.uk, 11 Sept. 2014. Web. 18 Jan. 2015.

# Half Bad

**Author:** Sally Green (b. 1961)
**Publisher:** Viking (New York). 416 pp.
**Type of work:** Novel
**Time:** Unknown
**Locale:** England

(Courtesy of Viking)

*A young-adult paranormal novel,* Half Bad
*(2014) relates the struggle that Nathan Byrn
endures due not only to his mixed heritage,
but also to the fact that his father is the most
notorious Black Witch in known history.*

**Principal characters:**
NATHAN BYRN, a young man who is half
 Black Witch and half White Witch
MARCUS EDGE, his father, a notorious Black
 Witch
CELIA, his jailor and teacher
ARRAN BYRN, his half brother
GABRIEL, a Black Witch stuck in human form
ELSIE ASHWORTH, his grandmother and legal guardian
MERCURY, a black market practitioner of witchcraft whose twin sister was killed years
 earlier
JESSICA BYRN, his half sister, a Hunter of Black Witches
DEBORAH BYRN, his half sister
ANNALISE O'BRIEN, his first love

In *Half Bad*, Nathan Byrn lives shackled in a cage somewhere in rural England. He is
guarded by a fierce woman named Celia, who trains him how to fight and who alter-
nately treats him with kindness and brutal violence. The reader soon learns that Nathan
is the son of Marcus Edge, an infamous Black Witch known to have committed several
murders of White Witches. Nathan's mother was herself a White Witch who killed
herself under mysterious circumstances, leaving Nathan and his three half siblings,
who are all pure White Witches rather than a "Half Code" like Nathan, in the care
of their maternal grandmother, Elsie Ashworth. As the youngest, Nathan watches as
each of his half siblings eventually turns seventeen and receives the gifts and familial
blood that will unlock their own powers as witches. Before he comes of age himself,
however, Nathan is forcibly taken from his family by the Council that governs matters
pertaining to witches. Although the Council would like to kill Nathan outright, they
instead decide to train him as a weapon to lure and kill Marcus, since no one else has
been able to do so. They assign Celia as Nathan's guard and teacher, and the two live
alone in an isolated location where he is subjected to a brutal physical regimen.

As Nathan matures, the Council begins to assess his physical and magical abilities more frequently. Because he is now separated from his grandmother and cannot receive the necessary gifts and blood, Nathan is uncertain what will happen on his seventeenth birthday, having heard that whets, or underage witches, who do not receive their gifts on time usually die within a year. Desperate, Nathan finally escapes from Celia and the Council and makes contact with an underground network with the hope of obtaining his gifts from a black market practitioner named Mercury.

The overarching theme of *Half Bad* is the notion of good versus evil, particularly when the division is not as clean cut as it might at first seem. The White Witches consider themselves to be pure and good, but the physical torture they seem to enjoy inflicting on Nathan from a young age proves that many White Witches are anything but benevolent. With the exception of Annalise, a White Witch with whom Nathan falls in love at a young age, the O'Brien family is particularly sadistic. When they discover that Nathan and Annalise have been meeting secretly, Annalise's brothers use a knife to carve the initials *B* and *W* into Nathan's back, creating large permanent scars by using a powder to prevent Nathan from healing naturally. Similarly, even though Celia is uncomfortable with the Council's extreme treatment of Nathan, she thinks nothing of slapping him whenever he says something she does not like, and he is often unable to predict what will set her off.

In addition to physical cruelty, the Council seems to wage a campaign of terror against anyone who does not strictly conform. Beginning from Nathan's infancy, the Council enacts decrees designed to restrict not only Nathan's freedom, but that of his family, even though they are all "pure" White Witches and have been complying with the Council's edicts all along. Nathan learns that the Council may be responsible for his mother's suicide and that they regularly use threats against loved ones and other psychological tactics to maintain their unchallenged rule over witch matters. Readers will notice the similarities between the Council members and members of the Nazi Party in mid-twentieth-century Germany. Registers, for example, are kept to track the purity of bloodlines, and the magical, bone-deep tattoos to permanently brand Nathan are reminiscent of the identification numbers that were tattooed on the arms of individuals in Nazi concentration camps.

*Sally Green lives in northwest England. Half Bad, the first book in a projected trilogy, is her debut novel and has been translated into forty-five languages. The sequel,* Half Wild, *is scheduled for publication in 2015. A film adaptation of* Half Bad *is in production.*

Another theme that the author explores is that of familial loyalty. Nathan learns early on that in order to protect himself, he must answer any questions about his father by saying that he despises him. In reality, however, Nathan often fantasizes that his father will come to rescue him, first from his stifling home life lived in fear of the Council and later from the literal cage in which the Council imprisons him. Naturally, Nathan wonders whether his father's past actions could be considered self-defense or have other justifiable motivations. In addition, Nathan tries to analyze which traits he has inherited from his father and which from his mother. As Nathan's critical seventeenth birthday draws near and he becomes more and more frustrated, he finds himself giving in to rage more frequently, and he wonders whether he is perhaps as inherently bad as his father is believed to be.

Nathan also experiences varying degrees of loyalty from his own family. Jessica, his oldest sister, aspires to be a Hunter, or a White Witch who dedicates his or her life to tracking Black Witches. Even when Nathan is barely old enough to walk, Jessica constantly tells him that he is to blame for their mother's death. Later, she uses her gift, which enables her to disguise herself as anyone, to try and trick Nathan into saying things that could be construed as sympathetic toward Marcus. It is clear that Jessica would betray Nathan as a way to ingratiate herself with the Council. Deborah and Arran, however, are supportive and recognize that, regardless of his father's identity, Nathan is the same boy that they have watched grow from infancy. Nathan's grandmother, too, does everything she can to protect him from the Council.

As in J. K. Rowling's Harry Potter series, *Half Bad* depicts the world of witches as hidden among humans, who Green refers to as "fain." Similarly, the novel is set in contemporary England, but witches generally keep to themselves and eschew modern technology. Nathan himself is particularly sensitive to cell phones and computers, which create a jarring static in his head. In fact, the part of his nature that is influenced by his Black Witch heritage makes it impossible for him to stay indoors at night because walls interfere with his connection to the land and the moon. Imprisonment is therefore another method by which the Council can torture Nathan.

One of the more unique aspects of this novel is the author's use of the second-person point of view for those chapters in which Nathan describes his incarceration and training at the hands of Celia. This technique lends immediacy to this portion of the narrative. Nathan copes by mentally dividing his repetitive days into discrete chunks of time with particular activities that he looks forward to and others he attempts to get through quickly as possible. Nathan also tries to escape, but each rebellious act leads to more painful and severe measures designed to secure him. Because Nathan is imprisoned with Celia for well over a year, they develop a strange captor/captive relationship, and both are forced to acknowledge a grudging mutual respect. Unlike the chapters written in second person, other sections of the novel are related differently to the reader and have a distancing effect. When Nathan learns about his father and other ancestors from stories told to him by Jessica, Celia, Mercury, and his grandmother, Nathan's feelings of isolation and bewilderment are emphasized as is the feeling that he is being punished and tortured for past events over which he had no control.

Although Nathan continues to love Annalise despite never having had much opportunity to spend time together, the most important relationships in Nathan's life are with other males. For instance, although Marcus and Nathan have not yet met face-to-face, Marcus's influence on Nathan's life is pervasive. More immediately, however, Nathan's half brother, Arran, is the first person Nathan believes will continue to love him even if his inherited dark nature emerges. Later, while seeking an audience with the elusive Mercury, Nathan is befriended by Gabriel, a Black Witch who is stuck in the form of a fain. Nathan does not recognize until it is pointed out to him that Gabriel appears to have fallen in love with him. Nonetheless, when Nathan must go on the run again at the end of the book, Gabriel is the first person who comes to mind for help.

The women in Nathan's life, on the other hand, affect him in more practical ways. His grandmother, for example, does her best to help him navigate the society that despises him, and Celia in her own misguided way trains Nathan to the best of his abilities. Jessica's hostility and deceit teach Nathan at a young age to be wary. Mercury is perhaps the strangest female influence in Nathan's life. Like the Council, her own personal goal, fueled by revenge, is to use Nathan to kill Marcus. By the time Nathan meets Mercury, however, he has learned to recognize other people's motives and how to appease them and appear to go along with them even when he has his own goals in mind.

The first book in a projected trilogy, *Half Bad* provides little resolution to Nathan's story. He ultimately meets his father and receives the necessary coming-of-age gifts, but the brief glimpse that Nathan and the reader get of Marcus is not enough to ascertain whether Marcus is truly as evil as everyone believes. Through the compelling story arc of Nathan's desperate situation, the reader is a witness to his physical and emotional growth as he matures from a passive boy to a young man who learns how to affect his destiny.

*Amy Sisson*

**Review Sources**

Bradburn, Frances. Rev. of *Half Bad*, by Sally Green. *Booklist* 15 Feb. 2014: 74. Print.

Grossman, Lev. "Rough Magic." Rev. of *Half Bad*, by Sally Green. *Time* 17 Mar. 2014: 70. Print.

Rev. of *Half Bad*, by Sally Green. *Kirkus Reviews* 15 Feb. 2014: 73. Print.

Rev. of *Half Bad*, by Sally Green. *Publishers Weekly* 23 Dec. 2013: 52. Print.

Mills, Annette M. Rev. of *Half Bad*, by Sally Green. *Library Media Connection* Oct. 2014: 37. Print.

# History of the Rain

**Author:** Niall Williams (b. 1958)
**Publisher:** Bloomsbury (New York). 368 pp.
**Type of work:** Novel
**Time:** The early twenty-first century
**Locale:** Faha, Ireland

*In* History of the Rain, *a bedridden nineteen-year-old woman chronicles her family's history and life in a rural Irish community.*

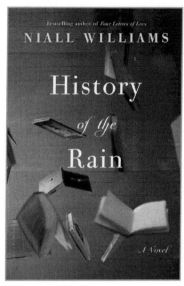

(Courtesy of Bloomsbury Publishing)

**Principal characters:**
RUTH LOUISE SWAIN, a nineteen-year-old woman who is bedridden due to a blood disorder
AENGUS "AENEY" SWAIN, her twin brother
VIRGIL SWAIN, her father
MARY MACCARROLL SWAIN, also known as MAM, her mother
ABRAHAM SWAIN, her paternal grandfather
MARGARET KITTERING SWAIN, a.k.a. GRANDMOTHER, her paternal grandmother
FIACHRA MACCARROLL, her maternal grandfather
BRIDGET TALTY MACCARROLL, a.k.a. NAN, her maternal grandmother
MRS. QUINTY, her former teacher and frequent visitor
VINCENT CUNNINGHAM, her friend and would-be suitor

The ninth novel by Irish writer Niall Williams, *History of the Rain* (2014) begins in an attic room in the rainy rural community of Faha in Ireland's County Clare, where nineteen-year-old Ruth Swain is confined to her bed. The young woman has returned to her parents' home after collapsing while away at Trinity College Dublin; doctors have determined that she has some kind of blood disorder, but the exact nature of her illness remains unclear. Now living in her childhood bedroom, Ruth, a voracious reader, surrounds herself with the nearly four thousand books that made up her father's library, telling frequent visitor Mrs. Quinty that she hopes to read all of them before she dies. She is particularly fond of and often references the nineteenth-century British writer Robert Louis Stevenson, who wrote some of his best-known works while bedridden and whose initials Ruth shares. Ruth believes strongly in the power of stories, which she says human beings tell "to stay alive or keep alive those who only live now in the telling." Inspired by this belief, by her most-loved books, and by her need to come to a better understanding of her father, she begins to recount the story of the Swain family, a long tale filled with beauty, tragedy, and, most of all, water, in the forms of both the ever-present rain and the nearby River Shannon.

Ruth begins with the story of her paternal grandfather, Abraham Swain. The son of an English reverend who gave his family what Ruth calls the "Swain Philosophy of Impossible Standard," Abraham initially planned to follow in his father's footsteps and join the clergy. However, he never felt called to that vocation, and when World War I broke out, he enlisted. He was nearly killed in battle but was helped by a German soldier and later by a British medic. After the war, Abraham moved to Ireland, where he developed a deep devotion to salmon fishing; he recorded his fishing data in his salmon journals and later wrote a book on the subject. Ruth notes that those texts are among the books in her collection. Abraham eventually married a woman named Margaret Kittering and had four children with her, the youngest of whom was Ruth's father, Virgil. Shortly after completing his book on Irish salmon, Abraham died of a heart attack while fishing.

Much like his daughter, Virgil had an intense love of books and learning from a young age. He particularly enjoyed Herman Melville's *Moby-Dick* (1851), a book that Ruth argues epitomizes the Swain Philosophy of Impossible Standard. After the death of his father and then his mother, Virgil, who apparently inherited Abraham's attachment to the water, joined the merchant navy and left Ireland for a time. After his return, Virgil encountered Mary MacCarroll while standing on the bank of the River Shannon. Mary was the daughter of Fiachra MacCarroll, said by some to be a descendant of Irish folk hero Tuan MacCarrill, and the feisty Bridget Talty, whom Ruth calls Nan. Virgil and Mary wed after a courtship that involved many walks along the river, and after years of speculation as to when they would have children, Mary eventually gave birth to twins, Ruth and Aengus. Fittingly, the two were conceived by the River Shannon, and Ruth likens their birth to swimming downriver.

The four Swains and Nan lived together in a small house near the river in Faha, where Virgil took up writing poetry. Over the following years, he passed his devotion to books on to his daughter and his hereditary attachment to water to his son. Aengus's devotion to the river ended in tragedy when he drowned in it on his and Ruth's last day of primary school. This loss had a strong effect on the family and particularly on Ruth, who, years later, still feels grief at the loss of her twin—a loss in which she "lost more than half the world." Her father lost his ability to write poetry for a time following Aengus's death, and although Ruth and Mary compiled Virgil's poems into a manuscript titled *History of the Rain* and sent it to publishers in an attempt to lift his spirits, they were unable to secure its publication. Although he eventually resumed writing, Virgil later threw his pages in the river. Not long after, Ruth found him dead at his writing desk. Although deeply saddened by her father's death, Ruth was heartened when she found notes for a poem she had asked him to write for her among his belongings. To preserve her father's memory, she resolved to write a book about her family's history that, like her father's unpublished manuscript, would bear the title *History of the Rain.*

Ruth intersperses her story with events occurring in the present, recounting her conversations with visitors about such topics as Irish folklore and the existence and nature of heaven. She also documents her doctor's appointments and trips to the hospital, recounting the banter between ambulance operators Timmy and Packy, and her encounters with Vincent Cunningham, a young man who has harbored romantic feelings for her since childhood. But Ruth always inevitably returns to her long narrative, which twists and meanders much like the river that has become so entwined with her family's history.

In *History of the Rain*, Williams constructs a complex narrative that, though at times straightforward, is characterized by its numerous tangents and digressions. Ruth acknowledges this and comments on its intentionality: "This, Dear Reader, is a river narrative. My chosen style is the Meander." This narrative style suits the novel's plot, which by necessity moves fluidly between past and present, and by describing her chosen style, Ruth, as narrator, underscores Williams's intentions. The meandering nature of the narrative serves a number of purposes in the novel. By recounting present events, Ruth both demonstrates how the events of the past continue to affect the Swain family and hints at events that occurred in the past

*Niall Williams is the author of nine novels, including* Four Letters of Love *(1998) and* John *(2008), as well as various nonfiction books and plays.*

before explaining them; for instance, Aengus's absence is palpable long before Ruth reveals that he is dead and explains the circumstances of his death. At the same time, telling the story of the past from the present allows Ruth to view past events, many of them tragic, with a degree of perspective. She notes that over time, the difficult events in a story can be turned "into fairy tale"; likewise, by transforming her family's history into a story, she lessens the pain of its many tragedies.

In his author's note, Williams mentions that his father loved books and instilled a love of reading in his son, to whom he left his books after his death. The influence of Williams's experience is evident in *History of the Rain*, both in the specific details—a love of reading runs in the Swain family, and Ruth inherits Virgil's books after he dies—and in the novel's deep connection to literature. Ruth makes frequent references to the many books she has read, comparing the people and events in her life to characters and situations in books and engaging in various discussions about literature and storytelling. One particularly striking feature of the book is the use of parenthetical references to books in Ruth's collection; after quoting the nineteenth-century English poet Gerard Manley Hopkins, for instance, Ruth includes the citation "(Book 1,555, *Poems & Prose*, Penguin, London)." This both demonstrates the breadth of her reading—and, by extension, Virgil's reading, as the books come from his collection—and gives the reader a more concrete understanding of the importance of books in her life.

According to the author's note, one of the books Williams inherited from his father was titled *The Salmon Rivers of Ireland*. This too is echoed in *History of the Rain*; indeed, the novel even includes a brief excerpt from Abraham's own book on Irish salmon. The novel as a whole is full of mentions of salmon and, more prominently, the rivers where such fish live and other waters. Water imagery permeates *History of the Rain*, from the titular rain itself to the river that claims the lives of Abraham and Aengus, nearly floods the Swain home, and provides Ruth with the narrative motion of the story. Ruth's family's connection to water seems to be more than just an inherited predilection; it is something ancient and bone-deep. In one of the present-day conversations she documents, Ruth learns about Irish folklore from Tommy Devlin, a cousin of her maternal grandmother. According to his stories, when a great flood overtook Ireland, some of its people survived by becoming either birds or swimmers. Later, a man named Tuan MacCarrill survived a disaster by transforming into a salmon. Ruth's mother's family, the MacCarrolls, supposedly are descended from Tuan Mac-Carrill and inherited his affinity for the river; thus, the attachment to water flows to Ruth from both sides of her family. These deep ties contribute to the overall sense of history and inheritance that fills the novel.

*History of the Rain* was well received by critics and was included in the long list for the 2014 Man Booker Prize, a prestigious award for English-language novels. Critics praised the novel's powerful narrative, which, although deeply tied to Ireland and the particulars of Ruth's family, is nevertheless deeply relatable. In his review for the *Santa Barbara Independent*, Brian Tanguay commented that the story Ruth tells is truly "everyone's story," a narrative "about how we aspire and endure." The prose itself was received positively as well, although Catherine Taylor, in her review for the *Guardian*, argued that Ruth's style of narration, with its fanciful descriptions and non-standard capitalization, can at times become "cloying." Indeed, her voice and many other aspects of the prose are undoubtedly unique, but critics generally agreed that this only adds to the novel's charm. In his review for the *Sydney Morning Herald*, Peter Pierce particularly called attention to Williams's subtle use of colloquial language, which colors what he calls the "eloquent plainness" of the novel. All of these elements combine to create a novel that is lyrical and sharp, tragic yet hopeful, and steeped in the rains and rivers of Ireland.

*Joy Crelin*

### Review Sources

Rev. of *History of the Rain*, by Niall Williams. *Kirkus* 15 Apr. 2014: 156. Print.

Rev. of *History of the Rain*, by Niall Williams. *Publishers Weekly* 3 Mar. 2014: 43. Print.

Pierce, Peter. Rev. of *History of the Rain*, by Niall Williams. *Sydney Morning Herald*. Fairfax Media, 27 June 2014. Web. 18 Dec. 2014.

Tanguay, Brian. Rev. of *History of the Rain*, by Niall Williams. *Santa Barbara Independent*. Santa Barbara Independent, 25 June 2014. Web. 18 Dec. 2014.

Taylor, Catherine. "Pure Eccentric Entertainment." Rev. of *History of the Rain*, by Niall Williams. *Guardian*. Guardian News and Media, 7 Aug. 2014. Web. 18 Dec. 2014.

Wade, Francesca. "Otherworldly and Quaint." Rev. of *History of the Rain*, by Niall Williams. *Telegraph*. Telegraph Media Group, 19 Aug. 2014. Web. 18 Dec. 2014.

# Hold the Dark

**Author:** William Giraldi
**Publisher:** Liveright (New York). 208 pp.
**Type of work:** Novel
**Time:** Present
**Locale:** Keelut, Alaska

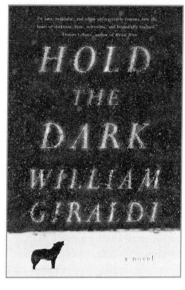

(Courtesy of Liveright)

Hold the Dark *is a novel rich with violence, wilderness, and sin, and will make readers feel the desolate chill of rural Alaska.*

**Principal characters:**
RUSSELL CORE, a wolf expert and nature writer
MEDORA SLONE, a Keelut native whose son, Bailey, has disappeared
VERNON SLONE, Medora's husband, a Keelut native and military service member

*Hold the Dark* is William Giraldi's second novel. His first, *Busy Monsters*, was a loopy-lingoed take on the classic picaresque narrative—an episodic quest undertaken by an unlikely, and sometimes unlikable, hero. The book was funny and largely well-received; Fiona Maazel, in her review for the *New York Times* wrote that it "abounds in antics and satire." Ron Charles of the *Washington Post* described it as a romance with a "delicate sweetness" and "one of the weirdest comic novels of the year." However, *Hold the Dark* is none of these things. Indeed, readers of *Busy Monsters* will be surprised to find that the two books were written by the same hand. Then again, in an interview with journalist David Cameron for the blog *Talking Writing*, Giraldi reveals that he had something more spiritual to get off his chest. "The novels that are most important to me are in some ways both religious and social," he said. "By 'religious,' I mean the mythological or spiritual, not the doctrinal or dogmatic." In its own way, *Hold the Dark* represents Giraldi grappling with something larger than himself.

In the tiny village of Keelut, Alaska, many hours away from the nearest town, children are taken by wolves in the middle of the night. Among the missing children is Medora Slone's six-year-old son, Bailey. After Bailey disappears, Medora tells "her fellow villagers how she had trekked over the hills and across the vale all that evening and night and into the blush of dawn with the rifle across her back and a ten-inch knife strapped to her thigh. The revenge she wanted tasted metallic." Medora, like all of the ghostly residents of Keelut, is resourceful and tough. She wears boots that she made herself out of caribou hide and gave birth to her son with only some ointment from a wolf's organs to protect against the pain. Still, for all of her self-sufficiency, Medora decides she has reached an impasse.

Her fellow villagers refuse to go after the wolves, believing them to be possessed by evil spirits. Her husband, Vernon, is at war, but he is coming home soon. Without any remains, what will she offer him to bury? She must recover Bailey's bones, and she decides, improbably, to contact Russell Core, an author and wolf expert who lives thousands of miles away. As a person with a less magical view of the wolves, Core refuses to kill one of them either. Wolves would only kill a human child if they were starving, he reasons. Wolves are not natural enemies to humans, but like sharks (and polar bears before them), they have gotten a bad rap in popular culture. Core has his own problems, however. He agrees to visit Keelut and help Medora locate her son's body, and perhaps even kill the wolf that took him, to avoid the supreme grief of caring for his wife, who has recently suffered a life-altering stroke.

*Hold the Dark* is William Giraldi's second novel. His first, Busy Monsters, was published in 2011. He is the editor of the literary journal AGNI at Boston University.

Core is a stranger in a strange land: he is logical, inquisitive, and, in Keelut, often afraid—all of the things that Medora and the Keelut natives are not. Filtered through his eyes, Keelut emerges as a visceral place—though its customs remain tantalizingly oblique. "He'd been deep into the reaches of Montana, Minnesota, Wyoming, Saskatchewan, but no place he could remember matched the oddness, the otherness he felt in this place," Giraldi writes of Core. Keelut is "a settlement at the edge of the wild that both welcomed and resisted the wild." When Core arrives, Medora's behavior is erratic. She tries to seduce him and then rubs her skin raw as she bathes in the bathtub. She speaks in strange aphorisms—all of Giraldi's characters are self-reverential, speaking in heightened, hushed tones. "This wildness here is inside us," she tells him. "Inside everything."

Core embarks on his mission into the tundra, promising himself not to kill the wolves, though he hopes to recover some part of the boy. He encounters the pack of wolves and, after briefly entertaining the thought of suicide-by-wolf, fires a warning shot in the air sending them scattering away from the village. He returns to Medora's home with nothing. Prepared to comfort Medora, he is shocked to find that no one is home. In the course of his search for her, he discovers the frozen body of Bailey Slone—a truly shocking revelation that sparks a chain of events bloody enough to atone for Bailey's bloodless death. Medora's husband, Vernon, comes home and embarks on a quest to find his wife, who seems to have vanished into the thin air. Unable to bring himself to leave, Core becomes enmeshed in the search for Medora and Vernon, leading an expedition akin to the one he arrived in Keelut to undertake in the first place.

Keelut is not a real town, though *keelut* is a real Inuit word. It refers to an evil mythical beast, a hairless creature that resembles a dog or a wolf. But Giraldi is skilled in conjuring a sense of place. His Keelut is desolate and unforgiving. "If dust jackets were more than paper and ink," John Wilwol wrote in his review of *Hold the Dark* for the *New York Times*, "this one would bear blood and frost." Readers will feel the cold but might also recognize the lack of police oversight that contributes to a larger sense of isolation. The Slones' chase across the barren landscape is a well-wrought escalation of the action, though much of it can be reduced to a neat line of severed limbs and dark, pulpy entrails on the white snow. *Hold the Dark*'s graphic violence is effective at first. The moment is jarring, but Giraldi cannot sustain tonally the bloodbath. Every interaction becomes inevitable, descriptions become redundant, and the act of killing becomes a parody of itself. Comedy—at which Giraldi is certainly adept, as evidenced by his first novel—does not seem to be the aim here, yet his real goal is unclear.

Nick Ripatrazone, in a review for the *Millions*, called *Hold the Dark* part of a "new Catholic fiction, one forged in the smithies of writers who reject belief but retain reverence for religious language." Ripatrazone concludes that Giraldi's goal "appears to be searching for transcendence in a world plagued with evil. . . . It is a violent, dark novel, written by a man who thinks 'knowledge and art are survival,' someone who still considers sin real." *Hold the Dark* is full of sin, though Giraldi seems preoccupied with only one. Matricide is not the crime in question here; this is not a book about mothers and children, or about animals, survival, or war—though at various points throughout, it may appear to be about any one of those things. Indeed, the secret sin at the heart of the novel is quite different than what readers will expect.

Giraldi's prose is forceful. His sense of pacing is strong. Yet *Hold the Dark* is actually less than the sum of its parts. The friction between Giraldi's dual goals—"literary thriller," as Ripatrazone accurately described it, and morality tale—fails to ignite. In making a serious argument that Keelut (or the world) is truly evil, he robs the town of any complexity and, with it, the book of any substantive story. Rather than choose to make the alien familiar, Giraldi chooses to make the alien more alien, and the sense of unreality creates a distancing effect. The best stories about the supernatural say something about what it is like to live in the real world. How do people survive on the brink of civilization? What animal characteristics must they adopt to survive? Giraldi toys with these questions, but the conclusion he works toward undercuts them. After all, animals have no human sense of right and wrong—another compelling line of inquiry that Giraldi establishes early on. That Giraldi returns to the theme of a human moral code is curious, as he seems to say that all the crimes perpetrated within the book could be attributed to the fact that the criminals were just sinners all along.

*Molly Hagan*

## Review Sources

Ripatrazone, Nick. "Heart of Darkness: On William Giraldi's Hold the Dark." Rev. of *Hold the Dark*, by William Giraldi. *Millions*. MMIX The Millions, 11 Sept.

2014. Web. 23 Jan. 2015.

Taylor, Elizabeth. "Editor's Choice." Rev. of *Hold the Dark*, by William Giraldi. *Chicago Tribune*. Chicago Tribune, 4 Sept. 2014. Web. 23 Jan. 2015.

Wilwol, John. "Hour of the Wolf." Rev. of *Hold the Dark*, by William Giraldi. *New York Times*. New York Times, 5 Sept. 2014. Web. 23 Jan. 2015.

# How to Be Both

**Author:** Ali Smith (b. 1962)
**Publisher:** Pantheon (New York). 372 pp.
**Type of work:** Novel
**Time:** ca. 1470s; 2013–14
**Locale:** Bologna, Italy; Cambridge, England

*This novel in two parts tells the separate but entangled stories of a young, contemporary British girl and a fifteenth-century Renaissance painter. The novel pushes the boundaries between history and fiction, past and present, and life and death as it unfolds these stories of a tortured adolescent and an ambitious painter, both navigating the pitfalls of love and loss and exploring ambiguous gender and sexual identities.*

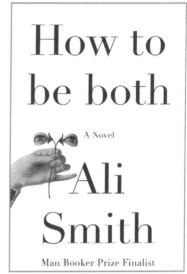

(Courtesy of Pantheon)

**Principal characters:**
FRANCESCO "FRANCESCHO" DEL COSSA, an Italian Renaissance painter of great skill
BARTOLOMEO "BARTO" GARGANELLI, an aristocratic friend of his
COSIMO "COSMO" TURA, his rival, an artist of some acclaim
BORSO "BORSE" D'ESTE, the Duke of Ferrara, patron of his most significant work
GEORGIA "GEORGE" COOK, an adolescent girl dealing with aftermath of her mother's death
CAROL MARTINEAU, her deceased mother, a political journalist
NATHAN COOK, her father
HENRY COOK, her younger brother
HELENA "H" FISKER, a classmate of hers
MRS. ROCK, her high school counselor
LISA GOLLIARD, a mysterious friend of Carol's

Short-listed for the Man Booker Prize, Ali Smith's *How to Be Both* (2014) is an experimental novel that pushes the boundaries of its genre while testing the minds and imaginations of its readers in an exhilarating fashion. The novel is divided into two halves, both of which are titled "One." One half of the book centers on a teenage girl who goes by the name George during the first year after her mother's sudden death. Amid pangs of teenage angst, George's half of the novel is dedicated largely to thoughtful reflections on the nature of human mourning, the limits of memory (whether personal or historical), and the experience of love across space and time. The other half of the book is narrated by the long-dead Renaissance painter Francesco (or Franchesco) del Cossa, about whom little is known in reality. The artist's half of the novel is largely self-reflective and autobiographical, containing thoughtful passages concerning the creative spirit, the nature of art, and the power of realism in art.

The two halves of the book reconcile with one another through many layers of connection that only gradually become intelligible to the reader. Still, the novel is designed to keep many of its meanings and interrelationships well hidden, perhaps only to be divulged on multiple read-throughs. Likewise, it resolutely keeps secrets, mysteries, and fissures between its two halves, confidently reminding the reader of the limits of human understanding. One such trick of the book is that in half the printed copies, George's story comes first, and in the other half, Francescho's is first. The experience of reading the novel, and even the reader's perception of who is the main character, is influenced by the order in which the halves are read. As reviewer Arifa Akbar commented in the *Independent*, this technique allowed *How to Be Both* to demonstrate "that the arrangement of a story, even when it's the same story, can change our understanding of it and define our emotional attachments."

The title of *How to Be Both* reflects the structure of the novel as well as several conceptual themes that are explored throughout the text. Most prevalent among these is the book's exploration of gender ambiguity. In Smith's version of Francescho's story, the painter is eventually revealed to be a woman passing as a man in order to get work as an artist, a fact that is only known to a very small number of close confidants. Francescho's mother dies when the child is still quite young, and in order to help Francescho emerge from a traumatic phase of mourning, her father decides to help her fulfill her potential as an artist. In order to achieve this goal, she must don her older brother'sclothes, conceal her femininity, and take on a new name. This gender bending is not immediately apparent to the reader, who never learns Francescho's original given name. The secret gradually becomes apparent as the story unfolds, adding complex twists to the artist's personal friendships and professional endeavors. As Francesco del Cossa was a real Renaissance painter, Smith here takes liberties with the legacy of the artist. It is true that little is known about del Cossa's life, and likely Smith wanted to demonstrate the possibility of taking such historical flights of fancy and the ability of fiction to remove a literary character from the confining historical limitations of factual biography. Still, some information about the real del Cossa, in a foreword, footnote, or otherwise, might have been worthwhile to call out Smith's distinction between art history and fiction.

Like Francescho, George also lives on a border between gender norms. The ambiguity of her chosen nickname is, perhaps, the first hint of the uncertainties with which she is struggling. As she develops a close female friendship with a classmate named Helena, who goes by "H," and contemplates the possibility of her own lesbian inclinations, George attempts to come to terms with her deceased mother's fling with Lisa Golliard while also pursuing the historical mysteries of the Renaissance painter del Cossa, whom she instinctively believes could have been a woman. Francescho and George both offer their individual meditations on their sensations of dual identities.

This theme of paired dualities is much larger, though, than the central focus on gender ambiguity. Indeed, perhaps more satisfying are the moments when this same theme is used to draw connections between the living and the dead, the past and the present, or art and life.In its largest sense, Smith uses this concept to suggest the universal connections that bind each element of the fabric of the world. At the end of Francescho's half of the book, for example, is a poem that concludes by arriving at this concept with the lines

> hello all the everything
> to be
> made and
> unmade
> both.

Francescho's discussion of painting the frescoes at the Palazzo Schifanoia presents another thoughtful instance of reflection on this same theme. Although works of art present illusions, Francescho reminds the reader that they are still real, material objects with their own presence; thus, a hand or a foot "coming over the edge . . . into the world beyond the picture" emphasizes that "a picture is a real thing in the world." Similarly, as Francescho's painting develops on the walls of the pleasure house, the artist realizes that the work has come to take on an existence of its own, wholly separate from the creative act. This is evocatively captured as Francescho describes the moment when she examines her painting by torchlight and realizes that its figures have come to life: "I saw they were escapees: they'd broken free from me and from the wall that had made them and held them and even from themselves." The figures, dancing in the nighttime illumination, become animated with a life that their own creator did not anticipate.

*How to Be Both* also offers thoughtful reflections on remembrance and mourning. A thin thread separates life and death in much of the book. Francescho cannot remember her own death and questions if it actually happened; uncertainty about the artist's death, which is presumed to have occurred during an outbreak of plague, is raised again as George, her mother, and H all attempt to uncover more information. Perhaps inspired by the voice of an epic narrator, guide, or hero, the character of Francescho offers a wise narrator's voice. Now a disembodied observer of the experiences of a mysterious young woman (eventually revealed to be George), Francescho also explores the inner recesses of her own biography. Like George, Francescho mourns the early loss of her mother. Other memories haunt and plague the artist, who describes having attempted ceremonies to wipe clean her own slate of memory in order to banish the tormenting memories of life's unhappiness. George, meanwhile, struggles with how to finalize the loss of her mother and move

*Ali Smith has published several acclaimed novels and collections of short stories, including* There but for The *(2011),* The First Person and Other Stories *(2008), and* Girl Meets Boy *(2007). She has been short-listed three times for the Man Booker Prize and has received numerous other awards and acclaims, including the Orange Prize for Fiction, the Goldsmiths Prize, and the Costa Book Award for novels.*

forward while still living with the memories. She resolutely works her way through narratives and dialogues with her mother, translating all of her mother's wisdom and opinions into the past tense because she is dead. As any teenager would be, George is troubled by her own conflicted relationship with her mother and burdened by the guilt of having been uncooperative with many of her mother's desires in the last few months of their lives together. Throughout, she wonders about the continuities between life and death. She queries, "Do you think, when we die, that we still have memories?" over and over again, likely wondering if her own mother can still remember her, or how long her memories of her deceased mother will themselves survive. Perhaps most poignant is the moment when George sends a text message offering a Latin translation over which she has long been laboring, on the subject of enduring love. In it, she confesses that although she has offered the translation, "I can't mean any of them because right now for me they are just words." Shortly thereafter, she admits to her counselor, Mrs. Rock, that she sent this message to a cell phone number that no longer exists, a number that the reader knows once belonged to her mother.

Throughout these complex tales of transience, loss, and memory, the paintings of Francesco del Cossa are the most pervasive motif. Carol Martineau, George's mother, becomes drawn to a reproduction of one of the frescoes at the Palazzo Schifanoia, and shortly before her death, she takes her two children on a brief trip to Italy to see the works in person. She can uncover little about the artist and cannot even remember his name during the visit, but nonetheless their collective encounter with the work is profound, and some of the most vivid memories of recent conversations with her mother that George recounts come from this trip. Naturally, many of Francescho's own narratives have to do with the creation of this work and the substantial attention that it received during her lifetime. Another work by del Cossa, this one a panel painting in the National Gallery of Art in London and the first piece described by Francescho, becomes a significant tool to George's process of healing: after many months of sinking further and further into mourning, George finds the painting and begins to visit it regularly, sitting for hours in the presence of this work by an artist to whom her mother was drawn. She develops a rapport with the saint in the painting, whose gaze always looks resolutely past her; she begins to regard him as an "old friend" and is grateful that his disregard for her presence seems to remind her, "You're not the only one, as if everything isn't happening just to you. Because you're not. And it isn't." She is hardly out of the woods as she comes to these experiences, a fact that is emphasized by the many days of school she misses in order to study the painting, but for the first time it seems that she might move on.

*How to Be Both* is a challenging but rewarding novel. It contains moments of exquisite description and thoughtful reflection on the meaning of art, seen through the alternate illusions of literary fiction and painting. Through its painful explorations of the mourning process and the challenges of aging, it also captures experiences of broad relevance with both grace and beauty.

*Julia A. Sienkewicz*

## Review Sources

Akbar, Arifa. Rev. of *How to Be Both*, by Ali Smith. *Independent*. Independent.co.uk,
    14 Aug. 2014. Web. 9 Feb. 2015.
Charles, Ron. Rev. of *How to Be Both*, by Ali Smith.*Washington Post*.Washington
    Post, 2 Dec. 2014. Web. 9 Feb. 2015.
Gentry, Amy. "*How to Be Both*: Ali Smith's Coin Flip." *Chicago Tribune*. Tribune
    Interactive, 12 Dec. 2014. Web. 9 Feb. 2015.
Ulin, David. "Ali Smith Has Double Vision in *How to Be Both*." *Los Angeles Times*.
    Los Angeles Times, 28 Nov. 2014. Web. 17 Jan. 2015.

# How to Build a Girl

**Author:** Caitlin Moran (b. 1975)
**Publisher:** HarperCollins (New York). 352 pp.
**Type of work:** Novel
**Time:** 1990–93
**Locales:** Wolverhampton and London, England

(Courtesy of HarperCollins)

*Caitlin Moran's first novel,* How to Build a Girl, *tells the story of a smart but unhappy, pudgy girl from a British working-class background who reinvents herself as a ferocious teenage music critic. As the heroine joins the world of Britain's rock-and-roll scene in the early 1990s, she experiences a sexual awakening.*

**Principal characters:**

JOHANNA MORRIGAN, also known as DOLLY WILDE, the daughter of a large British hippie family who becomes a teenage rock music critic
PAT "DADDA" MORRIGAN, her father, a disabled, failed rock musician
KRISSI MORRIGAN, her elder brother, who slowly accepts his homosexuality
ALI, her standoffish cousin, who has shifting musical tastes
LUPIN MORRIGAN, her younger brother
JOHN KITE, a fictional British rock musician famous for his sad songs
TONY RICH, a Harvard-educated upper-class British music critic
KENNY, the bald gay editor of a British music magazine

British newspaper columnist Caitlin Moran's first novel, *How to Build a Girl*, tells the amazing story of how an unhappy, pudgy girl from a dying industrial city in England turns herself into a fearsome teenage rock-and-roll critic writing for a London music magazine. Despite the author's disclaimer, the story is fairly autobiographical. As such, it has been told by the author before in her two nonfiction works, *How to Be a Woman* (2011) and *Moranthology* (2012). Yet *How to Build a Girl* still works well as a touching, if deliberately rude, coming-of-age story.

At fourteen, in the spring of 1990, Johanna Morrigan feels unloved, "fat," and longing for her first kiss from a boy. To compensate, she has turned to masturbation. Her family is large, poor, and dependent on government benefits for her disabled and often drunk father. They live in Wolverhampton, a desolate city in the British midlands north of London. After a humiliating experience on local television, Johanna decides to rebuild herself as a "self-made woman." Inventing the persona of Dolly Wilde for herself, she is ready to take on the world of rock and roll.

From the start, Johanna's first-person narration is designed to shock the reader through an explicit tale of an awkward sexual situation. This technique is repeated consistently throughout the novel, so readers can decide right away how comfortable they are with it. The same holds true for ironic, but graphic sexual scenes accompanying Johanna's eventual sexual awakening.

The novel's beginning is perhaps a bit over the top. After shocking some readers by relating briefly a particular sexual incident, Johanna remembers how that afternoon, her father, Pat "Dadda" Morrigan, made a drunken fool out of himself. She tells how, after a two-day binge, he brings home "a young disheveled man, carbuncular." Her description contains a clever allusion to the young man carbuncular in the "Fire Sermon" of T. S. Eliot's modernist masterpiece poem *The Waste Land* (1922). As Johanna is a precocious reader of British classics, this is nicely in character—allusions like this are sprinkled throughout the narrative. Yet the ensuing scene, where Dadda mistakes the man for a rock music talent scout and plays him his awful demo tape before throwing him out in a rage, appears overwritten. It turns out the man was just a cutlery salesman anyway.

The early focus on Johanna's Dadda and his antics and her dysfunctional family threatens to make *How to Build a Girl* appear more like a British picaresque novel, which it is really not. As Johanna's own story gathers speed, those farcical incidents about her father, or a visiting nurse mistaking fourteen-year-old Johanna for the mother of her twin baby siblings, fade away. Her love for her younger brother, Lupin, and her desire to bond with her older brother, Krissi, remain in the background of her musings. It turns out Krissi has issues of his own to work through. He is just beginning to understand his homosexuality. Yet soon, Johanna's own teenage fears and obsessions, about her first kiss or losing her virginity, begin to take center stage.

Painfully insecure, Johanna secretly looks up to her cousin Ali, who has embraced a persona as a goth and is hanging out with a goth group. Initially, Johanna lacks the courage to join her. Instead, she explains more of her modes of masturbating. With typical humor, she tells that she would not use a blue roll-on deodorant bottle as a sex toy, as this "would be like having sex with a Smurf." American readers may warm to Johanna's subtle, rather British sense of humor, though she is not a character who speaks lines that would trigger the laugh track of an American situation comedy.

When Johanna believes her loose lips have endangered her father's disability benefits, she seeks to make amends by trying to earn some money. She wins a poetry contest for £250 (about $375). As with many occurrences in Johanna's life, this instance is modeled on Moran's experience. However, when given the chance to read her poem on a local TV show, Johanna embarrasses herself so badly she decides to "upgrade" herself. Thus, the true action of *How to Build a Girl* begins.

First, Johanna chooses a new name. After discussing alternatives with an amused Krissi, she settles on Dolly Wilde, the name of Oscar Wilde's niece—an "'amazing alcoholic lesbian who was dead scandalous.'" Next comes her physical transformation. She begins by dressing all in black and dying her hair black. When Johanna tries out her new persona on Ali and her goth friends, she fails miserably to join their crowd. Thwarted, she visits a record store and picks up a free music magazine. Perusing its pages, Johanna suddenly decides she wants to become a rock music writer, as she believes, "I could easily write this stuff."

The narrative jumps forward to October 1992, when Johanna is almost seventeen. Amazingly, the twenty-seven music reviews she has submitted to the British music magazine *Disc & Music Echo* (*D&ME*), earn her a position as a freelance contributor. One of the male writers has made a bet that Dolly Wilde would turn out to be a man, and he has to pay the winner when the teenage girl appears. It is details like this that give the nascent career of Johanna/Dolly its special touch; this scene also represents another episode closely related to Moran's autobiography.

On November 1992, accompanied by her father, Johanna attends her first gig in Birmingham for a review, which is published, instilling great confidence. Her success persuades her to drop out of school in February 1993, a turn many readers may feel unfortunate. Eventually, her parents let her drop out, and she embarks on her career as teenage music writer in full force.

(Credit: Mark Harrison @ Lucid Representation)

*At sixteen, Caitlin Moran became a reviewer for Great Britain's* Melody Maker *music magazine. Soon, she became a television music show host and then a newspaper columnist. She published her memoir,* How to Be a Woman *(2011), to great acclaim, followed by her essays in* Moranthology *(2012).*

In spring, on a trip to Ireland, she develops a massive crush on the melancholic singer John Kite, whose concert she is flown in to cover. Spending a chaste night in his hotel room talking until 5 a.m., Johanna/Dolly writes a gushing story about Kite and his music. This earns her the enmity and scorn of her editor Kenny, who demands harsh, cynical criticism from his writers. For a while, Johanna/Dolly's assignments dry up. Eventually, Johanna/Dolly ends up in Kenny's good graces again.

*How to Build a Girl* also talks with irony but quite graphically about how Johanna explores her sexuality with various men throughout the summer of 1993. Yet her attempts to become girlfriend of the twenty-three-year-old Harvard-educated fellow music writer Tony Rich, a scion of an upper-class family, fail miserably. This, and her longing for John Kite, propels Johanna into her first existential crisis at the climax of the novel.

There is a clever narrative ploy: occasionally, Johanna makes clear she is writing from the perspective of an adult. For instance, Johanna tells the reader that "Years later . . . I realized there were no demons" in the music she begins to listen to. This can explain the occasional break in the narrator's voice into one that sounds suddenly much older than the teenage protagonist. A case in point is her later homily against cynicism and her advice to "Live a kind and gentle life." These lines sound like jarring discontinuities in tone, explicable only by the interjection of an older self of the protagonist.

For all its narrative spunk and originality, there remains one major critical problem with Moran's novel. This is, as courageous critics such as Liz Jones from London's *Evening Standard* and many reader-reviewers on the Internet have pointed out, that much of its material can already be found in Moran's previous two nonfiction books. In her author note preceding *How to Build a Girl*, Moran states that while she shares some background with her protagonist, "Johanna is not me . . . it is all fictitious." Yet many of Johanna's experiences resemble very closely those of her author, which Moran relays in her first book, *How to Be a Woman*. In addition, Johanna/Dolly Wilde's job interview at the fictitious music magazine *D&ME* resembles Moran's own job interview at the real magazine *Melody Maker* that Moran wrote about in *Moranthology*.

There is nothing wrong about writers using their own lives as inspiration for their fiction. What has disappointed critics such as Jones is that Moran has told her own teenage life story before, so that *How to Build a Girl* can appear like a sexed-up repetition of the same story. However, readers who have either not read Moran's nonfiction accounts of her teenage years or become so fascinated that they are delighted to revisit them with some added fictional touches will enjoy *How to Build a Girl* tremendously. This is evidenced also by many positive professional reviews and some glowing reader responses.

*R. C. Lutz*

**Review Sources**

Friedman, Ann. "About a Girl." Rev. of *How to Build a Girl*, by Caitlin Moran. *New York Times Sunday Book Review*. New York Times, 10 Oct. 2014. Web. 4 Jan. 2015.

Gilbert, Lauren. Rev. of *How to Build a Girl*, by Caitlin Moran. *Library Journal* 15 Sept. 2014: 70. Print.

Jones, Liz. "Sorry, Caitlin, But This Isn't How to Be a Novelist." Rev. of *How to Build a Girl*, by Caitlin Moran. *Evening Standard* [London] 26 June 2014: 42–43. Print.

# If the Tabloids Are True What Are You?

**Author:** Matthea Harvey (b. 1973)
**Publisher:** Graywolf (Minneapolis). 160 pp.
**Type of work:** Poetry

*Poet Matthea Harvey's fifth collection of poetry and illustrations,* If the Tabloids Are True What Are You?, *strengthens Harvey's position as a successful experimental poet and illustrator.*

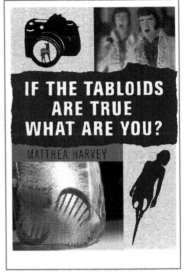

(Courtesy of Graywolf Press)

Matthea Harvey is firmly located in the postmodernist tradition begun in the twentieth century. Her work does not usually rely on forms, nor is she fastidious about punctuation or line breaks. She favors prose poems, made popular by the nineteenth-century symbolist poet Charles Baudelaire; more than half of the poems in her new collection, *If the Tabloids Are True What Are You?* (2014), are prose poems. Although written in paragraphs rather than in lines, they still rely on typical poetic devices such as rhyme, alliteration, and personification. These lines from "The Radio Animals" illustrate Harvey's style:

> When a strong sunbeam hits the cloud, the heat in their bones lends them a temporary gravity and they sink to the ground. Their little thudding footsteps sound like "Testing, testing, 1 2 3" from a faraway galaxy. Like pitter and its petite echo, patter.

Yet Harvey also demonstrates her skill with traditional forms with the collection's lone sonnet, "Michelin Man Possessed by William Shakespeare." Fittingly, it follows the prescribed rhyme scheme of a Shakespearean sonnet.

The poems in *If the Tabloids Are True What Are You?* would indeed be suitable tabloid fodder, with titles such as "Using a Hula Hoop Can Get You Abducted by Aliens" and "Woman Lives in House Made of People." The collection opens with a series of nine prose poems about mermaids, a theme Harvey has used before. Full-page silhouettes of mermaids with various implements in the place of tails accompany each of the poems, which range from thirteen to twenty lines. The tools are obliquely alluded to in the partner poem; for example, the tail of the silhouette paired with "The Backyard Mermaid" is shaped like the tines of a rake. Some of the connections are more obvious than others. In "The Objectified Mermaid," the mermaid poses like a model, prone on her stomach with her spork-shaped tail in the air, and the poem begins, "The photographer has been treating her like a spork all morning." Other poems are not as clear or successful.

For Harvey, the use of a hybrid form—the prose poem—pairs well with works about hybrid creatures such as mermaids. (The topic of the hybrid, a being of two different worlds who belongs to neither, is a recurring theme in Harvey's work; in her 2007 collection, *Modern Life*, she focused on another such being, Robo-Boy, devoting seven prose poems to his various mishaps and deformities.) Later in this collection, five poems combining animals and family members are also accompanied by silhouettes, though these are used as background for the poems' titles. Of the five, all are free verse except "My Wolf Sister," which is a prose poem.

Harvey's poems have a playfulness and a love of language about them, as "My Owl Other," one of the animal poems and the first one she wrote, demonstrates. Not only is the word "owl" frequently repeated, it also

*Matthea Harvey has published five books of poems.* Modern Life *(2007), her third collection, won the 2009 Kingsley Tufts Poetry Award and was a finalist for the National Book Critics Circle Award, in addition to being chosen as one of the* New York Times' *notable books of 2008. She teaches at Sarah Lawrence College.*

appears in the middle of numerous other words, including "fishbowl," "prowling," "fowl," "scowl," "growl," "owlets," and "bowl." In addition, words that use the same three letters in a different order to create assonance, such as "hollow," "shallow," and "willow," dot the poem. The following excerpt shows Harvey's skill with this poetic device:

> Scowl and growl are owl eggs
> with terribly tough shells—how
> do owlets peck their way out into
> the world with those introspective beaks?

"My Owl Other" is an elegy for Harvey's German grandmother, whom she called Omi Eule, German for "Grandmother Owl." The poem also references her grandmother's nickname for her, Matty Maus:

> You're gone too, my Owl Other,
> My mother's mother, who called me
> Mouse but never thought me a mouthful

This is one of the few poems to include a personal element. Harvey is at the other end of the continuum from the confessional poets of the 1950s and 1960s, such as Sylvia Plath. Although some more contemporary poets, notably Sharon Olds, continue to use the confessional style, Harvey generally keeps her distance and maintains an impersonal tone, less confession than commentary on the absurdity of life. The poems in her latest collection reveal to the reader very little about her as a person.

Harvey devoted seven years to crafting this collection. It is the first to include her own visual art, though she created the art for the cover of *Modern Life*, and the illustrations accompanying Harvey's written work are as intriguing as the poems themselves. The images grew from an initial impulse to use art as the title of a piece, which she has done in some of the poems; strange objects are beautifully framed in elaborate gilt frames and photographed. The poems that make up "Inside the Glass Factory" feature color photos of bottles filled with liquid of varying shades. There is also a series of miniature objects, including chairs and human figures, photographed inside ice cubes, with no accompanying text except for the word "stay" written on the first ice cube.

Perhaps most unique among the illustrations are the linen handkerchiefs that Harvey embroidered to accompany *Telettrofono*. A project for the Solomon R. Guggenheim Museum, *Telettrofono* was recorded with sound artist Justin Bennett over several summer weekends in 2012 as part of a soundwalk—a self-guided tour—of Staten Island. The work celebrates Italian immigrant and inventor Antonio Meucci, who created a working telephone nearly twenty years before Alexander Graham Bell but was not granted a patent. This poem includes a mermaid chorus, as a nod to the rumor that Meucci's wife had been a mermaid.

By no stretch of the imagination is this a traditional poem. Its directions and subheadings, such as "Preset Verifiable Fact Mode" and "Preset Math Problem Mode," no doubt make more sense in the audio tour, which lasts a bit more than an hour, but they can be distracting to someone trying to read the work on the page. The slower pace of spoken word, mixed with sound effects, might be a useful aid. Like many of the pieces in this collection, the work was first published in a periodical, in this case *Poetry* magazine. Harvey's poems have appeared in sources ranging from the venerable *Harvard Review* to the avant-garde *Bomb* magazine website.

Harvey often collaborates with others; much of the work in this collection demonstrates that. The partnerships work in both directions. For example, the Poetry Radio Project—itself a collaborative effort between the Poetry Foundation and American Public Media's *Performance Today*—asked Harvey to create a work to accompany a multidisciplinary performance of Philip Glass's String Quartet no. 5. Performed by the Miró Quartet, Glass's work is accompanied by the five poems that make up Harvey's "Inside the Glass Factory." Artist Jeff Koons illustrated "The Straightforward Mermaid" for the *New Yorker* and "The Inside Out Mermaid" for the *New York Times*. In addition, other artists have used Harvey's poetry to spark their own work. Filmmaker Ani Simon-Kennedy used "The Straightforward Mermaid" as the basis for a short film, *Sea Full of Hooks*, which was selected to be screened at the 2011 Cannes Festival's Short Film Corner.

Another collaborative work in *If the Tabloids Are True What Are You?* is "M Is for Martian," commissioned by artist Adam Schecter to accompany his show *Last Men* at the Eleven Rivington gallery in New York. The poem is an erasure; Harvey took seven pages from Ray Bradbury's short story "R Is for Rocket" and covered most of the text with correction fluid, leaving a spare poem consisting of just a few words per page. Harvey is no stranger to this technique, having composed her 2011 poetry collection, *Of Lamb*, entirely from erasure, using David Cecil's biography *A Portrait of Charles Lamb* (1983). Unlike the poems in *Of Lamb*, which were accompanied by paintings by Amy Jean Porter, "M Is for Martian" has no illustrations, only the pages with most of the text "erased."

Critics are both delighted and happily perplexed by Harvey's style. Writing in *Library Journal*, Barbara Hoffert called the collection "inventive and disturbing," and a reviewer for *Publishers Weekly* noted that "Harvey's work rarely strays far from whimsy, but she manages to channel her playfulness for complex and even wrenching effects." Daniel Handler, reviewing the collection for the *Los Angeles Times*, was bemused but largely appreciative. He cited a section of "Inside the Glass Factory," when the factory workers have "the same idea at the same time— / to make a girl out of glass," as "a terrific moment" of interplay between text and accompanying image, and he found the mermaid poems particularly effective in this respect as well: "Both image and text look askance at the narrative of a typical mermaid; rather than slinky, aquatic male fantasies, these beings are textured with the grit of real life." However, he questioned the purpose of some other images, such as the one illustrating "Michelin Man Possessed by William Shakespeare," and admitted that *Telettrofono* and its embroidered handkerchiefs "lost [him] completely," writing, "Even as I stared, fascinated, I didn't know where we were."

Harvey is not conventionally accessible; not everyone will appreciate the close reading and rereading that her poems require. This has been true since her first published collection. For readers diligent and patient enough to give the sometimes-opaque poems full attention and multiple readings, however, the words sparkle like a mermaid's tail.

*Judy A. Johnson*

**Review Sources**

Brodeur, Michael Andor. Rev. of *If the Tabloids Are True What Are You?*, by Matthea Harvey. *Boston Globe*. Boston Globe Media Partners, 4 Oct. 2014. Web. 1 Nov. 2014.

Handler, Daniel. "Matthea Harvey's *Tabloids* Mashes Word Pictures with Imaginative Art." Rev. of *If the Tabloids Are True What Are You?*, by Matthea Harvey. *Los Angeles Times*. Los Angeles Times, 14 Aug. 2014. Web. 1 Nov. 2014.

Hoffert, Barbara. Rev. of *If the Tabloids Are True What Are You?*, by Matthea Harvey. *Library Journal* 15 May 2014: 81. Print.

Rev. of *If the Tabloids Are True What Are You?*, by Matthea Harvey. *Publishers Weekly* 16 June 2014: 54. Print.

# The Impossible Knife of Memory

**Author:** Laurie Halse Anderson (b. 1961)
**Publisher:** Viking (New York). 400 pp.
**Type of work:** Novel
**Time:** The present
**Locale:** Belmont, New York

*In* The Impossible Knife of Memory*, Laurie Halse Anderson chronicles the devastating effects of post-traumatic stress disorder on seventeen-year-old Hayley and her veteran father.*

**Principal characters:**
HAYLEY KINCAIN, a seventeen-year-old girl who has enrolled in high school after years of homeschooling
ANDREW "ANDY" KINCAIN, her father, a US Army veteran who has post-traumatic stress disorder
FINNEGAN "FINN" RAMOS, her friend and eventual boyfriend
GRACIE RAPPAPORT, her friend, the daughter of divorcing parents
TRISH, her father's former girlfriend, a recovering alcoholic

(Courtesy of Viking)

The author of several acclaimed young adult novels, Laurie Halse Anderson has become known for writing about difficult subjects that, though sometimes considered taboo in teen literature, are nonetheless major areas of concern for many young people. Her novel *Speak* (1999) follows the aftermath of a teenage girl's sexual assault, while *Wintergirls* (2009) deals with eating disorders. *The Impossible Knife of Memory* (2014) continues in this socially conscious vein, calling attention to the damaging effects of war-induced post-traumatic stress disorder (PTSD) on both the veterans who struggle with it and the people who love and care for them.

Senior year of high school can be a time of difficult transitions for many students, but it is especially hard for seventeen-year-old Hayley Kincain, who spent the previous five years being homeschooled by her truck-driver father, Andy, as they traveled throughout the United States. Wanting to give Hayley a traditional senior-year experience, Andy decided to relocate to the upstate New York town of Belmont, where he grew up and where Hayley spent her first years of life. In addition to encountering the predictable difficulties of tough classes, unlikable classmates, unreasonable teachers, and meddling guidance counselors, Hayley faces challenges that many teenagers never experience. Her father, a veteran of the United States' military campaigns in Afghanistan and Iraq, is deeply traumatized by his experiences at war, and since returning from overseas he has struggled with PTSD that has gone almost entirely untreated.

His flashbacks have grown worse over time, although he refuses to admit it, and it is only for his sake that Hayley agreed to settle in Belmont.

Andy's instability is an ever-present feature of Hayley's life; each day, she must navigate her father's mood swings, calm his self-destructive behavior, and deal with the consequences of his spotty employment and self-medication with alcohol. These issues are exacerbated by the absence of Hayley's mother, who died when she was only a toddler. Although Andy was at one time in a serious relationship with a woman named Trish, who raised Hayley while he was overseas, she likewise succumbed to alcohol abuse and left Andy after his return. Hayley's memories of Trish and Andy's fights and her feeling of abandonment by the woman who had become her de facto mother further contribute to her protectiveness of her father and her detachment from many of the typical elements of high school life.

Once in Belmont, Hayley quickly rekindles her friendship with Gracie Rappaport, a friend from her early childhood. Although Hayley considers many of her classmates to be mindless "zombies" forced to conform by an oppressive schooling system (as opposed to the not-yet-zombified "freaks"), she establishes a small circle of friends that includes Gracie and her boyfriend, Topher, as well as Finnegan "Finn" Ramos, who convinces her to write for the fledgling school newspaper in exchange for help with precalculus. Hayley struggles academically, not because of a lack of scholastic aptitude but because of her disillusionment with traditional schooling, her tendency to talk back to teachers, and her constant anxiety about her father's well-being. Although she hopes that life in Belmont will bring Andy a measure of stability, he continues to experience flashbacks, self-medicate with alcohol and marijuana, and grow increasingly unstable. A visit from some army friends improves his morale briefly, but his condition worsens after they leave.

As Andy's mental state continues to decline, Hayley attempts to balance her responsibility to her father with her budding relationship with Finn, whom she agrees to date after a series of "antidates." As the brother of a drug-addicted young woman who has manipulated and stolen from their family to feed her addiction, Finn is uniquely suited to be Hayley's confidant; however, she remains reluctant to tell him, or anyone, about her father's condition or her own trauma. This lack of communication is a cause of stress in their relationship, and Hayley opens up to Finn only after he witnesses her father's destructive behavior firsthand.

*Laurie Halse Anderson is the author of several young-adult novels, including* Speak *(1999) and* Wintergirls *(2009), and numerous children's books. She received the American Library Association's Margaret A. Edwards Award for her contributions to young-adult literature.*

Just when Hayley's home and school lives seem to be improving, she discovers that Trish has traveled to Belmont to meet with her father, who neglected to warn her that Trish was coming. The arrival of her former mother figure unearths painful memories in Hayley, and she worries that Trish will harm Andy or trigger a violent psychological episode. However, Trish is a changed woman, having completed treatment for her alcoholism and pursued higher education in the years since leaving Andy, and she remains with the Kincains for a time while searching for a job. Hayley begins to adjust to Trish's presence, but when Andy refuses to seek any kind of treatment, Trish leaves again. Several days after Christmas, the crisis in the Kincain household comes to a head, and Hayley must face her worst fears to save her father—and herself.

Anderson has stated in interviews that *The Impossible Knife of Memory* was inspired in part by her firsthand knowledge of the effects of war on veterans. She has recalled that one of her nephews, a veteran of the United States' twenty-first-century wars, had a difficult time adjusting to civilian life after returning home. Anderson's own father was a World War II veteran who witnessed the horrors of the Dachau concentration camp and who later lost his job because of his alcohol use. PTSD is a constant force throughout the novel, and its influence extends beyond Andy and affects all who care about him. The novel's title itself refers to a repeated image within the narrative: a knife that Hayley describes as tearing through the barriers between the past and the present, allowing unwanted memories to enter the mind.

In many ways, the novel is truly less about Andy's PTSD itself and more about Hayley's emotional and psychological response to it. Andy has been through a war, but Hayley's daily battle with her father's demons is likewise a traumatizing conflict. Like her father, whose bloody memories appear as brief first-person vignettes scattered throughout the book, Hayley has attempted to suppress the memories of the bad times but has ultimately forced herself to forget positive memories as well. The good parts of her childhood, and particularly of her time living with Trish, have been drowned out by her memories of the later fallout. As Hayley admits at the novel's conclusion, her attempts to hide from her memories have made her as much a "zombie" as the classmates she looks down on.

As a narrator, Hayley is initially a bit difficult to connect with, as she projects a tough, somewhat cynical exterior. It soon becomes clear, however, that Hayley's hard outer shell is in fact a protective one designed not only to keep the dangers of the world out but also to keep painful memories in. Her true character is revealed through her relationship with her father, for whom she takes on an almost parental role. Although their life experiences have been very different, the Kincains are at heart quite similar. Andy's refusal to begin therapy or seek medical treatment for his psychological difficulties is mirrored in Hayley's own reluctance to tell her friends about her home life. Although Hayley seems to believe that she is alone in her attempt to save her father, she is not truly without emotional support; rather, she unconsciously rejects it. Gracie, whose parents are going through a contentious divorce, would be an ideal candidate for Hayley to talk to about her father and Trish; however, Hayley never broaches the subject. Similarly, Finn, whose sister's struggles with addiction have significantly affected his family, would understand Hayley's complicated feelings about her father's alcohol and drug use better than anyone. Despite their romantic connection, Hayley does not seem to even consider telling her boyfriend about Andy's history. Much as her father rejects the treatments and resources available to him as a veteran, Hayley refuses to acknowledge her options for support, not out of stubbornness but because she is unable to recognize that such options truly exist to begin with. Both Kincains are so overwhelmed by their trauma that they are unable to envision a way out of it, and this characterization proves crucial to the novel's climax.

*The Impossible Knife of Memory* was received well by critics, who praised Anderson's sensitive and complex depiction of PTSD and its effects on veterans and their caregivers. In her review of the novel for the *New York Times*, novelist Jo Knowles praised the book's raw honesty, particularly in regard to the horrors of war. Indeed, *The Impossible Knife of Memory* is respectful of Andy's military service, but it never glorifies or sugarcoats war, nor does it attempt to argue for or against the legitimacy of the conflicts in which Andy served. Instead, the novel simply documents the devastating, long-lasting effects of war on soldiers and, in so doing, presents a compelling argument in favor of more and better care, resources, and opportunities for veterans.

Reviewers likewise praised the novel's strong, well-defined characters and their complex relationships with each other. Chief among those is the relationship between Hayley and her father, which forms the foundation of the narrative. Writing for the *Times Union*, Lyn Miller-Lachmann noted that Hayley and Andy's close relationship has led Hayley to absorb many of her father's qualities, including "the hyper-alertness, paranoia, and emotional numbness and detachment characteristic of PTSD." As damaging as these characteristics are to Hayley, they prove essential to her and her father's survival. The connection between father and daughter plays a crucial role in the novel's conclusion, demonstrating that even in the face of deep psychological trauma, a strong human connection can cut through the fog of memory and point the way to a brighter future.

*Joy Crelin*

## Review Sources

Chilton, Martin. Rev. of *The Impossible Knife of Memory*, by Laurie Halse Anderson. *Telegraph*. Telegraph Media Group, 17 Sept. 2014. Web. 26 Nov. 2014.

Rev. of *The Impossible Knife of Memory*, by Laurie Halse Anderson. *Kirkus Reviews* 1 Nov. 2013: 211. Print.

Rev. of *The Impossible Knife of Memory*, by Laurie Halse Anderson. *Publishers Weekly* 21 Oct. 2013: 52–53. Print.

Kahn, Elizabeth. Rev. of *The Impossible Knife of Memory*, by Laurie Halse Anderson. *School Library Journal*. Library Journals, 7 Aug. 2013. Web. 26 Nov. 2014.

Knowles, Jo. "Line of Fire." Rev. of *The Impossible Knife of Memory*, by Laurie Halse Anderson. *New York Times Book Review* 12 Jan. 2014: 16. Print.

Miller-Lachmann, Lyn. "The Hidden Costs of War: A Review of *The Impossible Knife of Memory*." Rev. of *The Impossible Knife of Memory*, by Laurie Halse Anderson. *Times Union*. Hearst, 14 Sept. 2014. Web. 26 Nov. 2014.

# In Paradise

**Author:** Peter Matthiessen (1927–2014)
**Publisher:** Riverhead Books (New York). 256 pp.
**Type of work:** Novel
**Time:** Winter 1996
**Locale:** Oswiecim, Poland

*A Polish American professor and poet with a mysterious family history attends a Zen Buddhist retreat at the former site of the Auschwitz-Birkenau death camp in Oswiecim, Poland.*

**Principal characters:**
DAVID CLEMENTS OLIN, an American literature professor and poet in his mid-fifties
GYORGI EARWIG, a combative retreat participant with a mysterious background
SISTER CATHERINE, a nun in her twenties
BEN LAMA, the middle-aged Zen Buddhist retreat leader
DR. ANDERS STERN, an evolutionary biologist and self-professed "Nordic Jew"

(Courtesy of Riverhead Books)

It is the winter of 1996 in Oswiecim, Poland. During World War II, the sleepy hamlet was the home of the Auschwitz-Birkenau concentration camp, which oversaw some of the most horrific crimes in human history; now, the site remains as a museum and memorial. Dr. David Clements Olin has just arrived from the United States and sits in a corner café drinking black coffee. The day is his to while away, but two zealous young Polish people, Wanda and Mirek, intrude on his solitude. They make a valiant effort to entertain their American guest, but Olin's inability to relate to them and Wanda and Mirek's disturbingly innocent view of their town's dark past make for a concise introduction to Peter Matthiessen's *In Paradise* (2014), a novel about the fading horrors of the Holocaust and what it means to "bear witness." Wanda and Mirek offer to drive Olin to Auschwitz, where he is staying at the old SS quarters. When Mirek pulls the car up to the building's entrance, Olin speaks from the backseat:

> In a voice gone hoarse, the passenger inquires, "How do you feel? Being here, I mean? How does it feel to come to such a place? In your own country?" The young Poles exchange looks of alarm. Why would their guest ask them such a thing so many years after those shrouded times that even the old people claim they can scarcely remember?

Olin's misguided attempt to chastise his hosts demonstrates one of the book's central questions: How should one confront the physical space that saw the deaths of so many people—and by extension, the atrocity of the Holocaust itself? In anger? In reverence? In repentance?

Though Wanda and Mirek do not know it, Olin is staying at Auschwitz as part of a Zen Buddhist retreat. He is there not as a participant but as an onlooker, completing research for a monograph he is writing about Polish writer and former Auschwitz inmate Tadeusz Borowski. Borowski, who was not Jewish, survived imprisonment at Auschwitz and Dachau and wrote a book of short stories called *This Way for the Gas, Ladies and Gentlemen* (1959) before taking his own life in 1951 at the age of twenty-eight. Borowski's accounts of the death camps are unique among Holocaust literature in that he pointedly acknowledges his own complicity within the Nazi killing machine. Polish critic Jan Kott has described Borowski's choice to present his work as thinly veiled fiction as a moral decision, "an acceptance of mutual responsibility, mutual participation, and mutual guilt for the concentration camp."

Matthiessen's constant evocation of Borowski raises another thorny issue, one that Matthiessen attempts to address through the mental anguish of the cerebral Olin, about survivor's guilt and those things that one must do (often to the detriment of one's fellow humans) to survive. Matthiessen's characters are interested in the nature of evil and how, when, and why it takes root in the human heart. Olin struggles with a quote from the Russian writer Aleksandr Solzhenitsyn, who was imprisoned in the Soviet gulag. "If only it were so simple!" Solzhenitsyn wrote. "If only there were evil people somewhere insidiously committing evil deeds, and it were necessary only to separate them from the rest of us and destroy them. But the line dividing good and evil cuts through the heart of every human being. And who is willing to destroy a piece of his own heart?"

Philosophical questions fuel *In Paradise*, but while many are raised, few are answered. The 140 retreat participants—which include a Zen Buddhist spiritual leader named Ben Lama, a mysterious and combative figure called Gyorgi Earwig, an evolutionary biologist named Dr. Anders Stern, two young nuns, and a few survivors and descendants of Nazi guards—take turns bearing witness each evening on a makeshift stage, but their testimonies often dredge up old prejudices and devolve into argument. Olin is skeptical of the whole affair. Even the term "bearing witness" seems inaccurate to him: "Excepting the few elderly survivors among them, what meaningful witness can any of them bear so many years after the fact? Witness to *what*, exactly? The emptiness? That silence? What can they hope to offer besides prayer in belated atonement for the guilt of absence, of having failed to share in unimaginable sufferings?"

At the camp, many of the book's characters claim to have visions of crowds or to have heard the footfalls of thousands of feet on wooden platforms. Often when Olin walks the grounds alone, the site roils with enough intensity to constitute a character—or many characters—in and of itself. Against this stark backdrop, Matthiessen constructs an unusual plot. On the first day of the retreat, Olin defends a duo of young nuns after Earwig insults them. However, Earwig's caustic and offensive remarks are oddly refreshing amid the aimlessness and passivity of the rest of the group, and Olin finds Earwig both admirable and distasteful.

Olin befriends one of the nuns, named Sister Catherine, and quickly becomes infatuated with her. Meanwhile, he embarks on a search for his mother, who was from Oswiecim and whom he has never met. These twin plotlines, the one involving Sister Catherine and the other involving Olin's mother, seem clunky laid atop Matthiessen's larger meditation on evil. Both women appear to be vessels for a deep yet vague yearning that exists within Olin, one that is variously channeled through his waffling resolve to find his mother and to not find her and his desire to be with Sister Catherine and to not be with her. Olin's inability to take decisive action in either endeavor only to muddies the thematic waters. As a character, Olin is his own worst enemy, but what this means in terms of the larger story of *In Paradise* is unclear.

Matthiessen is most successful in developing evocative images that demonstrate the ambiguity of the retreat's goal to "bear witness." The book's most powerful scene involves the retreat participants joining hands in a spontaneous and ritualistic song and dance. The moment echoes the Anna Akhmatova poem that Matthiessen chose for the book's epigraph:

> And the miraculous comes so close
> to the ruined dirty houses—
> something not known to anyone at all
> But wild in our breast for centuries.

The dancers are exhilarated by their brief and unplanned moment of unity, which they later refer to cryptically as "it." The dance is euphoric but also a powerful expression of grief, as is a mural that Olin describes, painted in the cellar of a survivor named Malan. Malan, who was imprisoned in the concentration camp for five years, returned to Oswiecim at the end of his life out of a perverse homesickness. Only when he completes the mural, he tells Olin, can he die in peace. The painting itself is a nightmare rendered in black and white, Olin observes. "Here they are, he thinks, all the hungry ghosts, the silenced voices, not descending from the heavens but arising from the dark."

In 1996, the year in which the book is set, Matthiessen embarked on the first of the three Zen Buddhist retreats he would attend at Auschwitz. Matthiessen, a cofounder of the *Paris Review* magazine and a prolific journalist and writer, considered writing a nonfiction account of his experience there, but as a non-Jewish American, he felt his own point of view was inadequate. In her review for the *New York Times Book Review*, Donna Rifkind quotes Matthiessen's explanation of his decision to write a novel instead: "Only fiction would allow me to

> *Peter Matthiessen was a prolific author, with thirty-three books to his name, as well as the cofounder of the* Paris Review *magazine. He was the only writer to win the National Book Award in both the nonfiction and fiction categories, for* The Snow Leopard *(1978) and* Shadow Country *(2008). He died in April 2014, only a few days before* In Paradise *was released.*

probe from a variety of viewpoints the great strangeness of what I had felt." Indeed, all of the characters in *In Paradise* appear in half-light, as if placed in the novel only to contain the multitude of sensations Matthiessen felt on his own retreat. Still, he does not take many liberties with Olin, who is an uneasy narrator, insisting that too much has been written or said about the Holocaust for him to contribute anything of value. Perhaps this is true, but it is an unwelcome (or, at least, not very fruitful) sentiment to come across in a novel about the Holocaust. "*In Paradise*, like its protagonist, is so suffused with qualms about its legitimacy that it stifles its own anguish," Rifkind wrote in her review. In addition, Olin's non-romance with Sister Catherine hijacks *In Paradise* as it approaches its unsatisfying conclusion. Moments of clarity salvage the book, but one wishes that it were Matthiessen, not Olin, bearing witness in its pages.

*Molly Hagan*

## Review Sources

Charles, Ron. Rev. of *In Paradise*, by Peter Matthiessen. *Washington Post*. Washington Post, 5 Apr. 2014. Web. 30 Oct. 2014.

Cheuse, Alan. "In *Paradise*, Finding Understanding in the Ruins of Horror." Rev. of *In Paradise*, by Peter Matthiessen. *NPR*. NPR, 8 Apr. 2014. Web. 30 Oct. 2014.

Olidort, Shoshana. Rev. of *In Paradise*, by Peter Matthiessen. *Chicago Tribune*. Tribune Interactive, 18 Apr. 2014. Web. 30 Oct. 2014.

Ransley, Lettie. "*In Paradise* Review: Peter Matthiessen Addresses the Holocaust." Rev. of *In Paradise*, by Peter Matthiessen. *Guardian*. Guardian News and Media, 7 June 2014. Web. 2 Oct. 2014.

Rifkind, Donna. "Let Us Remember." Rev. of *In Paradise*, by Peter Matthiessen. *New York Times Book Review* 27 Apr. 2014: 22. Print.

# In the Kingdom of Ice
## The Grand and Terrible Polar Voyage of the *USS Jeannette*

**Author:** Hampton Sides (b. 1962)
**Publisher:** Doubleday (New York). Illustrated. 480 pp.
**Type of work:** Environment, history, nature
**Time:** July 1879 to spring 1882
**Locales:** Arctic; Bering Strait

*Funded by the publisher of the* New York Herald, *the ship captain, George De Long, and thirty-two men set off to follow supposed warm water currents in a polar expedition to the North Pole. The story provides a tale of challenge and misfortune, reminding the reader that when humans are pitted against nature, nature wins.*

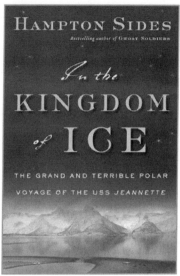

(Courtesy of Doubleday)

**Principal personages:**
JAMES GORDON BENNETT JR., the owner, publisher, and editor in chief of the New York Herald, who funded the expedition
GEORGE WASHINGTON DE LONG, the naval lieutenant who led the polar expedition
GEORGE MELVILLE, the engineer on the expedition, among the survivors who returned with the story
AUGUST PETERMANN, a German cartographer whose belief in a warm current passage to the Arctic became the basis for De Long's voyage
EMMA DE LONG, the wife of George De Long and source of much of the latter's strength and determination

The 1870s began a period of exploration for the United States as it emerged from a civil war. With the completion of the transcontinental railroad, the western frontier no longer generated the same level of excitement in exploring the unknown. Instead, the country began to look to the north. Secretary of State William Seward had arranged for the purchase of Alaska from Russia in 1867, and while it was referred to as Seward's Folly by those questioning its cost, others looked both to it and to the North Pole beyond, as the next unknowns open for exploration.

Two factors were necessary for such an expedition into the region of ice: those who looked for such a challenge, and a source to fund it. Lieutenant George De Long wanted that challenge. His interest in the Arctic was spawned by a rescue with which he was associated in 1873. At the time, De Long was second-in-command of the USS *Juniata*, a ship traveling along the coast of Greenland on a mission to rescue any surviving passengers from a ship lost somewhere north of the Arctic Circle. When the

*Juniata* could travel no farther, the captain requested volunteers for a smaller boat to navigate the ice for another four hundred miles. De Long was the first to reply. While they were unable to locate any survivors—unknown to the captain, they had already been rescued—De Long became mesmerized by the Arctic, becoming what Arctic scientists called a "pagophile."

The other necessity, a source of funding, was supplied by James Bennett Jr., owner and publisher of what many considered the most influential newspaper of the time. Bennett was of the opinion that a newspaper should do more than simply report stories: the newspaper should also create its own stories. Several years earlier, Bennett had funded an African expedition, led by Henry Stanley, to locate the explorer David Livingston. Stanley's dispatches created a sensation—and sold papers. Bennett was considered the third-wealthiest man in New York for good reason. Examples of his eccentricity provide much of the lighter side of the story.

Other explorers had previously attempted to penetrate to the Arctic, though rarely sailing beyond the eightieth parallel before encountering ice so treacherous they were not able to proceed. Some were never heard from again. Why would De Long think he could be any different? He became convinced by an idea: that the region of the North Pole was an "open polar sea" surrounded by an "ice-belt." If one could penetrate that belt, particularly during the summer, one would encounter only water. Historical thought supported this theory as far back as the late sixteenth century. Maps produced by the British admiralty, as well as United States naval charts, included an open sea. Two additional sources reinforced De Long's belief. The first was an article written by a naval officer, Silas Bent, in 1869 for *Putnam's* magazine. Bent was familiar with a warm Pacific Ocean current called by the Japanese Kuro Siwo, a counterpart, so to speak, of the Atlantic Gulf Stream. Bent believed the current flowed into the Bering Strait off the coast of Alaska, and from there worked its way into the Polar Sea. Bent referred to the portal that would be created as the Thermometric Gateway.

The other source with which De Long was familiar was the work of the German cartographer August Petermann. Long considered among the most talented in that profession, Petermann had almost an obsessive belief in an open portal sea. His maps, then considered "second to none" in their reliability and timeliness, to say nothing of their beauty, indicated such. Furthermore, Petermann considered himself an expert on the Arctic. Nearly every book on the subject was found in his extensive library.

*Hampton Sides is editor at large of the adventure magazine* Outside. *His previous books include* Stomping Grounds *(1992),* Ghost Soldiers *(2001),* Americana *(2004),* Blood and Thunder *(2006), and* Hellhound on His Trail *(2010). Several have been the basis for television documentaries. He has also contributed articles for periodicals and magazines.*

There was another reason for Petermann's interest as well: his belief in the existence of a landmass off the coast of Siberia called Wrangel Land. In Petermann's theory, Greenland contained an extension that crossed the Arctic to link up with Wrangel Land, forming a continent Petermann called Transpolarland. It was his belief that a specially built ship would be capable of penetrating the "ice-girdle" into the open sea, not only reaching the pole, but confirming his belief and the accuracy of his maps.

All of this—Bent's article, the maps and charts, the existence of Wrangel Land—was theoretical. No explorer had actually seen an open sea or explored such a landmass.

Once a decision for the expedition was made, it only remained to locate a ship able to survive the polar ice and a crew capable of manning the ship. De Long located the former in England, a steam-powered British naval vessel called the *Pandora* (by then privately owned), which had survived several trips into the polar ice. The *Pandora* was purchased by Bennett, rechristened the USS *Jeannette* after Bennett's sister and, after final preparations at the port of Le Havre, was ready to sail. A crew was brought onboard and, on July 15, 1878, set sail around South America to San Francisco. After eighteen thousand miles and 166 days on the ocean, they arrived.

While in dry dock, the ship underwent the extensive repairs and refitting necessary for the voyage. De Long handpicked his crew: George Melville as engineer, an expert seaman and savant in repairing boilers; Dr. James Ambler, an experienced surgeon and war veteran; John Danenhower, the navigator who more than once on the voyage from France was critical in saving the ship; and twenty-nine other officers, seamen, scientists, and crew. In July 1879, the ship began its voyage to the Arctic. By then, Congress had declared the expedition—known officially as the US Arctic Expedition—and De Long as the official captain, with all the authority over the crew inherent on an American naval vessel.

It was well supplied, particularly in the context of the time. In addition to the steam-powered engine, it carried eight tons of foodstuff (including Budweiser beer), assorted equipment—sixty arc lights from Thomas Edison to illuminate the ship during the long nights, two Bell telephones, scientific equipment, and even a portable darkroom.

It required thirty-five days, but by mid-August the *Jeanette* had reached the Alaskan coast, where De Long had originally planned that they would acquire the last store of coal and prepare to once again head north. Instead, however, he had received orders to first learn the fate of a Scandinavian explorer, Adolf Nordenskiöld, who had earlier disappeared. Orders were orders, and a critical week was wasted in learning Nordenskiöld did not need finding. A month later they caught a glimpse of Wrangel Land, but the ever-thickening ice kept the ship moving toward the northeast, away from land. By September 7, the ship was imprisoned within the solid ice. Not only had they not found any evidence of a warm undercurrent, unbeknownst to the explorers, earlier that summer scientists commissioned by the US Coast and Geodetic Survey had determined the Kuro Siwo was significantly weaker than had been thought. There was no warm current and no open polar sea, a fact that De Long eventually came to realize. Petermann's Transpolarland was likewise shown to be a myth. There was no land connection with Greenland, and Wrangel Land was found to be an island surrounded by the ice.

For twenty-one months, the ship was locked in ice. From the journals maintained by De Long and several members of the crew, for a time they could entertain themselves through the long night. But while the crew remained alive and generally healthy—disease and lead poisoning aside—it was inevitable that the long odds against their survival would begin to tell. First was sheer boredom during the long nights—Edison's arc lights simply did not work. But the worst happened once the spring and summer 1881 arrived. The *Jeanette*, as strong and reliable as it had been, at last could not withstand the enormous pressures of the freezing ice. In June, the ice completed its stranglehold and the thirty-three men were forced to abandon ship, some seven hundred miles from their destination at the pole. Reaching the coast of the closest landmass—Siberia, some one thousand miles distant—was the sole possibility for survival before their food ran out. As De Long wrote, "Our outlook was not encouraging."

De Long did whatever was humanly possible, dividing the men into three groups, each with their own tasks. But whatever could go wrong seemed to go wrong. Whether it was moving on ice flowing in the wrong direction or the inevitable blizzards once the weather began to cool—a relative change given Arctic conditions—the end for some was inevitable.

Still, there were survivors who managed to return to civilization. Melville, William Nindemann, and James Bartlett buried De Long and nine others at the site named Amerika Khaya (America Mountain) by the Yakuts. Melville and his colleagues then continued along the coast to Russia, and after a journey of twelve thousand miles that took them through Moscow, Berlin, and finally, England, their voyage ended in September 1882 as their ship, *Parthia*, entered New York harbor. Thousands were there to greet them; Bennett was not.

This was not the end of the story, however. Melville brought with him the story of the ill-fated journey: articles, charts, and, most important for history, De Long's journals and personal diary. De Long himself, along with his colleagues at Amerika Khaya, were later sent back to the United States to be reinterred in a Bronx cemetery.

Included in the extensive number of sources used in the story, Sides has drawn on contemporary writings and even first-person accounts—Melville himself published a work—to produce as detailed a tale as is possible. As a history, it summarizes some of the more important explorations that preceded the De Long expedition. Among those sent out in a rescue attempt was John Muir, the naturalist and preservationist. The consequence of American civilization on Alaskan Native tribes mimicked that for American Indians on the Plains. Bennett may have been one of the more colorful characters in the story, providing Sides an opportunity to employ droll humor that the *New York Times Book Review*'s Robert Harris found notable, but the tragedy which surrounded Petermann and, indeed, the ill-fated crew, brings a human touch as well.

*Richard Adler*

## Review Sources

Harris, Robert. "Abandon Ship!" Rev. of *In the Kingdom of Ice*, by Hampton Sides. *New York Times Book Review* 17 Aug. 2014: 12. Print.

Krist, Gary. Rev. of *In the Kingdom of Ice*, by Hampton Sides. *Washington Post*. Washington Post, 1 Aug. 2014. Web. 7 Jan. 2015.

Price, Matthew. Rev. of *In the Kingdom of Ice*, by Hampton Sides. *Boston Globe*. Boston Globe, 2 Aug. 2014. Web. 7 Jan. 2015.

Rev. of In the *Kingdom of Ice*, by Hampton Sides. *Kirkus Reviews*. Kirkus Reviews, 5 June 2014. Web. 7 Jan. 2015.

Tobar, Hector. "'Kingdom of Ice' Uncovers a Polar Adventure Frozen in Time." Rev. of *In the Kingdom of Ice*, by Hampton Sides. *Los Angeles Times*. Los Angeles Times, 1 Aug. 2014. Web. 7 Jan. 2015.

# In the Wolf's Mouth

**Author:** Adam Foulds (b. 1974)
**Publisher:** Farrar, Straus and Giroux (New
  York). 336 pp.
**Type of work:** Novel
**Time:** 1942
**Locales:** North Africa, Sicily

*Focusing on the Allied invasion of North Af-
rica and Sicily in 1942,* In the Wolf's Mouth
*explores the impact of war on both combat-
ants and civilians by tracing the activities
of an American infantryman, a British civil
affairs officer, and several Sicilians whose
lives have been affected by the Fascist takeover of their island before the war.*

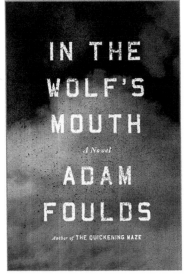

(Courtesy of Farrar, Straus and Giroux)

**Principal characters:**
PRINCE ADRIANO, a major Sicilian landowner
PRINCESS LUISA, his daughter
ANGILÙ CASSINI, a shepherd who becomes manager of his estate
CIRÓ ALBANESE, a Sicilian returned from exile in America with the Allied forces
RAIMUNDO "RAY" MARFIONE, an Italian American infantryman

WILLIAM WALKER, a British civil affairs officerThe appearance of a new novel by Adam
Foulds is certain to attract significant attention. His first novel, *The Truth about These
Strange Times* (2007), won a Betty Trask Award, given to Commonwealth writers un-
der age thirty-five, and earned him the designation Sunday Times Young Writer of the
Year in 2008. His second novel, *The Quickening Maze* (2009), was short-listed for the
Walter Scott Prize as well as the Man Booker Prize, the most prestigious honor given
to a Commonwealth novelist. Between these novels, he published *The Broken Word*
(2008), a long poem—a rare undertaking in contemporary times—that was recognized
with a Costa Poetry Award (formerly the Whitbread Prize), a John Llewellyn-Rhys
Memorial Prize, and a Somerset Maugham Award. Foulds was named a fellow of the
Royal Society of Literature in 2010.

Praise for *The Broken Word*, which uses the Mau-Mau uprising in Kenya during
the 1950s as its backdrop, and *The Quickening Maze*, a novel set in nineteenth-century England, suggests that Foulds has found his comfort zone: historical narrative.
*In the Wolf's Mouth* (2014) gives further evidence that such is the case. The novel
deals with events of World War II, specifically the Allied invasion of North Africa and
Sicily in 1942, when forces from the United States and the British Empire mounted
their first major combined offensive aimed at what British prime minister Winston
Churchill called the soft underbelly of the Axis powers. That theater of operations was

the proving ground for American general Dwight Eisenhower and British field marshal Bernard Montgomery and provided the first real test of American forces against veteran German troops and their Italian compatriots in arms. Allied victories signaled to the world that the Nazi war machine could be defeated.

Reading *In the Wolf's Mouth*, however, one may not realize the high stakes involved in this multinational conflict. Foulds deals with little of the grand strategy involved in the Allied campaign. Instead, he creates a group of fictional characters who are at best bit players in this great drama of liberation. In a series of vignettes, Foulds weaves a tale of warfare and survival that asks, and in some cases answers, larger questions about the impact of democracy on civilizations that have existed since long before this latecomer to the political scene emerged in the West.

Foulds's major figures are an eclectic group, intended to represent the countries and cultures involved in the conflict. Ray Marfione, an American infantryman of Italian descent, sees his share of action in skirmishes along the North African coastline and later in Sicily. Like millions of soldiers, his principal concern is survival. William Walker, son of a British veteran and hero of World War I, has dreams of making a difference in this conflict but ends up serving in rearguard positions. He relieves his frustrations by looking for opportunities to demonstrate his patriotism, sense of duty, and initiative.

Four Sicilians become involved with the Allied forces that land on the island in 1942. Prince Adriano, a major landowner whose family has ruled its little piece of Sicily for centuries, seems unfazed by either Fascist rule or Allied liberation. His daughter Luisa, however, sees the coming of the Allies as a chance to break away from the cloying atmosphere in which she is forced to live; privilege, apparently, comes at a price. The two other Sicilian characters are or were in Adriano's employ. Angilù Cassini begins life as a shepherd but eventually becomes manager of Adriano's estate. He is promoted to that position because his predecessor, Ciró Albanese, is forced to flee Sicily when the Fascists come to power in 1926. Perhaps the most interesting character in the novel, Albanese is a member of the Sicilian Mafia. Threatened by the Fascists, he escapes to the United States, where he gets a job on the New York waterfront.

*Adam Foulds is a British poet and novelist. He has won several awards for both prose and poetry, and his 2009 novel* The Quickening *was short-listed for the* Man Booker Prize. *In 2013 he was included in* Granta *magazine's list of the best young British novelists.*

The novel opens in 1926 with a prologue describing Albanese's departure and Cassini's elevation by Adriano to estate manager. The two major sections of the book focus on the Allied invasion of North Africa and Sicily. The horrors of combat are viewed through the eyes of Marfione, who sees one after another of his squad members die in battles that make no sense to him. Walker appears in North Africa as a member of a military team sent in to reestablish order and return the region to its status as subservient to the European powers that have ruled there for centuries. Albanese does not make a reappearance until the action shifts to Sicily, whereupon readers learn that he has been recruited by the Allies to reestablish a government in Sicily once the

Fascists and their German allies are expelled. Nothing could please him more, as he sees this offer as a chance to return to his homeland, reclaim his wife (who has remarried in his absence), and regain the respect he once had as a Mafia leader.

While *In the Wolf's Mouth* has its share of action, the novel's principal focus is on the impact of war on the people involved in it. Although Foulds may not appreciate the comparison, the structure of the novel is similar to that of thriller writer Tom Clancy's first best seller, *The Hunt for Red October* (1984), with scenes shifting quickly to provide snapshots of each character's actions, thoughts, and emotions. A number of reviewers have called attention to Foulds's ability to capture the chaos of war in prose that borders on the poetic. Equally noteworthy is his exceptional talent for vivid, realistic descriptions. One of the more memorable (and more brutal) scenes is the killing of the Cassinis' dog; with a kind of Hemingwayesque attention to procedural detail, Foulds explains how Albanese's stepson creeps up on the sleeping canine, holds its mouth, slits its throat, then carries the bloodstained carcass to the Cassinis' doorstep to leave the dead animal as a warning of what will follow if Angilù fails to vacate the home that was once Albanese's.

If there is a dominant mood to the novel, however, it is certainly irony. *In the Wolf's Mouth* is filled with instances of dramatic and cosmic irony. Individual scenes make discerning readers aware that beneath surface gestures and formal conversations, an ironic subtext is being played out before them. Will Walker's visit to Prince Adriano's palatial country home is a particularly good example. The point of view in the scene is Walker's, so it is not at all surprising that he reads the nods and gestures of the prince and his daughter as signs that the Allies are most welcome. By the time this visit occurs, however, readers know that Prince Adriano is a survivor; he remained untouched by the Mafia's activities before the Fascists came to power, he survived during the Fascist regime, and he is confident he will still be around—and still living the life of luxury he has always enjoyed—after the Allies leave the island.

Exploring the activities of the liberation forces and those they have come to liberate allows Foulds to expose a larger ironic truth about modern wars, especially those fought in the name of democracy. Many people in the West share Walker's naïve belief that people released from the chains of a totalitarian regime will rush to embrace democracy, but the Sicilians seem unimpressed by the idea; once the Fascists have gone, they quickly move to reestablish a *status quo ante*, returning to the social structures depicted in the prologue. It is almost as if the war never happened.

The title of the novel carries in it the ironic stance Foulds wishes to establish in his narrative. It is taken from an Italian expression, "May you be in the wolf's mouth." Though the origins of the phrase are open to debate, it is commonly thought to be a backhanded way of wishing someone good luck. To be in the jaws of a predator hardly suggests that one is in propitious circumstances, so to escape unharmed is a sign that one is indeed fortunate. Certainly Ray Marfione has found himself "in the wolf's mouth" and survived, though not intact; the war has scarred him, and at one point, when he sees a friend blown to pieces by an explosive device left behind after the fighting has ceased, he deserts his post and hides out at Prince Adriano's house. Cared for by Luisa, he struggles with the temptation to remain out of harm's way. Ultimately, he decides to rejoin his unit, and in the novel's closing scene he engages in a brief conversation with an investigator who questions him about the circumstances of his temporary absence. This exchange—another example of Foulds's debt to Hemingway—is pregnant with meaning:

> "Look, don't worry." The man sat back from the typewriter, his hands on his lap. "I don't think there'll be trouble. You were gone awhile but you're back. Happened to a lot of guys. Coming back is not desertion, is it?"

> "No, it isn't. I didn't."

> "Like I said. Now, you said there was a blast?"

> "That's right."

> "So. Amnesia. And now you're back."

> "I'm back. I see. That is what happened. It is. That's what happened."

> "Fine. Tell me from the beginning."

> "We came through the fighting. We got lost. We were really lost."

> "Okay. Go on."

On the immediate level of the story, the investigator's directive is intended to get Ray to continue his narrative. On a deeper level, "go on" is what Ray must do with his life now that he has been through the war. The entire passage can be seen as a summation of the experience of war by the common soldier on whom victory or defeat ultimately depends. Deftly combining an exploration of personal struggle with an examination political philosophy, *In the Wolf's Mouth* is a novel that is sure to linger in the mind after the last page is turned.

*Laurence W. Mazzeno*

## Review Sources

Abrams, Rebecca. Rev. of *In the Wolf's Mouth*, by Adam Foulds. *FT.com*. Financial Times, 7 Feb. 2014. Web. 23 Jan. 2015.

Akam, Simon. "Write What You Know—Especially If It's the Second World War." Rev. of *In the Wolf's Mouth*, by Adam Foulds. *Spectator*. Spectator, 25 Jan. 2014. Web. 23 Jan. 2015.

Gatti, Tom. "Lambs to the Slaughter: *In the Wolf's Mouth* by Adam Foulds." Rev. of *In the Wolf's Mouth*, by Adam Foulds. *New Statesman*. New Statesman, 6 Mar. 2014. Web. 23 Jan. 2015.

Lenarduzzi, Thea. "Left in Suspension." Rev. of *In the Wolf's Mouth*, by Adam Foulds. *Times Literary Supplement*. Times Lit. Supp., 5 Feb. 2014. Web. 23 Jan. 2015.

Manning, Kate. Rev. of *In the Wolf's Mouth*, by Adam Foulds. *Washington Post*. Washington Post, 14 Aug. 2014. Web. 23 Jan. 2015.

Manguel, Alberto. Rev. of *In the Wolf's Mouth*, by Adam Foulds. *Guardian*. Guardian News and Media, 15 Feb. 2014. Web. 23 Jan. 2015.

# The Invention of Wings

**Author:** Sue Monk Kidd (b. 1948)
**Publisher:** Viking (New York). 384 pp.
**Type of work:** Novel
**Time:** 1816–ca. 1840
**Locales:** Charleston, South Carolina; Philadelphia, Pennsylvania

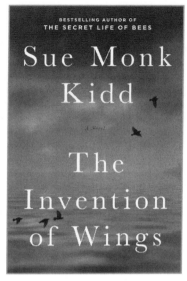

(Courtesy of Viking)

*This historical novel, set in antebellum Charleston, South Carolina, centers on the intertwined lives of Sarah Moore Grimké, daughter of a well-established lawyer, and Hetty Handful Grimké, the young slave gifted to Sarah on her eleventh birthday. The story follows Sarah into her vocation as an abolitionist leader and feminist advocate, while Handful struggles to gain freedom and agency.*

**Principal characters:**
SARAH MOORE GRIMKÉ, the daughter of a wealthy Southern family who becomes an abolitionist and feminist
ANGELINA GRIMKÉ, her sister, who joins her as an abolitionist
HETTY HANDFUL GRIMKÉ, a slave of the Grimké family
CHARLOTTE SUMMER GRIMKÉ, Handful's mother, also a slave of the Grimké family
DENMARK VESEY, a free African American resident of Charleston who plans a slave revolt
THEODORE WELD, an abolitionist leader who marries Angelina
LUCRETIA MOTT, a leading Quaker, abolitionist leader, and feminist who befriends Sarah

*The Invention of Wings* (2014), set primarily in antebellum Charleston, South Carolina, concerns itself with the oppressive nature of slavery at both the societal and the family level. Intertwined with this theme is an exploration of the constraints on female freedom and the female experience of a life confined to a golden cage. Two central protagonists advance the story of the novel in their own voices. Sarah Moore Grimké is the main protagonist, a fictionalized version of the known historical figure of the same name. The book follows her from age eleven through midlife, when she becomes a renowned advocate for abolition and women's rights. Sarah and her young sister Angelina become exiles from the South, publishing compelling pamphlets in support of their cause and speaking to large audiences throughout the North. The second protagonist is Hetty Handful Grimké, born into slavery in the Grimké household. Handful is a purely fictional character, though her experiences are built on historical information about slave life in the South. Along with her mother, younger sister, and other members of the African American community with whom they develop secret bonds and friendships, Handful sustains her life through beliefs and activities that fly below the radar of her masters. Ultimately, this novel is about how these women, both imprisoned to varying degrees by the limitations placed on them by society, find new lives, independent voices, and freedom despite the odds.

One of the strengths of *The Invention of Wings* is that Sue Monk Kidd's dual protagonists enable her to explore two different sides of the Southern household: the white world and the slave world. Though they occupy the same home and their lives are in many ways linked, these two growing women experience the world very differently.

Handful is, of course, at the beck and call of the white owners of the house, but her world revolves primarily around her close relationship with her mother, Charlotte, who is a talented seamstress and thus occupies a position of some status within the household.

(© Roland Scarpa)

*Sue Monk Kidd authored two previous novels,* The Secret Life of Bees *(2002) and* The Mermaid Chair *(2005). She has also written several memoirs focused on spiritual discovery and inspiration, including* Traveling with Pomegranates: A Mother and Daughter Journey to the Sacred Places of Greece, Turkey, and France *(2009), coauthored with her daughter, Ann Kidd Taylor.*

Through her mother, Handful learns stories about the ancestral life in Africa, including, most significantly, her grandmother's tales of people in Africa who could fly. These stories sustain both Handful and her mother, and later in life, Handful learns to interpret them as promises of the enduring strength of the spirit.

The two women chafe at the limitations placed on them within the household structure, and Handful's mother incrementally seeks ways to defy the Grimkés and to gain greater freedom. This leads to a crucial decline in their situation when Handful inadvertently causes one such defiance to be discovered and her mother is violently and publicly punished. Eventually, Charlotte strikes up a relationship with the free black man Denmark Vesey, to whom she introduces Handful; then, tragically, she disappears. Handful follows in her mother's footsteps, clandestinely pursuing friendships and allegiances outside of the Grimké household, first by attending the African Methodist Church and then by increasing her bond with Vesey and his circle. Through her new connections, Handful becomes both witness to and active participant in the attempts to lift the chains of bondage. When Vesey's planned slave rebellion fails and he is executed and buried in an unmarked grave, Handful realizes the full power of white oppression to crush the spirit and strangle opposition. Nevertheless, she continues to fight for herself, her family, and, eventually, freedom.

Sarah Grimké is a figure of relative privilege. Nevertheless, Kidd shows how the spirit of an intelligent, precocious young woman is stifled within a social system that allows its women only the option of marriage and family life. At an early age, Sarah believes that she will follow in her father's footsteps and become a lawyer. She learns the hard way, through family ridicule, reprimand, and punishment, that no such opportunities are available to women. Although she loves learning and is a better student than either of her brothers, she watches her older brothers go off to college and find professional fulfillment, while she is punished with banishment from her father's large library and relegated to texts that are deemed proper for a young woman. She has inwardly rebelled against the violence and oppression of slavery since she was four years old, when she witnessed a slave being brutally whipped on her mother's orders. Initially, she believes that her father also supports her antislavery sentiments, but in this hope she is eventually proved wrong. Frustrated and entrapped within her life, Sarah endures lengthy periods in which she literally loses her voice, which will come and go from her capriciously. Her indignities compound when she enters into an engagement with a man of lower stature who, as it turns out, is also a lying rogue.

Sarah finds an opportunity for an alternative future when she is forced to accompany her dying father to Philadelphia in the hope of finding him a cure. There, she encounters Quaker culture and values and experiences a life away from her mother's orders and the rigid lockstep of Southern society. After her father's death, Sarah gradually builds a new life for herself in the North, and her younger and equally outspoken sister Angelina eventually joins her. As the book ends, they have successfully begun their lives as abolitionists and feminist advocates. Although banished from the South and feeling the loss of their mother and siblings, they have found a way to have a voice.

The relationship between Sarah and Handful brings the two halves of the book together. Handful is Sarah's signature gift on her eleventh birthday. Although Sarah is already an outspoken voice against slavery, her parents nonetheless follow the tradition of giving her a personal slave in the same year that she will begin to appear in society. Forced into owning a slave and forbidden from freeing her, Sarah seeks alternative ways to grant Handful her freedom, such as teaching her to read and write. In the process of becoming Handful's teacher, Sarah also becomes her friend, though the imbalance of power and agency between them places strong limitations on this friendship. The two young women grow apart as puberty and social status lead them to face different sets of struggles. Nonetheless, throughout the book they offer each other favors both small and large, and the chasm that separates their lives can at times be bridged through their mutual humanity. Ultimately, although Handful defaults to being a Grimké family slave, Sarah maintains her feelings of responsibility for Handful and is instrumental in helping her find a way to escape toward a new and better life.

Though the reader of *The Invention of Wings* will primarily be drawn into the individual dramas of lives and experiences within the novel, it is the encounters with significant historical personages and movements that make this book of particular note. Kidd's decision to focus on the Grimké sisters introduces into popular consciousness two remarkable female leaders of the antebellum period. It is somewhat unfortunate that the intertwined stories of Handful and Sarah shifts the focus of Kidd's novel to the early period of Sarah's life. For this reason, much of the novel concerns itself with Sarah's efforts to find her own voice and develop agency within society, and while this coming-of-age process is interesting within the scope of a novel, it is less significant in terms of getting to know Grimké as a historical figure—particularly since much of it is speculative on Kidd's part. Thus, the actual rise of the Grimké sisters into the national eye is somewhat muted within the novel, taking place only in the final few chapters of the book. The reader must turn to the concluding author's note to gain a more rounded perspective on the sisters and their achievements. In this note, Kidd also admits that she borrowed somewhat freely between the achievements of the two Grimké sisters in order to support the structure of her novel, which focuses so fully on Sarah and very little on Angelina. Though the boundaries between fiction and history are blurred in a novel such as this one, Kidd's decision in this case to privilege the compelling nature of her fictional narrative over historical fact seems unnecessary.

In addition to the Grimké sisters themselves, Lucretia Mott (who helps Sarah find herself anew in Philadelphia), Denmark Vesey, and Theodore Weld (who marries Angelina at the conclusion of the novel) were all significant historical figures of the nineteenth century. Mott, though an important abolitionist and advocate for women's rights, is known within the book only as a supportive figure to Sarah Grimké. Undoubtedly it would have muddied the narrative to more fully pursue Mott's own significance, but some gesture in this direction would have added richness and complexity to the story of the fight for abolition and women's rights. Theodore Weld is introduced in the story as an already-significant leader in abolitionism, though his work and perspective enter into the novel only as they pertain to the Grimké sisters. Specifically, his reluctance to allow the Grimkés to pursue the feminist agenda that they wish to introduce in their own speeches and publications is used as a way to highlight the fact that oppression and silencing of women existed even among the most liberal-minded of leaders in this period. Again, though, it would have been interesting to follow the intertwined narratives of Angelina, Sarah, and Theodore more fully in order to give the reader a better understanding of their individual and collaborative contributions to this significant cause.

Other than the Grimké sisters, Vesey's character receives the most elaboration within the novel. Narrated through Handful's eyes, his story is certainly not told in full, but it does present him as a powerful historical figure and a charismatic leader. Kidd also does well to use Handful's own experiences in order to show how the South Carolina community worked to obliterate the memory of this leader, whose legacy, through the empowerment of slaves, could be so damaging to the extant slave structure.

Overall, *The Invention of Wings* has much to offer a reader interested in the deep history of the fight for social equality for women and minorities in the United States. Kidd's fictionalized approach to history allows her to tell the story of these two causes as intertwined in ways that can be enlightening, though she has done well to avoid any potential impulse to portray the constraints placed on women as equal to those placed on slaves. The story of the Grimké sisters has not been remembered in popular history, and Kidd's excavation of it here may well invite readers to learn more about them and the other historical figures who populate this novel. More broadly, through this story of resistance and advocacy, Kidd also provides a formula through which her readers can be inspired to find their own voices, even if they challenge the parameters of social convention.

*Julia A. Sienkewicz*

**Review Sources**

Berne, Suzanne. "Taking Flight." Rev. of *The Invention of Wings*, by Sue Monk Kidd. *New York Times Book Review* 26 Jan. 2014: 15. Print.

Dumas, Bobbi. "Finding Flight in *The Invention of Wings*." Rev. of *The Invention of Wings*, by Sue Monk Kidd. *NPR*. NPR, 11 Jan. 2014. Web. 3 Nov. 2014

Wrinkle, Margaret. Rev. of *The Invention of Wings*, by Sue Monk Kidd. *Washington Post*. Washington Post, 6 Jan. 2014. Web. 3 Nov. 2014.

# The Invisible Bridge: The Fall of Nixon and the Rise of Reagan

**Author:** Rick Perlstein (b. 1969)
**Publisher:** Simon and Schuster (New York). 880 pp.
**Type of work:** Biography, history, politics, sociology
**Time:** 1910s to the late 1970s
**Locale:** United States

The Invisible Bridge: The Fall of Nixon and the Rise of Reagan *offers a biography of Ronald Reagan that helps set his life in social, cultural, and political context in order to explain his second run for the presidency—a campaign made possible by the collapse of the Nixon presidency.*

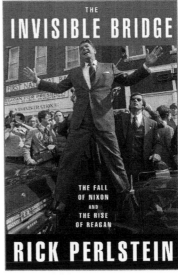

(Courtesy of Simon & Schuster)

**Principal personages:**
RONALD REAGAN (1911–2004), fortieth president of the United States
RICHARD NIXON (1913–94), thirty-seventh president of the United States
GERALD FORD (1913–2006), thirty-eighth president of the United States
JIMMY CARTER (1924– ), thirty-ninth president of the United States

Rick Perlstein's *The Invisible Bridge: The Fall of Nixon and the Rise of Reagan* is a massive book that offers an overview not only of the two men mentioned in its title (especially Reagan) but of the times in which they grew up and flourished. It is clearly written and wide ranging. Perlstein is interested not only in Nixon and Reagan as individuals but in the social, cultural, economic, political, and military history of the United States during most of the first seven or so decades of the twentieth century. Washington, DC, is one of the book's main settings, but so are all the various places Reagan lived as a boy and worked as an adult, particularly Hollywood. As various reviewers have noted, Perlstein relies mainly on secondary sources (especially newspaper reports, autobiographies, histories, and biographies written by other authors), and he and his publisher have been roundly criticized for putting his notes on a website rather than including them in the book itself. Arguments can be made for and against this decision, but it sets a poor and troubling precedent. Persons who actually take the trouble to examine the notes online may be surprised by how little original research Perlstein did.

Anyone who lived through the 1960s and 1970s (the decades of greatest interest here) may find the book a bit padded, especially with details about the pop culture of the time. Younger readers, however, including Perlstein's own contemporaries, may be thankful for this everything-including-the-kitchen-sink approach. It brings the period alive for lay readers, and the book is clearly intended more for a broad audience than for academic specialists. Perlstein is less a pioneering historian interested in uncovering new facts by patient sleuthing than a journalist interested in producing good, readable copy about the past. This text is a sequel to two preceding books (one on Barry Goldwater and the rise of conservatism and the other on the Nixon presidency), and surely it will be followed by another volume focusing on Reagan's years as president. Anyone seeking to understand why and how Reagan was in a position to even become president will probably want to read *The Invisible Bridge.*

All the standard claims and phrasing about Reagan appear in Perlstein's text (including the inevitable need to call him Ronald Wilson Reagan). Reagan is presented as simple-minded, unable to appreciate complexities, ignorant of many important facts,

*Rick Perlstein, a widely published journalist, is the author of several well-received books on the rise of the American conservative movement, focusing particularly on the political careers of Barry Goldwater, Richard Nixon, and Ronald Reagan.*

and given to exaggeration, if not outright dishonesty. In other words, he is the anti-Perlstein. Small details help shore up this unflattering picture; they suggest that Perlstein has really done his homework rather than merely rehashing what others have already written. At one point, for instance, Perlstein illustrates how Reagan allegedly played fast and loose with the facts to criticize the *Republican Party* in the late 1940s:

> Noting "an Associated Press dispatch I read the other day," he introduced America to one Smith L. Carpenter, who "retired some years ago thinking he had enough money saved so that he could live out his last years without having to worry. But he didn't figure on this Republican inflation which ate up all his savings. So he's gone back to work." He paused for ironic effect: "The reason this is news is Mr. Carpenter is 91 years old."

"Here," Perlstein notes,

> was that soon-to-become trademark Reagan skill: illustrating abstract questions of public policy with true heart-tugging stories from genuine folks. Or rather, apparently true. Generations later, when a wondrous technology would let the complete contents of dozens of newspapers be searched in less than a second, the fact could be told. And that fact is that none of these dozens of newspapers ran any Associated Press dispatch about

someone named "Smith L. Carpenter," nor anyone else who went to work when he was ninety-one years old because inflation ate up his savings.

One can almost hear Perlstein using against Reagan almost the same line Reagan used so effectively about Jimmy Carter's alleged dishonesty: "There he goes again."

But in fact there was indeed a ninety-one-year-old man in 1948 named Smith L. Carpenter, and his plight was indeed widely reported in numerous newspapers at the time thanks to a United Press (not Associated Press) dispatch from August 1948, and printed in the *Camden (Arkansas) News* on page 3: "Smith L. Carpenter, 91, retired since 1925, is going back to work, he says, because inflated prices have used up all his old-age savings." The same article can easily be found in at least eighteen different newspapers of the period, sometimes with many additional details and quotations; for instance, the front page of the July 29, 1948, Eufaula, Oklahoma, *Indian Journal* quotes Carpenter at length.

This is just one example among many in which Perlstein either relies on secondhand accounts or the accounts of interested parties; fails to do his own homework; or allows his own predilections to determine the judgmental tone and sometimes flawed substance of his writing. He thus often seems guilty of some of the same faults he alleges against many of the book's major figures. For example, at one point Perlstein accuses Reagan of getting his facts wrong when discussing government regulations that had supposedly delayed the availability in the United States of an antituberculosis drug that might have saved thousands of lives. "In fact," Perlstein writes in a favorite phrase of his, "the drug, rifampin, had been on the market since 1971—and the FDA had approved it even before the manufacturer submitted the application."

Once again, then, Reagan may sound ill-informed (if not actually dishonest), but he may have been relying on the findings of such distinguished academicians as Dr. Stephen DeFelice and professors Sam Peltzman, Milton Friedman, and Murray L. Weidenbaum, whose opinions about the issue are not at all hard to trace thanks to e-books. (See, for instance, page 244 of the 1974 book *Pills, Profits, and Politics*.) For Perlstein, Reagan's assertions about rifampin imply that he was either a wily yarn spinner or an uninformed politician who did not wish to "honor truth" (a nice way of putting it). But the facts of the debate were more complicated than Perlstein suggests, and they could easily have been discovered by anyone interested in knowing why Reagan would say something so apparently alarmist and incorrect. Perhaps he had simply read *Pills, Profits, and Politics*.

Reagan is continually portrayed as a person either incapable of appreciating complex truths or as habitually disposed to fudge facts. But Reagan is hardly the only figure who emerges from *The Invisible Bridge* looking either stupid or mendacious. Jimmy Carter does not come off very well, either, nor unsurprisingly do Lyndon Johnson and Richard Nixon. Surprisingly, George Wallace is presented somewhat sympathetically as a victim of Carter's deceit. This is a warts-and-all (but mostly warts) account of the history of the period, with few people given credit for having honest motives or trying to engage in principled disagreements.

Much is implied by the verbs Perlstein uses when he describes Reagan speaking. Reagan rarely "declares" or "asserts" or "argues." Instead, with his suspiciously dramatic, self-promoting instincts, he often "scowl[s]," "bark[s]," "peddle[s] fairy tales," "bray[s]," "rant[s]," "bray[s]" again, and so on. He often seems either hypocritical or merely confused—a man on the make from at least his days at college, a failed husband and father, a B-grade actor who was soon washed up in Hollywood (even though at least five hundred luminaries turned up for his birthday party after Perlstein says his career had tanked), and so on. Die-hard Reaganites may sense that Perlstein is biased, but fans of various liberal stalwarts such as Jimmy Carter and Frank Church will not be entirely happy either. Ultimately, many readers will finish the book feeling that few people meet Perlstein's exacting standards. Ironically, fans of Reagan may actually find the book far fairer, at least in the blame it dishes out to almost everyone, than they might have expected.

Nevertheless, during the course of his text, Perlstein does offer a vivid sense of what it was like to be alive in the decades he covers. All the old controversies loom large once more. All the old personalities (many of them long forgotten) come back to life. Admittedly, Perlstein sometimes errs on the side of bad taste (as when he notes that Vice President Rockefeller "croaked" not long after taking office), but in general this is a lively, spirited account of the period and its personalities. It has been widely praised by numerous reviewers. Adjectives used to describe it include "epic," "kaleidoscopic," "remarkable," "delightful," "enthralling," "entertaining," "charming," "irresistible," "erudite," "meaty," "nuanced," "engrossing," and so on. One hopes, however, that Rick Perlstein will in future books make better use of the Internet and other kinds of research sources than he has made in *The Invisible Bridge*.

*Robert C. Evans*

## Review Sources

Bobelian, Michael. Rev. of *The Invisible Bridge: The Fall of Nixon and the Rise of Reagan*, by Rick Perlstein. *Forbes*. Forbes.com, 4 Sept. 2014. Web. 14 Dec. 2014.

Boot, Max. Rev. of *The Invisible Bridge: The Fall of Nixon and the Rise of Reagan*, by Rick Perlstein. *Wall Street Journal*. Dow Jones, 1 Aug. 2014. Web. 14 Dec. 2014.

Brands, H. W. Rev. of *The Invisible Bridge: The Fall of Nixon and the Rise of Reagan*, by Rick Perlstein. *Washington Post*. Washington Post, 1 Aug. 2014. Web. 14 Dec. 2014.

Martin, Jonathan. "When the Silent Majority Finally Began to Speak." Rev. of *The Invisible Bridge: The Fall of Nixon and the Rise of Reagan*, by Rick Perlstein. *New York Times*. New York Times, 28 July 2014. Web. 14 Dec. 2014.

Packer, George. "The Uses of Division." Rev. of *The Invisible Bridge: The Fall of Nixon and the Rise of Reagan*, by Rick Perlstein. *New Yorker*. Condé Nast, 11 Aug. 2014. Web. 14 Dec. 2014.

Rich, Frank. "A Distant Mirror." Rev. of *The Invisible Bridge: The Fall of Nixon and the Rise of Reagan*, by Rick Perlstein. *New York Times*. New York Times, 31 July 2014. Web. 14 Dec. 2014.

# The Invisible History of The Human Race
## How DNA and History Shape Our Identities and Our Futures

**Author:** Christine Kenneally
**Publisher:** Viking (New York). 368 pp.
**Type of work:** History, science
**Time:** Prehistory to the present day
**Location:** The world

*Drawing on cutting-edge research, Christine Kenneally explores the fields of genetics, psychology, sociology, medicine, and economics to discover the forces that have molded and continue to shape individual families, as well the human species as a whole.*

**Principal personages:**
MADISON GRANT, American lawyer and eugenicist who advocated racial purity
ADOLF HITLER, Anti-Semitic Nazi leader
NINO VOIGTLÄNDER and HANS-JOACHIM VOTH, German researchers who traced centuries-old roots of anti-Semitism
PETER DONNELLY, STEPHEN LESLIE, and WALTER BODMER, Oxford geneticists who employed genetic markers to establish ancient British migration patterns

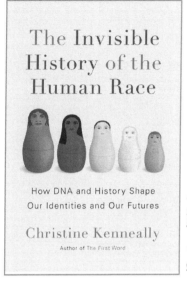

The Invisible History of the Human Race

How DNA and History Shape Our Identities and Our Futures

Christine Kenneally
Author of The First Word

(Courtesy of Viking)

Public interest in genealogy has exploded in recent years. Subscription-based Ancestry.com, located in Provo, Utah, boasts more than fifteen billion online records, and has more than two million members. Founded in 1845, the New England Historic Genealogical Society (NEHGS) has collected more than 200 million records for New England, New York, and other states. In addition to family history organizations such as Ancestry.com and NEHGS, television programs have also popularized genealogical research. *Who Do You Think You Are*, a British documentary series, features celebrity "guests" whose family histories are explored in detail. This popular series has spawned similar programs in several other countries, including Canada, Australia, Ireland, and the United States. The American version, produced by Lisa Kudrow, was nominated for an Emmy Award in 2012. A similar PBS program called *Finding Your Roots*, hosted by distinguished Harvard professor Henry Louis Gates Jr., also delves into the ancestry of famous people and has been enthusiastically received.

Although genealogy has been a popular hobby for centuries, there is more to the field than accumulating ancestors on a family tree, as Christine Kenneally demonstrates in *The Invisible History of the Human Race*. Profound questions concerning individual and corporate identity, cause and effect, and cultural legacies shape her narrative. How are companies like Ancestry.com preserving family history? Can beliefs such as anti-Semitism or character traits like trust survive in cultures over hundreds of years? How does the vertical transmission of family and cultural history affect our sense of national, ethnic, and individual identity through time? Finally, what role does DNA play within our present genetic framework? Each topic could easily fill the pages of a book of its own. Kenneally, however, gracefully ties them all together to create an intriguing biological, sociological, cultural, and psychological mosaic.

*Christine Kenneally is an award-winning journalist who has written for the* New York Times, *the* New Yorker, Slate, Time, New Scientist, *and other publications. She is the author of* The First Word: The Search for the Origins of Language, *which was a finalist for the* Los Angeles Times Book Prize. *She lives in Melbourne, Australia.*

Kenneally did not embark on her own quest for her ancestors with such grand ambitions in mind. Her foray into the past began with a simple second grade assignment in a Melbourne, Australia, classroom. She reminisces about the day when her teacher asked class members to interview their parents and then draw a family tree. Kenneally was excited to begin her project, but her parents' reaction was unexpected. They reluctantly shared limited information and then refused to talk further about the subject. It was only years later that her father revealed to Kenneally and her siblings that he was the illegitimate son of the woman he grew up thinking was his sister. Her father's painful admission not only affected how his own life unfolded but also caused his children to question the truth of everything else they had been told about their family background.

The unwelcome revelation of family secrets is only one possible drawback to the pursuit of genealogical research. Looking back to colonial America, Kenneally notes that establishing "pedigree" in the New World was just as important as in the old. Tinged with elitism, the practice of forging a connection to one's illustrious ancestors—the province of the rich and powerful—reinforced the existing class system. Unlike the wealthy, ordinary laborers had neither the time nor the means to research their origins and then embroider family trees on wall hangings. Kenneally says of the time, "Truly, the more class-conscious a society is, the more likely it is that genealogy will be used against the people of lower classes." The use of genealogy to underscore the idea that an accident of birth makes one person inherently better than another clearly has social, cultural, and moral implications that go far beyond individual vanity.

Kenneally does not shy away from the dark side of genealogical research. One of the more disturbing aspects she covers is the eugenics movement, which was influenced by the ideas of Madison Grant (1865–1937). A lawyer, conservationist, and eugenicist, Grant promoted the idea of racial purity. He was an advocate of the "one-drop rule," a concept where "race was reduced to a formula based on parentage," which became law in the segregated American South. Kenneally also credits Grant with coining the term "the Nordic race," which he applied to people with blond hair and blue eyes.

Grant's lionization of racial purity found an audience in Adolf Hitler and Nazi Germany. Although the persecution and brutal extermination of Jews is well known, the means by which the ethnicity of a person was evaluated and documented is less so. Kenneally reveals the chilling story of how genealogy and eugenics became inextricably linked in a sinister government program. In an effort to force Germans to prove their Aryan ancestry, the Nazis issued the *Einheitsfamilienstammbuch*, a government generated genealogical register, where Germans were required to record their family history going back hundreds of years. Anti-Semitic in intent, the purpose of the document was to weed out anyone who did not descend from pureblooded Germans. Those who could not prove undiluted German ancestry were sent to the Nazi death camps.

Insidious misuse of family history records was not limited to the Nazis. Kenneally recounts the heartbreaking story of Geoff Meyer, a man who grew up in Australian orphanages and foster homes. He had no idea why he had become a ward of the state, and no one would tell him anything about his birth family. Kenneally notes, "Group homes operated like totalitarian states within a democracy. As well as being places of mental and physical torture, the institutions systematically controlled children's access to information while they were institutionalized as well as once they left." In contrast to the Nazis' insistence on meticulous documentation of family history, Meyer's familial past had been stolen from him by the state's policy of secrecy. Kenneally discusses other instances of information suppression that have ripped the past from whole populations. Totalitarian regimes like North Korea and China, European slavers who kidnapped Africans from their homeland, colonial governments—including democracies such as the United States and Australia—that took indigenous children from their families and placed them in group homes, and others all have committed what Kenneally calls "cultural genocide."

The ill effects of such egregious crimes are apparent, but often the root causes of injustice are buried for centuries. In a disturbing analysis of the origins of anti-Semitism in a small German village, Kenneally cites a study conducted by Nino Voigtländer and Hans-Joachim Voth which peels back the layers of hate to uncover reasons for the townspeople's prejudice. In one case, the researchers traced anti-Jewish sentiment back to 1348 when Agimet, a Jewish man who was tortured, falsely confessed that he had poisoned town wells. His alleged mischief was thought by his Christian neighbors to have caused the Black Death. Since the origin of the plague was unknown in the fourteenth century, it was easy to blame the spread of the disease on the Jews, a much-maligned minority. This resulted in devastating pogroms. To the researchers' surprise, the prejudice and hatred that spawned the attacks persisted among citizens six hundred years later. Those villages where pogroms did not occur had a much lower rate of anti-Semitism.

If some paths of genealogical research paint to a malignant portrait of human nature, others illuminate national and world history in new and beneficial ways. An important tool used in such studies, DNA is employed to determine the genetic and cultural history of populations going back hundreds and even thousands of years. Kenneally thoroughly covers the genetic sequencing and chromosomal structure of DNA. Her explanation of how specific biological markers—including the male Y chromosome and female mitochondrial DNA—are passed down through the centuries in an unbroken line suggests stunning possibilities in the quest to unearth the hidden histories of ancient human populations. She cites a study by Oxford geneticists Peter Donnelly, Stephen Leslie, and Walter Bodmer, who employed genetic markers to differentiate between ancient groups such as Britons, Scots, Picts, Saxons, and others, and determine where in the British Isles they lived during the Roman occupation. In an account rivaling an engrossing detective story, Kenneally recounts how the Oxford team sifted through thousands of genomes to discover and trace the genetic history of Britain. Their groundbreaking analysis overturned entrenched beliefs and, when their genetic map was compared with archaeologist Mark Robinson's historical map, answered enduring questions about the end of the Roman occupation. Kenneally notes that the team's findings "essentially turned the light back on in the Dark Ages."

Academics are not the only group that has benefited from technological advances in genealogical research. For most of human history, establishing an accurate lineage required a painstaking search of the official records of libraries, churches, towns, and other repositories. Now millions of documents are online, so anybody with Internet access can easily find information. Ancestry.com offers a spectrum of services to the general public to help subscribers track down family lines. In addition, individual DNA testing, which was once limited to medical and biological research, is now available to the general public for a reasonable fee through companies such as Family Tree DNA and 23andMe.

Kenneally praises the benefits that such organizations have made available. However, there are drawbacks she does not adequately address. Because many public and private family trees on Ancestry.com are user-generated, some information may be inaccurate. If a subscriber makes an error, that mistake can be compounded exponentially as multiple users insert it into their own family trees. For serious amateur genealogists, verifying Ancestry.com content against established records is essential. Also, although the accuracy of individual DNA testing is improving, it is possible that different companies could achieve varying results. For example, two pie charts from competing laboratories may display the same admixture, but the percentage of each ethnicity may not match. Nonetheless, DNA testing remains one of the most reliable methods available to prove ancestry.

At the heart of Christine Kenneally's *The Invisible History of the Human Race* lies a persistent question: Who *are* we—as individuals and as a species? It has taken us millennia to get this far in our quest to discover the answer, but her masterful study takes us further along the road to decoding our true identity.

Pegge Bochynski

## Review Sources

Dobbs, David. "The Story of Us." Rev. of *The Invisible History of the Human Race*, by Christine Kenneally. *New York Times Book Review* 19 Oct. 2014: 1–22. Print.

Hughes, Virginia. "Learning Our Roots, Inside and Out." Rev. of *The Invisible History of the Human Race*, by Christine Kenneally. *New York Times* 2 Dec. 2014: D5. Print.

Rev. of *The Invisible History of the Human Race*, by Christine Kenneally. *New Yorker* 3 Nov. 2014: 95. Print.

Rev. of *The Invisible History of the Human Race,* by Christine Kenneally. *Publishers Weekly* 4 Aug. 2014: 40. Print.

Rev. of *The Invisible History of the Human Race,* by Christine Kenneally. *Kirkus Reviews* 1 Sept. 2014: 62. Print.

Kramer, Eileen H. Rev. of The Invisible History of the Human Race, by Christine Kenneally. *Library Journal* 1 Oct. 2014: 106. Print.

# J

**Author:** Howard Jacobson (b. 1942)
**Publisher:** Hogarth (New York). 352 pp.
**Type of work:** Novel
**Time:** The late twenty-first century
**Locale:** Port Reuben, England

(Courtesy of Hogarth)

*In his thirteenth novel, Howard Jacobson describes the effects of anti-Semitism, both subtle and overt, even in a society with the best intentions for its members. The humor for which Jacobson is best known becomes increasingly dark in this treatment of a postapocalyptic world.*

**Principal characters:**
KEVERN "COCO" COHEN, a solitary man who teaches at a community art center
DENSDELL KROPLIK, his neighbor, a barber and local historian
AILINN SOLOMONS, his girlfriend, an orphan newly arrived in town
ESME "EZ" NUSSBAUM, an older woman who befriends Ailinn and brings her to the village
EDWARD EVERETT PHINEAS ZERMANSKY, a professor of art at the community center
EUGENE GUTKIND, a detective inspector and conspiracy theorist
ROZENWYN FEIGENBLAT, a librarian

Howard Jacobson's novel *J* (2014) is a postapocalyptic tale set in the aftermath of a vaguely remembered cataclysm. In the second decade of the twenty-first century, England suffered some sort of catastrophe from which it is still reeling two generations later. The nature of the catastrophe is not quite clear—it is only ever referred to as "WHAT HAPPENED, IF IT HAPPENED"—but word has come down of "hate gangs" and conspiracy theorists who overran the capital city, where bank failures and the collapse of great businesses brought down the country's economy. From hints dropped about ordinary people in Port Reuben, a seaside community in the west of England, it appears that their ancestors experienced a destructive wave of anti-Semitism, a pogrom, if not a full-scale holocaust.

Rather like Germany in the late twentieth century, the England of *J* is officially attempting to make amends, even as anti-Semitic stereotypes still linger in the national consciousness. In an attempt to avoid repetition of the past's unspeakable horror, the government launches Operation Ishmael, based on the proposition that the country's Jewish population will become indistinguishable if every person and place is given a Jewish-sounding name. If everyone can say, "Call me Ishmael" (or Isaac or Jacob), and if everyone hails from a town with a name like Port Reuben, there will be no fingering of aliens in the population. At least, that is the theory.

Kevern Cohen and Ailinn Solomons have typically Jewish surnames, but they only start to suspect that they are actually of Jewish extraction after they meet and fall in love. Though they never take their relationship for granted, they know that they are suited to each other because they are both unsuited to the social life of English society at large. What makes them so unsuited—Kevern's extreme fearfulness and Ailinn's complete lack of living relatives—are problems that are known to afflict the children of Holocaust survivors.

*J* is divided into three numbered sections. The first describes Kevern's life in the cottage where he was raised and shows the influence of his equally fearful father, who provides Kevern's main connection to the twentieth century and its culture. This section brings him together with Ailinn and takes them on a first visit to the capital city, which Kevern's father ominously called the Necropolis and warned him never to set foot in. It also introduces a dim-witted detective named Eugene Gutkind who regards Kevern as a social misfit and therefore a likely suspect in a double-murder case, which everyone else regards as a murder-suicide. The detective breaks into Kevern's cottage while the lovers are out of town, and the evidence of his visit, noticeable due to a trick Kevern learned from his father, throws the young man into a state of heightened panic.

*Howard Jacobson has written numerous comic novels, starting with 1983's* Coming from Behind, *as well as nonfiction books such as* Roots Schmoots: Journeys among Jews *(1993) and* Whatever It Is, I Don't Like It *(2011), a collection of his occasional journalism. His* Finkler Question *(2010) won the prestigious Man Booker Prize for Fiction.*

The plot darkens in the second section. While Kevern's boss attempts to put Gutkind off the case, his neighbor Densdell Kroplik abets the detective, with whom he shares a passion for the outlawed work of Richard Wagner and German culture in general. Separated from Kevern, Ailinn receives a packet of letters written by her grandmother at the time that her own mother was born. In the letters, Aileen's grandmother tries to explain to her own parents her reasons for marrying a Christian missionary and refusing to accept their fears for the future. Kevern, meanwhile, is told by librarian Rozenwyn Feigenblat that pogroms are not as "medieval" as he thinks and that Port Reuben has seen warnings to people of his "kind." The young couple begin to suspect the people who take the most interest in them. Ailinn wonders how her benefactor, Esme, has come into possession of the letters; Kevern fails to understand why his supervisor, Everett, has no interest in the sketches that his mother made in Port Reuben, sketches that Everett privately considers "primitive," "modernist," and "degenerate."

Then, in the brief third section, the humor begins to brighten. If Kevern's and Ailinn's friends are plotting something—if even they still believe the old stereotypes—it does not necessarily follow that the country wants to eliminate everyone of their "persuasion." It may be that those in charge want to preserve their culture, rather as they might wish to preserve an exotic species of bird. The novel does not draw this last analogy, but it does cast the strangely naive Kevern and Ailinn as members of an endangered species, though ones able to think about their options and communicate with each other—at least to some extent.

The novel takes its title from a game that Kevern's father taught him to play. Whenever either of them would speak a word that began with the letter *j*, he would first have to put two fingers across his lips so that the consonant was muted. In the American edition, this half-stifled letter is shown with heavy erasure on the dust jacket and with fingers across it on the title page. In the text, initial *j*'s are superimposed with two short horizontal lines, like an equals sign, whenever the narration is from Kevern's point of view—a reflection of the fact that Kevern continues this practice long after his father's death, much as he continues his father's habit of rumpling the silk runner in the front hall before leaving the cottage. He stops crossing his *j*'s only when he gets the joke. The equals signs also appear in the margins surrounding one-page excerpts, seemingly torn out of library books, that discuss details of past atrocities committed against Jews.

The words "Jew" and "Jewish" never appear in the book, but readers will be in on the joke long before the isolated and trusting Kevern. Even those unfamiliar with Jacobson's other published work will come to the novel with more knowledge of Jewish history than is available in a postapocalyptic England where only a few Jews still remain alive, Internet usage is banned, and details of Jewish history and culture are routinely removed from library books. Esme struggles to learn about matrilineal heritage or even chicken soup. Everett simply falls back on the prejudices of an earlier generation.

The blindness of central characters to values their society once held is the same as that found in the novels to which *J* has been most often compared: Aldous Huxley's *Brave New World* (1932) and George Orwell's *Nineteen Eighty-Four* (1949). Such novels are commonly described as dystopian because they present the opposite of a utopia (or eutopia)—that is, a "good place." Utopian novels ask readers to believe, as a starting premise, that there is a place outside the known world where life is or once was distinctly better. Examples include the moral and intellectual utopia of Atlantis in Plato's *Critias* (fourth century BCE), the scientific utopia of Thomas More's *Utopia* (1516) and Francis Bacon's *New Atlantis* (1627), or the feminist utopia of Robert Graves's *Seven Days in New Crete* (1949), also known as *Watch the North Wind Rise*. Dystopian novels, by contrast, are based on the premise that something negative has happened to the known world: industrial mechanization and genetic engineering in *Brave New World* and authoritarian government and social engineering in *Nineteen Eighty-Four*, for example. Margaret Atwood's dystopian novel *The Handmaid's Tale* (1985) starts from the premise that nuclear war has left only a few women capable of bearing children. Ray Bradbury's *Fahrenheit 451* (1953) supposes the existence of a totalitarian state in which all books are subject to burning.

Another description that might be applied to the novel is "alternate history," a term widely used of *The Plot against America* (2004), Philip Roth's disturbing account of rampant anti-Semitism under a 1930s-era president with strong Nazi sympathies. Some British reviewers have complained that England in 2014 is hardly in the same position as Germany after the burning of the Reichstag in 1933. In the same way, it could be said that England in the Victorian age was far from inventing a steam-powered computer, as envisioned in *The Difference Engine* (1990), by William Gibson and Bruce Sterling. Jacobson has responded indirectly, in an article printed in the October 11, 2014, edition of the *Guardian*, by insisting that *J* is not a prophecy but a story of things that "are, in a sense, still happening—in that we remain marked by them, troubled by memories that are not always our own."

*J* has had a mixed reception throughout the English-speaking world. It received high praise in the *Lancet* from Terry Eagleton, one of the Great Britain's best-known literary critics, who called it "a rare combination of moral vision and subtle emotional intelligence." Another British critic, John Sutherland, noted in the London *Times* how "distinctively British" the novel's anti-Semitism is made to appear. Other reviewers found the novel hard to follow, vague and diffuse due to the lack of either an omniscient narrator or a character with a clear understanding of what is happening, let alone what has happened before.

As with the darker films of Woody Allen, such as *Crimes and Misdemeanors* (1989) or *Match Point* (2005), critics often profess to miss the earlier funny stuff. Although they admire the novel's artistry, many do not like the result. James Walton, reviewing the novel for the *Spectator*, argued that while the plot is "deft," the underlying premise is not. *Washington Post* reviewer Ron Charles, pondering Jacobson's relative lack of popularity in the United States, suspected that American audiences might be uncomfortable with the author's tendency to combine humor with serious issues such as anti-Semitism; he concluded that "*J* is unlikely to change that reception" because despite being Jacobson's "most serious novel," it is "also his most disquieting."

The irony of suppressed information about Jews in a society where everyone has a Jewish surname is tragic. The England depicted in *J* needs the Jewish population that it decimated early in the twenty-first century because it needs to know what it is not, that being English means being non-Jewish. Knowledge is necessarily limited; there are always "iffers" who qualify any comments about "WHAT HAPPENED" with the big *if*: "IF IT HAPPENED." Attempting to discover the past, Esme wishes for less evasion and denial: "Not WHAT HAPPENED but WHAT HAD BEEN DONE." Readers of Jacobson's journalism know that he is concerned about the growing anger displayed toward Israel in the popular press and its possible side effects. Readers of this what-if novel are obliged to consider what could happen in our time.

*Thomas Willard*

**Review Sources**

Charles, Ron. "*J*, by Howard Jacobson, Is a Chilling Tale of Our Anti-Semitic Future." Rev. of *J*, by Howard Jacobson. *Washington Post*. Washington Post, 14 Oct. 2014. Web. 22 Dec. 2014.

Cummins, Anthony. "Howard Jacobson's Disturbing Dystopian Vision." Rev. of *J*, by Howard Jacobson. *Guardian*. Guardian News and Media, 17 Aug. 2014. Web. 22 Dec. 2014.

Eagleton, Terry. "A Dark Dystopian Tale." Rev. of *J*, by Howard Jacobson. *Lancet*
    384.9951 (2014): 1337. Print.
Sansom, Ian. "Post-Shtick Notes." Rev. of *J*, by Howard Jacobson. *New Statesman*
    29 Aug. 2014: 47. Print.
Sutherland, John. "Don't Mention the J-Word." Rev. of *J*, by Howard Jacobson.
    *Times* [London] 9 Aug. 2014, Features sec.: 16. Print.
Walton, James. "Howard Jacobson's *J* Convinced Me That I'd Just Read a Master-
    piece." Rev. of *J*, by Howard Jacobson. *Spectator*. Spectator, 13 Sept. 2014. Web.
    22 Dec. 2014.

# John Quincy Adams
## American Visionary

**Author:** Fred Kaplan (b. 1937)
**Publisher:** HarperCollins (New York). 672 pp.
**Type of work:** Biography
**Time:** 1767–1848
**Locale:** United States, Great Britain, France, Netherlands, Prussia, Russia

*In his biography of John Quincy Adams, the sixth president of the United States, Fred Kaplan traces Adams's lifelong commitment to the principles of national unity and his belief in the power of diplomacy to settle both national and international disputes.*

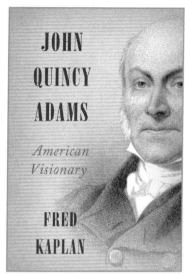

(Courtesy of HarperCollins)

### Principal personages

JOHN QUINCY ADAMS (1767–1848), sixth president of the United States
LOUISA JOHNSON ADAMS (1775–1852), his wife
JOHN ADAMS (1735–1826), his father and the second president of the United States
ABIGAIL ADAMS (1744–1818), his mother
THOMAS JEFFERSON (1743–1826), third president of the United States
JAMES MADISON (1751–1836), fourth president of the United States
JAMES MONROE (1758–1831), fifth president of the United States
ANDREW JACKSON (1767–1845), seventh president of the United States

Early in his biography of John Quincy Adams, Fred Kaplan quotes from a letter Adams wrote in 1846 to the abolitionist Joseph Sturge. Writing out a portion of William Collins's 1746 poem "How Sleep the Brave," Adams tells Sturge that, though he learned these lines while still a child, "the impression made upon me by the sentiments inculcated in these beautiful effusions of patriotism and poetry" have remained with him. Then he asks rhetorically, have these encomiums on heroism "ever shaken my abhorrence of war? Far otherwise. They have riveted it to my soul with hooks of steel." Kaplan observes that, "The metaphor 'hooks of steel' aptly represents the tightly connected elements of family, community, and values that became the essence of John Quincy's sense of himself and his relationship with his country." These are the primary themes that run through Kaplan's *John Quincy Adams: American Visionary*, a well-researched, well-written, sometimes apologetic yet always respectful account of the sixth president of the United States, whose life was inexorably bound up in the founding and early growth of the nation.

The son of two towering figures from America's revolutionary era—John and Abigail Adams—John Quincy, as Kaplan refers to him often to distinguish him from his father, began his education in national politics and international diplomacy in 1778 when, not yet eleven, he accompanied John Adams to Europe. While the elder Adams struggled to get the French to support the American colonists in their rebellion against Great Britain, John Quincy went to school in more ways than one. As a teenager, he traveled again to Europe as part of his father's diplomatic entourage; by the time he entered Harvard College he had spent time in France, the Netherlands, Russia, Finland, and Sweden. Although he pursued a career in the law, he knew he was destined for politics. When called, he served as George Washington's minister to the Netherlands, his father's minister to Prussia, Massachusetts state senator, US senator, the first US minister to Russia, minister to Great Britain, and the US secretary of state. In 1824, he won a disputed election to serve as the country's president. Like his father, however, he served only one term, defeated in 1828 by populist demagogue Andrew Jackson. While most men leaving the presidency before and after him have been content to return to private life, Adams accepted a nomination to run for a seat in the US House of Representatives, beginning an eighteen-year stint that ended upon his death.

> *Fred Kaplan, distinguished professor emeritus of English at Queens College and the Graduate Center of City University of New York (CUNY), is the author of biographies of Abraham Lincoln, Mark Twain, and others. His 1984 biography of Thomas Carlyle was a finalist for the National Book Critics Circle Award and the Pulitzer Prize.*

In Kaplan's appreciative and at times argumentative study, the hectic events of Adams's political career are woven into a larger narrative that includes extensive coverage of his childhood and his marriage to Louisa Johnson. Their married life was hardly idyllic. Though far from poor, they were constantly worried about finances, especially debts owed by Louisa's deceased father, for which Adams felt responsible. Louisa had four miscarriages before bearing her first healthy child, and more later in life; they had three sons and one daughter, who died while still a toddler. Kaplan provides ample evidence of Adams's life as father to three sons who disappointed him more than they made him proud (although, as Kaplan records with great subtlety, the youngest, Charles Francis, eventually distinguished himself as a historian, politician, and diplomat). Kaplan also describes in some detail Adams's brief career as professor of rhetoric and oratory at Harvard, a position he held from 1805 to 1809 and one that he seemed genuinely reluctant to give up when appointed minister to Russia.

Another of Adams's lifelong interests that Kaplan centers on is his love of literature, and Kaplan's prior experience as a biographer of such great authors as Charles Dickens and Henry James comes to the fore in his close analysis of John Quincy's writings. Adams's taste predictably ran toward those authors whose works illustrated and upheld the high moral values that he cherished. Adams appreciated the time he spent reading classical and modern authors, from whom he learned much about life and from whom he was able to borrow an occasional quote to give just the right touch to speeches, letters, and essays, which he wrote prolifically throughout his life. Kaplan interrupts the historical narrative on numerous occasions to analyze some of Adams's more important speeches and publications, in almost every instance pointing out how consistent and effective he was in promoting national unity, advocating for a strong federal government, and championing the abolition of slavery. On the other hand, Kaplan's defense of Adams as a fine poet may be less convincing.

From Kaplan's perspective, John Quincy's political career was one that constantly demanded his full attention to national unity and international diplomacy. On the national level, this often meant demanding the supremacy of the federal government over individual states. Unfortunately, his strident calls for a strong federal government put him in opposition to the prevailing trend in national politics. By the time Adams entered the US Senate, a coalition of states-rights legislators (and judges) dominated the federal government. Led by Thomas Jefferson, the Democratic-Republicans had already triumphed over the Federalists, the party of Adams and his father. Over forty years Adams changed political affiliations several times but never compromised his position on the role he felt government should play. In Kaplan's narrative, Adams becomes the tragic hero battling against forces that were leading the country in what he was certain was the wrong direction.

However, Kaplan's staunch defense of Adams and his career becomes a weakness when he succumbs to portraying Adams's political rivals as villains. If John Quincy is the hero of this tragic drama, there must be villains, and Kaplan finds them among southern politicians, several of whom serve as foils for the Adams in Kaplan's portrayal. Chief among these foes is Jefferson, to whom Kaplan consistently attributes base, sometimes nefarious motives, for virtually every political decision he made. Kaplan is quick to point out that Jefferson was heavily reliant on electoral votes from states that could count its enslaved population as three-fifths of a person, a constitutional quirk that gave southern states greater clout than seems fair in hindsight. Kaplan notes that Adams had the courage, however, to break with his Federalist colleagues and support Jefferson's deal to purchase the Louisiana Territory because he thought it in the best interest of the country. Where he parted company with Jefferson and especially Andrew Jackson was in the methods employed to annex territory and create new states. Adams wanted the citizens of those lands to have a vote on joining the Union; his political opponents saw no reason to extend that courtesy to inhabitants of any new lands acquired by the United States. However, while Kaplan offers an in-depth examination of Adams's motives and his overall career, he often succumbs to one-sided portrayals of Adams's political rivals.

James Madison fares somewhat better than Jefferson, though he is still viewed by Adams and Kaplan with distrust. James Monroe comes in for some praise—Adams seems to have changed his mind about Monroe, whom he initially distrusted, perhaps because he made Adams his secretary of state, the lone Federalist in a staunchly Democratic-Republican cabinet. Kaplan is quick to find instances that illustrate Adams's important role in shaping America's national and international policy. He devotes considerable attention to Adams's successful diplomatic efforts to acquire Florida from Spain, avoiding a costly war over the disputed territory. Kaplan carefully lays out evidence to argue that the famous Monroe Doctrine proclaiming America's right to interfere anywhere in the Western Hemisphere to protect threats to its safety was largely the brainchild of Adams, who argued vociferously that a strong stand against auto-cratic governments and colonial powers was the only way to preserve both America's independence and affirm its republican form of government. While some might take issue with the claim that Adams was, as one reviewer of Kaplan's book describes him, "perhaps the greatest secretary of state in American history," Kaplan's portrait of Adams's service in the office does nothing to challenge that assessment.

The Virginians were Adams's political enemies because of both their opposition to strong federalism and support of slavery. All these reasons and more made Andrew Jackson a particularly dangerous foe to Adams's political career. In Kaplan's telling, Jackson comes across as a particularly venal and self-aggrandizing political boss bent on destroying all that Adams and his father stood for. Jackson's political machine, unable to stop Adams's election in 1824, apparently vowed to make him a one-term president; with a majority of Jackson supporters and anti-Federalists dominating both houses of Congress, Adams was largely ineffectual during his four years in office. Upon his election to the House of Representatives in 1830, Adams did what he could to defeat Jackson's antifederalist agenda, but as Kaplan records with a tinge of sad-ness, his efforts were not enough.

Adams's term in the House was also characterized by opposition—this time to southern politicians who insisted not only that slavery be retained in the states where it was sanctioned by the Constitution in 1789 but also in new states being created to the west. Adams became the champion of abolition, introducing bills to prevent the exten-sion of slavery and repeal it where it existed. Although his efforts frequently came to naught, in this instance he was on the right side of history. His greatest triumph for the abolitionist cause came in 1841, when he appeared before the US Supreme Court to represent Africans taken from the slave ship *Amistad* to argue that they had been cap-tured illegally and had the right to be released. Kaplan also points out that in Adams's last term he was joined in the House by young Illinois Congressman Abraham Lincoln, suggesting that Adams surely influenced his young colleague in this early stage of Lincoln's political career.

In his introduction and again in his concluding pages, Kaplan suggests that Ad-ams's political career has lessons to offer for twenty-first century Americans. Not everyone will find the parallels pointed out so directly as reviewer Thomas Mallon does, who observed that "one can almost see Sarah Palin in a coonskin cap when the Jacksonians arrive on the scene." Nevertheless, the informed reader can see similari-ties between Adams's idea of the role of government and those of progressives who followed him into American politics and recognize in the Jefferson-Jackson faction the support for limited government and strong states rights that are hallmarks of conserva-tive politicians who rose to prominence after the election of Ronald Reagan in 1980. Many may come away believing, as reviewer David Holahan remarked in a review for the *Christian Science Monitor*, that *John Quincy Adams: American Visionary* "should be required reading inside the Beltway" for its rich portrayal of Adams's career and of the formative decades of government in the United States.

*Laurence W. Mazzeno*

## Review Sources

Dunn, Susan. "Angry, Icy, Enlightened Adams." Rev. of *John Quincy Adams*, by Fred Kaplan. *New York Review of Books*. NYREV, 5 June 2014. Web. 31 Oct. 2014.

Holahan, David. "'John Quincy Adams': Often Forgotten Yet Highly Distinguished." Rev. of *John Quincy Adams*, by Fred Kaplan. *Christian Science Monitor*. Christian Science Monitor, 26 May 2014. Web. 31 Oct. 2014.

Landers, Robert K. Rev. of *John Quincy Adams: American Visionary*, by Fred Kaplan. *Wall Street Journal*. Dow Jones, 28 May 2014. Web. 31 Oct. 2014.

Mallon, Thomas. "Born to Do It." Rev. of *John Quincy Adams: American Visionary*, by Fred Kaplan. *New Yorker*. Condé Nast, 5 May 2014. Web. 31 Oct. 2014.

Mazur, Louis P. "Sacred Duty." Rev. of *John Quincy Adams*, by Fred Kaplan. *Los Angeles Review of Books*. Los Angeles Review of Books, 14 Aug. 2014. Web. 31 Oct. 2014.

Merry, Robert W. "A Principled Warrior." *New York Times Book Review*. New York Times, 2 May 2014. Web. 31 Oct. 2014.

# Kinder than Solitude

**Author:** Yiyun Li (b. 1972)
**Publisher:** Random House (New York). 336
 pp.
**Type of work:** Novel
**Time:** Present
**Locales:** Beijing, China; United States

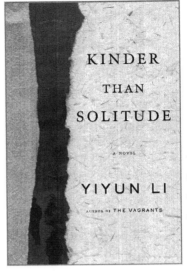

(Courtesy of Random House)

*Kinder than Solitude, a novel set in contemporary Beijing and the United States, is the story of the effects of a murder that left a young woman comatose for more than twenty years before her death. It focuses on the ways in which a life unlived can impact those around it.*

**Principal characters:**

SHAOAI, a recently deceased woman who
    was poisoned more than twenty years ago
BOYANG, a successful Beijing businessman who helped care for her
RUYU, a woman who was sent to live with Shaoai's family as a young girl
MORAN, a childhood friend of Boyang and Ruyu

*Kinder than Solitude* opens with the cremation of Shaoai, who had been brain damaged and uncommunicative since she was poisoned in 1989, more than twenty years earlier. Neighbors vividly remember that year not only because of Shaoai's poisoning in the fall but because of the afternoon in May when an army tank was burned nearby and because of the day in June when a townsman "pedaled three bodies on his flatbed tricycle from the Square to the hospital." The way in which these events are linked in memory is representative of the way in which the lives of the novel's four friends are linked by tragedy.

The poison that slowly killed Shaoai was put in her drink, a glass of Tang, and was stolen from one of the labs where Boyang's mother worked, which subsequently ended her career. Similarly, Shaoai's college career had recently ended when she was expelled from the university for her protest activities, which led the police to at first believe that her poisoning was a suicide attempt. That theory was quickly ruled out. Unable to solve the mystery of the poisoning and to pinpoint a perpetrator, no charges were filed and the suspects were free to go on with their lives.

But what will those lives be like? Will those most intimately acquainted with Shaoai go on to live full lives with their potential realized, or will they go on to live lives as blighted as the life of Shaoai? As the novel progresses all three of the remaining teenage friends have grown to be adults with unenviable lives that are loveless and lonely. They are no longer friends because Shaoai's poisoning has left them estranged from one another and, in many ways, from themselves. Boyang has helped to care for Shaoai over the years, and it is he who attends the crematorium to see to her ashes. That same day, he visits his mother who asks who would want to kill Shaoai and why, which are questions that have haunted the novel's characters for two decades.

Although Shaoai is poisoned in the same year as the Tiananmen Square massacre, when dreams for a revolution were quashed, the novel is not political in nature and does not dwell on the protests from April through June 1989. Rather, the protests and massacre are used as a backdrop for the lives of these friends. It is significant, however, that the references to the Tiananmen Square student protests are framed in relation to the protesters' shattered hopes, which then parallel the shattered hopes and promise of the lives of Shaoai, Boyang, Ruyu, and Moran.

None of the characters escapes scrutiny. Readers learn, for example, that Shaoai is slightly older than Boyang, Ruyu, and Moran and that when Ruyu is sent to live with Shaoai's family, Ruyu and Shaoai must share a room. Shaoai is caustic and cold toward Ruyu and ridicules her for not knowing how to stop an unwanted sexual advance. It is not until after Shaoai has been terse with Ruyu that she begins to consider Ruyu's background and her very sheltered life. The fact that the poison Shaoai drinks is delivered in her morning Tang is illustrative of the dichotomy between the two girls' lives: Tang was a rare commodity in China and difficult to come by.

*Yiyun Li's award-winning first collection of short stories,* A Thousand Years of Good Prayers, *was published in 2005. It was followed by* Gold Boy, Emerald Girl *(2010) and her debut novel,* The Vagrants *(2011). She is a MacArthur Fellow and the recipient of the PEN/ Hemingway and the Frank O'Connor International Short Story Awards.*

Ruyu is first introduced to the reader as she travels to Beijing to live with Shaoai's family. Ruyu is an orphan who was raised by two elderly and secretly Catholic sisters whom she refers to as her grandaunts. Ruyu is relieved when she and Shaoai recognize one another at the train station, but she is also surprised that Shaoai has a picture of her and decides it must be a copy of the official birthday portrait she has taken each year. Ruyu has been raised as a Catholic and her future plans, as determined by her grandaunts, include a place in the church. She is in Beijing because of the educational opportunities available to her there and has secured a place in the local school based on her musical abilities with the accordion.

Although Shaoai rejects Ruyu, Moran and Boyang welcome her. The three become good friends, but hostility grows between Ruyu and Shaoai; therefore, it is Ruyu who is initially suspected of slipping the poison into Shaoai's drink. Ruyu insists that the poison was stolen from her room, and more than twenty years later, the truth behind the poisoning is still not known. At the time of Shaoai's death, Boyang is divorced and living in Beijing while Moran and Ruyu are living in the United States. The three friends are in contact with each other except through a brief monthly e-mail Boyang sends from an account that is not his normal account.

Critics have positively reviewed *Kinder than Solitude*. Some refer to the ways in which the personal tragedy of Shaoai mirrors the tragedy of the blighted hopes of Chinese dissidents. In a review for the *New York Times*, Jess Row alludes to the way in which the neighbors remember Shaoai's poisoning within the context of events that occurred in that same year, "Notice that beneath the passivity there's a withering, vibrating sarcasm at work in the juxtaposition of national and personal tragedies. Is that all, Li seems to be asking. Should the teenagers of the Tiananmen era really be expected to trade the pursuit of happiness for 'the belief in feeling less, suffering little'?"

It is left to Boyang to comment on contemporary China because both Ruyu and Moran have left the country long ago. He recalls Shaoai shouting at her father about "our revolution" and that it is "going to be completely different from yours," explaining that her father's revolutions "came from following the lead without thinking." Boyang's awareness of the changes that have taken place in China since Shaoai was poisoned and, as Row describes, his observations of the "rootless, vacuous, ahistorical . . . twenty-somethings around him" adds poignancy to the novel. As Li writes, Boyang understands that "what happened twenty years ago was as ancient as the events of two hundred or two thousand years ago."

David Ulin, in a review of the novel for the *Los Angeles Times*, addresses *Kinder than Solitude*'s place of history when he points out that "what makes it so vivid is its humanity, the idea that nationality and history are less important than the vagaries of the heart." He further explains that, "for all three [remaining friends], the events of late 1989, when Shaoai was poisoned, linger as a backdrop, a shared experience they can neither process nor put away." Li, through the character of Moran, reflects that "those seeking sanctuary in misremembering did not separate what had happened from what could have happened."

Marie Arana, reviewing the novel for the *Washington Post*, addressed the damage done to all four of the friends: "For Shaoai, the damage is physiological, shutting down her body's faculties one by one until she is trapped in bloated flesh, where she will languish for twenty-one years before her murder is finally consummated. For the others, the poisons will be more subtle. Each will erect an emotional wall, a hermetic husk, and, in the end, each will be as unrecognizable as a victim."

The inability to escape the past without being affected by it and the struggle to find a way to move beyond what has occurred in order to map out a future is the core theme of *Kinder than Solitude*. It is also a novel set in contemporary China that takes the country's political past and weaves it into the stories of individuals who have moved beyond that past and into their personal futures. The novel is not angst-ridden in the traditional sense, but it does display an underlying disconnect between what once was, what was anticipated, and what currently is. This disconnect is accentuated in the book in that the time between the Tiananmen Square protests and the current, present-day time is left vacant because of imprisonment, illness, or estrangement. In coming home, the characters are forced to deal with the reality of today on both intensely personal and societal levels. What, the novel seems to ask, are the effects of the wrecked political hopes of the past? How do these dashed hopes intertwine with the everyday lives of the people from that time? Is this impact really so different from what has been felt by past generations? Will history repeat itself and play out again for a new generation? As Ulin explains, "We are all children once, and we all participate in things, see things, that we carry with us for the rest of our lives. 'One life had ended,' Li writes, 'and none of them was innocent. That must be something. No?'"

*Gina Hagler*

## Review Sources

Allfrey, Ellah. Rev. of *Kinder than Solitude*, by Yiyun Li. *NPR Books*. NPR, 16 Apr. 2014. Web. 12 Feb. 2015.

Arana, Marie. "'Kinder than Solitude' Dives into the Weight of Memory." Rev. of *Kinder than Solitude*, by Yiyun Li. *Washington Post*. Washington Post, 17 Mar. 2014. Web. 11 Feb. 2015.

Rev. of *Kinder than Solitude*, by Yiyun Li. *Kirkus*. Kirkus, 25 Feb. 2014. Web. 12 Feb. 2015.

Rev. of *Kinder than Solitude*, by Yiyun Li. *Publisher's Weekly*. PWxyz, Feb. 2014. Web. 12 Feb. 2015.

Row, Jess. "Strangers to Themselves." Rev. of *Kinder than Solitude*, by Yiyun Li. *New York Times*. New York Times, 7 Mar. 2014. Web. 16 Feb. 2015.

Ulin, David. "Yiyun Li's 'Kinder than Solitude' Deals with Poisoned Past in China." *Los Angeles Times*. Los Angeles Times, 28 Feb. 2014. Web. 12 Feb. 2015.